Good Night,
Sweet Prince

THE LIVELY ARTS SERIES
FROM MERCURY HOUSE

LILLIAN GISH *The Movies, Mr. Griffith, and Me*

JEAN RENOIR *Renoir, My Father*

JOSEF VON STERNBERG *Fun in a Chinese Laundry*

GENE FOWLER *Good Night, Sweet Prince: The Life and Times of John Barrymore*

JOHN GIELGUD *Early Stages*

LYDIA SOKOLOVA *Dancing for Diaghilev*

ALSO BY GENE FOWLER

Trumpet in the Dust   *Shoe the Wild Mare*

The Great Mouthpiece   *Timber Line*

Father Goose   *Salute to Yesterday*

The Great Magoo (a play, in collaboration with Ben Hecht)

Illusion in Java   *The Jervis Bay Goes Down* (poem)

A Solo in Tom-Toms (privately printed)

Treasure Bad.
'54

John Baughman

The Lively Arts

Good Night, Sweet Prince

THE LIFE AND TIMES OF *John Barrymore*

by

GENE FOWLER

Mercury House, Incorporated
San Francisco

First published in 1944 by Viking Press, New York. This trade paperback edition published in 1989.

"Good Night, Sweet Prince (The Life and Times of John Barrymore)" © 1943 and 1944 by Gene Fowler; renewed 1970 and 1971 by A. Fowler, G. Fowler, Jr., J. F. Morrison, and W. Fowler. Reprinted by permission of the heirs of Gene Fowler.

Published in the United States by
Mercury House
San Francisco, California

Distributed to the trade by
Consortium Book Sales & Distribution, Inc.
St. Paul, Minnesota

Mercury House and colophon are registered trademarks of
Mercury House, Incorporated

Manufactured in the United States of America

Library of Congress Cataloging-in-Publication Data

Fowler, Gene, 1890–1960.
  Good night, sweet prince : the life and times of John Barrymore / by Gene Fowler.
      p.   cm. — (The Lively arts)
  Reprint. Originally published: New York : Viking Press, 1944.
  ISBN 0–916515–56–7 : $12.95
  1. Barrymore, John, 1882–1942.   2. Actors — United States — Biography.   I. Title.   II. Series.
PN2287.B35F6   1989
792'.028'0924 — dc19
[B]   88–7855
                                                                  CIP

TO HIS GREAT FRIEND

Edward Sheldon

John Barrymore's favorite lines
from Shakespeare

O! what a rogue and peasant slave am I:
Is it not monstrous that this player here,
But in a fiction, in a dream of passion,
Could force his soul so to his own conceit
That from her working all his visage wann'd,
Tears in his eyes, distraction in's aspect,
A broken voice, and his whole function suiting
With forms to his conceit? and all for nothing!
For Hecuba!
What's Hecuba to him or he to Hecuba
That he should weep for her? What would he do
Had he the motive and the cue for passion
That I have? He would drown the stage with tears,
And cleave the general ear with horrid speech,
Make mad the guilty and appal the free,
Confound the ignorant, and amaze indeed
The very faculties of eyes and ears.
Yet I,
A dull and muddy-mettled rascal, peak,
Like John-a-dreams, unpregnant of my cause,
And can say nothing; no, not for a king,
Upon whose property and most dear life
A damn'd defeat was made. Am I a coward?
Who calls me villain? breaks my pate across?
Plucks off my beard and blows it in my face?

Tweaks me by the nose? gives me the lie i' the throat,
As deep as to the lungs? Who does me this?
Ha!
Swounds, I should take it, for it cannot be
But I am pigeon-liver'd, and lack gall
To make oppression bitter, or ere this
I should have fatted all the region kites
With this slave's offal. Bloody, bawdy villain!
Remorseless, treacherous, lecherous, kindless villain!
O! vengeance!
Why, what an ass am I! This is most brave
That I, the son of a dear father murder'd,
Prompted to my revenge by heaven and hell,
Must, like a whore, unpack my heart with words,
And fall a-cursing, like a very drab,
A scullion!
Fie upon't! foh! About, my brain! I have heard,
That guilty creatures sitting at a play
Have by the very cunning of the scene
Been struck so to the soul that presently
They have proclaim'd their malefactions;
For murder, though it have no tongue, will speak
With most miraculous organ. I'll have these players
Play something like the murder of my father
Before mine uncle; I'll observe his looks;
I'll tent him to the quick: if he but blench
I know my course. The spirit that I have seen
May be the devil: and the devil hath power
To assume a pleasing shape; yea, and perhaps
Out of my weakness and my melancholy—
As he is very potent with such spirits—
Abuses me to damn me. I'll have grounds
More relative than this: the play's the thing
Wherein I'll catch the conscience of the king.

Hamlet, ACT II, SCENE II

Contents

CANTO FOUR

THE STAG AT EVE

The Illustrations

The illustrations selected for this book are indicative rather than definitive in the sense of pictorial or chronological sequence. They are the less frequently seen photographs of the man Barrymore taken at the flood of the personal, in contrast to the artistic, events in his life. Here are his own favorite photographs and some that have not become clichés of publication. These pictures were chosen from the collections of Melbourne Spurr, Spencer Berger, John Decker, Jane Parlan, John Ellis, and from Columbia, Warner's, M.G.M., and R.K.O. Studios.

1. BARRYMORE'S FAVORITE PHOTOGRAPH OF HIM-SELF

    When John Barrymore was forty-three years old he sat for a photographic portrait by Melbourne Spurr of Hollywood. There were two exposures made on glass plates. These poses were closely similar, yet not identical, as could be seen when examined by persons familiar with the flashing variations of mood expressed in Barrymore's face. The photograph reproduced in this book is little known. The reason for its obscurity is that it was Barrymore's favorite photograph of himself, and he did not wish it to be scattered in the manner of confetti on the mantelpieces of the land. It essentially was a non-actorish study of a man in love with one woman, Dolores Costello, and was intended to be shared only with that woman. The negative of this picture survived merely because Mr. Spurr was not called upon to surrender other than old celluloid to the "scrap drive" for war materials. The photographer was at some pains to find the plate and make a print for this book.

2. AS FRANÇOIS VILLON IN *THE BELOVED ROGUE*

  Barrymore was then forty-four years of age, and notwithstanding his abiding habits of physical neglect, his natural ath-
leticism is apparent. This photograph from the John Decker
Collection was taken on the motion picture set of United Artists.

3. WITH DOLORES COSTELLO IN *THE SEA BEAST*

  Barrymore and Dolores Costello were in the first months of
their great love in 1926 when this photograph was taken during
the filming of *The Sea Beast* at the Warner Brothers Studio.
This picture, from the Spencer Berger Collection, represents
much more than a scene posed by actors.

4. AS CAPTAIN AHAB IN *THE SEA BEAST*

  Barrymore regarded this motion picture as the best one he
ever made. (From the John Ellis Collection.)

5. IN GALSWORTHY'S PLAY, *JUSTICE*

  When playwright Edward Sheldon persuaded Barrymore to
leave inconsequential, comic stage roles and do Galsworthy's
Justice, the actor took his first great stride in serious portrayals.
We see him as William Falder, beating at the door of his prison
cell—a great moment in the theatre. (From the Spencer Berger
Collection.)

6. HAMLET

  This was John Barrymore at the time of his New York
Hamlet, when he played one hundred and one successive performances on Broadway, a continuity record in depicting the
melancholy Dane. The younger Booth appeared in this part
one hundred times on the same street. (From the Spencer Berger
Collection.)

7. AS THE DEAD HAMLET

  Barrymore as the dead Hamlet (at the Haymarket, London)
and the actor's favorite theatrical photograph of himself. This
seldom seen picture was taken when the actor was in his forty-
third year and at the noonday of his dramatic renown. It was
also his last great time on the boards.

8. WITH GRETA GARBO IN *GRAND HOTEL*

  It was after this love scene that the Swedish star kissed Barrymore for having afforded her the opportunity to play opposite
a flawless artist. (From the Spencer Berger Collection.)

bloodshot sorrow of the eyes and the sallow skin of the aged wanderer on the heath.

The first sheet drawings are reproduced from original sketches by John Barrymore.

Good Night,
Sweet Prince

Overture

A STRANGE thing happened to me shortly before I decided to undertake this work: several strange things. I hesitate to speak of them. Indeed, if I lacked witnesses to certain of these happenings, I should not care to risk my liberty during a time of bovine opinions and slaughterhouse verdicts. I shall cite only one event in detail.

During our last journey to Camp Baldy in the California mountains, Barrymore sat beside the fire as the rain drummed against the scantlings of our cabin. John Decker, the artist, and his wife had gone to an adjacent cabin, for it was deep into the hours, and we sat there, Barrymore, my younger son Will, and myself.

"The rain," said Barrymore, "beats with the persistence of an unpaid madam at our door." Suddenly he grew solemn as if a question had been asked. "Certainly I believe that ghosts communicate with those who stay on earth. And when I come back, don't stand and gape. Be hospitable to my shade."

He unreeled a forefinger that seemed prodigiously long in the firelight. "If you think I'm jesting about the visitation, *wait!*"

Now he dozed fitfully. He murmured in his sleep, as he often had, "Mum Mum." That is what he called the woman he loved best, his grandmother, Louisa Lane Drew.

He didn't have long to live, this man who had thrice hurled away the years. John Sidney Blythe Barrymore died at ten-twenty o'clock the night of May 29, 1942.

During the last days at the hospital, I had asked Decker if he would make a sketch of our friend. I showed him where I should like to hang it on a wall in the room where this is being written, near Barrymore's *Richard III* sword given me by him some years

3

ago. Then I chanced to note that the picture would be in awkward juxtaposition to a cuckoo-clock.

"Oh, let the clock stay," the artist said. "It's fairly well carved and Jack liked it."

"Well," I replied, "the clock hasn't been in running order for two years. When Jack dies—as this time it seems he must—I'll set the hands at the hour of his death."

I didn't sleep all night after Barrymore died. I had had a great deal to drink, yet I couldn't get drunk and I couldn't sleep. I kept thinking of other friends who had gone before their time. I walked the garden with my dog. Jack had loved her, as he had loved all creatures that did not talk. I felt alone. I went indoors at last, for the mounting sun hurt my eyes.

I came into this room, where I now sit, and found a leaf of manuscript long mislaid, something I had written on Fire Island years ago:

> Today the leaves of the huckleberry bushes are a warm russet, like the hair of my first girl. The cranberries are plentiful in the hollows. The wind is from the west, and we'll have no rain tomorrow. The sea is piling in beneath the whiplash of the west wind. Is it lonesome here on Fire Island? you ask. It is lonesome everywhere, my friend.

Decker came up from Bundy Drive with the death-bed sketch of our friend. The artist had framed it hurriedly. He placed it on the wall between the *Richard III* sword and the clock. And now I remembered my intention to set the clock-hands at the hour of Barrymore's death. As I moved to do so, I found there was no need.

The hands of the clock had stood for more than two years at ten-twenty.

CANTO ONE

Songs of the Morning

I.

At Rise of Curtain

I WAS a reporter for the *New York American* at the time, and not entirely in the good graces of the city editor. I had come to the newspaper in 1918 under the sponsorship of Damon Runyon, and to do sports. I did them—but not always in print. Mr. Runyon shuddered at the trapeze solos of his protégé and others less tolerant than he leered in the direction of certain Park Row gutters, but Mr. Hearst refused to permit his field-marshals to cashier me. But I was transferred for cause by Caleb Van Hamm, the distinguished managing editor, to the city staff where, it was anticipated, I soon would be court-martialed by a lieutenant-general known for his antipathy to young men of uncorked vigor.

One of my few admirers on the *American* staff at the moment was John McMahon, the new drama editor. (Alan Dale was our frenzied critic during that glamorous epoch.) McMahon thought highly of me because I chewed tobacco when writing poems. "It shows you just don't give a damn," he said. "I used to be that way."

To help free me from the kennels of the city editor's displeasure, McMahon sometimes asked that I be "lent" to his theatrical department to write feature stories, gestures of good will in behalf of various impresarios whose plays needed tonics beyond the postage-stamp advertisements in the amusement columns.

One November day McMahon borrowed me, saying: "Arthur Hopkins has a play that is not catching on. *Redemption.* Don't bother seeing it. It gives you the creeps. But Arthur is a prince. Get an interview with John Barrymore. He's in it, poor guy."

I visited Mr. Barrymore in his dressing-room after the matinee performance. He was perspiring and swearing eloquently, while molting a false beard. I never had seen him before, on or off stage.

"What in hell do *you* want?" he said, without turning in his chair. My reportorial eye caught his in the mirror. We exchanged glares by means of the looking-glass, after which he wheeled about, rather happily I fancied, to ask, "Where were you last night?"

"At Lipton's saloon, then at the Murray Hill Baths. Where were *you?*"

He rose, cinched his belt. "I was with the Baron."

He began to put on a coat that seemed, in shape and size, to be the property of someone larger-bodied and less solvent than himself. Before the somewhat seedy coat had enveloped him, I saw with an eye of prize-fight camp and baseball club-house experience that he was athletic, had an extraordinary sense of balance, and moved on the balls of his feet like Benny Leonard. He was slim, well proportioned, and had a slight "hang" to his shoulders, as have most good punchers of middle weight. His forearms were those of a stroke-oar.

"Who is the Baron?" I asked, as a button fell from Mr. Barrymore's coat. I moved to pick the button up from the floor, but he restrained me.

"That button," he said, "has been hanging for a year, like a moose's lavaliere. The Baron is my only true friend."

The star of *Redemption* now put on a fedora, a vintage number in every respect. It might have been forest-green once. But as he adjusted the crown, giving it certain deft tugs and pats, it suddenly took on a quality of magnificence.

I have known but four men who could wear hats becomingly: Grover A. Whalen, James J. Walker, Damon Runyon, and Barrymore. And of the four, I think Barrymore the champion, because the other gentlemen had the benefit of new and expensive beavers, whereas Barrymore's appeared to have been obtained from the city dump.

Barrymore's father, it is recalled, could make senile headgear mean something. According to Jack, his amiable sire permitted pet squirrels to nest in his sky-piece.

"The only reason why a man should pay the least attention to a hat," said Mr. Barrymore, as we went outside the theatre, "is that it is something one tips to a lady."

It was twilight now and the last of the matinee-goers were turning to look at the eminent actor. We walked into the West Forties where stragglers from other playhouses gazed upon him. In this decent era autograph seekers had not yet begun to pounce like gadflies upon their celebrities. Barrymore caught the attention of the Broadway pedestrians but did not take much notice of them. Vanity was not among his vices.

We at last arrived at an old and sepia-colored boardinghouse in West Forty-First Street. Barrymore entered it with some zest, happily sniffing the stale air of a tunnel-like hallway. When asked concerning the identity of this cavernous place, he replied, "We are in a sepulcher of dynastic majesty. The Valley of the Kings."

A rotund lady materialized from the catacombs. She manipulated a drop-cord electric light, peered at us through silver-rimmed spectacles, then embraced and was embraced by Mr. Barrymore, who called her "Marie, my Blossom!"

Over Marie's shoulder, and from among a hayloft of gray hair, he testified, "She's one of my father's old flames. Bequeathed her to me."

Marie tittered uneasily and pushed him away. "He's always making these jokes. You see, I was Richard Mansfield's wardrobe mistress."

"Please," said Barrymore, "omit the word 'wardrobe.'"

Marie shook a fat finger at Mr. Barrymore. A glum mood abruptly possessed her. In the stingy light from the one lamp she seemed a drowned doll, waxy and bloated.

"I'll have to ask the Baron to leave," she intoned. "Him and his dog."

"What!" roared Mr. Barrymore, advancing on her, and she retreating as if hobbled in a barrel of lard. "Oust a philosopher? A savant? A seventh son of a seventh son? Where is your sense of values?"

Marie, firm in her resolve, replied, "Him and his awful dog!"

Mr. Barrymore stiffened, rolled his eyes upward, unhinged his jaw, and gasped, "A pound of flesh!" He glanced at her appraisingly, then added, "In fact, a ton of it!"

"And." Marie now waggled a sausage of a thumb in my direction, "I want no more weak-minded hoofers owing *me* money."

Mr. Barrymore came out of his swoon, then gently took her partly in his arms.

"Marie, drain that ice water from your veins. Be warm again, as you were when you were Mansfield's mistress . . ."

"John Barrymore," and she broke his inadequate embrace, "I was Mansfield's *wardrobe* mistress, and nothing more."

"That," said he, "is a matter strictly between you and your Maker." He lifted a hand. "No *double-entendre* implied." He took on the air of a special pleader. "Marie, I ask you to trust the Baron one more week."

"It's already been five," she said morosely. "Him and that nasty old dog!"

"One more week," said Mr. Barrymore. "I may say, with all truth, that I am now in the chips. A gambler named Arthur Hopkins is grubstaking me. You shall be paid."

Marie paused, relenting a little. Mr. Barrymore went on: "Marie, all nature is waiting with finger on lip for your decision. I appeal to your better side, the real you, to permit the Baron, one of the greatest alchemists since Trismegistus, to continue his experiments among the alembics and test tubes." He turned to me. "The Baron is seeking the philosopher's stone."

"The Baron," said Marie, "is making gin."

A weak bark sounded from the end of the Stygian corridor. Mr. Barrymore pushed Marie aside, then guided me along the hallway.

"You will love the Baron," he said. "I am convinced that Robespierre was his father."

Without knocking, Mr. Barrymore opened a door to reveal in the room beyond it a small, bald fellow with protuberant black eyes and jackstraw habiliments. He was leaning over a gas plate balanced upon the lid of an elderly and well-labeled trunk. A spicy mist rose from a dented tin utensil.

"Baron!" said Jack, moving to hug the good wizard.

"I'm cooking some chili," the Baron said in a furry voice. "I am making it extra hot because you . . ."

The Baron's words foundered in the clinch. His guest of honor kissed him on the bald spot. As the Baron turned politely to me, I saw a man of perhaps seventy years. His hands were thin, long fingered, and curiously young. He held a tarnished spoon in one of them. With the other he flicked a tear from his eye. He seemed easily roused to tears, either from sentiment or too much grog.

"You are a friend of Mr. Barrymore?" he asked of me lugubriously.

The actor interposed: "Everybody's friend, Baron. Mr. William Randolph Hearst's in particular. Advises him on all political moves.

Forms the entire policy of the Hearst publications, from coast to coast."

Our host shattered me with the gentle, child-spoken inquiry, "Do the Hearst papers *have* a policy?"

"I am only a reporter, Baron," I replied.

"Throw aside that false modesty," said Barrymore. Then he sidled over to the gas plate, sniffed eagerly, and now the Baron's dog rose from a dark corner and slowly arrived at the actor's feet.

The Baron began to weep anew. "Jim hasn't stirred all week from his gunny sack. Look! Look! He has walked all the way across the room to greet Mr. Barrymore."

Jim was an old animal, the first and last pug dog I ever encountered in the East. Indeed, I had not seen one anywhere since my own pug had gone mad and been chloroformed when I was a child. Jim's gingerbread body sagged in the middle. His tail was looped like a stale cruller over his hind parts. And one of his eyes was closed in a perpetual wink.

This dog, flatulent and stiff with years, seemed suddenly in paradise. The star of *Redemption* was on the bare floor, his face near Jim's muzzle, and Jim's tongue was out like a fireman's shirt-tail, licking Barrymore's chin.

"Jim's a little old," the Baron said, as if in a soliloquy. "Like myself, I suppose. One day we are up and frisking about. Then suddenly we awaken one morning, and we are stiff and old and things have passed us by."

The chili began to boil over. The Baron turned to look after it, lowering the flame, then plumbing the thick stew with his spoon. A tear dropped into the aromatic caldron.

Barrymore at length deposited Jim on what once may have been a divan, and asked the chef, "What wonders have you performed today in your bathroom?"

Our host's eyes were moist onyx knobs as he promised, "Prohibition enforcement will not find me napping." He turned out the gas, and lifted the pot of chili from the makeshift stove, using an old waistcoat on the hot bail. "I have some bang-up gin ready for dilution."

He set the stew on a backless kitchen chair near the divan, studied it a moment, then turned, beckoned, picked up a half-filled glass jug, and led us outside to a bathroom of the President Garfield era.

It was a small room with a zinc tub and could not accommodate all of us at one time.

"You see," said Barrymore, "the Baron is also prophetic. The Elijah of the latrines."

The actor insisted on staying outside while the Baron diluted the alcohol and flavored it with juniper essence. Not wishing to endanger a scientific effort, I also remained at the threshold of the bathroom, watching the celebrated alchemist at his labors.

"I don't think you'll find many pug dogs left in the whole world," Barrymore said to me. "Do you remember the pug dog at all?"

"I had one," I replied.

He now looked at me with genuine interest. His bantering manner fell like a bullfighter's cape. With almost naïve tone he asked, "You really owned one? Tell me about him."

"There's not much to tell," I said. "I was living with my grandmother . . ."

"You *were?*" he asked, with such emphasis that I believed him to be pulling my leg. I hesitated a moment. "Is there anything remarkable about having lived with one's grandmother?"

"Yes," he said quietly. "Yes, there is." There was no mistaking his sincerity. "You see, the only bringing up I ever had was by my grandmother, Mrs. Drew. So great, so sweet she was, inside the armor of her great dignity. So able. We called her Mum Mum."

He seemed to catch himself being sentimental. He called to the Baron, "Are you dissolving a pearl?"

"All in good time," the Baron replied gently. "All in good time."

I found Barrymore studying me in the half-light from the bathroom door. After a pause he said, "I interrupted you. The pug dog?"

"He went mad," I replied. "I couldn't understand why they had put him under a wooden wash-tub, then placed a rag soaked with something beneath the tub, and my uncle standing there like an elephant hunter being photographed after the kill."

"What did you do?" he asked slowly, as if to test my character.

"I did nothing, except yell my head off, and try to get loose from my grandmother's grip."

"But afterward," he persisted, "what did you say to her?"

"I said that I'd never forgive my uncle."

"What was her attitude?"

"She was a religious woman," I said. "She told me what a sin it was not to forgive—anything. She pointed out to me that Jesus always had forgiven, even when nailed to the Cross. I remember how terribly shocked she seemed when I blurted out, 'Yes, but Jesus never had a dog.' "

Until now we had not shaken hands, nor had Barrymore even asked my name. He put out his hand, and said, "Hello!"

The Baron, carrying a filled jug, and chuckling, emerged from the bathroom. His tears had evaporated. There was an aura of ecclesiastical peace upon him. We followed him back to his quarters.

After sampling his experimental nectar, we discovered that Jim had eaten the whole of the chili!

The Baron walked over to Jim, who somehow had slyly crawled down and up again onto the divan. He shook a finger at the venerable thief, who lay distended on the lumpy couch, both eyes closed.

"Jim! Jim!" scolded the Baron. "You have eaten Mr. Barrymore's chili. I made it especially for him. How could you?"

Jim didn't bother to open his openable eye. The Baron turned to his guests, shrugged, grew tongue-tied.

Barrymore was greatly amused. He helped himself to another portion of synthetic gin—from a china cup with no handle, and a crack in it.

"Food," said he, "is all right in its place, and its place correctly is in the belly of our friend Jim." He studied the cracked cup, then said reverently, "The Liberty Bell on tour."

Now Nature and Jim came to sudden grips.

I do not know how much time we had spent at the bathroom, nor how long it takes for peppery foods to stimulate a slumbering raider of stew-pots; but I do know that Jim now roused, opened his good eye, growled apprehensively, then lay back like the Lion of Lucerne.

But not for long. The next time around, both for our drinks and for Jim's gastric eccentricity, the aged thief leaped like an acrobat of the Keith-Albee circuit, roared, came to the floor, and made himself into an exploratory crescent.

The attacks now recurred with greater violence, like the more spirited parts of a Russian concerto. Jim began to snap with futile amazement, chase his tail, plunge like a lassoed elk, and bare his gums, where only three teeth remained as yellowed badges of the emotions.

"Christ! What a performance," said Barrymore. "Perhaps I should have chili an hour before curtain time."

He tried to soothe the galvanized victim. "We must get him something instantly." Then to Jim, "No encores. Pay no attention to the applause."

Attracted by the strange bedlam, Marie appeared in the doorway to call out, "*Now* what!"

Barrymore seized her. "Go to the nearest drug store. Get some limewater. Whites of eggs. . . ." His voice trailed off as he propelled the confused landlady down the hall.

Jim kept up his prancings and bull-bellowings until Barrymore reappeared with a mixture in a bowl, and some eggs. He administered the potion to the dog, and whatever it was, the remedy seemed to quiet him within fifteen minutes. During that time Barrymore held the spent and panting animal in his arms, as if it were an ailing child.

Suddenly Barrymore remembered that he was due at the theatre. "Good God!" he said, carefully placing Jim on the divan. "Time to smear on the paint and pretend I'm somebody else."

On our way back to the theatre, I remembered that I had been sent by McMahon to get an interview. Barrymore was most evasive, said he hadn't the slightest idea what the play was about, and, on parting, asked me to swear not to waste my time in seeing *Redemption*.

"Save your groats for more pleasant stimulants than our drama," he counseled. "Or," he added in parting, "even if you are given a free pass to the playhouse, where I gibber with the accents of a pushcart peddler and cavort within the parentheses of Mr. Tolstoy's minor deliriums, I recommend suicide as the lesser of two evils."

2.

The Coming of Greengoose

A GLASSED-IN carriage with an Irish coachman drew up at the entrance of the old Chestnut Street wharf. It was St. Valentine's Day, 1882. The ice had all but cleared from the Delaware River in front of and below the city of Philadelphia. The iceboats had retired to seasonal moorings downstream, and their crews been paid. The skippers were shouting good-bys to winter, and to one another, from the pilothouses.

A small wind carried random snorts of rain from the northwest, puddling the streets. There had been an epidemic of cholera in the East, and the harassed contractors in charge of street cleaning were being attacked by the Press for permitting quagmires to accumulate. There were hints of political laxity.

The rain made a gutter of the coachman's hatbrim. It trickled inside the collar of his black oilskins as he climbed down to tie a hitching-strap to a rusty post. He swore without moving his lips, so as not to be overheard by his employer. Nothing is as restless as a wet Irishman.

The crewmen of the ice-breakers sloshed past the somewhat dainty conveyance on their way to a tavern on the waterfront, there to solicit new employment and drink to last year's snows. They noticed the smart brougham, so out of place in the wet, prosaic ruts of the wharfside.

Indeed, this seemed a valentine itself, the little black vehicle, notwithstanding the fouled spokes and hubs, the clogged accouterments, the mire streaks on the plate-glass windows, and the slyly profane banshee at the bridle bits of the wilted hackneys. Perhaps the carriage itself would not have supplied such a valentine quality had it been unoccupied. A smallish woman sat upright in the brougham. Even the dullest beer-guzzler among the passing river men could sense that she was a personage.

This poised lady, caped with a dolman of embossed black velvet, did not seem her sixty-two years, although there were inferences of iron-gray hair beneath a plum-colored turban and white plume. To the mire-heeled river men, she didn't appear to be of Rittenhouse Square origin, despite the social accents of the brougham. Rather, she brought reminders of the Queen Victoria of calendar chromos, but less plump. There was an implication of authority in the way she sat on the broadcloth cushions of the closed carriage, a regal fire in the large, bright blue, slightly bulging eyes.

One of the thirsty captains recognized her as Louisa Lane Drew, Mrs. John Drew, manager of the Arch Street Theatre, and, of late, Joseph Jefferson's famous Mrs. Malaprop in *The Rivals*. The wet-jowled skipper touched his cap with a hooked forefinger, received a nod from the lady and the flutter of a lace-mittened hand, then sidled with needless self-consciousness into a saloon. A male chorus sounded in a rummified anthem from behind a pair of swinging doors.

Mrs. Drew's black brougham was awaiting the arrival of the steamboat *John A. Warner*, expected up from Wilmington to re-new its yearly traffic. On this first voyage of the season, it would be carrying among other passengers a hard-working Philadelphian. He had been summoned home by Mrs. Drew, as if by royal com-mand, from emergency labors in Delaware.

This passenger was Dr. J. Nicholas Mitchell, eminent homeopath and cousin of the distinguished Dr. S. Weir Mitchell, neurologist and man of letters. The fact that Dr. J. Nicholas Mitchell's illus-trious cousin was an allopath had not marred their devotion to each other. In fact, both practitioners had been fighting cholera in Dela-ware for the past two weeks, each applying his own distinctive sys-tem of medicine, when Mrs. Drew's telegram had reached the homeopathic member of the Mitchell family.

Her younger daughter Georgianna, wife of actor Maurice Barry-more, was expecting a third child on this St. Valentine's Day in 1882. The confinement may have been uppermost in the mind of Mrs. Drew as she awaited the coming of the good homeopath. Her pres-ence at the waterfront on a muddy, rainy afternoon would support such conjecture. Still, the Drew family were a capricious, wander-thought folk, and it may have been that she did not focus exclu-sively on the anticipated valentine.

Mrs. Drew sat erect, so as not to disarrange her half-hoop skirt, or "tilter." There was a dream of remembrance in her large eyes. It is possible that she thought about her beginnings, her many trials, her family's long theatrical history. For almost a century her people had been on the stage. She herself was in her fifty-seventh season of footlights and grease paint. (And before the dark angels would come to her one day in 1897, she would have completed seventy-two years as an active artist.)

She might have been thinking of how her mother and father, players of provincial reputation in Lambeth Parish, London, had brought her at the age of seven from England to Philadelphia. She had been born the same year as Jenny Lind, 1820, the year fuddy old King George III had died. And here at the Chestnut Street Theatre she had played all five roles in *Twelve Precisely* on January 5, 1829. A critic had extolled her as "this astonishing little creature"; but the event she liked best to recall was that a veteran of the Revolutionary War had come backstage to hold her on his knee and share some candied cherries with her.

She *was* history, this woman. She had listened to the Liberty Bell tolling in 1834 for the death of Lafayette; and a year afterward heard its last note, as the great bell cracked while sounding the requiem for Chief Justice Marshall. And the old theatre she had managed since 1861 was no slight part of an historic environment. A block to the east of the Arch Street Theatre lay the wise bones of Benjamin Franklin, and a square beyond his grave the Betsy Ross house. Four squares to the south, the clock of Independence Hall showed a brave face to the wondering world.

Now Mrs. Drew was home again after thirteen weeks with Joseph Jefferson, the fourth of the theatrical Jeffersons and the third of the Josephs. And, to think, she had even played as a girl with Jefferson's grandfather! She had appeared also with Forrest, Macready, and the eccentric Junius Brutus Booth. She had been in Booth's *Hamlet* company at Natchez the night a cock had crowed during *Ophelia's* mad scene. The elder Booth had become so distraught as to scamper up a ladder into the "flies." Nor would he come down, to quote Mrs. Drew, "until the manager had promised to permit him to resume his high position on the ladder and remain there until Jackson was re-elected President."

The chorus, more earthy than before, was braying in the tavern. Mrs. Drew smiled knowingly. Was it the song of the drinkers that amused her, or was she recalling her five months' marriage to a Mr. George Mossop in 1848? That actor had been a devoted bottle-man, and one evening arrived on-stage in Buffalo after a dinner of foods laced with onions. He was less than steady in his scenes. As his wife returned to the wings, she overheard a member of the company remark: "He's drunk again. Poor Mrs. Mossop!"

She turned upon the gossiper with a sprightly: "Yes. And tonight with *onions!*"

After Mr. Mossop had climbed into his urn in Albany, Louisa met John Drew, a native of County Clare, Ireland. They were married in 1850, and had four children in the following five years: Louisa, John, Georgianna, and Sidney.

The elder Drew was a portrayer of Irish roles. He was handsome, strong, and Mrs. Drew used to tell her grandchildren: "Your spirited grandfather was one of the fine actors of his day. Had he lived to be forty-five, instead of thirty-four, he would have been great. But too early success was his ruin. It left him nothing to do."

The coachman came from the tavern with the intelligence that the *John A. Warner* had been reported a quarter of a mile from port. He handed Mrs. Drew a rain- and beer-stained copy of the *Philadelphia Ledger* to occupy her until the boat arrived. She examined the front page briefly, yet long enough to see that the advertisement for her Arch Street Theatre had not been omitted from page one, column one. The advertisement informed the public that Mr. Sol Smith Russell was appearing that night in his new comedy, *Edgewood Folks.*

A whistle sounded offshore. Mrs. Drew stirred from her reflections. The coachman opened the door to announce, "She's a-dockin'! The *John A. Warner's* a-nosin' in."

When the craft had been made fast, Dr. Mitchell came ashore. He carried a battered clinical valise and an umbrella. This Aesculapius was a man of perhaps fifty-six, large bodied, and wore burnsides which, when dampened by the rain, had the effluvium of sheep-dip.

The physician went at once to the carriage. The coachman untied the now sleepy horses, climbed wetly onto the box, and drove the expectant grandmother and the learned homeopath through the rain to Number 2008 Columbia Avenue.

Dr. Mitchell held his umbrella over Louisa as they crossed the sidewalk to the entrance of the three-story brick house. It was not a building of great consequence, such as might have been expected of the successful manager of a famous theatre, one who maintained a coachman and brougham, a cook and maids. Still, it was not a commonplace home, if one bears in mind that Philadelphia residences had a biscuit-like similarity: flat roofs, metal cornices, plain façades. There were white stone lintels over the slim windows, and block-marble steps at the front doorway, four of them, and a threshold, daily scrubbed in fair weather and cowled with wooden treads in winter.

Mrs. Drew was prospering at this time. An adroit actress-manager, she had in 1861 assumed a property built in 1827, a Philadelphia version of a Greek temple. She found it in straits, borrowed to renovate it and to pay her actors, then persuaded Edwin Booth, Jefferson, and others of public favor to appear before her footlights. Her shrewdness brought the theatre from the shadows, and her achievements as an actress enlarged her personal income.

Mrs. Drew had an iron-bound manner, was reserved even in her own home, yet underneath the armor plate of her dignity she had a warm generosity. She lived in the style of a lavish Victorian. Her several successive homes sheltered her children and theirs, and were sanctuaries for an assortment of waifs and poor relations. Always she shared her purse and herself. Perhaps she regarded the saving of money too lightly for her own eventual needs, an amiable quirk that became manifest in her talented descendants.

As Mrs. Drew entered the hallway, Polly the maid helped her remove the dolman. "Mr. Sol Smith Russell is in the parlor, waitin'. He's excited."

Mrs. Drew removed her plumed turban. "Never mind Sol Smith Russell. How's Georgie?"

"She's havin' pains."

Mrs. Drew turned to the doctor who, having wrestled off his galoshes, was eying the clinical satchel. She gestured with a long hatpin. "I think you know the way, Doctor."

The big homeopath began to climb, Mrs. Drew following after him. Halfway up the staircase, and with a swish of her voluminous skirts, Mrs. Drew leaned over the banister to ask Polly, "Where are the children?"

"With Mr. Sidney," said Polly.

"Oh," said Louisa, in a tone that might have meant anything. "I hope their feet are dry." She paused on the stairway, as if making up her mind about something, perhaps Sidney.

Sidney Drew, her favorite son, was a young man of extraordinary skill at games of billiards or pool. He had abilities as an actor, particularly as a farceur, but preferred to win side bets from strangers and at pool. He was so artful at the green table that friends declined to play against him. So also did strangers, once they had seen him cue in hand. He now was virtually compelled to usurp a technique known to a few other virtuosos: to enter contests with out-of-towners and between trains. Sidney would lose consistently, and for small bets; but when the greedy opponent suggested a sizable prize for a "last game," Sidney would reluctantly consent, and then suddenly reveal himself as a master of the varicolored globes and win the game with a flourish. Sometimes his flabbergasted dupes grew nasty and violent.

While Mrs. Drew paused on the stairway, a finger to her lip, Mr. Sol Smith Russell emerged from the parlor to call up to her, "It's awfully important that I talk with you."

Mrs. Drew raised an eyebrow. "I'll see you in a few moments, Mr. Russell."

"It's about the scenery," said Mr. Russell, a thin comedian who resembled a rural Rameses II. "My cliff has been lost."

But Mrs. Drew had gone upstairs.

Mr. Russell aggrievedly returned to the parlor. He began absently to examine an encased medal presented by the late Edwin Forrest to Louisa Lane in 1828. She had appeared as Albert to Forrest's William Tell, and when but eight years old.

While Mr. Russell's pharaonic nose was hanging above the medal, Sidney Drew appeared in the hallway carrying three-year-old Ethel, kicking and squealing, and followed by four-year-old Lionel, grinning and burbling happily.

"How are you, Sol?" asked Sidney, who was known to the children as "Uncle Googan."

"I've lost my cliff," said Mr. Russell, solemnly eying the children, "and your mother pays no attention whatsoever."

Sidney had set Ethel on her feet and was trying to mollify her with a piece of sugar from a pocket supply he kept for horses.

"Uncle Googan won four dollars," Lionel confided to Mr. Russell. "Hooray!"

"Sh! Sh!" warned Sidney, glancing at the stairs. "Mustn't tell Mum Mum."

But Mrs. Drew, now in the bedroom of her daughter Georgie, was holding in her arms a new baby boy.

"He looks like little Greengoose," she said. "The pretty lad in the story book."

3.

Silk Topper and Gaslight

MAURICE BARRYMORE had been in America almost
seven years at the time of the birth of his younger son
John. The father had crossed the sea from Liverpool to
New York in the spring of 1875.

His fellow-passengers accounted their twenty-eight-year-old ship-
mate an amiable dandy. These voyagers themselves were mostly of
English or Continental stock, and therefore uncritical of Barrymore's silk hat and monocle as he went ashore to clear the customs
at Castle Garden.

He decided not to ride the horsecar, but walk uptown to the
Hoffman House. He struck out briskly across Bowling Green at
the evening hour when frosty halos rested on the gaslights. The
benchwarmers, a rank of frowsy goblins along the old park railings, squinted at the high hat and monocle. An occasional catcall
rose from these chilled and vagrant cynics as the alien swell marched
past. He walked confidently up Broadway as if on a familiar round.

The advent of Mr. Barrymore to the famed Hoffman House Bar
assuredly was that of a gentleman. The monocle and silk topper
seemed a guarantee of elegant docility; yet there was a don't-tread-
on-me nuance to his gaze, an implied belligerence in the considerable chest.

He appraised in the mirror the reflection of a ceiling-high painting opposite the bar, artist Bouguereau's *Nymphs and Satyr*. Four
roistering nudes framed in gilded perpetuity were playing tug-of-
war with a strangely reluctant demi-god of the glades.

Mr. Barrymore ordered a whisky-and-soda—without ice. His
speech was as neatly clipped as the hedges of Oxford University.

The chief bartender, who looked like something out of the State
Department, pretended not to notice the eyeglass, the silk hat, or
the un-American request for no ice. The foreman of the drink-
mixers was an astute stoic, used to almost any sudden puzzle. Likewise, his subordinates in white were tactful and impassive. They
could listen with sacerdotal patience to woozy confessions, advise

customers on matters of criminal law, extra-marital relationships, self-cures, all without loss of poise or patronage.

These sage tapsters masked their concern over the newcomer's aversion to ice; but as much could not be said of the guests in this best of all possible bars. Many of them stared, others nudged their companions, and pursed their lips. A group of three nearest the ice-less Mr. Barrymore were not satisfied to let him mind his own thirst. They smirked, turned up their mustaches, and made fruity sounds.

The leader of this trio was well known to this drinking ground of professors from Wall Street, the theatre, the prize ring, the horsy set. This bulking boyo was Herman Oelrichs, of the New York and Newport whirl, renowned swimmer, all-round athlete. He had for his companions Billy Edwards, former lightweight champion, hired by the Hoffman House management to safeguard the art gallery of the barroom against the walking sticks of intoxicated guests, and a high-stake gambler, Jerry Dunn, who at the moment was saying pointedly, "I niver murthered a man in me whole endurin' life, but I've kilt eleven."

Mr. Barrymore gazed at the lethal gambler as if at an art object. His monocled serenity impressed the slayer of eleven. Mr. Oelrichs now placed a silver dollar in his eye, leaned toward Mr. Barrymore, and drawled, "I say, Percy, I suppose this is the *English* way? Wot?"

"Oh, no," replied Mr. Barrymore, removing his eyeglass, and settling the silk hat brim to his head. "Allow me to show you." His fist traveled a short, jolting arc. "*This* is the English way!"

Mr. Oelrichs dived without benefit of springboard, and lay like a dissected frog on the tiles, the dollar spinning musically to a stop beneath the picture of the satyr and the buxom nudes.

During this tornado the Barrymore hat remained as solidly on his head as a cornice. The spectators sucked in their breaths. Oelrichs responded to cracked-ice massage, was lifted to his feet and informed by Billy Edwards where he was, blinked, then put out his hand to Barrymore, who took it while the patrons cheered with ringside sincerity.

Oelrichs ordered drinks for everyone, and, as a symbol of esteem, decreed that no ice be served for the first round. Barrymore stayed on until late next morning, and remained Oelrichs' friend for as long as he lived.

The vanquished sportsman was delighted to learn that his conqueror had been amateur lightweight champion of England during his student days at Oxford. When he told Oelrichs that his first name was pronounced "Morris" in England, the American chose to call him "Barry" instead. He became Barry to Broadway and to the theatre, an institution he was to adorn until after the turn of the century, a much-loved, sometimes envied man of wit, charm, and outstanding physical endowments.

During this well-resolved night, and on other evenings at the Hoffman House, Barrymore's friends learned many things concerning him. He had been born in a dungeon of the old fort of Agra in India, in 1847, as Herbert Blythe, son of an army officer, afterward a judge in the courts of Madras.

It had been a time of unrest in the United Provinces of Agra and Oudh. The women and children of Europeans in that district sought refuge inside the red sandstone fortifications. And there Barrymore's mother delivered him into the world.

In 1857, during the Sepoy Mutiny, Herbert once again was quartered behind the ramparts of the fort. The boy witnessed brave sallies of the besieged garrison, saw the European quarter of the city burned and men killed before Colonel Greathed marched to the relief of the fort.

"Yet," he used to tell his children, "I also could see in the distance the white glory of the Taj Mahal, the Pearl Mosque of Shah Jahan. And such things are always important."

Young Blythe moved to England for his formal education. He entered a boys' school at Blackheath, afterward attended Harrow, and finally matriculated at Lincoln College, Oxford, where he occupied the rooms of John Wesley.

Upon leaving Oxford, the young man's relatives undertook to advise him as to a career. Among these counselors was Henry Wace, Prebendary of Canterbury Cathedral, eventually its dean. The Reverend Mr. Wace, brother-in-law of Herbert's sister, Mrs. Eva Wace, took great interest in the bright, athletic Oxonian. Prebendary Wace concurred in the family decision that Blythe read for the law, which he proceeded to do. Yet his heart and mind were not with the law books, although he at length qualified for a call to the bar. He really wished to be an actor, an ambition that horrified his elders.

The need to choose between a make-up box and a briefcase

weighed upon young Blythe. He went down to Brighton one day late in the season of 1874, there to walk beside the sea and think things over, whether to be a lawyer or a player.

While enjoying some fish and chips, his attention fell upon a passer-by, a young woman of more than ordinary attractiveness. She was holding the sleeve of a stoutish man of middle years. Blythe recognized her escort as the comedian Charles Vandenhoff.

Two ruffians were following the actor and the young woman, heckling them with alcoholic proverbs. Blythe heard them advise the lass to sever her December-and-May ties and come with them at once. They gave reasons. The girl was obviously embarrassed, her escort at a loss to do more than protest.

Blythe confronted the toughs, advising them quietly to trot their insults back to the pub. He was set upon, but decided to beat his assailants into a pair of blood-puddings. Upon completing this calisthenic, the Oxonian doffed his bowler to the young woman and her escort, and turned to leave. The comedian detained the Galahad, inviting him to dinner. In the conversation that followed, Blythe confided his personal problem, that of choosing between Blackstone and the Bard.

"You have a presence for the stage," Vandenhoff said.

Blythe made up his mind to try his luck at acting, and returned to London to assume the stage-name Maurice Barrymore. He had seen this name on an old playbill hanging in the foyer of the Haymarket Theatre. He soon toured the provinces with Vandenhoff's company in the role of Cool in Dion Boucicault's *London Assurance*.

After a series of family harangues against theatricals, Barrymore left England for America. He remained in New York for a time, occupying a hall room, for his means soon became scanty. He proceeded to Boston and made his American bow in *The Shaughraun*, another of the fecund Boucicault's products.

In the autumn of 1875 Barrymore became a member of the famous stock company founded by Augustin Daly. It was at Daly's Fifth Avenue Theatre in New York that he met the twenty-two-year-old John Drew, himself only ten months away from Philadelphia and Louisa's apronstrings. Together they appeared in support of Edwin Booth's Hamlet in October of that year. Maurice was Laertes, and Drew was Rosencrantz.

This was Booth's eighty-fourth time as Hamlet, and his return to New York after an absence of two years. The celebrated tragedian was a month this side of forty-two years of age, and in the topmost branches of the Shakespearean bay tree. He had been engaged for a season of eight performances at Daly's. His moody presence was an "event" in the seventh season of the Fifth Avenue Theatre.

There had been a delay in this Shakespearean presentation. Booth had been thrown from a carriage and suffered a fracture. During the *Hamlet* rehearsals he carried his right arm in a sling.

Barrymore found Booth "considerate and kind." He was to play several times with the great tragedian, again that fall in *Richard II*, and afterward in *Othello*, *Cymbeline*, and *Richelieu*.

There is no critical mention extant of Barrymore's first Laertes. His new-found friend, John Drew, however, had sprung from such an illustrious theatrical line that critic William Winter thumbnailed him:

> The gentleman who played Rosencrantz evidently had an engagement with a friend after the performance, so hurried was his speech and so evident his desire to get through with his part.

This carelessness of speech had been remarked by Drew's mother during her son's debut in Philadelphia. The elocutionary defect, as well as Drew's self-assurance, may have caused Louisa to fling her badly chirping chick into the cockpits of New York.

During young manhood Drew had spent many evenings behind the scenes at his mother's theatre. By day he was a clock salesman at Wanamaker's. He did not care for the life among the pendulums and gongs. He frequently cited his dramatic birthright, so his mother finally permitted him to play the part of Plumper, a minor role to be sure, in *Cool as a Cucumber*, in March of 1873. To give her son encouragement, Louisa herself appeared on-stage as his maid.

As she retired to the wings Mrs. Drew was heard to remark: "What a dreadful young man! I wonder if he ever will amount to anything? He has too much confidence."

This noun-swallowing descendant of the Drews was to become one of the most accomplished readers on the American stage. His youthful conceit was remedied eventually, perhaps by Mum Mum's great friend, Joseph Jefferson. One day that star took John aside.

"Young man," he said, "when I was your age I was so conceited as to be sure that every one knew me. I believed that I had made

Washington Irving famous by my playing of Rip van Winkle. I entered the Fifth Avenue Hotel one day, and a stocky, undersized man with a grizzled beard saw me in the lobby. He looked at me for some time, then asked, 'Are you an actor?' To which I replied testily, 'I believe I am.' Then he asked if I were at present playing any of the theatres. This nettled me, because I assuredly was known to all mankind as the creator of Rip, and was playing the part then. I am afraid I did not reply to the meddlesome question. After the man had left the lobby, I asked a bell boy, 'Who was that doddering old nincompoop?' To which the shocked lad replied, 'Why, *that* was General Ulysses S. Grant!' "

At the close of the Booth engagement John Drew said to Maurice, "I'm going home for the week end. Like to come along?"

Barrymore accompanied his friend to Philadelphia, there to meet Georgianna Drew, John's younger sister. They fell in love. Mrs. Drew did not entirely bless the suit. First off, she regarded Maurice as an amateur. She had little respect for any actor whose family had not undergone at least fifty years of professional campaigning. Then, too, she believed no one good enough for her favorite daughter, particularly a bouncing, irresponsible chaser of dreams. Yet, after a swift courtship, Georgie became Mrs. Maurice Barrymore.

Mrs. Drew never upbraided her daughter for her wild choice, but she could not and did not show her son-in-law any affection. She would not call him by name, and when she addressed him at all, it was as "you." Nor did he feel safe to address her by any term other than "Ma'am." He may have been amateur lightweight champion of England, but in Mrs. Drew's house *she* was the champion.

In 1876, the year of her marriage, Georgie took the place of Miss Jeffries Lewis in a play called *Pique*, acting the part of Mary Standish. Afterward she appeared with her husband and her brother.

She also played in companies supporting such eminent portrayers of tragic roles as Mme. Helena Modjeska, Edwin Booth, and Booth's co-star, Lawrence Barrett, and with the robust John Edward McCullough during that artist's last season. But Georgie became best known for her abilities in comedy parts, and by the nineties had established herself in public favor as a member of the Palmer Stock Company. Mrs. Barrymore was one of the best comediennes of her time, according to the dean of all drama critics, Ashton Stevens.

While strumming his treasured banjo (on which he is a virtuoso) Mr. Stevens recently said: "I've never been quite just in notices about any member of the Barrymore family, because of my un-yielding prejudice in favor of them. I saw Jack's mother beautifully underact the Widow with William H. Crane in *The Senator* before I had attained the age of publicity; and I knew and wrote about Maurice Barrymore when I first took pop-gun in hand and he played a gentleman of considerable importance with Rose Cogh-lan in *A Woman of No Importance.*"

Of her mother, Ethel Barrymore says: "She was a natural actress, so restrained in word and action that many persons, reared on arti-ficial acting, could not appreciate her art. She was twenty-five years ahead of her time. As to her personal appearance and manner in our home, my mother was blond, fair, and gay."

4.

The Tomb of the Capulets

PHILADELPHIA houses stiffly complied with a tradition of design manifest in the sameness of square after square of flat roofs and trite façades. It was obvious that someone less im-aginative than Sir Christopher Wren had set the peas-in-a-pod style for the city's dwelling places. Perhaps some ancient maker of peach-crates imposed a pet theory upon the amiable Quakers at a time when the best brains of the community were preoccupied with the Declaration of Independence and the Bill of Rights.

Mrs. Drew had no choice but to occupy successively several of these outwardly unromantic warrens. Her four children were born in one of them. The back door of that house gave upon a cemetery of heroes of early American wars.

The Ronaldson cemetery was the oldest nonsectarian graveyard in the city, a green-sodded burial ground shaded by ash trees. The Drew children, playing as in a park, romped here among the tombs of almost everybody's ancestors.

Mrs. Drew's South Tenth Street house was near St. Stephen's Protestant Episcopal Church, where she had been a communicant since 1835. The Drew children were christened there. Georgie Drew

taught Sunday school in this church, before her conversion by Mme.
Helena Modjeska to Catholicism.

Mrs. Drew appeared at services with Victorian propriety on the
arm of son John, a handsomely mustached young man in morning
coat, pin-striped trousers, a flower in his lapel. The daughters de-
murely followed after them, like ladies-in-waiting. Sidney Drew cus-
tomarily was late for church, possibly because of his exacting labors
at the billiard parlor.

Mrs. Drew was a burden bearer. No matter how many relatives
or waifs thronged her household, she never complained. When the
increase became a strain on domestic comfort, she promptly moved
to more commodious quarters.

Lionel and Ethel were born at Number 119 North Ninth Street.
Neither of them remembers this house at all, nor does Lionel recall
anything of the Columbia Avenue birthplace of his brother John,
other than one yammering incident at a time when John was learning
to walk. The future Hamlet fell from the second-floor nursery window upon an array of flowerpots. He cut his chin and banged his head.
His howls were horrendous. He bled like a sacrificial goat. Uncle
Googan set off with such speed for Dr. Mitchell's office that John
Drew remarked: "Heavens! What a magnificent quarter-miler was
lost to the University of Pennsylvania when Sidney decided to stay
illiterate."

The children, all three, remembered best the next house leased by
Mum Mum. That was Number 140 North Twelfth Street, the largest
of all the Drew residences, a three-story building with cavernous
halls, monastic rooms, a nursery known as "The Annex," and two
attics. The boys sometimes slept in one of the attics.

A stonecutter did business across the street from the house in
North Twelfth Street. This Sicilian Phidias, a sallow dwarf with a
weather-vane mustache, was a carver of tombstones. Numerous
pieces of his handiwork, stolid angels and emaciated doves, occupied
the sidewalk in front of his establishment. In deference to this morbid bric-a-brac, Georgie Barrymore named their new home "The
Tomb of the Capulets." This house no longer is standing except in
memory.

The old Arch Street Theatre, too, has been razed. Its site is now
a parking lot. Yet on the brick flanks of once adjacent buildings
there still may be discerned the slanting evidences of a balcony
among remnants of Pompeiian pink plaster. And one thinks of For-

rest, McCullough, the Booths, Jefferson, Ada Rehan, the Drews and the Barrymores. One vicariously relives the days when Lincoln visited the theatre of his friend Mrs. Drew, and in imagination sees Charles Dickens during his second American tour, and the King Lear whiskers of Walt Whitman who, on the evenings before his paralysis, crossed over from Camden as a welcome though non-paying patron of this storied playhouse.

"Poets," said Mrs. Drew, "neither should be given money, nor money taken from them."

John Drew well remembered the day he ran home from the Episcopal Academy to inform his mother of the death of Abraham Lincoln. Mrs. Drew was, of course, greatly shocked by the news.

She asked her twelve-year-old son, "Are you sure?"

Then she sat wordlessly for a long time, looking at the well of purple ink on her desk. Now she brought from a drawer a letter Lincoln had written in 1862, thanking her for providing the Presidential party with seats at the Arch Street Theatre.

After gazing at the letter for a time, she said slowly, without raising her eyes, "Who did such a monstrously wicked thing?"

"Mr. Booth's brother," said John.

His mother was incredulous. "No!" she exclaimed. The gentle, talented kinsman of the slayer had been a star at Mrs. Drew's playhouse and often a guest in her home. "No! It is unthinkable! The brother of one so kind . . . Will our profession ever atone?"

The Drew-Barrymore family was not a brawling clan, notwithstanding the long list of physical clashes attributed to their menfolk. These individualists were unusually polite in their own home, almost formal. Maurice, although by nature a firebrand, could reveal the manners of a gentleman of abundant native charm.

It just seemed to happen that when these outward Victorians got in the way of adventure, gunpowder began to explode. These turbulences usually occurred during chivalrous crises, such as the incident of an injury to John Drew's eye. According to Jack Barrymore, Drew lost the sight of his right eye while fencing. Yet here we encounter a surge of poetic license on the part of our legend-loving protagonist.

Drew didn't have a sword with him; not even a poniard. He had been skylarking with cronies, and on his way home encountered a gentleman jabbing a lady with a walking stick. Mr. Drew made gallant remonstrance. His intentions earned the sudden ire of both parties, as often happens when a stranger seeks to solve the plane‹ tary relationships of Mars and Venus. The lady rewarded Mr. Drew's efforts with an eloquence usually associated with the fo'c'sles of cattle-ships. Her escort turned the ferrule of his cane from its soft target to Mr. Drew's eye.

This injury might have permanently retired from the boards any other leading man, but nothing less than the grave has ever been known to snuff out a Drew or a Barrymore. Uncle Jack's sightless eye went unnoticed by most playgoers, so diverting was his theatrical craftsmanship.

This was not the only mishap to the family's men-folk during the season. Papa returned home with a dented noggin after a tour with Lillie Langtry. Maurice and Robert Hilliard had been supporting the "Jersey Lily" in repertory during her Canadian triumph.

While in the city of Toronto, Mrs. Langtry received a round-robin mash note from all the members of a visiting hockey team. It was beneath this titled beauty, a former protégée of Edward, Prince of Wales, to reply to a letter written by amorous commoners.

That evening after the play—and also after the hockey game— Barrymore and Hilliard were having nightcaps in the hotel bar. The hockey team, carrying sticks and other equipment, entered for a drink before train time.

One of the players, said to be the goalie, suddenly announced to his colleagues in a loud voice: "I think I'll let you fellows take the train without me." He squinted toward the ceiling. "I plan on going upstairs to call on Lillie Langtry."

Mr. Hilliard had had enough drinks to feel a spell of nobility coming on. "That is not a gentlemanly remark," he admonished the goalie, "and I shall ask you to retract and apologize at once."

Hockey sticks began to fall against Mr. Hilliard's ribs. His friend Barrymore joined the fight, managed to floor the pleasure-loving goalie; but a few whacks on the head put him out of the lists.

At matinee time next day the Jersey Lily looked with genteel amazement at her battered actors. She discharged them on the spot.

"That," said Barrymore, "is poetic justice. We never should have gilded *this* Lily."

A third fracas enlivened the family history this year. It seems that Uncle Googan had been in need of a few dollars, which of course meant a visit to the pool hall. Several strangers had been reported waiting there between trains. Uncle Googan took Lionel and Jack along as mascots.

At the doorway of the pool hall a friend hoarsely warned him not to come in. "The fellow you beat so bad two years ago has come back," said Uncle Googan's informant. "You know? The big bloke from Kansas City?"

Uncle Googan peered through the window to see a huge, bull-necked man gesticulating near a cue rack. Uncle Googan noted that the aggrieved fellow was delivering uppercuts in the air.

"He says he's going to beat your brains out," Uncle Googan's informant continued. "God! What a grudge!"

Uncle Googan turned to the children. "Now you both keep out of the way. Stay right here, but at one side of the door."

He stepped briskly into the parlor. There was a lethal silence. The shot-makers stopped their play. Not even the squeak of chalk on cue tips was heard. The colored attendant paused in the task of racking the fifteen balls on one of the tables, a massive green plateau near the door. Uncle Googan whistled a little hornpipe. The Kansas City giant began advancing toward Uncle Googan.

Suddenly Uncle Googan left off whistling. He plucked a shining hard ball from the table. He wound up like Amos Rusie, then fired the missile. It struck the Kansas City man's head, bounced off and hit the colored attendant in the leg. The wounded flunky cried out and did a stork dance; but the Kansas City grudge bearer didn't seem to feel the projectile at all. He kept right on walking in slow, heavy golem fashion.

Uncle Googan was fascinated in a frozen sort of way. It was unbelievable that anyone had a head that hard. Uncle Googan couldn't retreat, a catalepsy having seized him. Nor could he manage to reach for another ball. He stood his ground like a stuffed bantam rooster and gazed wide-eyed at Kansas City.

Then, just as the onlookers were expecting the golem to pulverize Uncle Googan, another amazing thing happened. The man from Kansas City smiled in a silly grimace, then collapsed beefily to the floor.

Uncle Googan shrugged, turned to the doorway to call out, "You may come in now, children, and watch your uncle shoot a little pool."

5.

Of Mice and Lionel

W AS the Tomb of the Capulets haunted? We shall see. People of the theatre have an absorbing respect for the supernatural; nor should workaday outsiders pooh-pooh such psychic overtones as fill the ears or minds of phantom-conscious artists. The ladies and gentlemen who walk enchanted boards are not to be dismissed as mere interpreters of poems or animators of dreams.

These gallant mimes have a mediumistic quality. They may often tiredly wish to cast aside this mystic burden as they shed their wigs and masks when the curtain falls. Yet they cannot. And who are we insensate worldings to gainsay the superstitions of actors or ridicule their fears?

Perhaps the array of tombstones on the sidewalk across the street from the Drew home in North Twelfth Street prepared the week-end guests for morbid imaginings. At any rate, Mrs. Drew's actor-visitors quaked at night-time noises heard within these walls. They whispered to their colleagues that the premises were haunted.

The trills of a little bell addressed their ears at lonely hours, like distant tinkles of a spirit-world sleigh ride. The guests confided to their fraternity brothers that the bell phenomenon was not the only evidence of nasty wraiths in the Drew house. There was yet another fearsome intrusion on sane repose. Rasping sounds, as if Old Scrapey himself were whetting his iron tail off-scene, issued from the wainscoting of a back bedroom, which happened to be Uncle Googan's.

These tinklings and raspings seemed commonplace enough to members of the household. But a jittery guest could not abruptly exchange a lifetime of fairy-tale philosophy for the pewter-cool logic of Sir Isaac Newton.

The family had become used to the bell. It never crossed their minds that a guest, liverish with terror, might mistake it for a tin-tinnabulation from the Great Beyond. No explanations were asked, and none given.

The bell rang from above, no question about that, yet not from astral heights. Had the quaking guests dared explore a certain bedroom, they might have found the belfry and its charming sexton, Eliza Lane Kinloch.

Mrs. Kinloch was Mrs. Drew's mother, and great-grandmother to the Barrymore children. During the night hours, and whenever the bedridden old lady needed attention or grew lonesome—which was often—she would tinkle a little bell like that used by Punch in the old puppet shows.

The aged Eliza lay with matriarchal unrest in a boudoir next to Uncle Googan's. There were mementos of her theatrical past on the tables and walls and within range of her still beautiful eyes. She had been a sweet singer of ballads in the provinces of England, where she was born in 1799.

On the wall at the side of Eliza's bed there was an oval-framed keepsake, a tintype of a St. Charles spaniel. Lionel and Jack seemed especially fond of this picture. Whenever they sought a pretext for staying up beyond the curfew Mum Mum had prescribed, the boys would visit Great-grandmother's room for the customary kiss, then conveniently spy the St. Charles spaniel as if for the first time.

"What a beautiful doggie!" Lionel would enthuse.

"Tell us, Grandma," Jack would say, "tell us all about him."

The little old lady in the tatting-edged nightcap of Irish linen would sigh prettily. "Oh, *that* was darling little Grimaldi. He was named after Joseph Grimaldi, the greatest of the clowns. I saw him perform so many times at Sadler's Wells. They called him Little Joe. Born the same year as I, he was."

"The doggie, Grandma?" Jack would ask with the innocence of Dick Turpin.

"No! No! Not the dog. The clown Grimaldi." She would pause. "I loved him so very much."

"Loved the clown, Grandma?"

"No! No! No! Not the clown. It was your great-grandfather I loved. Only your great-grandfather. A most jealous man he was. What a splendid figure! . . . Isn't it time to say your little prayers?"

"Tell us about the doggie first, Grandmother," Lionel would prompt.

The dear old lady was easily sidetracked from prayers. "Well, then, Grimaldi used to travel with us everywhere. Guarded Louisa like a tiger. He once bit a costermonger. He! He! But a careless maid dropped a heavy kettle on him. Stupid bitch that she was! . . . Now say your little prayers."

The boys would kneel to say the prayer their father had been at solemn pains to teach them.

"God bless Mother, and Papa, and Mum Mum, and Grandmother, and Uncle Googan; and please, God, make Uncle Jack a good actor."

"Now run along, dears," Great-grandmother would say. "Run along."

After they had gone, she would begin tinkling her little bell. Polly the maid, her hair in curl papers, would bring hot tea, and Great-grandmother would keep later hours than anyone except Maurice. Then, after Polly had returned to her quarters, the boys would reappear at Great-grandmother's door, and induce the forgetful old lady to begin all over again the story of the St. Charles spaniel.

The spooky noises from the wainscoting of Uncle Googan's room, used as a guest chamber during Sidney's frequent absences, actually arose from a subhuman, rather than a superhuman, source. If Lionel had honorably obeyed Mrs. Drew's decree in regard to ridding the place of his white mice, the séance-minded guests would have had but one disquieting mystery, the bell, to derail their dreams, alcoholic or otherwise.

Lionel's snowy rodents were fruitful. Their attic cages had become overcrowded tenements. One of the pets escaped to scurry into the kitchen as Annie the fat cook was preparing Mrs. Kinloch's fifth round of pekoe. Annie screamed, broke a Royal Doulton teacup, and next day threatened to give notice.

"I'm disp'r'tly afeared of mice," she informed Mum Mum. "And white they be, I'm more afeared than brown. The lad either rids this house, that's been me pride and joy, of the mice, or by the saints, I go meself!"

Mum Mum conferred with Lionel. She recited Annie's good qualities as a domestic. Mrs. Drew was not afraid of mice, or much of anything else, but it would be best for Lionel to do away with the white multitude. Lionel entered a somewhat oblique defense of his little animals by questioning the character of the cook. He summed up by charging that Annie often displayed a heartless side.

"She pulls my ears," he cited. "Ask Jack."

"She pulls them with reason," said Mum Mum. "And besides, if she pulls them hard enough, you'll look like a faun when you grow up."

It seemed so exciting, the prospect of turning into a faun, that Lionel yielded. He promised to liberate the mice. He kept his word technically, freeing them in Uncle Googan's room. Little John wept to see them disappear in the holes of the mopboards. But Lionel winked like a faun, and was not sad at all.

There was a difference of four years in the ages of the brothers. Greengoose seemed a pain in the neck to a mature custodian of mice, yet Lionel permitted Jack to accompany him to Uncle Googan's room each afternoon, there to attend the white rodents. Lionel would set out a plate of uncooked cereal, go "cluck! cluck!" and the mice would pop out from the wainscoting as if in response to the Pied Piper.

The new freedom of the mice in no way lessened their fertility. They struck up promiscuous friendships with wild brown natives of the woodwork. Soon there were to be seen mice of fascinating markings. Some of them wore white targets on brown backgrounds. Others were blazed, piebald, calico, half-and-half, pink-eyed but brown-bodied; and one of them, a favorite of the brothers, was entirely white except for a dashing brown mask like a highwayman's, and fierce dark eyes.

Even when Lionel appeared in the bedroom with no food at all, and clucked, the army in assorted uniforms would scamper into view as if to assembly blown on the bugle. Of course, all this supplying and reviewing of troops had to be done secretly, and after a guest-occupant of the room had risen for breakfast at noon.

It was not until Lionel had had another brush with fat Annie that his control over the mice suggested a means of getting rid of guests entirely, so that the brothers could enjoy the luxury of Uncle Googan's bed themselves when he was away on tour.

One afternoon Lionel returned home from the Episcopal Academy where he attended grammar school. It was winter and the great snow plow, drawn by twelve snorting horses, had been clearing the street. When Lionel tracked the newly scrubbed kitchen floor, Annie seized one of his ears. Faun or no faun, it hurt. The cook led him upstairs, still holding him by the ear, to shut him in Uncle Googan's room, supperless. Little Jack sat up in bed, peering with goggle-eyed interest from beneath his black bangs.

The downstairs front door was heard to open. Mum Mum's

quick, firm footsteps could be recognized on the stairs. Annie gave the resentful faun's ear another tug, but Lionel cunningly refrained from yowling. He made a "cluck! cluck!" sound instead.

The loyal mice responded. They began to charge from four directions, scampering across the floor like part of an Asian migration. Annie gasped, crossed herself, then collapsed on the bed, pinning little Jack beneath her. He began to yell helplessly.

The mice, unused to such an unorthodox reception, streaked back to their joists and rafters. Then Mum Mum entered the room to investigate.

"What on earth?" she asked.

"I don't know," Lionel said gravely. "I'm afraid Annie has had a drop too much to drink."

Mum Mum first released Jack from the human landslide, then sniffed at Annie's breath. Fortunately a slight odor of spirits could be detected.

Annie revived, calling out, "Spotted mice! Spotted mice! By the saints, I seen 'em with me own two eyes!"

Mum Mum advised her, "Annie, perhaps you should take off your apron and go immediately to Father O'Reilley to sign the pledge."

This incident convinced Lionel that his and Jack's occupancy of Uncle Googan's room might be guaranteed. The wicked faun began the practice of slipping into the chamber and uttering "cluck! cluck!" to harass a sleeping guest. Such a victim invariably arose early next day, pale and shaking, to make excuses for leaving the haunted house.

As for Uncle Googan, he didn't mind the mice at all. He thought them fascinating, and brought delicacies from the free-lunch counters to feed them by hand.

"Mice," he said, "keep Philadelphia from being dull."

Ethel seldom joined in the robust didos of her brothers. More weighty matters, such as her future, preoccupied her mind. Frequently she stood before an early picture of Mum Mum, a composite engraving of five Louisas in various costumes, at the age of nine and in her multiple roles of *Twelve Precisely*.

"Here I am," Ethel confessed to her brothers, "getting old, and nothing done."

An acquaintance of Mrs. Drew one day intruded gratuitously into the affairs of Lionel the mouse-tamer. He happened into the parlor-office to announce: "Mrs. Drew, I owe all my success to a public school, the Race Street public school, to be specific. Your grandson Lionel is dawdling along at the Episcopal Academy. Learns nothing. How *can* he? Send him to the public school, Mrs. Drew. It will make a man of him."

Lionel next day was summarily removed from the Academy, then enrolled at the Race Street public school.

One night Lionel appeared at the kitchen door to greet Annie with the only thing he really had learned in the cradle of self-made men: "Hello, Annie, you old sonofabitch!"

He was hastily rescued from the Race Street school and enrolled in a Catholic institution. His sister Ethel had been for some time in a similar school, the brown-front convent of Notre Dame in Rittenhouse Square. Jack also was attending a Catholic school supervised by the Convent sisters at the rear of the main building where Ethel was receiving her early education. Jack's classmates, boys less than seven years old, were taught by Sister Vincent, a nun with a Della Robbia face of sweetness and piety.

Mrs. Drew neither approved nor opposed her daughter's change of creed. She believed wholeheartedly in freedom of worship. As for Maurice, it made no difference to him so long as Georgie was satisfied.

In the late afternoons Polly would escort the children to the second-floor library, and draw the portieres to screen the room from the head of the stair. The children would select from the shelves one of several illustrated volumes, more often than not *The Ancient Mariner* or *Picturesque America*, then rest their elbows on the rug to look at the pictures. As a literary finale they would open an enormous religious volume and turn apprehensively to a full-page woodcut showing the Lord floating in mid-air above a chasm inhabited by winged serpents and fiery dragons. Was there no escape from this eternal pit of monsters if one sinned? Perhaps there was a smaller pit for children.

Each day at teatime the boom of the front-door gong would shatter the spell of the gulf of punishment. Then a man's voice would come as if in response to a tuning-fork:

"God damn it, Mrs. Drew! I've had the God-damnedest busy day of it!"

The children would peer from behind the brown velure curtains to see the full-chested visitor, Mr. Riter. This erect gentleman was entirely bald, but had a cascade of white whiskers and the most compelling black eyes since those of Saladin the Sultan. He carried himself and his epithets with the aplomb of a retired admiral.

Mr. Riter, principal stockholder in the Arch Street Theatre corporation and chairman of its board of agents, also owned the Dollar Store. The children feared for his safety if the monsters of the book were to overhear him as he "God damned" himself into the parlor, there to discuss business of the theatre with Mrs. Drew.

Soon Polly in cap and white apron would appear with an antique silver tea service of vintage pattern. Embossed grapes and vine leaves clustered on the sides of the teapot, the creamer, the sugar bowl, and even the small slop-cup.

Mr. Riter occasionally brought with him his daughter, who sang sentimental ballads after tea. If Maurice happened to be home—which was seldom—he would sit beside the box-like Steinway piano and shed real tears while the young woman sang his favorite, "The Garden of Sleep."

After the tea had been sipped and the songs of yearning hearts sung, and the door closed on the owner of the Dollar Store, Polly would climb the stair to feed the children. After their supper she would chaperon them to Mrs. Kinloch's bedroom, and stand squinting at the scene while the little ones kissed Great-grandmother. Polly permitted one story of Grimaldi and the St. Charles spaniel, waited stoically until after the prayer for Uncle Jack Drew's artistic improvement, then hustled the young Barrymores off to bed.

Only five years ago, Lionel Barrymore received a letter bearing a San Francisco postmark. He opened it to read:

> I recently attended an auction and purchased a lovely silver tea-set. It was a grape pattern. I happened to find the name "Drew" engraved upon it. Could this by any chance have belonged to a member of your family? And, if so, would you like to own it?

We had tea from this old service at Lionel's home in Chatsworth just recently. The teapot brought memories to him of Mr. Riter's visits in the happy times of long ago. These memories inspired others of a later day, and he said, "I have something to show you. I have just completed a manuscript concerning Jack's and my times together."

Lionel then brought a manuscript from a briefcase. It is not a literary work, but a musical composition called "In Memoriam." It contains nostalgic melodies of Lionel's own contrivance; and through it there persist gypsy airs, both sad and gay, and a little song, "Blue Forget-me-nots," which the brothers used to hear at the Café Boulevard in New York when they were young and eager and touched with dreams.

"Unless my friend Eugene Ormandy and his Philadelphia Orchestra play it," said Lionel, "we'll just file it away. Ormandy would understand better than anyone else what it means."

Lionel looked for a time at the score of the memorial music, then said, "To write this was like having a long visit with Jack."

6.

The Wings of St. Michael

WHENEVER Maurice played the Arch Street Theatre the three little Barrymores behaved as if Mrs. Drew had done them a personal favor. Of course the iron-encased business woman did not see eye-to-eye with the children in this respect. She really was booking the best available attractions for her playhouse, and if such an attraction happened to be Modjeska, and Maurice Barrymore tagged along with the company of the talented Pole, well, Mr. Riter, we must take the bitter with the sweet.

But the children had a more joyous view of their father's engagements at Mrs. Drew's theatre. It meant that Papa really had come home for a season, and would not flit in and out of their lives.

If not otherwise occupied after the night performance Papa would pay surreptitious visits to the attic. There would be suppers of smuggled food at late hours in violation of Mrs. Drew's strictest orders against waking or stuffing the children after they had gone to bed. The happy rule-breakers would lick their chops, promise not to make any sound that might bring Mum Mum or Polly or Annie up the narrow staircase to spoil their fun.

Papa would tell stories of India. The boys considered his re-enactment of the siege of Fort Agra the masterpiece of the garret presentations, more bloodcurdling even than the picture-book tableau of the Lord in levitation over the pit of monsters. Papa acted out the Sepoy Mutiny, playing the parts of both armies. The defense of Fort Agra became the only military action in all history to be dramatized on tiptoe and in whispers.

If only they might find relief in one cheer! But no. Their yells were chained inside their skins, an emotional frustration that made their toes curl and their brains evaporate in smoke.

One night, when the garrison of Fort Agra faced liquidation, and with the relieving army of Colonel Greathed lost in a fog near the doorway of the attic-battlefield, the multitude that was Papa put on such a stimulating performance that his audience could hold in no longer. They began to jump up and down on the bed. Their vow of silence flew the coop. They cheered. The actor, by force of habit, took a bow. A dislocated bed-slat clattered to the floor. Papa laid a finger against his lip and hoped for the best. But the worst, the very worst happened. Someone could be heard scaling the heights otherwise known as the attic stairs.

Mrs. Drew, in negligee, entered from the direction of General Greathed's late bivouac near the doorway. Papa flinched. He wasn't acting now. Then nightgowned Annie came in too, looking like a shroud-maker in the suburbs of Fort Agra.

Mrs. Drew advanced on the guilty sentinel. "Well, you, is four o'clock in the morning the best time to scare the children?"

"I was only giving them a touch of India, Ma'am," said the dramatizer of British hollow squares and Sepoy hordes. "A soothing battle scene."

"I'd like to give you a touch of something," said Mrs. Drew, "a touch of intelligence perhaps." Her attention was being insisted upon by Annie, whose eyes were as large as carriage lamps. Annie made motions for Mrs. Drew to look at the bed, upon which the children were crouching in a guilty attitude. Mrs. Drew examined the bed, raised a brow, the left one, turned to Maurice to ask with menacing politeness: "In the future, could you manage to avoid such decisive battles until after the season of tropical rains?"

"Yes, Ma'am," weakly replied the former amateur lightweight champion of England.

What a gay companion Papa was, by night or by day, never

grouchy when the boys came shouting into his room of a morning! How full of life and high spirits he seemed even when asleep! He refused to wear custom-made nightshirts, such as Uncle Jack Drew disported, with maroon-piped seams, French-embroidered monograms, and hand-loomed linen kerchiefs tucked just so in the pockets. Not Papa, the hardy fellow!

He reposed in an undershirt, a kind of rowing-club jersey, always the same one, or at least of identical pattern, a sleeveless, sagging relic traversed by horizontal stripes. He never bothered with underpants.

Papa's extreme hairiness impressed his sons. Tufts protruded from the loopholes of his undershirt like the wings of St. Michael. What a brave apparition he seemed as he rose from tousled sleep! He would gulp some water, shudder, snort, as if returning to mortality, sit up on the edge of the bed, scratch his torsorial upholstery, then rise to stride up and down the room like a Roman senator in half a toga. He would point a long finger at his sons, glare with pretended ferocity, and recite excerpts from the Bard, such as "Sleep that knits up the ravel'd sleave of care."

Sometimes he would quote from lesser authors, as on the day he undertook to lecture his sons on financial ethics. Georgie had asked her husband to speak to the boys concerning larceny, embezzlement, and crimes that sprout from the roots of a petty theft. It seems that the boys had neglected to place their thank-offerings in the poor box; they had bought peanuts instead. Unknown to Georgie, Maurice had shared the peanuts, a delicacy of which he was notably fond. He raised his voice so that eavesdroppers would mistake the oration for a moral rebuke.

Maurice had but a hazy concept of money matters. Facts of any sort draped him on the ropes. Today as he munched what remained of his share of peanuts, he dismissed from his mind all references to coins or currency. He recited poems instead, among them the philosophical jingle:

> Tommy Trout, a man of law,
> Sold his bed, and slept on straw.
> Sold the straw, and slept on grass,
> To buy his wife a looking-glass.

Maurice loved his wife and children in his own will-o'-the-wisp fashion. If his waywardness seemed inexcusable to the Broadway moralists, his family (other than the stern Mrs. Drew) pleasantly conceded that Papa was not a homing pigeon.

When among his children, he suddenly seemed a doting parent and contentedly so, as if he never had been away at all. He entered into all their plans, elaborately suggesting what he and his young ones would do on a tomorrow that was to find him gone.

Maurice's wife, as beautiful as any of his admirers, possessed a superlative mentality that left her rivals in the lurch. She seemed serenely confident that no matter how far or for how long he might wander among the mirages, he would always come back to her.

On one of the belated homecomings, a Sunday morning, Maurice approached the Tomb of the Capulets as Georgie and the little ones were descending the marble steps. Georgie was carrying a rosary and the Holy Book, and obviously was off with her brood to Logan Square and the great brownstone Cathedral of Saints Peter and Paul.

"Why, hello, darling!" Maurice called out, with the overdone cordiality of the two-faced male. "I was delayed getting in from New York. Up all night with Wilton Lackaye."

"Until now," said Georgie, "I had always thought Wilton Lackaye to be a *man*."

Maurice sought to change the subject. "Where are you going, darling?"

"I'm going to Mass," said Georgie, leading the children away, "and you can go to hell!"

By now Maurice was an acknowledged figure in the theatre, although not eulogized by everyone. Certain American critics deplored his English accent. Upon his return to London, however, the play reviewers of that citadel of enunciation scoffed at his Yankee nasalities.

"Great God!" he groaned. "Must I be condemned for the rest of my life to giving recitations on ocean liners?"

Maurice had an abiding love for America. An English patriot once belittled his transplanted friend's admiration for the western world, remarking, "Why, we could go over and beat the daylights out of America any day." To which Maurice replied, "What, again?"

The theatrical craftsmanship of Barrymore, it would seem from the record, was never quite comparable to the burnished art of the younger Booth or the unvarying skill of Joseph Jefferson. Yet Barrymore had an arresting personality. There was more than medallion beauty to his presence on the stage. Away from the footlights he relaxed into an indifference of manner and dress, and seemed no more an artist than any other baseball fan whose main concern was to sit in the grandstand with a score card and a bag of peanuts in his hand.

In the limelight of the theatre, however, he became a dynamic Adonis. He possessed a disarming self-confidence, quite as effective in its own natural virility as the heavy egotism of Edwin Forrest or the aloof intellectuality of Henry Irving.

Such flaws as the critics found in Maurice Barrymore's portrayals failed to lessen the ardor of his partisans. The foremost actresses of that day, notably Olga Nethersole, Helena Modjeska, and Minnie Maddern Fiske, regarded him as first choice among their leading men.

His three children shared in ample inheritance their father's theatrical presence, his wit, his quick charm. They partook in varying degrees, however, of Maurice's off-stage attributes and deficits.

In appearance, Ethel and Lionel resembled their mother. John seemed a carbon copy of his father, amended somewhat by the Windsor Castle mannerisms of Uncle Jack Drew and the inherent spirituality of his mother. He possessed his father's physique, voice, alertness of movement. He received from Maurice not only the most electric stage presence since Edwin Forrest, but also many of his parent's epic frailties, the thoughtless behaviorisms, the capricious tendencies for self-ruination.

Like his impetuous sire, Jack was given to sudden exploits of generosity, and equally fitful moods of self-centered arrogance. In Jack there was repeated the father's complexity of hot-and-cold blowings, the quicksilver humor, the chronic deafness to opinions of others, and a constant tragic restlessness. Both father and son seemed forever to be seeking something—God knows what—some great intangible. Perhaps they were searching for themselves. They were as angels in revolt against a God too bountiful with gifts denied most other men.

Maurice appeared in Philadelphia one week end to announce that he would take his wife and Lionel on a tour with Mme. Modjeska. Sometime during this journey, perhaps out West, he said, he would present a play he had written for the Polish star. In fact, he added, he might become a playwright exclusively, perhaps a producer. He had grown a little tired of taking orders—as if he ever had!

The name of his play, he revealed, was *Nadjezda*. It had a prologue in which a woman marketed her honor to a spidery cynic. Then, in the play proper, the seducer of the mother tried to practice an immoral encore on her daughter. Much coquetry, terror, and some retributory blood-letting had been incorporated in the drama to give Modjeska an opportunity to parade her emotions.

While Maurice was aggrandizing his plans, Uncle Googan interrupted with competitive enthusiasm, "I, too, am writing a play."

Eyebrows were raised. Uncle Googan seemed to his relatives more natural with a cue in hand than a quill. Mum Mum, although extremely fond of Sidney, asked with mischievous interest, "Does someone in your play get killed with a billiard ball?"

"I have been working on my melodrama secretly," Uncle Googan persisted, "laboring over it for months. How do you like this title, Maurice? I call my play *Odd, To Say the Least of It.*"

"I think," Maurice replied, "that you have been wise to work in the greatest secrecy. And I earnestly recommend you continue in the same way."

The children rejoiced over Papa's becoming a playwright. To think, he not only could recite brave words but write them as well, anything that he wished, and not depend merely on Shakespeare or Dion Boucicault!

They saw in their father a magnificent success. How in the world could such an otherwise infallible oracle as Mum Mum be deferential to the pronouncements of occasional household guests such as Joseph Jefferson, Edwin Booth, and Lawrence Barrett, and now be sitting complacently at her desk, her back turned to their father and his genius?

"Mme. Modjeska," Mrs. Drew said over her shoulder, "is deserving, after all she has suffered, of the cream of the gentleman's efforts in her behalf."

After a somewhat stormy beginning as Modjeska's leading man in 1882, Maurice now was regarded as a splendid necessity in her company. At first his painstaking employer complained about his lazy gaiety. He sometimes neglected to memorize his lines. He also would contrive amazing excursions from the text.

Indeed, one evening Maurice suddenly slipped away from the scene at hand and into an entirely different play. The startled Modjeska thought her ears had gone on a holiday. She studied the impassioned wanderer for a moment, then joined the wool-gathering venture. She played the alien scene with such artistic vigor that the audience wildly applauded.

After the curtain calls, Mme. Modjeska rebuked her leading man. "Now look, Mr. Barrymore, you must not be so careless again. Please remember who made it possible for you to rise to such fame as you may think you own."

This was no way to address a Barrymore. "Madam, I was quite well known to the American public at a time when they thought Modjeska the name of a tooth-wash."

On his homecoming to Philadelphia, Maurice revealed to his family that the great American tour would extend to San Francisco, the Golden Gate. He announced that William Muldoon, the champion wrestler of the whole world, would accompany the Shakespearean troupe. The Greek-bodied bone-crusher had been engaged to play the part of Charles the Wrestler in *As You Like It*, Papa to be Orlando. These opponents would contend in lion skins, giving Papa's striped undershirt a recess.

"Who'll win, Papa?" Lionel asked.

Maurice winked at his son. "Don't be absurd. Your father always comes out on top. Now run along to school."

A deflated Lionel returned that afternoon. Papa and Uncle Googan learned from him that he had suffered a social reverse at the home of two schoolmates, occupants of a mansion in Rittenhouse Square. He had dropped in on them to play with their magic lantern.

While manipulating the lantern slides in a darkened room off the library, Lionel overheard the remarks of the head of the house, a rotund distiller with blue-book aspirations.

The maker of spirituous delicacies was instructing his elder son: "You must quit encouraging that Barrymore boy coming to this house, Milton. Confine your visits to the school. Yes, speak to him on the street, but remember who you are, Milton, and what sort of boys you invite here. We have a position to uphold, and . . . well, his people are *actors*. . . ."

Upon receiving Lionel's blubbering report, Maurice prepared to descend violently on the distiller, but Uncle Googan intervened. "Let me cope with this, Barry. The situation requires more than brute force." He turned to Lionel. "Come with me. We shall rehearse."

The next day Lionel appeared at the home of the aristocratic blender of booze. He prevailed upon the butler to show him to the library. He found the plump manufacturer reading the financial columns of the newspaper. The host lifted a disapproving eye from his journalistic barricade and said, "Well, young man, what do you want?"

"I hardly know how to say it," Lionel began with fake emotionalism. "It . . . it . . ."

The blue-blood candidate riffled his newspaper with impatience. "Now! Now! Get it over with." A note of sadistic hope crept into his tone. "Are you in some kind of a nasty mess? Father drunk all the time, eh?"

"No one in my family touches the stuff, sir," said Lionel. The distiller winced. Lionel took advantage of this reaction to blurt out: "It's this way, sir . . . well, you see I'm very fond of your boys, cross my heart, and when I think of *never* being allowed to see Milton again and the magic lantern . . ."

"Here, now," the distiller said, returning to the Wall Street reports, "stop sniffling . . ." He lifted his glance from the newspaper to see Lionel wiping his eyes. "You must learn to accept facts as they are." Then back to his journalistic survey, mumbling as he read: " 'Steel one and a half points down' . . . My boys have a social position to uphold . . ." He smiled with the sincerity of a mortician. "I'll say good day now. Good day."

A sob from Lionel roused the distiller from his stock market abstractions. "You still here? Now run along. You have your place in the social scheme, a fairly honest one, as things go, and in spite of your environment of actors and other degrading . . ."

"Yes, sir," Lionel interrupted shakily, "that's just what I mean. My family forbids my coming here any more, and will beat me with a club if I ever . . ."

"What?" asked the puzzled sponsor of John Barleycorn, half rising from his Morocco-bound chair. "Your family *what?*"

"My Uncle Googan says that I must remember who I am, a Barrymore. And that a Barrymore—even a Drew—must never associate with anyone in *trade!*"

The creator of intoxicants wheezed like the noon whistle over the vat-room. His neck expanded, his paunch oscillated. He half rose, then subsided rumpily among the cushions.

Jack and Ethel Barrymore huddled in the background of the Reading Station while Papa and Mama prepared to take Lionel on the great tour. They followed Lionel's actions with wide appraising eyes. They marveled as he moved about like a world traveler, conferred with the man at the ticket gate, advised the porter as to proper handling of luggage. A windfall of grandeur blessed him.

During one of Lionel's whisking errands past their bench the children spied a price tag on the tail of their brother's new reefer. Should they call Mother's attention to it? Perhaps not. It would be impolite to bother her while she was busy at the ticket window rectifying Papa's mistake in reserving two places instead of three in the Pullman car. They could, of course, apprise Lionel of the tag which was bringing titters from station-mongers. But he floated about the premises with such self-assurance as to discourage minor criticisms.

When the sniggers of tourists persisted, Lionel descended from his cloud to wonder if he were missing some joke. He at first pretended that he was in on the fun, but his fellow-travelers pointedly refrained from giving him a hint as to the cause of their growing amusement. It finally occurred to him that he himself might be the source of the merriment.

Lionel whistled his way adroitly to the gentlemen's washroom. He consulted one of those perjuring wall-mirrors that hang like dingy satirists over the cracked and homely porcelains. He stood on his toes to seek information from the looking-glass, but was unable to find in it other than a blur of nose and ears and a piece of fog that ought to be his chin. Nonetheless, he built up enough evidence to satisfy him that nothing at all was wrong with his appearance.

While Lionel was formulating this self-assurance, a rude fellow emerged from a shuttered booth, rinsed his hands, looked for a towel, which even a fool never expects to find in these ammoniac grottos, then spied the price tag. His maniacal laughter sent Lionel out of the washroom more confused than before.

Only the sight of Mr. Muldoon saved Lionel from a plunge into melancholia. The Solid Muldoon, bending over like an arch of triumph, was shaking hands with little Jack. Just as Lionel planted himself within range of Mr. Muldoon, Mother touched his reefer and said in a stage whisper, "Good gracious, Lionel! One would think you were for sale."

She took him aside to unfasten the label which had a crossed out $6.70, and below the canceled price an interesting revision that read $4.99.

Mr. Muldoon's questions, addressed to Jack, came over this scene. "What are you doing in school, young man?" the eminent rib-twister was asking.

Jack replied, "Nothing."

This candor appalled the Solid Man. He was about to forfeit a fall, in a manner of speaking, when Mother interrupted her price-tag plucking to offer some irrelevant advice to her younger son.

"I wouldn't spend *all* my time sketching in class, Jack, if I were you. Sister Vincent informs me that you scrawl constantly on the blackboard, even the walls. Pictures of the Bad Man. Monsters, too! Is it nice to frighten the other children?"

Jack smiled up at his mother. "No, Mamma."

Mr. Muldoon nodded with magisterial gravity. "Then why," he asked of Jack, "*do* you draw pictures of the Bad Man and these—ah—these monsters?"

Jack looked Mr. Muldoon squarely in the eye. "Because I see them in my sleep."

"Tell Mr. Muldoon what your lesson was," Mother said to ease the tension. "Speak up, son!"

"I don't remember," Jack replied.

"Yes you do now," Mother corrected him gently. "Sister Vincent told me you were studying the Knights of . . . Remember it now? The Knights of . . ."

Mr. Muldoon saw a chance to exercise his own literacy. "The Knights of the Round Table? Eh, young man?"

Jack nodded reluctantly. "I guess so . . . Mamma, may I have some lemon drops all my own?"

Mr. Muldoon said to Maurice. "I find relaxation in history myself, Barry." He wheeled on Jack "Did you come across Lancelot in your lessons?"

Lionel at last saw an opportunity to get into the Muldoon colloquy. "Jack had to stay in after school for something he said about King Arthur—and who killed him."

"You did?" the frowning wrestler asked of Jack. "Who *did* kill King Arthur?"

The boy replied with sudden authority, "Henry Irving."

The call of "All aboard" interrupted this. There was a last embrace by Mamma, then Ethel and Jack stood watching the lucky ones disappear through the ticket gate.

Then they turned wordlessly to go outside where Mrs. Drew's Irish coachman was waiting to drive them home. Ethel took Jack's hand, and they walked slowly, like Hansel and Gretel, to the brougham. The coachman helped Ethel into the carriage where she sat upright and regal, as Mum Mum always did, and Jack climbed onto the box beside the driver and from time to time held the reins when the roadway became clear of traffic.

The Philadelphia fortunes of Mrs. Drew began to pale in the late eighties, and her home began to lose its familiar members. The tinkle of Great-grandmother Kinloch's little bell no longer was heard. Uncle Googan had married Gladys Rankin, daughter of McKee Rankin, and had gone with his pearl-handled cue and a fragment of *Odd, To Say the Least of It* to New York. Uncle Jack Drew had become a permanent resident of that metropolis.

The city was moving away from the Arch Street Theatre. Yet the courageous little manager would not leave the vicinity of Independence Hall and the historic neighborhood of Betsy Ross. Her board of agents showed a worried loyalty, and the older tragedians still answered her calls when rheumatism and ague permitted.

Mr. Riter stood gallantly behind the efforts of his friend, but was growing too old to remain active. "God damn it, Mrs. Drew," he said, "I'm getting tired." Then he sighed until his whiskers bobbled like a frosty nest, and recited from Heine, " 'Other times, other songs.' "

When Papa decided to take his three children to live in New York, Mrs. Drew showed no tears. The family had outgrown the Tomb of the Capulets, and never again would be gathered together for long at any one time except among the pages of the encyclopedias.

7.

The Entrance of the Little Fauns

LIONEL was eleven years old, Ethel ten, and Jack seven when in 1889 they moved to New York, then a city of almost one million four hundred thousand population. It was the Horatio Alger time of luck and pluck, of rags and riches. So much to be seen and heard in this Manhattan of adventurous growth!

Each afternoon a parade of great names moved along Broadway, a procession that lasted regularly until milk-man time next morning. During the Barrymore children's first stroll in this street of fickle luster, they glimpsed a succession of magnificos, among whom they admired most of all Papa's friend, John L. Sullivan, the heavyweight champion.

The Boston Strong Boy set the fashion for gentlemen who regarded themselves athletic. On this day he had on a dark blue pea-jacket, tight trousers of robin's egg blue, and a high silk hat, which he tipped to little Ethel and bellowed, "Hello, sis! Happy to meet you!"

When John L. lifted his silk tile to Ethel and she saw the close-cropped skull, the child naturally believed him to be Genghis Khan. She fled behind her father's coat tails. Mr. Sullivan turned to Lionel. "And what's your name, lad?"

"Lionel," said the boy, panting with hero worship.

Mr. Sullivan grunted. "It is, eh? *Lionel!* Huh!" He looked at Maurice accusingly, grunted again, then squinted at Jack and said cryptically, "Well, well, well!"

Jack at this time was less than prepossessing. He seemed as slim and pale as a church candle, wore black bangs, and looked like a Siamese office boy. He had nothing about him to indicate that he would grow up to be a new Apollo.

Mr. Sullivan poked Jack gently with his stick, merely knocking the boy's wind out, then said to Maurice in parting, "Fine family, Barry! Fine family!"

The first Manhattan home of the Barrymore children was a brownstone house at Number 1564 Broadway, afterward the site of the Palace Theatre, shrine of vaudevillians. On occasional week ends Mum Mum would come from Philadelphia to see her grandchildren. During one of these visits she reported the death of her great friend Mr. Riter, whose last words, of course, had been, "Well, I'll be God damned!"

Papa took the children to the zoo on Indian Summer days. He knew a great deal about animals because of his experiences in India. His lectures enchanted other zoo visitors, and before long a crowd would be following him and his charges from cage to cage.

One day he decided to discuss the habits of the llama at the Central Park menagerie. "It is a domesticated variety of the guanaco," he said, "and spits in your eye if he doesn't like you. The first dramatic critic was a llama. The great-grandfather of William Winter was one. Llama meat is not good for the dinner table. Tastes like a forgotten sponge."

A tall aviary stood next to the llama corral. Aquatic birds, cormorants, pelicans, storks, herons, and their cousins occupied this great cage. Perhaps it was hard for attendants to keep the place clean; at any rate the perches, bars, and dirt floor showed gray-white with birdlime. The winged captives interested Jack more than did the expectorating llama. He kept tugging at his father's sleeve, interrupting him.

"Tell us about the birds, Papa," he said. "Look at 'em!"

"Presently," said Maurice. "You must learn all about the llama first. Would you believe it? He is of the same family as the camel."

"Please, Papa," Jack persisted, pointing to the cage. "What kind of birds are they?"

Maurice cast an appraising glance at the festoons of birdlime. "Presumably," he said, "they are birds of passage."

At about this time the newspaper men began to pepper Maurice with inquiries about his play *Nadjezda*. It had enjoyed a favorable première in San Francisco during the late "great tour." Now, a year or more after that presentation, Sarah Bernhardt was appearing in *La Tosca*, the work of the French playwright Victorien Sardou. Certain of Barrymore's friends charged that the French academician had plagiarized Barrymore's basic idea.

Maurice ignored the issue until informed by a reporter at The Lambs bar one day that Sarah Bernhardt had said, "An idea sometimes is suggested to a dramatist by an obscure source. Sardou is a master; the man who accuses him insignificant."

"I hold a man no less a thief," Barrymore remarked, "if he steals from his own hat-rack my cane, which I have confidently placed there, and proceeds to build upon it an umbrella."

The Police Gazette, a pink package of flamboyant engravings and frisky body type to be found in every barbershop of America, wrote up the *Nadjezda* controversy. Its drama critic buttonholed Maurice in the doorway of Rector's one evening.

"Did you see the piece I wrote about you in *The Police Gazette* this week?"

"No," Maurice replied. "I shave myself."

If Maurice Barrymore was regarded as the first wit of The Lambs, a similar position was accorded by The Players to his brother-in-law, John Drew.

Drew not only was a humorist of repute but became noted as an unfailing gentleman, meticulous of dress and elegant of conduct. He did not enjoy off-color stories or smutty remarks. When an acquaintance one day dealt him a salty tale at the bar, Drew said, "I do not think you know me well enough to tell that kind of story."

Drew maintained a Victorian deportment even when partaking liberally of the bottle. Politeness on Drew's part began at home, where he always took pains not to astound Aunt Dodo, a foe of the demon rum, with exhibitions of elbow-bending. He practiced elaborate ruses to conceal the domestic nipping. He placed stimulants in vases, or hid his bottles behind a swollen Buddha on top of the trophy cabinet.

One evening Uncle Jack entertained Nat Goodwin, celebrated comedian and cork-puller, at the Drew home. Goodwin told stories of his father, a New England gambler. Nat had not long since revisited Boston, the city of his birth, and been given a dinner.

"I am happy," he said to the banqueters, "to come back to a place where I dwelt and my father dealt so long."

This story sent Aunt Dodo to bed. Drew brought some bottles from exile, and the good companions sat down to drink the healths of an alphabet of friends. At dawn Goodwin remembered that he had to catch a morning train. He would not leave, however, without first assisting his drowsy host up the staircase to his room. On the way Mr. Drew slipped, and crashed down the stairs. Without a moment's hesitation, he looked up from the floor to inquire of his innocent guest: "May I give you a hand, Nat, old man? Sorry to mention it, but I'm afraid your fall has disturbed my wife. Light sleeper, you know."

"Perhaps," says Lionel, "Uncle Jack Drew deserves the highest honors of all the male members of our family; for it is so much harder to be a great gentleman than to be a great actor."

Sometimes Papa would take Jack for a stroll, informing Mother that they would be back in a few minutes. But Maurice's time-sense was in keeping with his other views toward responsible conduct. More often than not the strollers would return home at three o'clock the next morning, Jack asleep in his father's arms.

Jack described a situation of this kind during a speech he made in 1939 at The Lambs, where he was guest of honor after an absence of more than twenty years.

"When I was a little shaver," he said, "my father used to bring me to this club and check me in the cloak-room. My mother would be worried along about one o'clock in the morning, and would telephone The Lambs to ask, 'Is that bastard there?' Now please understand me, gentlemen, she was not referring to me, but to my father!"

As children, the Barrymores were timid with strangers. Indeed, an inward shyness possessed them during their subsequent private lives, notwithstanding their ease on the stage or in other public collisions. The Barrymores were slow to admit anyone to their confidence. However, once you had gained passport, you stayed their friend; and never could you have found gayer, more affectionate companions, were you to live to be seven hundred and ninety-four.

To protect their mental privacy, each child set up his own kind of barrier. Ethel, notwithstanding her usual graciousness, could become a bundle of claws when approached clumsily. As for Lionel, he might do either of two things to a well-meaning dullard: punch him in the nose, or retreat into an ossified cocoon and glower at him. Jack, after adolescence, concealed from the world his sensitivity and his daydreams by assuming an ebullient façade, together with cock-o'-the-walk mannerisms and prussic-acid humor. He could be tactless at times, abruptly ironical, or unexpectedly aloof, and too often closed the door on those who otherwise might have come to know the wild yet child-sweet spirit of the man, his surpassing inner decencies, his star-lit charm.

The Barrymores, when among strangers, made a practice of using a code, words or lines taken from plays, to convey private messages. For example, whenever Ethel entered a floor-gazing trance in the presence of guests, the code words were "Look up, Pauline," a speech from Bulwer's *Lady of Lyons*.

Because of the irregularity of their theatrical duties, their frequent tours, the elder Barrymores decided to send Ethel back to the convent and place the boys in Catholic boarding schools. Jack went to Georgetown's elementary school near Washington, and Lionel to Seton Hall College at South Orange, New Jersey.

Jack did not stay long at Georgetown. It seems that some older boys thought that an actor's son should know more about life than he apparently did. They took the wide-eyed neophyte to a sporting house one evening; but when a warning reached the canny proprietress that an inquisitive priest was about to nab her young customers, she sounded a signal and they all fled into the night— all but Jack.

The priest collared the lad, and invited him to tell the names of his companions. This he refused to do, and the school promptly dismissed him. His preceptors notified Papa that Jack had been cast out for a "serious breach of conduct," and advised the culprit to explain that statement to his father as best he could. The lad shivered all the way to New York.

That night he went falteringly to Maurice's bedroom to find Papa in no mood for nasty tidings.

"Well," asked Maurice, "why were you hurled out of school? For selling French postcards to Congressmen?"

Jack hinted at erotic high jinks in the brothel, but added hastily, "I didn't do anything in that house. I mean . . ."

"I know precisely what you mean," Maurice said. "Didn't do anything, eh?" Then he roared, "Why not?"

It was agreed that Jack go to Seton Hall. Maurice accompanied his younger son to South Orange. There they toured the campus with the head of the school, Father Marshall, and Lionel.

Father Marshall had a serene personality, dignified and reserved, and the face of an ascetic Spanish nobleman. In the gymnasium, he indicated the parallel bars. "Have you ever exercised on the horizontal bars, my son?"

"Yes, Father," Jack replied. "Lots."

"Then get up on the bars and try the giant swing, my son."

While Father Marshall, Papa, and Lionel looked on, Jack got up, then went heels-up into the air, standing on his hands on the bars. Suddenly from his pockets there showered some curious keepsakes, including a razor, a loaded pistol, a pack of playing cards, and a pair of dice.

Father Marshall picked up the contraband, saying matter-of-factly, "I don't think you will need these articles *here*, my son."

8.

The Violin String

CIGARETTE smoking in the early nineties was regarded as a vice. Cigarettes were called "coffin nails," and the users known as "fiends." American women, other than habitués of love bazaars, did not smoke. When a boy began this habit he had to go through more dodges in hiding his bronchial debauchery than a two-minded husband trying to conceal an extra-marital letter.

The young students of Seton Hall found the locker room of the gymnasium a comparatively safe place for their smoking exercises. One afternoon they came to this sanctuary after baseball practice to open a box of Sweet Caporals, a brand of lung-foggers that had as a premium in every package a colored picture of some famous athlete or actor.

To the astonishment of the Barrymore boys, the card in today's cigarette box contained a bright miniature portrait of Georgie Drew in an evening gown.

"It's Mamma!" Jack shouted. "Look, everybody!"

"It's Mamma, all right," Lionel said. "What an honor!"

One of the baseball players, a boy of such severe moral restraints as never to countenance the locker-room vice, was dressing some distance away from the secret smokers. He pointedly had not come over to examine the picture card, so Lionel took it to him.

"Isn't it wonderful?" Lionel asked. "She's my mother."

The scandalized puritan glanced at the card, then said slowly, "I think it's disgusting."

Lionel stared incredulously at the critic. Then he became furious, and knocked the boy down. The lad's head struck against the edge of the locker. He lay quite still. The victim, when taken to the infirmary, still failed to open his eyes. Lionel was ordered to the infirmary, and warned not to leave the premises. The school physician informed him that the boy might die.

"Even if he dies," Lionel blurted out, "he never should have said my mother was disgusting."

When Lionel tried to leave the infirmary he found a big policeman from Newark sitting outside the door. The officer stayed on guard all week, and only when the injured boy roused at last from unconsciousness did the authorities permit Lionel to return to his own dormitory.

There was an older boy at Seton Hall well liked by everyone until he became an assistant instructor at the seminary. He suddenly took on airs of stern magnificence. One day he reprimanded Jack for reading *Buffalo Bill's Adventures* behind an opened textbook. During this rebuke the assistant instructor placed a hand on Barrymore's head. That night Jack composed a letter to Mum Mum:

> I was attacked by this huge fellow and without cause. And, as the great brute advanced toward my desk, I tried to placate him; but he struck me, and as I reeled beneath the cruel blow the world went black before my eyes. . . .

When Mum Mum read this curdling document, she hastened to New York. She displayed the letter to Uncle Googan, commanding him to find Maurice. "Here's something, for once, that he can take care of."

Sidney commissioned his brother-in-law in Mrs. Drew's name to punish the great brute of Seton Hall. When Jack got wind of his father's coming visit, he ballyhooed the event to his schoolmates, promising them: "My father's on his way to beat seven kinds of hell out of the entire faculty. Blood will flow from here to Newark. God, what a fiend he is in a crisis like this!"

Jack and a gallery of expectant fellows waited in the shrubbery to witness the arrival of the fierce avenger. Finally a carriage drew up with a sturdy yet seemingly carefree Mr. Barrymore. Jack stepped from behind a lilac bush to wave to Papa. Maurice paid not the slightest attention to his son. Obviously he didn't see him. Papa entered the building where Father Marshall had an office.

"He didn't speak to you," a boy said to Jack. "How's that?"

"He don't look so tough to me," said another pal. "Not mad at all."

"Hah!" snorted Jack. "A lot you know about *real* fighters. They have a graveyard smile just before they mangle everybody in sight. You'll see."

The boys listened for the beginning of the battle. "It's mighty quiet in there," said one of them. "Mighty quiet."

"Just wait," Jack advised. "My father is studying the situation, like Chinese Gordon always did. In a minute the whole damned building will fly to pieces, with priests sailing out of doors and windows, their ears torn loose."

But silence, except for laughter, continued over this scene. The boys left the bushes to peer through a window. To Jack's astonishment, he saw his amiable father seated opposite Father Marshall discussing the Carlyle Harris case, a murder in which Harris, a student at the College of Physicians and Surgeons, had poisoned his schoolgirl wife.

After the priest and the actor had debated the motives and the degree of guilt of Harris, Mr. Barrymore and the head of the school walked arm-in-arm out of the building and past the group of gaping schoolboys to Maurice's carriage.

Papa again failed to see Jack. The son was so let down by his father's fistic neglect, as well as by the collapse of his own advertisement of the decimation of the faculty, that he had no voice left to call out to him.

Maurice waved to Father Marshall from the carriage, then drove off entirely delighted by his visit with the intelligent man, of whom he afterward said: "A priest so honest that Diogenes would have put away his lantern, and so learned that Plato would have kicked Socrates in the behind."

Late in the summer of 1891, Lionel and Jack were astounded to see Papa and Richard Mansfield cycling along Riverside Drive. It was not the pedaling of the two eminent actors that entranced the children, but the fact that both were dressed alike in remarkable costumes: black tights, fur jerkins, zouave sashes, and astrakhan hats of flower-pot contour.

Mansfield, extremely proud of his legs, had designed the cycling costume himself so as to accentuate the symmetry of his calves. He insisted on presenting Maurice with a similar uniform, and together they appeared on the boulevards like a pair of variety acrobats.

Papa waved to his sons, and his cycling comrade drew alongside to invite the boys to the Mansfield home that evening. He said he was giving a stag party. Papa and Mr. Mansfield then rolled onward in carrousel grandeur.

At the Mansfield home that night the boys found themselves apart from the men and in an upstairs room, a kind of study. They ate sandwiches and cake, and drank beer.

A large divan stood at one side of the oak-paneled study, and over it a framed portrait in oil of a grave-faced, prissy man, staring in a frightened sort of way through gold-rimmed spectacles.

"He looks like a clown's kidney," said Jack.

They were laughing and making more jokes about the portrait when one of Mr. Mansfield's guests, temporarily ill from too much refreshment downstairs, entered the room to lie on the divan. A sudden gripe caused the sufferer to sit up. The boys found that he closely resembled the portrait hanging above his head. He was grave-faced, prissy, and stared in a frightened sort of way through gold-rimmed spectacles.

Jack burst out laughing. The sick man squirmed, knocked against the picture frame, and the portrait descended with a great smash. The noise attracted the host and some of his guests. They came upstairs to find the woozy fellow and the picture on the floor. He was lifted to the divan and the picture set to one side.

"What in hell happened?" Maurice asked his sons. "Did either of you hit him?"

Lionel replied, "He couldn't help being struck by his own likeness, Papa."

In 1892 Georgie Drew went to Philadelphia to keep an engagement at the Arch Street Theatre in *Wilkinson's Widows*. She caught cold, and Dr. Mitchell forbade her to go to the playhouse for the opening performance. She insisted upon taking her place, however, and became quite ill.

She returned to New York, where her health rapidly began to fade. Yet she kept in good spirits, and seemingly remained the same person that her daughter called "blond, fair, and gay."

Misfortunes other than the failing health of her favorite daughter now beset Mrs. Drew, the seventy-two-year-old burden bearer. Her elder daughter, Louisa, had died in Boston. Affairs at the Arch Street Theatre had worsened. The twelve successive seasons with Joseph Jefferson had reached a close at the old Baldwin Theatre in San Francisco. So Mum Mum returned to Philadelphia, gave up housekeeping, and moved to New York, sometimes to live in hotels and occasionally to reside with Sidney or John Drew.

Drew finally had left Daly's Company, the distinguished group with which he had been associated for sixteen years as co-star with the great Ada Rehan. A barrier of fancied wrongs separated Augustin Daly and John Drew. He now appeared as a star in his own right, with Maude Adams as his leading lady.

Drew's Victorian ethics did not permit him to visit Ada Rehan, although she was fond of the Drew-Barrymore family and they of her. If Drew wished any intelligence of Miss Rehan's activities, he would make inquiries through a mutual friend. Uncle Jack was a stickler for correct behavior, the sort of man who would not think of dying without first making an appointment with St. Peter.

New York physicians decided that Georgie must take an indeterminate rest, a cruise in warm waters.

One day in 1892 she sailed for the Bahamas. The children went to the North River pier to say good-by to their mother. They saw among the farewell party the gentleman who had been struck by his own likeness at the Mansfield home. He was a playwright, slightly more successful than Uncle Googan, and an earnest admirer of Mother as an actress. He had brought her a gift, a china teapot filled with chocolate creams and tied with a bon voyage ribbon.

Maurice was weeping. Georgie held his hand. The boys didn't know why their father should be so upset, for Mother was smiling all the time. In the hurry of the good-bys, she forgot to share the chocolates with the children. This, the boys thought, was so unlike Mother, who usually divided all good things with others. During her absence the boys kept thinking of the chocolates. Had Mother found them good? And how long had they lasted?

Papa placed the boys for the summer on a decrepit farm near Garrettson's on Staten Island. It seems, peculiarly enough, that he owned the place, although no one, including himself, had any clear remembrance as to how the title had been acquired or from whom.

A Negro tenant, Edward Briggs, did such farming as was done—meaning none at all—and took care of two Arctic dogs presented to Maurice by Robert Edwin Peary, the discoverer of the North Pole.

By the time the boys reached the farm, the dogs had increased from two to thirty-five. Briggs, known to the Barrymores as "Edward the Black Prince," managed somehow to keep the dogs and the boys reasonably well fed.

During this summer Jack left the farm temporarily to visit Mrs. Drew at North Long Branch, New Jersey, where Ethel was spending her vacation. Lionel went to the home of Joseph Jefferson at Buzzard's Bay to join the actor's son Willie, and while there sometimes rowed Mr. Jefferson and President Cleveland on fishing trips.

On one of his Buzzard's Bay visits Lionel shared in an historical confidence. He found President Cleveland recuperating at Mr. Jefferson's from a secret operation for a malignant condition of the palate. It was at a time when diplomatic relations between the United States and England creaked following a Venezuelan boundary dispute. A monetary panic also was in progress. Any public news of the President's malady might have shaken the world.

The Barrymore boys quite naturally liked Willie Jefferson because he was a problem child. He owned a rare cello made by some master of Cremona, and frequently lost it in saloons. On one of his trips to England he lost both his cello and his wallet. He cabled his eminent father, collect: "Send hundred dollars quick."

Mr. Jefferson cabled back: "For what?"

Willie replied, collect: "For Willie."

Mrs. Drew and little Ethel came to the Jefferson home this summer for a visit. One evening Ethel lay in a hammock while Grandmother and Mr. Jefferson talked. During their conversation the actor called Mrs. Drew by her first name, and the child suddenly realized that this was an "event." No one, other than Great-grandmother Kinloch, would dare do such a thing.

As if in telepathic accord with the child's wonderment, Mrs. Drew said to her long-time friend, "Joseph, it occurs to me that you are the only one left to call me Louisa."

There was a long silence. Then Mr. Jefferson replied, "Yes, Louisa. And you and I are the only ones still active of all our once-numerous assembly of artists."

When Georgie returned from the Bahamas, her sons were away at Seton Hall and Ethel at the Convent of Notre Dame. Mum Mum had accepted a short engagement in Boston. John Drew had gone abroad, and Maurice was with a stock company out West. It was a scattered family.

The sea journey had benefited Georgie somewhat, yet physicians now could diagnose her condition as tuberculosis in an advanced form. They decided to send the actress to Santa Barbara in California.

Who would go with Georgie, to watch over her during the then eight-day journey by train? The tradition of the theatre was severe. Its people must not miss a curtain; contractual obligations outweighed any personal problems of actors.

It seemed that no one other than Ethel, barely fourteen years old, was available for this duty. And it seems now, fifty years after that sad time, that Ethel always would be called upon to bear family burdens. She became a successor to Mrs. Drew in this and many other respects, a willing, dependable, uncomplaining refuge for madcap relatives in their hours of bewilderment.

Ethel left the convent to go on the long journey with her stricken mother. Without experience of the world of precise business contacts where service and courtesy are often modified by the amount of cash in view, the child had to make all arrangements for her mother's transportation and care. It was a shocking circumstance for a girl suddenly to exchange the cloistered serenity of Notre Dame for the shove-about rudeness of railway stations.

Ethel, her mother realized, was growing into a beautiful person, both in appearance and in character. Georgie remarked the long golden curls, the blue eyes that seemingly changed to gray or green or even midnight with the girl's moods.

"All my children," said Georgie, "have Drew eyes and Drew hair." Then she added, as if to herself, "and Drew courage."

Sometimes Modjeska visited her friend Georgie in the sanitarium. The Polish actress had been playing for several seasons with Edwin Booth, now in his own year of death. She resided, between Shakespearean tours, at her Anaheim home, which was not far from Santa Barbara. It became obvious to Modjeska that Georgie was gravely ill. She tried gently to prepare Ethel for the shock of her mother's death.

One July morning Ethel went to Mass. As she was returning to the sanitarium, one of the little girls of the neighborhood, skipping along happily, began a sing-song shout: "Your mother's dying! Your mother's dying!"

The shocking chant put Ethel in a state of agonizing suspense. She tried to run to her mother's room, but her feet were stones. She held her breath as she reached the doorway, from which a thin-faced doctor emerged to tell Ethel that it was true.

Ethel knelt beside the bed to hear her mother say, "What is to become of my poor little ones?"

Ethel undertook the task of arranging for the removal of the body to Philadelphia. To make herself appear mature the child did up her hair and bought a long black dress. She purchased a coffin from meager funds. She was sadly resolute. There now was no need for anyone to say to her, "Look up, Pauline." She assumed the burden, alone, and far from home. She would be a child never again.

Once more on the train Ethel sat for eight nights and days in a day coach. There had been no money available for a berth. She did not get out to dine at the railway eating-houses, as was the practice in those days. Occasionally someone thought to give Ethel a sandwich, but that was all. She was the kind of person even then who could share her joys with others but never her grief.

She had spent her last dollar on a telegram to Sidney Drew at North Long Branch. He would know how to break the terrible news of Mother's death to Mum Mum. Perhaps he could even find Papa, who had not been heard from for weeks.

At Chicago, between trains, and while Ethel was standing by to see the plain box wheeled from the baggage car, she heard her name called by a messenger boy. She signed for the message, sent by one of Maurice's best friends, Clay M. Greene, Shepherd of The Lambs: "Don't worry about a thing, little girl. We are trying to locate your father."

John Drew was in London when he received the news of his favorite sister's death. W. Graham Robertson, in his memoir *Life Was Worth Living*, describes Drew's sorrow.

Robertson was calling on Drew, and brought a message from Ada Rehan. He was discussing Drew's and Miss Rehan's last performance together in *As You Like It*, and recalling how she suddenly had been overcome by the thought of their parting and burst into tears on the stage. The arrival of word of Georgie Barrymore's

death interrupted this reminiscence. Robertson tells of Drew's reactions:

> It came to him as a great and unexpected blow.
> "I wish you would go and tell Ada," he said. "Don't let her
> read of it first in a newspaper, or learn of it casually."

Robertson went at once to Miss Rehan's hotel, and found her in
excellent spirits. They talked about various matters for a while,
then a strange sound, rather like the snapping of a violin string,
was plainly heard.

> Ada held up her hand. "Hush! Did you hear that?"
> I nodded. She walked to the window and stood looking out,
> her back turned to me for a long minute, then returned and
> sat down by me quietly.
> "Who is dead?" she asked. "You have come to tell me that
> someone is dead."
> "John's sister—Georgie Barrymore," I whispered.
> We sat in silence until she said slowly: "An old friend. I
> knew that it was an old friend. I have heard that sound several
> times, and always it has been followed by the news of an old
> friend's death!"

Lionel remembers that at his mother's funeral Maurice seemed
unable to believe that Georgie had died. He kept trembling and
denying the tragic fact. He had on a frock coat, the one he had
worn on-stage in *Frou-Frou*, and a high, stiff collar that irritated
his neck and chin.

Ethel and Jack went to the cemetery in a carriage with Mum
Mum, who, clad in black, looked gravely thoughtful, much as she
had in the portrait Sully had painted of her in 1864. Lionel rode
with his father and an actor friend, Eben Plympton. The friend
reached across Lionel's shoulders to place a hand on Maurice's
shoulder.

"Why don't you have a cigarette, Barry?" Plympton asked. "It
might settle your nerves a little."

Maurice stared at Plympton confusedly. "But would it be the
right thing to do?"

"Of course," said Plympton, providing Maurice with a cigarette.
Lionel lighted it for his father, but noticed that it hung loosely
from Maurice's lips, and soon went out.

After Georgie had been buried and the family were on their way to the New York train, Mum Mum said: "The greatest sorrow of all is for a mother to outlive her children."

9.

The Young Gypsies

THE Barrymore boys said good-by to Seton Hall; not, however, without a stimulating valedictory by Lionel. He managed before taking leave of the pleasant academy to bowl over, in a manner of speaking, the ghost of Thomas De Quincey. It was to be Lionel's farewell to the class of English literature where Father Brown long had officiated.

This modest priest, respected for his piety and admired for his scholarship, was not much given to talking; he preferred listening to recitations from the classics. Father Brown would sit in an uncushioned chair, close one eye, roll a pencil beneath the flat of his hand on the desk, and mutter an approving, "Precisely. Precisely." Or an admonitory, "Well, now. Well, now." Or a low-voiced prohibition, "Oh! Oh! Oh!"

He had an austere face like that of Saint Januarius. Upon it stood an ample nose, a weather vane of his moods. But size was not its chief attribute. The priest's cutwater drew attention mainly because of its ability to change expression. A recitation well given found Father Brown's nostrils dilated as if smelling a cowslip. A split infinitive brought severe lines, like a fallen frown, to either slope of his promontory. The clergyman's hypotenuse closely resembled that of Thomas De Quincey, Father Brown's literary lodestone.

The Seton Hall classicist admired the works of this prince of dreams. He especially prized De Quincey's *Confessions of an English Opium-Eater*, holding that work to be the ultimate in style and composition, and finding in its scope the full employment of two powers seldom exercised by one master: an ability to explore fantastic deeps and the talent to apply exacting logic to a splendid prose.

The *Confessions* headed the list of required reading in the Seton

Hall English course—that is, until Lionel tweaked the noses of De Quincey and Father Brown.

It had been the occasional practice of the reverend teacher to assign his boys to read aloud their favorite excerpts from the *Confessions*. Father Brown would seem his happiest during these times when students brought in their harvest of good phrases.

It came Lionel's turn to recite. He pounced upon a scene near the close of the first part of the *Confessions*, pertaining to the author's meeting with a girl of sixteen. No one in the class hitherto had discerned a provocative intimacy in De Quincey's association with "Thee, O noble-minded Ann." It remained for Lionel to remedy that oversight.

He read aloud to the class:

> Being myself at that time a peripatetic, or a walker of the streets, I naturally fell in more frequently with those female peripatetics who are technically called street walkers.

Lionel lifted an insidious eye, first to his classmates and then to Father Brown, who was rolling his pencil, wiggling his nose confusedly, and mumbling, "Oh! Oh! Oh!" It was now that an actor was born. Lionel found himself in command of an audience. He read on with crafty hallelujahs:

> Some of these women had occasionally taken my part against watchmen who wished to drive me off the steps of houses where I was sitting; others had protected me against more serious aggressions. But one among them—the one on whose account I have at all introduced this subject—yet no! Let me not class thee, O noble-minded Ann, with that order of women; let me find, if it be possible, some gentler name to designate the condition of her to whose bounty and compassion—ministering to my necessities when . . .

Father Brown lifted his pencil and his nose. "Class dismissed!"

The boys hastened to consult De Quincey again, this time more painstakingly, but the essays had been removed from the reference library shelves. Nor were they ever restored during Father Brown's occupancy of the chair of *belles-lettres* at Seton Hall.

Mum Mum, now seventy-three years old, undertook the temporary care of the children, pending a tour her son Sidney had planned. Uncle Googan, when times grew entirely bad, evolved bold schemes to refinance himself and family. He had a gay, brave quality about him, and was no more afraid of the great silver panic of 1893 than he had been of the Kansas City golem that day in the Philadelphia pool parlor.

He laid aside his pool-hall wand and also shelved temporarily his drama, *Odd, To Say the Least of It,* and formed a company to go on tour in Sheridan's *The Rivals.* This enterprise, he promised, would be managed efficiently. Among other economies, there would be no author's royalties. Besides, Mum Mum would revive the role of Mrs. Malaprop, a part she had so successfully portrayed for twelve seasons with Joseph Jefferson. And the character Uncle Googan planned to assume was none other than that of Bob Acres, hitherto the conceded domain of Joseph Jefferson.

Uncle Googan now had a son, Sidney Rankin Drew, known to the clan as "Little Kidney Stew." The Sidney Drews and Mum Mum were living at Madame Bourquin's boardinghouse near Fort Wadsworth on Staten Island, until time for the tour. The Drews and Barrymores in other years of theatrical wanderings frequently had stayed at Madame Bourquin's, where their credit always was good. This thrifty hostess knew that she would get the money eventually, with Mrs. Drew at the family helm.

A variety of citizens resided at the Bourquin pension, among them Phil Goldstone, the eminent pawnbroker, a corps of salesmen known as "drummers," shipping men, and two or three spinsters who found the sea air invigorating.

The principal attraction at Madame Bourquin's (aside from easy credit) was a bowling alley which the guests used free of charge. The children often polished and waxed the wooden fairway, and for this service were permitted to house a pet monkey in an upstairs room above the bowling alley.

During one of their visits to Madame Bourquin's, a dog chased the monkey into the water. The little fellow became quite ill from exposure and submersion. He coughed and whimpered. The children consulted with the boarders as to what they should do for their sick pet. Some misguided wag among the "drummers" solemnly advised them to take the monkey to Dr. Jenkins.

Dr. William T. Jenkins was Health Officer of the Port of New York and in charge of Quarantine. It so happened that at the time of the monkey's illness Dr. Jenkins, almost single-handedly, was resisting a cholera epidemic introduced by passengers of arriving vessels. He had quarantined so many ships in the congested harbor that their owners complained to the authorities, the mayor, and even to Washington.

When the three Barrymore youngsters appeared with their monkey at his besieged office he thought at first that the outraged shipping interests were practicing some kind of baleful trick upon him. Then he noticed Ethel's tears, heard Jack sobbing, and saw Lionel standing abjectly against the desk. The true situation suddenly revealed itself to the doctor; someone had been playing a joke on the children.

He accepted the monkey as a patient, tapped its chest, listened to its heart with a stethoscope, then said, "I can't give you much hope, children. It has a pneumonia."

Dr. Jenkins tiredly wrote a prescription. When the children said they had no money with which to buy medicine, the physician ordered a befuddled assistant to prepare a small bottle of diluted whisky and strychnine.

Dr. Jenkins patted Ethel's golden head. "Now don't cry, sister. Take the little fellow home and keep him as warm as you can."

The children returned to the room above the bowling alley, administered the medicine, and the monkey promptly died; but, as Jack once said, "it passed out stinking and happy."

At Mme. Bourquin's the young Barrymores appeared in their first dramatic effort, *Camille*. Ethel, as actress-manager, played the name role in her own version of the Dumas Fils story. She coughed so convincingly during the rehearsals that Mum Mum believed the child had a bone in her throat. Lionel, after much coaxing (for he always detested love scenes) undertook the part of Armand, and Jack that of the Count de Varville, with a swirling black mustache. Mrs. Drew, Uncle Googan, Aunt Gladys, little Sidney, a cross-section of pawnbrokers, out-of-work Hamlets, and a dozen pessimistic children of the neighborhood comprised the audience.

It was Jack's recollection that the young Barrymores frequently acted together in homebrew theatricals. Ethel, however, maintains that a single *Camille* was their only venture of the sort. Lionel thinks they managed one other *Camille*.

The young Barrymores, it appears, had no marked compulsion toward acting. A curious aversion was manifest in their respective attitudes when entering their profession. Their collective testimony reveals that they never had aspired to become actors, nor, once they had put on the paints and wigs, enjoyed their work; this notwithstanding the century and more of stage tradition on the Drew side of their house, and the mimicry bequeathed them by their handsome father.

"We became actors," Ethel says, "not because we wanted to go on the stage but because it was the thing we could do best."

While seventy-three-year-old Mrs. Drew once again gallantly was lifting the plumes and corset-stays of Mrs. Malaprop from the moth-balls, she heard rumors that Maurice had remarried. If true, this would complicate matters. Mrs. Drew's dream-minded son-in-law at best seemed an untrustworthy guardian; but newly married, he couldn't be depended upon to look after the children while their grandmother was on tour.

Lionel went to Manhattan to scout the situation. He found his father at The Lambs in the company of the new heavyweight champion of the world, James J. Corbett. Lionel saw his father and the current ruler of the heavyweights standing among a group of courtiers at the bar, the champion holding a conspicuous glass of milk in a hand that seemed fashioned for the playing of a violin.

Lionel's father appeared in bright spirits as he greeted his son with: "My boy, I am truly glad to see you. Suppose you come uptown with me. Want you to meet some old friends. Been staying there off and on, you know. Such hospitality!"

In a West Ninety-Seventh Street apartment, Maurice introduced his son with elaborate formality to a surpassingly beautiful young woman.

"Miss Floyd. My son. My good friend, Miss Mamie Floyd. May I present my older son, Lionel? . . . Miss Floyd's people have been wonderful to me, Lionel, simply splendid . . . Mamie . . . that is, Miss Floyd . . . well, Mamie, this is my son, Lionel, as I believe I have said . . ."

Maurice now believed he had gone far enough with evasive formalities. He abruptly went to the cupboard, produced a pail, and said, "Lionel, get some beer." He smacked his lips. "Mamie and I are married. Hurry back."

Mum Mum received the news calmly. "Marriage is a man's own business," she conceded, "only your steam-kettle father is not a business man."

Jack, it was decided, would go to live with his Uncle John Drew and Aunt Dodo. Lionel would tour with his grandmother, and make a stage debut in the small part of Thomas, the coachman, in *The Rivals*.

John Drew returned from London after Georgie's death to welcome his favorite nephew to his own rooms at the Marlborough Hotel. On fair week ends they stayed at Drew's cottage in Westhampton, Long Island. At a later and more affluent time John Drew acquired an ivy-covered house in Easthampton. He waggishly named it "Kyalami," which means "home" in Zulu.

Jack drew pictures much of the time. He said he wanted to be an artist. Aunt Dodo permitted him to sketch on anything other than the walls or table linen. He created the same kind of drooling monsters seen in his dreams.

Jack would go with his uncle to the studio of Augustus Saint-Gaudens, which was near their hotel, to observe the eminent sculptor at work on the equestrian statue of General Sherman, afterward unveiled in the Fifty-Ninth Street plaza. Saint-Gaudens informed Jack that the model for the Sherman horse was the thoroughbred Ontario. This experience delighted the boy. Saint-Gaudens proved generous with his comments. He told of his own beginnings as a cameo-cutter's apprentice at the age of thirteen.

Uncle Jack Drew patronized his nephew's passion for the drawing board and easel, yet adroitly sought to keep him on the path of family tradition. Drew saw in himself and others of his blood a theatrical dynasty, with no allowances made for abdication.

Mr. Drew, imprisoned in a stiff shirt-bosom and condemned to drawing-room dialogue, now graced the Standard Theatre under the management of Charles Frohman, whom he called "Coriolanus Rotundus." Before long he would move into the newly built Empire Theatre, there to rule the greenroom as the first gentleman of the American stage.

Jack took on many of his uncle's stately mannerisms, but with a tongue-in-cheek acceptance. As much as he respected his uncle, he did not always choose to be reminded of one's duty to the profession of acting.

He was a sit-down sort of boy at this formative period, shy and somewhat confused. Fleets of daydreams cast anchor in his mind, in contrast to the night-time regattas of the spooks. To heighten these confusions, doubts, and questionings that beset a young mind of unusual sensitivity, Jack's father unexpectedly urged him to become a priest. Whether or not this was a paternal whim, Maurice's holy recommendation puzzled the lad. He became an altar boy for a little while, yet religiosity, other than a kinship with the pageant beauty of ceremonials, never enchained his free soul. He was to remain always a pagan in the cathedral.

Sometimes the boy left off sketching and the sit-down hours of reverie to go like a young Shelley for long walks. He had a somnambulistic air during these journeys, unmindful of the crowds in the park or on the avenues.

One afternoon when Jack was walking along Broadway he felt himself seized from behind and lifted from the pavement. Then he heard and saw Papa who spun him about happily and greeted him with implications that they had had an appointment for this special place and this very hour.

As they stood there a bulking man walked slowly past them. A quality of loneliness seemed upon him in this busy street. Papa took a quick step toward the big man, calling out cordially, "Hello there, John!"

Mr. Sullivan paused, turned his great head slowly, as if he suspected some kind of mischief. Suddenly the gladiator's eye fired with recognition. "Aw, Barry! It's you. Guess I was just all wrapped up in myself too hard. Nice of you to speak to me."

The ex-hero resumed his gallant march down Broadway, the ghosts of former worshipers following his slow strides.

"Why did he say it was so nice of you to speak to him, Papa?" Jack asked.

Maurice had been looking after John L., a sadness in his eye. He turned to his son. "This is Broadway, the longest street with the shortest memory. I wonder if you remember the time I first introduced you to John L.?"

"Sure, I do," Jack said. "He knocked my wind out with his cane."

"Good God!" Maurice said. "One of the greatest fighters that ever lived, and all you remember is that he poked you with his stick! I suppose when you grow up and are asked what you remember of our great friend Joseph Jefferson, your wandering operetta of a mind will forget his *Rip van Winkle*."

"Oh, no, Papa," said Jack. "I wouldn't forget *that!*"

Maurice raised his brow. "Really? Well, just what *do* you remember about that classic portrayal?"

"The dwarfs with kegs on their shoulders," Jack replied.

"Good!" said Papa. "Is that all?"

"No, sir. I remember the dog Mr. Jefferson had in the play."

"My boy," said Papa, "may all your sorrows rest as lightly on your mind as your memories of great men. Let us have that beer, a short one for you, to match your powers of recollection."

While Mum Mum, Uncle Googan, and Lionel remained on tour, Jack Barrymore made two bang-up discoveries. He learned first of all that General Nelson A. Miles, famous Indian fighter, was practically a neighbor of Uncle Jack's on Long Island. The boy looked forward to breaking this news to Lionel, a superior sort of brother, who believed himself to be an Indian scout and planned secretly to join the Wild West Show of Buffalo Bill Cody.

The lad's second amazing discovery revealed that a five-cent cigar had been named for Uncle Jack! Certainly this great honor (the second time a family member had been canonized by the tobacco hierarchy) would impress even Lionel.

Uncle Jack did not seem happy over the cigar incident. It seems that, while in Washington, Drew had been celebrating something, perhaps Nat Goodwin's birthday. He over-celebrated and fell asleep, quite decorously of course. He awakened next noon in his room at the Raleigh Hotel, the tumult of a brass band serving as an alarm clock.

"Confound it," he told his nephews, "I am fond of the City of Magnificent Distances, you know. But there is one serious drawback. There *always* is a ghastly parade of some sort. Daughters or Sons of This-and-That, you know. Impossible to sleep decently of a morning. Well, at any rate, I looked out the window to see a band and marchers! And a huge banner on long poles, and on the banner my picture and the advertisement:

"THE JOHN DREW CIGAR
5 CENTS
WITHIN THE REACH OF ALL"

Mr. Drew remembered nothing whatever of having met a group of cigar manufacturers during his time of celebration, or giving his consent to the naming of the product for him.

In recalling his debut as a professional actor in *The Rivals*, Lionel says, "It was like trying to play a French horn while standing on my head."

He was fifteen years old at the time he appeared as Thomas before a painted curtain and on a narrow strip of stage during what is known as a "front scene in one." He dressed in livery, wore boots a size too small, carried a whip that tangled around his legs, and had a gray wig that he says made him look like a young-old flea. His voice was changing, his larynx full of rusty files. The matinee audience at the Kansas City première thought him bad; the evening patrons thought him worse.

Lionel entered his boardinghouse dormitory that night to find a letter on the counterpane of his bed. He recognized the purple ink and penmanship of Mrs. John Drew. He opened the envelope to read:

I sincerely wish I did not have to write this letter, for I want to spare your feelings. But, dear boy, I am compelled to inform you of the plain facts regarding your portrayal of Thomas. You were somewhat inadequate, and it is with the deepest regret that I convey the news that it is no longer necessary that you appear in the cast. I shall see you in the morning, dear boy. Until then, good night, and God bless you,

Your affectionate grandmother,
Mrs. Drew.

Instead of depressing him, the letter affected him like an Emancipation Proclamation. He ran from the room laughing and shouting. He hastened upstairs to Mum Mum's apartment. The old lady was having her nightly snack of cheese, two or three soda crackers, and a large tumbler of water with a tablespoonful of whisky in it. Mrs. Drew seemed a little astonished at her grandson's midnight hilarity.

"Didn't you get my letter?" she inquired.

His voice cracked up and down. "That's why I am so happy!"

"Happy!" she echoed. "Well, then, I am glad you are not unhappy." She squinted at him appraisingly. "Speak frankly, my boy. What portion of my letter exalted you?"

"All of it," he answered. "I can be a scenic artist now. I want to paint scenery."

"Here," she said, offering him a sip from her tumbler, "this will help settle your vocal cords."

Lionel stayed on with the company at the suggestion of Uncle

Googan. The budding muralist would interrupt his study of scenic design to procure Manhattan cocktails for Joseph Jefferson's competitor.

Three Manhattans, double ones, occasionally made Uncle Googan suspicious of the audience. He sometimes fancied that personal enemies had stationed themselves in the front rows. This deduction sprang from a lifetime review of his fracases and their tumultuous aftermaths. His past was always in the process of catching up with him.

One afternoon, after nine Manhattan cocktails, Uncle Googan fancied that he saw in the Kansas City audience the same man he had felled with the pool-ball in Philadelphia. The fellow did not applaud at any time. He just sat and glared fixedly at Uncle Googan as if trying to clarify a memory.

Uncle Googan told Lionel that his sinister observer had twice followed him down the street and to the stage door. "Something must be done about this," said the spunky little actor.

Lionel was waiting with a Manhattan in Uncle Googan's dressing-room that evening. Sidney came in late with a look of spontaneous combustion, and carrying what seemed to be a bunch of grapes in a sack, which he gave to Lionel. "Here, get rid of this!"

Uncle Googan dressed hurriedly to go on-stage. Lionel explored the sack to find a tied-up handkerchief, and inside of it two or three broken cocktail glasses. There seemed to be traces of blood on the fabric.

The Barrymore family members never asked personal questions of one another. It was not until the company had reached St. Louis that Uncle Googan volunteered to his nephew that he had carried the sack of broken glass solely in self-defense against his mysterious shadower in Kansas City.

"I don't know whether he was the same man I subdued with a pool-ball back in Philadelphia. It was kind of dark when he bumped into me near the stage door. But I couldn't afford to take any chances. So I just disparaged him."

Lionel returned to New York to join Jack on Long Island and learn that their father had sent them a pair of bicycles, a kingly gift.

"Now," Jack said, "we can ride over to Easthampton to see him."

"Is Papa in Easthampton?" Lionel inquired.

"Not Papa," said Jack impressively. "General Miles."

Lionel was incredulous. "It *couldn't* be the real general. Why, he's the most famous man in the world except Buffalo Bill."

"I'd prove it to you," Jack said, "only I'm an Apache myself, and I don't want to be captured."

"All right," said Lionel. "We'll ride over to Easthampton and you can show me the house. I'm a scout. General Miles will recognize me. I'm Kit Carson."

"I thought you were a scene painter?"

"A man can be both," Lionel said. "Come on!"

They set out bravely for the general's headquarters. Jack waited at a safe distance as his brother rode up to the front gate. Lionel uttered a few birdcalls and other signals known only to plainsmen.

The general himself looked out from the doorway, saw Lionel standing at salute, smiled, returned the salute, and beckoned.

Lionel saluted again. "I'm a scout, sir."

"Oh," said the general, pretending to recognize him. "Of course. Of course. And you've come just in time, Lieutenant."

Lionel's eyes were wide. "Lieutenant?" His voice went into an uncontrolled upper register. "Lieutenant?"

"Naturally," said the general. "For your gallantry in action against the Sioux and the Nez Percés in Montana. Or didn't the commission reach you?"

"No, sir," Lionel wheezed. "And I am glad to hear of it from you personally."

"Well, then, my boy—I should say Lieutenant—what is your name again?"

"Kit Carson, sir," said Lionel.

"To be sure. To be sure. Well, then, Kit—we can be a little informal when no one else is around—do you think you are sufficiently recovered from your wounds to undertake a dangerous mission?"

"My wounds?" Lionel asked.

"Yes," said the great Indian fighter. "Those twelve arrows through your chest. We thought we had lost you." The general brought a twenty-five-cent piece from his vest pocket. "You will have to brave all those lurking hostiles," and he pointed with the quarter toward the village, "and get me two ten-cent cigars and the newspaper. Be as fast and as careful as possible. Watch the trail for signs. There are bloodthirsty devils on every hand."

Lionel rejoined Jack, and they set out on this great adventure. They returned, breathless, and Jack again waited behind a tree while his brother delivered the cigars and the newspaper to the general.

"Did you contact the enemy?" asked General Miles.

"Oh, yes, sir," replied Lionel. "Great bands of them."

"What tribes?"

"Seminoles."

The general raised a military eyebrow. "Seminoles? A little far north for them. Hm! This means that *all* the tribes are now on the warpath. Good thing you weren't captured."

"I *was* captured, sir," said Lionel, "and tied to a tree."

"And tortured, of course?"

"Yes, sir. A fire was built around me."

"But you escaped, fortunately."

"Yes, sir."

"How?"

"I had a knife hidden in my teeth."

"Good! Good!" said the general. "That's very clever of you. You'll get a captaincy out of this, Kit."

"Really?" asked Lionel.

"Yes. That is, if you appear at about this time each afternoon to do some more important work for your Country."

The general now gave Lionel a nickel. "Here," he said, "is a medal for your great deed." He hastened to explain, "It is quite all right, under the circumstances, for you to exchange it for ice cream."

"Thanks," said Lionel, as the general turned to go indoors, "but I have some troops that deserve medals."

The General paused in the doorway. "Troops? How many?"

"One," said Lionel. "He's an Apache Indian." He hesitated, then waved toward Jack's hiding place. "But a friendly one. He's re-formed."

The general fished in his pocket, brought out another nickel. "On your recommendation, here is a medal for the friendly Apache."

Jack misinterpreted Lionel's waving and the general's peering in his direction to mean that he was being designated for immediate capture, to be followed perhaps by the death penalty. He leaped from behind the tree and onto his bicycle, and raced away.

When a young man begins to grow new teeth, he takes on the habits of the animal he most resembles at the time of dentition—the adolescent elk—frisking about, showing off, annoying the other sex.

Jack had eight new grinders, four above and four below. He had shed their predecessors by means of an unpremeditated plunge over the handlebars of his new bicycle. Now a ninth tooth, an upper canine, had become loosened, yet held on to his gum like a fouled anchor.

No lucky accident was to rid him of this tottering milk tooth. It had survived bean blowers, peppermint sticks, and Lionel. Jack suffered the necessity of pulling this cuspid or having it done for him.

Perhaps no mightier conflict of mind occurs ever again in a lifetime than that first decision to unseat one's own tooth. It is all very well for one's elders to say that it will not hurt, or that it will be over with in a moment. If it were *their* tooth, they would sing a quite different tune. It is well known that parents, like other politicians, seldom can be relied upon for exact statements of fact. And in respect to the tooth business, a boy finds himself suddenly adrift on a sea of irresolution.

Naturally, Jack received advice from the unlicensed experts. These laymen popped up everywhere with prescriptions. Uncle Googan volunteered to lash the tooth to a bedpost, then strike a match and thrust the flame suddenly in front of the boy's nose.

"The recoil will do the job instantly," he said. "Never fails."

Lionel offered to knock out the incisor with a boxing glove. Papa happened to drop in from New York to make a bid of ten cents for the moot fang, no matter how it be delivered.

Jack appealed to Mum Mum, the only relative he completely trusted. She tied a waxed white thread to the tooth, promising not to tug at it. She advised her grandson to wear this apparatus until he himself decided when and where to be brave about the extraction.

Jack went for a stroll with Papa, pondering the alternatives. The string trailed from his lips as if he had not entirely finished an Italian dinner. And now he saw a friend, Henrietta, the blacksmith's daughter, in her front yard, saw her in a new and pleasant light.

Jack had played with Henrietta during summer week ends in Westhampton, had liked her after a fashion, but hitherto regarded her auburn braids as a bit comic; they stuck out like pine cones from her freckled face. Recently Jack had pulled these folded pigtails during a surge of virility.

"Now you go 'way," Henrietta had threatened, "or I'll call my mother."

Today Henrietta and two other girls were playing "come-to-see." They had borrowed long dresses and done up their hair. Jack's heart bounced. He forgot for the moment his dental woes. He surrendered to the modish, bronze figure-eight piled high on Henrietta's head and the adult draperies that transfigured her into a gowned Aphrodite. He left his father's side to vault the picket fence and present himself among the group of young ladies. Maurice looked on with the manner of a coach of a freshman team.

The girls resented Jack's uninvited presence, and said so. He felt the need of some pixy gesture to offset the hauteur of the belles.

It was the time and place to be brave. He seized the string that hung wetly from his lips. He braced himself. He tugged, winced, and out flew the tooth. He held it aloft with restrained bravado, as if waiting for an ovation. But there were no huzzas, not even a giggle. The sacrifice had misfired.

One of the girls became turquoise blue. Another screamed and ran off as fast as her long skirts would permit. Henrietta stood flabbergasted; then, with the fortitude of a blacksmith's daughter, she rallied, turned up her nose, stomped her foot, and pointed toward the gate.

"Think you're smart, don't you?" said the embittered hoyden. "Well, you get out of my yard this minute!"

But Jack, with Papa looking on, felt that he must save face. The movement of Henrietta's hand in the direction of the gate released a sudden stimulus in the skull of the unhorsed knight. A magic flash of recollection supplied Jack's chance for rescue. It was as if Henrietta's hand pointed, not toward an exit, but to the young man's memory of a theatrical photograph upon the wall of Uncle John Drew's Westhampton cottage. This special picture revealed Actor Drew in striped satin knee-breeches, silk hose, pumps, a tricorn hat beneath his armpit, leaning over the hand of Virginia Dreker in a play, *The Country Girl*.

With an impassioned bow, Jack seized the hand of Henrietta, raised it to his lips, and kissed it. Henrietta was not a playgoer, had never seen *The Country Girl*. She couldn't comprehend what this clown was doing, or why, unless his deed were part of some new, eccentric travesty.

While her wooer was concentrating upon courtly address Henrietta raised a knee. It caught Jack in the pit of the stomach and knocked his wind out. He reeled about the yard, gaping like a beached seabass.

The damsel left the yard, her skirts swishing among the dandelions. Papa came through the gate to clap his son's back and flex his arms. On the way home Maurice said to the frustrated Lochinvar: "My boy, that kick was symbolic of what happens whenever men like ourselves fall in love. Remember from now on to keep your eye on 'em, before, during, and after you kiss."

10.

The Red Apple

GREAT swirls of snow spread a robe of innocence over the city. It had snowed all day, and at theatre hour was still snowing.

Broadway seemed a lane devised by the Brothers Grimm. The buildings assumed strange silhouettes with storm-made battlements of medieval mood. And along the road beneath these spellbound castles, the coaches and cable cars moved in the veiled reflections of street lamps and theatre lights like a slow procession of wedding cakes. The soft flakes of snow persisted, floating down from a windless, low sky like the little ghosts of unanswered love letters.

The voices of playgoers, the old and the young alike, had lyric accents. There was magic everywhere, it seemed, with wishes to be granted to all. Sorrow, poverty, viciousness, suddenly had gone from this world of white, this happy Broadway world on the night of January 25, 1894.

There were, to be sure, a few deterrents to this wintry carnival —mere symbols as in every fairy tale. An old witch in slattern's wraps was squatting on a nail keg near the entrance of the new Empire Theatre, and selling hothouse violets. A roast-chestnut vendor stood at the curb where the snow lay in pillow-thickness against the supports of his brazier. Teakettle vapors spouted from the nose of this sooty ogre who had on burlap leggings and a mustard-yellow beard worn like a poultice.

Said the old witch, over a corsage of violets in her clothespin fingers, "The Man-in-the-Moon's plucking a great goose in the sky."

Replied the chestnut vendor, stirring his charcoals, "Each snowflake is the soul of one who died without love, or with a song unsung."

A Salvation Army worker with tambourine stood beside the billframe of the Empire Theatre upon which one could read beneath a festoon of snow that Mrs. John Drew and an all-star cast were appearing again in Sheridan's *The Rivals*. On this night Ethel Barrymore, not yet fifteen, was making her New York debut as Julia.

Inside the theatre, on the make-up shelf in the dressing-room that Ethel shared with two women players of minor roles, there was to be seen a large red apple.

The red apple was a traditional gift. When John Drew was eleven years old—that would have been in 1864—and in attendance at a boarding school at Andalusia, Pennsylvania, his schoolmaster was in the habit of saying to the class: "If you learn your lesson well, you shall have a nice red apple."

After he had become a star, Drew began to send red apples to his relatives on the first nights of their respective bows as actors, or afterward whenever one of them appeared in a new play. The red apple became a signal of inter-family regard and a token of good luck as well.

It was not until 1896 that Ethel soared high by means of both talent and beauty as Priscilla, the country maid in *Rosemary*. Uncle Jack was Sir Jasper Thorndyke in this Parker Carson play, and Maude Adams was Dorothy Cruickshank. Mum Mum sent an especially large red apple to Ethel on this occasion of personal triumph.

Later that same year Uncle Jack, Ethel, and Grandmother Drew had a reunion on the road when the *Rosemary* company reached Chicago. Mum Mum was closing an engagement at another Chicago playhouse in an all-star resumption of *The Rivals*. Joseph Jefferson,

Nat Goodwin, Julia Marlowe, William H. Crane, Francis Wilson, and other luminaries were in this cast. Uncle Jack announced a dinner in honor of his mother.

Many stories of early times were told that night. Mr. Jefferson recalled that the elder Drew had acted under Jeffersonian management in Richmond, Virginia, in 1856. With a bow to the head of the table he added: "Mrs. Drew, it is my belief that since the time of the senior Tyrone Power there has been no Irish comedian equal to your husband. He touched every heart."

Mrs. Drew, moved by this tribute from her eminent friend, told of a time in the sixties when *The Rivals* had its American première in her own Arch Street Theatre. Her husband played Sir Lucius O'Trigger to Jefferson's Bob Acres.

She caused Jefferson to nod happily by telling the dinner guests of various criticisms Jefferson had drawn upon himself by making broad arnendments and cuts in the Sheridan play. Mr. Jefferson, in his version of *The Rivals*, had omitted several of the characters entirely, changed the endings of the first and second acts, and had the temerity to write an epilogue. Mrs. Drew described one of the critics as leaving the theatre in a dither, crying out: "Great Heavens! This reminds me of a line in Buchanan Read's poem, 'And Sheridan Twenty Miles Away.' "

Unknown to Ethel or Uncle Jack, as they sat at the happy party, this would be the last time they were to see Mum Mum as a member of a theatrical troupe.

Ethel left the *Rosemary* company in 1897 to go to England as Miss Kittridge in *Secret Service*, a play starring William H. Gillette.

Gillette, now forty-two years old, had been of the theatre for twenty-two years. He was slim, straight, had a face of tomahawk austerity, the manners of a curator, the mind of a professor of Romance languages. He had been educated to the hilt: forged at Hartford, tempered at Yale, sharpened at Harvard, and finally damascened at the Massachusetts Fine Arts Institute. He painted in oils and enjoyed a membership in the American Academy of Arts and Letters.

It is not generally known, but Maurice Barrymore created the part of Lewis Dumont in *Secret Service* some months before his friend Gillette presented it at the Garrick Theatre in New York

in October 1896. Gillette agreed to Barrymore's playing the leading role for a season of two weeks in Philadelphia. Barrymore contributed appreciably to the context of the final version as given in
New York.

Lionel and Jack accompanied Maurice to the city of their birth.
They spent most of their time in the hotel room while their elder
learned his lines. Maurice was a bad "study." When memorizing a
part, he would perspire like a steel puddler.

While their father was mastering the dialogue of *Secret Service*,
the boys held the manuscript, reading back the other parts or
prompting him. He paced up and down the hotel room—in his
striped undershirt, of course—scratching his hair tufts, batting his
eyes, and finally sitting on the bed, a beer glass in hand.

Papa's difficulty in learning a part offered an odd contrast to the
retentiveness of other members of the family. His children became
remarkable studies, as all the Drews had been. Ethel was the clever-
est in this respect; she could, and can, read a play two or three times
over and know her own part, letter-perfect, and the "sides" of
opposite characters as well. Lionel similarly possessed a talon memory, as did Jack until a lapse in 1933, a condition to be examined
within its chronological frame.

Maurice Barrymore and Gillette worked on the lines of *Secret
Service* at The Lambs during the hot months that found most actors
involuntarily off duty, many of them deplorably so. A group of them
one day were unveiling a painting in the main hall, a large daub called
"Summer."

Gillette and Barrymore were asked for suggestions as to how this
gilt-framed atrocity might be refused by the club without singeing
the feathers of the donor.

"The painter should be arrested," Gillette said.

"Just a moment, gentlemen," said Barrymore, eying his season-
ally unemployed colleagues. "I think the picture properly belongs
where it is, in an actors' club, a heartening reminder to us all that
summer is not as bad as it is painted."

Ethel Barrymore was not acquainted with Mr. Gillette personally, but had seen him from the audience. The sixteen-year-old girl
from the convent shyly admitted to herself that Mr. Gillette was
her ideal. Of course she believed her father the handsomest man
in the world (so many persons thought that) and Uncle Jack the
most accomplished; but in Mr. Gillette she saw a combination of

good looks, urbanity, and intelligence; actor, playwright, painter, savant. . . . She had a secret, schoolgirl's "crush."

To Ethel's great joy, yet emotional alarm, her work in *Rosemary* had brought not only an opportunity for her to appear in support of this beau ideal but also the chance to accompany his players to London. She had fearsome heart murmurs as she boarded the ship that would carry the actors across the Atlantic.

Ethel, introduced to Gillette, found him charming indeed. But, entirely unknown to himself, the alumnus of four cap-and-gown factories shattered the girl's illusions. He held Ethel's hand a moment too long!

John Barrymore spent the summer of his fifteenth year with his grandmother. They occupied a third-floor room and alcove at the old Bevan House at Larchmont, New York. The boy seldom left Mum Mum alone, for the seventy-seven-year-old actress now was afflicted with dropsy, her first devastating illness.

"I saw you come into this world," she said to her grandson, "and now you are seeing me out of it. A fair exchange."

It was an early, hot summer, notwithstanding the near reaches of the cool blue water of Long Island Sound. Each late forenoon, after Grandmother Drew had breakfasted, Jack would help her slowly down the several flights of steps, for there was no elevator in the old hotel. He would arrange cushions in a rocking-chair on a veranda overlooking the Sound. Then Jack would bring her one of the several paper-backed novels that she was reading concurrently, in what Jack called "platoon formation."

He would sit beside his grandmother, sketching seascapes, picturing the white sails spread hopefully in a small wind, or making outlines of beached craft nosed high on the sand, their bare poles rising in varnished authority like the batons of orchestra conductors. Sometimes an excursion steamer would send a long-delayed wake against the heads of red or black marker-buoys upthrust from the channel banks.

"Waves and actors," said the old lady, glancing up from her book, "are much alike. They come for a little time, rise to separate heights, and travel with varying speed and force—then are gone, unremembered. Our good friend Joseph Jefferson has correctly observed, 'Nothing is as dead as a dead actor.' "

Mrs. Drew would doze over the open book, then awaken to find her grandson sketching the clouds. Sometimes Jack portrayed these massed sky-banks as nuns at prayer, or again as warriors, fiercely commingling, or monsters astride the world. Mrs. Drew would study these drawings, then turn her eyes to the wool-pack clouds.

"Do not dream too long or too deep, precious Greengoose," she would advise him, "or you will be gravely hurt one day by the awakening. Now what would you say to a cup of tea?"

Word reached Larchmont one day that Ethel had become the most talked of young beauty in England. She had been instantly accepted overseas, professionally and socially.

Ethel had finished her season with Mr. Gillette at the Adelphi, and been engaged immediately thereafter by Sir Henry Irving for his Lyceum company to appear as Annette in a revival of Leopold Lewis's *The Bells*. Irving had first given this play in London in 1871, and employed it again for his American debut in 1883. Sir Henry now was fifty-nine years old; and two years before had achieved knighthood, the first actor to be honored in this manner.

"What a long way our profession has come," Mum Mum told Jack. "I can remember well when we players were held in disdain by society; quarantined, except for the patronage of an occasional playboy king. And now Irving has felt a sword on his talented shoulder—off-stage, too, for a change—and my darling, beautiful granddaughter is the friend of the Duchess of Sutherland. All the blue-blood bachelors will ask her to marry them. But of course she could not avoid their eyes and their hearts. There is starlight on her head."

The family once again had become widely scattered. John Drew was on tour with Maude Adams in the West, Uncle Googan somewhere with McKee Rankin, Papa in Kansas City, and Lionel preparing to play in a comedy, *Uncle Dick*.

Lionel came up to Larchmont to ask his grandmother's advice as to his career. He had undertaken several small roles, but still had no stomach for the stage. Like Jack, he wanted to paint something more objective than his own face.

Lionel was saddened to find his grandmother in constant pain. She made light of this ill health, but her doctor confided that Mrs. Drew could not live much longer.

After the physician had left the veranda, Mrs. Drew said to Lionel, "Whatever it was that the learned calomel merchant has been telling you, pay no attention. I shall appear for rehearsals next season as has been my custom for seventy-two years. Why not? An actress has no business being ill. . . . You're getting to be a real man, Lionel. Nineteen, isn't it? Are you in love? . . . Well, I shall send you a red apple on your opening night." She turned to Jack. "We must be sure to send one to Ethel. Can one cable an apple? We shall try."

Lionel left for New York City on the late afternoon train. Mrs. Drew looked out at Long Island Sound for a long time. Her large eyes seemed occupied with a dream. Jack placed an arm about her. "Isn't it time for you to go upstairs, Mum Mum?"

Her thoughts must have been far away as she said, "There are shadows on the water. And the sky is overcast. Perhaps we shall have a thunder squall."

Jack thought the sky unusually clear at approaching sundown, but, with the politeness that obtained in his family, did not contradict the musing actress.

She turned to him with a forced gaiety: "I prefer the sea when it is a bright blue-green in the sunlight. Your grandfather had eyes like the sea, the Irish Sea."

"He must have been gentle and kind," said the boy.

"He was an imp!" retorted Mrs. Drew. "Couldn't depend on him for five minutes. Darted about the world like an inspired hobo. He was an imp, and you are an imp." She paused, then, "And I love imps. They keep one guessing. Now lend me your arm, and we'll make our exit on that line."

They retired to their quarters. Mum Mum said that she would forego dinner this evening. She sat in an armchair silently for a time. Then she spoke of various scenes of her past, perhaps talking to conceal the increasing pain.

"The only thing I ever feared, actually feared," she told her grandson that night, "was the eyes of William Charles Macready. What a dreadful man he was to work with! He would press a hand on your head as you knelt in a scene, then in a low tone tell you to stand up. And you couldn't, with him leaning on you like Jumbo's hind foot. Did I ever tell you that the gentlemen of the old theatre had bad tempers? Yet they were artists, all of them. Well, nearly all. . . ."

Jack brought basins of warm water, as was his nightly custom, to bathe his grandmother's swollen ankles and feet. Then he helped her into her bed. He kissed her good night, and sat beside her. She reached out to stroke his face. Then her expressive little hand was returned to the coverlet.

And she fell asleep, never to awaken.

Of his grandmother, Jack said in after years: "If such a thing be possible, I know that at Heaven's Gate Mum Mum was given, not a red apple, but one of purest gold when she entered there."

CANTO TWO

The Sun on the Meridian

I.

Vine Leaves in His Hair

I FOUND a little bronze satyr in Pompeii. He wore an eaves-dropper's smirk and had vine leaves in his hair. Today, as I was assembling evidence to fix the time when John Barrymore became less of Shelley and more of Byron, the satyr fell from his pedestal to lie in an attitude of rigor mortis among some Chinese snuff bottles. I would not attribute this collapse to supernatural causes, although no mortal was near the woodland deity at the moment. I believe that he decided to abdicate, now that a more nimble satyr comes on-scene.

Those days when Jack joined hands with life became his gayest memories. After the passing of his grandmother he entered upon a bouncing behaviorism, together with spontaneous, often uncontrolled alliances, such as novelists call romantic and physicians diagnose as glandular.

We shall observe copious mischief in this man, yet, I think, never a grain of malice. Emotionally he proved himself unstable at times, but whenever he loved, he meant it in headlong terms. The pattern seldom was modified by forethought. And each of his passions expired with a violence of death rattles and great groans.

The tempests that so frequently swept over his life imposed a price. He paid that exactment, late or soon, as he ransomed every free breath he drew, and without bickering. He seemed the personification of all literature that sings of men and their hearts' desire. And, on the last night when he cried out like a child from the sleep that dark angels bring, it seemed that the theme of his life became, not that of Paradise lost, but of Paradise mislaid.

It happened during Jack's fifteenth year (according to his own detailed narration) that he experienced his first complete relationship with a woman. The strange circumstances attending this initiation of the adolescent dreamer, the impact of the event upon an imaginative mind, may provide the key to a better understanding of the emotional conflicts, the jealousies, the extreme behaviorisms that made a jig-saw puzzle of Barrymore's later years. It may well be that even his interpretation of Hamlet's problem rested somewhat upon the con-sequences of Jack's own debut in the bedroom of a young woman currently the loved one of Maurice Barrymore, his father.

The woman was unable to restrain her desire for the son of the man to whom she was supposed to be attached. Finally Jack's naïveté was caught up and borne under in a vortex of wild fevers. His com-panion in this adventure not only was ardent; she brought to the occasion a virtuosity that belonged to Persian literature.

Although Jack's was not a nature to harbor feelings of guilt of moral wrongs, it seemed from his own manner of referring to this cyclonic première that he *did* feel that he had let his father down. And it appeared that the inconstancy of this woman fixed in Jack's mind a suspicious fear that all beautiful women might be the same.

One of Jack's later romances (he was sixteen and increasingly handsome, now that his teeth were not too large for his mouth) concerned a policeman's daughter. It also threatened to concern the policeman. Lionel became worried, even if Jack didn't. The elder brother argued against an infatuation that easily might turn into an early marriage or a trip to the reform school.

Jack received Lionel's lecture with quiet courtesy. It was a life-time characteristic of Greengoose that if he raged or yammered in response to friendly counsel, something could be done to dissuade him from self-contrived catastrophe; but if he sat back and smiled in the manner of a well-fed abbot, nothing could be done for or with him.

He smiled when Lionel pointed out the incongruity of military weddings for civilians; the power of the police, especially in mat-ters of personal affront; the bad food that one might expect at the reform school. . . .

"But we are in love," Jack kept saying quietly. "That's all that counts."

It drove Lionel mad to hear the jargon his brother employed in prosecuting this dangerous affair over the telephone, a sort of babyish Esperanto. Lionel was reading *The Sorrows of Werther* at the time, and, as might be assumed, found in that early work of Goethe a phrase applicable to Jack's problem. When the young suitor finally surrendered the telephone, sighed, and sank back on the bed to lapse into a lover's coma, Lionel closed the book.

"This law enforcement officer's daughter," he began slowly, "is a wonderful little girl." Then he borrowed freely from Goethe, and fired from the hip, "But she smells of bread and butter."

Jack sat up, squirmed, and Lionel could see a great love die in his brother's eyes. Jack didn't telephone anyone for three days.

Between romances Jack stayed up nights with newspaper friends, a tribe that worked hard and slept lightly. These rugged historians, together with such artists and actors as lived by moonlight, might be found at Minnie Hay's boardinghouse in West Thirty-Fourth Street, or at various Broadway cafés and taverns.

When Ethel returned from London to find her younger brother doing nothing with, yet doing everything *to*, his life, she decided to remove Jack from an environment of saloons, garrets, and journalistic insomnia. His most recent antic had been to steal from Ethel a box of grapefruit, a delicacy presented by some love-sick aristocrat, and thereby become a hero at a Saturday night spree at Minnie Hay's. Then, after the sociabilities had collapsed, Jack and an assortment of newspaper men marched to Madison Square where the Dewey Memorial Arch rose in plaster-of-Paris grandeur.

These journalists, as often happened, were too stiff in all respects to climb the arch to remove the gilded Victory blade from the hand of a matronly goddess atop the memorial. They boosted Jack, received from him the sword, and then began a tour of the bars.

When a police sergeant made inquiries at Minnie Hay's next afternoon, and asked Jack if the commemorative weapon had been stolen "by any habitués of this place," Jack replied gravely: "There are no habitués here, officer. And I quote, 'Only sons of habitués.' "

Ethel shanghaied her brother, taking him to London. Perhaps he would improve himself when meeting some worthwhile persons. In London Jack promptly fell in love with a lady of rank, and she with him. Their meeting was entirely romantic. She saw him standing on a cliff overlooking the sea as she drove past in her carriage on the way to her castle. His collar was open, his hair flying with the wind, and the lady thought his the most compelling silhouette since Childe Harold's.

No sooner had Ethel extricated Jack from this situation (it took six weeks to do it) than he fell in love with an actress of magnificent face and figure. She had a husband of mellow years, but he became less mellow upon finding that he suddenly was wearing horns. He threatened a suit for divorce, but when friends pointed out to him how ridiculous it would seem for a man of years to name a "sapling" as co-respondent, the legal procedure evaporated.

Ethel played upon Jack's desire to be a painter; so for a time she managed to shunt him from the romantic track and into the Slade School. One of Jack's fellow-students at that art institute was William Orpen (afterward Sir William, Royal Academician).

Perhaps we should discuss Barrymore's easel abilities now and have done with it. He had an abiding passion for art, a driving imagination, a compelling sense of color. Yet he never approached, in terms of technique and fulfillment, the earnest accomplishments of Lionel, either in oils or at etching, mediums in which Lionel excelled.

Jack appeared at his best when he worked in the small, although he painted mural panels at Murray's Restaurant, a Doré-like series which architect Stanford White found attractive. Yet oil painting in general was beyond his proven scope. He summed up his talent himself, saying, "I might have been, but wasn't."

His water-colors were rather successful, several of them indicating superior taste and feeling. He was facile at sketching himself in various make-ups, employing this means to determine exactly how he would look in a contemplated part. One of these sketches, "King Lear," a combination of line and wash, demonstrates that the artist was no stranger to suffering, yearning, bewilderment, and graphically could record these torments of the soul. He also managed a folio of excellent illuminations on vellum, in the manner of medieval designers of mass-books.

During his attendance at the Slade School Jack became greatly influenced by Aubrey Beardsley. He endeavored to capture for himself the simple, eloquent line of that gifted apostle of the macabre, but could not. Barrymore said that he viewed the Beardsley work with objective admiration, yet admitted: "I also was fascinated by the race of this emaciated young artist against death."

Jack never met Beardsley, but discussed him many times with the English author and caricaturist, Max Beerbohm, one of Beardsley's intimates. Years afterward in Europe, during a Barrymorean domestic upheaval, Jack left his hotel to wander about in a cemetery. He fell asleep, then awakened to find himself at the tomb of Aubrey Beardsley.

It seems curious that Jack at no time could express women in pictorial phrases of warmth or animation. No doubt the psychoanalysts can explain this paradox. His female nudes might have been done by any studio capon; they were lifeless, there was a tired daffodil quality about them; they had no insides. A certain frozen grace was manifest in their postures, yet they remained as sexless as angels.

In none of John Barrymore's drawings can there be found a line of pornography, real or implied, whether among the crowded, random pencilings on the walls of his telephone nooks, or among his papers or canvases. This from a man deemed blatantly erotic by so many commentators.

Jack returned to America with a determination to combine his art with journalism. Newspaper life and newspaper men enchanted him. He wanted no part of the stage, although his Uncle Jack Drew kept reminding him of his "birthright" as an actor.

Maurice, who is said to have been completely color-blind, recommended that his son put aside pen and brush, saying, "Birthright has nothing to do with the case." He pointed a long finger at Jack. "Would you rather be an artist and daub, or an actor and have romance?"

"But artists have romance," Jack said. "Look at Monty Flagg."

"Very well then," replied Maurice, "go ahead and reek of turpentine and starvation."

Jack enrolled at the Art Students League, but attended only three classes. When his father heard of this absenteeism, he confronted his son. Before Jack had stumbled halfway through a spurious excuse, Maurice interrupted: "I don't want to know why you skipped classes. The thing that dumfounds me is how in hell you managed to go for as many as three times!"

When actress Cissie Loftus said to Ethel, "It's too bad that such a clever lad doesn't get on with his work," Ethel asked quietly, "What work?"

Jack did study art rather assiduously for a time with George Bridgman, brilliant colorist, and received ten dollars from Daniel

Frohman for a poster for E. H. Sothern's *If I Were King*. This was first blood. He felt convinced that he had earned the right to wear a smock.

With the ten dollars in his pocket, Jack went downtown. He sought out a saloon with sawdust on the floor and Bowery characters whose faces might inspire him artistically. He found such a resort alongside the approach to Brooklyn Bridge.

He bought a drink there, one of those doses of barrel-whisky that curdle the membranes and dissolve the spinal cord. His ten-dollar bill fascinated the bartender. It also commanded the interest of the only other person then in the place, a rough-visaged fellow with long, thick arms, and a chin like the Flatiron Building.

The bartender retired to some secret niche to find enough change for the ten-dollar bill. He returned to count out the currency and silver on the bar. The chinny patron was edging over to Barrymore. Jack did some fast thinking.

With a croupier's flourish, he pushed the bills and silver toward the fellow. "Old man, would you do me a great favor? I'm a little under the weather. You keep it for me. We'll have some drinks, then you can return what is left when I get home."

Jack's companion revealed that he was Buffalo Costello, former pugilist. Early in the morning they arrived at Uncle Googan's, where the ex-boxer tenderly put the young artist to bed.

The next day Jack had a call from Buffalo Costello, who gave him a dollar bill. "I found this here plaster in me kick. I couldn't hold out on a swell kid like youse. See?"

Barrymore obtained a fleeting job on the *Morning Telegraph*, then went to work for Arthur Brisbane, the dome-browed savant who edited Hearst's *Journal*. Mr. Brisbane had such a high regard for Ethel that he waived his usual practicality and assigned Jack to the task of illustrating weekly editorials, occasional court stories, and the Sunday poems of Ella Wheeler Wilcox.

Jack, however, did not seem to realize that newspapers had to be published on time. He was consistently late with his copy. He also disregarded the text of articles he was supposed to emblazon.

Mrs. Wilcox at length complained of the irrelevancy of the pictures to her dithyrambs. When Jack attached a sketch of a hangman and a victim of the noose to one of her *Poems of Passion*, Mrs. Wilcox telephoned Mr. Brisbane, demanding an interview with "this

Barrymore person, who apparently is too senile, and too far gone with dissipation, even for the reading of a poem, not to mention the illustrating of metrical thought."

When Jack announced himself at the Wilcox home, she asked: "Didn't your father have the courage to face me? Is he a coward as well as a simpleton?"

When Jack disclosed that it was *he* who had been illustrating the poems, Mrs. Wilcox became suddenly charmed. She asked Jack to stay to tea. The poetess soon afterward wrote to Mr. Brisbane, confusing him no little by the insistence that no one other than young Barrymore ever be permitted to illustrate her work.

Jack's access to the regard of Ella Wheeler Wilcox merely delayed his journalistic annihilation for two weeks. Brisbane not only was exasperated by the young man's chronic tardiness but also by his failure to synchronize the illustrations with Brisbanian versions of the encyclopedia and the works of Sir Francis Bacon.

While hanging on the lip of the abyss, Jack one day created a picture that miraculously satisfied Mr. Brisbane. It showed mankind in the chains of dope and liquor habits. But after the first edition reached Park Row newsstands, the picture was found to be published upside down!

Although Jack in nowise could be held accountable for this mishap in the mechanical department of the newspaper, Mr. Brisbane's magnificent forehead became wrinkled with outrage. He called Barrymore to his office.

"I believe," he said to Jack, "that all your family were, or are actors?"

"Yes, sir," Jack replied.

"Then shall we allow the Fourth Estate, or anything else, to spoil that splendid record?"

Mr. Brisbane turned to examine some circulation figures, and Jack went from the office to Luke O'Connor's bar at the Columbus Hotel in Greenwich Village, a rendezvous for journalists, artists, and others who "slept under the sun and lived beneath the moon."

The list of Jack's colorful friends at Luke O'Connor's bar and at Minnie Hay's boardinghouse seems today a roll-call of the gods. Some of these great spirits are forgotten, and many never attained celebrity, yet each in his own fashion contributed to the announcement of a new century.

Young Barrymore was introduced to Luke's by Jack Francis, police reporter for the *Morning Telegraph*. Francis was a galvanic news hound assigned to duty at the West Thirtieth Street Police Station, fortress of the Tenderloin. It was in this Nineteenth Precinct that the late Alexander Woollcott, as a police reporter for the New York *Times*, began his metropolitan career.

The bartender at Luke O'Connor's was not a good bartender. Yet he was a remarkable fellow withal, a dreamer and word-smith, of the sort that commanded the lasting regard of O. Henry and Stephen Crane, and of many others less celebrated than these flag officers of the literary fleet.

This man, then known to his customers as John Hunter, had come to Greenwich Village from a clipper-ship voyage in the South Seas. He was affably quiet, studious, and managed to learn from Jack Francis how to mix a cocktail. He was fond of broiled fish, and his loving manner of preparing and eating them was the first thing about John Hunter that impressed Barrymore.

At dawn, an hour that found Hunter at his intellectual peak, some fish were bought at Jefferson Market and prepared in Luke O'Connor's kitchen. Hunter, Jack, and Francis then sat down to breakfast. Jack saw that Hunter ate the skins of the fish with great relish.

"Won't it poison you?" Jack asked.

"Don't be silly," replied the bartender. "The skin contains the iodine of the sea."

O. Henry, residing at the Columbus Hotel for the months before he moved to Irving Place, saw in Hunter a man of imagery, philosophy, spirit, and perception. "I think," O. Henry remarked to his companions at Luke's, "that we shall reckon with this good fellow one day."

Mr. Hunter somewhat fulfilled O. Henry's prediction in after years, when, under the name of John Masefield, he became poet laureate of England.

Sometimes Jack would go with Hunter, O. Henry, Francis, and reporter Charlie Summerville to a German hotel where pigs' knuckles and lager beer were exploited. Jack was particularly fond of Summerville, a journalist of parts who, like Barrymore, had suffered a *contretemps* with Arthur Brisbane.

Mr. Summerville was essentially a writer, but one day in the *Journal* office, between editions, he sat at his desk drawing a caricature of his chieftain. Upon completing this portrait, he put a horizontal line across it, dividing the St. Peter's dome of a skull from the precincts of the mouth. Then he labeled the upper half of the picture, the cranium, "A," and the lower portion, the lips, "B." Next he wrote a caption beneath this handiwork: "A does not know what B is doing!"

And now from over Summerville's shoulder there came an announcement from Mr. Brisbane himself: "Summerville, you are fired!"

Perhaps Jack's closest comrade at this time—at least he spoke of him more often than of any other person of the period—was Frank Butler, a bulking, eloquent, unpredictable reporter for the *Telegraph*. Butler looked like Ysaye, the Belgian violinist. He was the son of actress Rose Eytinge, a black-eyed beauty of startling resolution, and a descendant of General Benjamin Franklin Butler, known to residents of New Orleans during the War between the States as "Beast" Butler.

Lionel introduced Butler to Jack in some saloon unremembered by the elder brother. Butler had given up journalism for a time to play a minor role with Uncle Googan and Lionel in McKee Rankin's stock company. During a summer season in Minneapolis, Butler's heavy drinking and light acting outraged Mr. Rankin. He gave the sack to the descendant of "Beast" Butler one Saturday night.

Between then and Monday, Butler orated himself into a job on one of the Minneapolis newspapers, substituting for the drama editor who had gone on a holiday. This turn of events proved calamitous to the manager of the troupe. His former supernumerary loosed upon the company such bombastic attacks as seldom had been composed since the days of Dean Swift.

McKee Rankin importuned Lionel, who was rooming with Butler, to induce the bitter journalist to withhold his vitriol. Butler replied to this plea in print, attacking Lionel in particular, at the opening of the next week's play:

> Stay away from any theatre where McKee Rankin's heavy hand falls. Go into the parks, and enjoy the sunshine or the moonlight instead. Last night's play was the most atrocious event since the Massacre of the Innocents. But with all this criminality of stage-management and inferior playing, a curi-

ous thing was brought home to me: as bad as the company was in toto, a small part played by a man whose name is vague to me—Lionel something-or-other—this tiny role, I say, somehow of itself was so manhandled and debauched as to destroy an entire evening.

The newspaper discharged Butler after he had written an article called "Five O'clock." It described a magic-carpet tour of world capitals at that evening hour, the absinthe sipping on the Boulevard des Italiens, the gypsy music in Budapest, the sundown drinks at the Raffles Hotel in Singapore. Finally the author wrote that he had returned to Minneapolis "by a circuitous route," and concluded his article by asking:

And, home again from my glamorous experiences, what did I find was happening in the City of Minneapolis at five o'clock? I shall tell you: nothing. Not one blessed thing!

Lionel introduced Jack to the descendant of "Beast" Butler, and a monumental friendship was established. While waiting for the drinks, Butler said that he had a bothersome duty to perform. He called for writing paper, and composed and read a note addressed to Rudyard Kipling: "I have read *The Vampire*, you self-sufficient, soul-deficient, Saxon dastard!"

An artist, of course, needs a studio. Jack managed to find a narrow room with north light on the top floor of a brownstone house that once had been a mansion. It stood on the uptown side of Fourteenth Street, near Sixth Avenue.

When Jack informed his father that he now had a studio, Maurice promised to send him some furniture. The studio was bare, except for a sink, a gas-plate, and an old stew-pan. Jack had to sleep on the floor, and on cold nights wore his overcoat with newspapers tucked inside it.

The "furniture" that Maurice finally sent his son consisted of about a hundred books, including several ancient cookbooks, and nothing else. One evening, toward midnight, Jack came upon his newspaper friend, the huge Frank Butler. He learned that the journalist had been evicted from the Aulic Hotel for non-payment of rent.

Butler had pawned the removable gold crown of a front tooth for seventy cents. Now he had but fifteen cents left of this treasury.

He had spent the rest for drinks. He was hungry, and had no place to sleep on this chilly night.

"If you will feed me," Jack said, "I'll shelter you at my studio. You'll fall in love with the place."

"I accept the proffer," said Mr. Butler. "It is my winter of discontent."

Against Jack's better judgment, Butler insisted upon buying a copy of the *Telegraph,* a newspaper which cost ten cents before midnight and five cents in the morning. A newsstand dealer insisted on charging Butler ten cents, but after the journalist assured him that he was Mr. Blakely Hall, owner of the newspaper, the dealer grudgingly accepted a nickel.

With but ten cents left, the friends decided that Butler go to a lunch room where hot cakes and two cups of coffee might be had for a dime. Jack was to wait outside, drooling, until Butler ordered the second cup of coffee and finished half the portion of cakes. This was done, then Jack entered the lunch room excitedly to whisper into Butler's ear. Butler seemed stunned for a moment, then sprang from his stool, calling out, "No! My God! It can't be! My poor, poor, sainted mother!"

Jack then sat down, gulped the residue of cakes and coffee, and endured heartburn for six hours.

When Butler arrived with Jack at the studio and saw its lack of furniture, he bellowed, "Sold out! Rooked!" But he finally lay down on the floor among Maurice's books, and next day sold a story of his "experiences amidst old authors."

There was but one other tenant in the old house, Dr. Mundy, a specialist in social diseases and birth control. Dr. Mundy, sallow and thin, behaved furtively, as if his pillow whispered to him of nights.

It seems that Butler at some ancient day had been a non-paying patient of Dr. Mundy, and that the medico had set bill collectors on the Butler trail. When the pair met again on the stairway of the house in Fourteenth Street, Butler said to his former physician, "I would have paid you, sir, if you had not behaved like a grasping harpy during my indigent days of convalescence."

The former practitioner stared at Butler. "You are a deadbeat and a welsher, but it makes no difference to me now, for I am no longer practicing medicine. I am an undertaker."

Butler put out his hand. "Congratulations! I am happy that you have not seen fit to change your profession."

Butler's appetite for food and liquor was large and his income incredibly small. When solvent, he redeemed a frock coat, a fancy vest, a cape, and an opera hat from the pawnbroker. He also reclaimed the removable gold crown. When penniless, which was often the case, he dressed like a westerner, with a broad-brimmed Stetson hat.

Mr. Butler frequently appeared at various bars done up in bandages and smelling of arnica. It seems that strangers, including ladies, did not appreciate his bombastic sarcasms, and liked to beat him up. Although he was a weighty fellow and stood well above six feet two inches, and plunged into battle after two drinks, Butler simply did not know how to fight. Nor could he learn how to duck or slip blows, even from little antagonists. This lack of prowess unjustly earned him the reputation of being a bit of a coward. Jack Barrymore decided to do something about his battered chum's predicament.

"At least," Jack told Butler, "we can manage to repair your unfortunate reputation."

Jack looked up his pugilistic pal, Buffalo Costello, a panther-muscled person known for quick-tempered dealings with pedestrians whether on the Bowery or Broadway.

"Costello," Jack said, "for the large fee of two dollars, would you do me a great favor?"

Mr. Costello appraised his friend through slitted eyelids. "You got two dollars?"

"For the moment, no. Left it in my other pants."

"You got other pants?"

Barrymore seemed pained. "Let us not wander off into sartorial discussions. I am trying to cure a dear friend of his morbidities."

"Where's the two bones come in?"

"Confidentially, Buffalo, people think that he's yellow. But he's not really, and if you could see your way clear to let him knock you down . . ."

Costello grunted an interruption. "I'll tear his head off. See?"

"I shall try to put it more simply, Buffalo," said Barrymore. "As you know, the newspaper boys usually foregather in front of the Albermarle Hotel at five o'clock. If you will bump into my friend . . ."

Costello again cut in. "I'll break him in half! See?"

"Please," said Barrymore. "I have two dollars for you, if you allow my friend, Mr. Butler, to slug you in the kisser. It will restore his prestige."

"I'll moider his prestige!"

It took a long while for Barrymore to rehearse Buffalo Costello, but at last it was arranged for him to simulate defeat at the Albermarle.

"I hates to do all this on the cuff, see?" Mr. Costello observed. "But two bucks is two bucks." Then he advised his employer, "And I better be paid soon's I take the dive."

That afternoon a gallery of newspaper cronies saw Frank Butler and Buffalo Costello collide. The onlookers shuddered to think of their blundering pal in terms of sudden mincemeat. They further deplored Butler's inciting tirade: "Can't you see where you are going? You frowsy dullard! Must a busy citizen be at the mercy of an ape-faced bum?"

Butler followed this declamation with a roundhouse right which Costello permitted to light upon his Flatiron Building chin. The ex-fighter adroitly flopped to the gutter and lay there, while the incredulous newspaper men gaped.

Mr. Costello, helped to his feet by Barrymore, whispered, "Where's the two bucks?" He was whispered to hurriedly, "I'll have it for you in an hour." One of the astounded journalists asked Butler if he knew the desperate character of the man he had hit!

"It makes not the slightest difference to me," Butler replied grandly. "As a man of honor, I always defend myself." Then to Costello, "You had better move along, my seedy sir. Hop it, or I'll *really* trounce you."

The stupefied journalists decided to fete the suddenly potent Butler, a gesture of apology for their formerly low opinions of his fistic assets. They trooped after him into the Albermarle bar.

From the Albermarle, the celebrants went to Kid McCoy's Rathskeller at Fortieth Street and Broadway. Butler, glass in hand, reenacted his victory over Costello for such scribes and actors as had missed the Homeric encounter. During one of these recitals, a bar-fly interrupted the hero to say that a gentleman was waiting upstairs to confer with Mr. Butler.

"Tell him I cannot be annoyed," Mr. Butler said in a regal voice. "Send him packing."

At this moment Mr. Costello himself charged down the stairs. He was shouting, "Where's my two bucks?" He spied Butler. He sank a short left to the reporter's whiskers. Butler's gold tooth flew out like a grain of corn. The journalist himself sank like Admiral Cervera's fleet off Santiago.

Costello waited with black impatience until an emergency collection of $1.85 had been taken. Then he departed the scene. Mr. Butler, his prestige back where it had started from, stood limply against the bar, wearing the expression of the martyred St. Denis, who, if we are to believe Fortunatus, always appeared after the decapitation with his head beneath his arm.

"I am not a constant reader of the calendar," John Barrymore said to Lionel one day, "but Uncle Jack informs me that I am twenty-one years old."

"What do you propose to do about it?" asked Lionel. "Vote?"

Jack replied sadly, "It begins to look as though I'll have to succumb to the family curse, acting."

Lionel was properly sympathetic. "I know just how you feel." He sighed like a ferryboat. "There is no escape for us. We are in the cul-de-sac of tradition." Lionel had a drink of red wine, then asked, "Did Uncle Jack finally influence you?"

"Partly Uncle Jack, but also my stomach. It abhors a vacuum."

The brothers were sitting in the Café Boulevard on Second Avenue. They did not meet often, but when they did, they always came to the Café Boulevard. There were three reasons for their patronage of this particular café: the Hungarian food, the gypsy music, and two sisters from Budapest, twins.

The Barrymore brothers never visited these sweethearts elsewhere than at the Café Boulevard. The romance carried over from one visit to the next, no matter for how long a time the young men might fail to appear. It seemed an ideal arrangement, poetic.

Whenever the Barrymores bobbed up, the twins lost interest in other suitors. They would join the brothers, have red wine, and the orchestra would play "Blue Forget-me-nots."

The personnel of the orchestra constantly changed, but the white hussar uniforms did not. Consequently, these garments never fitted the wearers, except in the case of Prince Driga. The prince was first violinist and a fixture at the Café Boulevard. He had married into money, and wore many rings and smelled oppressively of perfume. He was delighted because the Barrymores had learned from the twins how to ask for "Blue Forget-me-nots" in Hungarian.

The Barrymores were a little sad tonight. First of all, the twins were absent. It seems that they had been offended by something Jack had done the last time he and Lionel had visited the café. Jack had brought a Scotch girl with him.

"They are terribly jealous," Prince Driga informed the brothers. "In our country, sweethearts are sweethearts."

"But the Scotch girl was only my model," Jack told Prince Driga. "In fact, the only model in town I can get to pose free of charge. Besides, she brings oatmeal for breakfast."

"It makes no difference," Prince Driga replied.

"Look here, Prince," said Lionel. "I didn't bring anybody to this place, Scotch or otherwise. Where's my girl?"

The prince flourished his bow. "Gone! Gone!"

"Gone where?" asked Lionel. "It's ridiculous!"

The prince's gestures perfumed the whole café. "Who knows? Maybe to buy a dagger. Maybe to the river . . ." and he made a diving motion.

"But why both of them?" asked Jack. "Lionel isn't to blame. The Highland Fling was my own idea."

Prince Driga began tuning his instrument, plucking the strings with each word. "In our country when both sisters love, both sisters also hate, and also kill, or die."

"But is everybody a sister there?" Jack asked.

"Oh, yes," and the prince tucked the violin between his chins, "women in love always are sisters, I think." He had a far-away look. "I shall play something for your lost love? Yes?"

"Hell, yes!" said Jack. He had some red wine, then said above the gypsy music: "Lionel, if I do stumble onto the stage, I'll not be any good. Then I'll *have* to come back to painting."

Lionel had some more red wine. He smacked his lips, wiggled his brows, then said, "You'll certainly fail, unless you try. But if you try . . ." he paused for a long moment, then repeated, "if you *try* . . ." another pause, "you're hooked forever."

"Let's go drag the Hudson River for our little sweethearts," Jack said. "Maybe we can resuscitate at least one of them."

2.

The Garden of Sleep

THE first great bell-beat of tragedy sounded for John Barrymore in 1903, the year that saw him at last on the New York stage. The sudden, evil occurrence was the collapse of his father's once brilliant, gay mind. The bleak overtone of this breaking of his parent's reason never quite died away in Jack's thoughts. It echoed, knell-like, again and again in after years to plague his soul; and toward the end of his own life provoked the only discernible fear in an otherwise exceptionally brave character.

It seemed Maurice's sardonic lot to reach his topmost place in the theatre just before the world went dark for him. He had magnificently enacted the part of Rawdon Crawley in support of Mrs. Fiske's Becky Sharp. His depictment of the scene wherein he received a letter from his son won sanction even from such a praise-saving critic as William Winter. The irony of all this underlay the fact that the actor was not entirely simulating the frenzies of this stage-role, but giving to it the outcries and the agonies of his own mental disintegration.

Reporter Jack Francis one afternoon in late autumn came upon the Broadway-beloved player. Francis had been gathering precinct news from Police Captain James Price. He was on his way out of the West Thirtieth Street Station to go to the Haymarket on the corner of Sixth Avenue up the street from the station house.

As Francis was leaving the doorway of the white-painted brick station house, he observed Maurice Barrymore sitting on the cast-iron steps. The actor was staring fixedly at a sign across the street that advertised a Negro mission on the second floor of a frame building:

> *All Ye That Enter Here,*
> *Leave Sin and Care Behind.*

Francis asked if he might be of some assistance. Maurice did not reply at once, but kept on staring at the sign across the street.

"May I take you home, Mr. Barrymore?" Francis asked. "You look kind of sick."

Maurice glanced up at the reporter. "Home?" he asked. "Is there such a place?"

Barrymore rose slowly, then lurched. Francis caught his arm before he could fall. Now Jerry the Lug, a Tenderloin hack driver, drove alongside the curb.

"Why, hello there, Mr. Barrymore," said Jerry. "Ain't seen you since . . ."

Francis interrupted, "Let's take him home, Jerry."

But when the cab reached the place where Maurice was living, the actor refused to get out. He said he wanted to go to Moran's bar, or to Jim Corbett's in Herald Square.

The worried Francis instructed Jerry to drive the hack to Bellevue Hospital instead. Barrymore didn't appear to mind. Perhaps he had forgotten where he had wished to be taken. He became incoherent at times, then returned abruptly to his usual bright manner and held onto his thoughts for a minute or so. Among other things, he recalled that his friend Wilton Lackaye recently had placed a note on the bulletin board of The Lambs: "Lost: one cufflink. Will buy or sell."

Then, as the cab arrived at the foot of East Twenty-Fifth Street, Barrymore began to hum a tune. He broke off to remark: "I like that song very much, 'The Garden of Sleep.'"

At the hospital the examining physician advised Francis that it would be best for the stricken man to remain at Bellevue for observation in the psychopathic ward. This was done.

Ethel and Lionel were out of the city at the time, and Francis was unable to locate Jack. After several days some of Maurice's friends came to the surface to procure his release. Yet they soon conceded that the actor, now in his fifty-sixth year, was deranged. Finally it was recommended that he enter a private sanitarium.

And now the family burden bearer, Ethel, arrived home to take her father to a place in Amityville, Long Island. As in the death of her mother, this, too, became a grievous journey for the beautiful young woman. Yet again she did not shirk her duty. She comforted her father on the way to Long Island; she hid her inner torment from him when he turned to her as if she were the parent and he the child. She assumed all the expenses, and made all the arrangements for the care of the once-gay, life-loving man.

Occasionally a few of Barrymore's friends visited him at Amityville. Sometimes he conversed with such sustained animation that it was felt he should be released. Then he would plunge back again into the repetitious ululations characteristic of his malady.

Among the long-time comrades to call at Amityville was Frank Case, proprietor of the Hotel Algonquin. When Frank Case last saw Maurice alive, he found the actor in comparatively high spirits. Many sheets of manuscript lay on a table in Barrymore's room. He was writing swiftly, and with much interest.

"I have a new play," he told Case. He gathered some of the sheets together, and handed them to his visitor. "Run your eye over this."

Case was disturbed by what he read. He finally got hold of himself. "I think it is fine, Barry. Perfectly fine."

Maurice seemed pleased, then entirely forgot the play, and apparently even the identity of his caller. Case was so upset by Barrymore's condition, and by what he had seen on the pages, that he cut short his visit.

There had been but one sentence written on the many pages, a statement repeated again and again: "It was a lovely day in June."

Maurice died in March 1905, and the men who loved and admired him, among them Willie Collier, say that Jack Barrymore would sit turning the pages of books that had belonged to his father, particularly the ancient cookbooks.

He kept these cookbooks until the close of his own life. And sometimes, when too ill to eat, would create menus based on the old recipes, and grace the lettering with ornate initials, then add the notation: "See if my lawyer thinks I can afford all this."

At the beginning of Maurice Barrymore's illness, his younger son was on the stage, yet hardly of it. He had revealed little evidence of the powers locked inside himself. Yet his personality attracted almost everyone off-stage, and, as Ethel says, "He inspired love." Jack was the readiest to admit that his early theatrical feints were "shoddy and indifferent."

He appeared twice as a professional actor before his New York debut. The first time was for a single night when he substituted for Francis Byrne at the Philadelphia tryout of *Captain Jinks of the Horse Marines*. The hastily rehearsed Jack blew up in his lines. His sister Ethel, a principal in *Captain Jinks*, went into an hysterical state which Jack described as "a cross between hilarity and strangulation." Her brother muffed his lines, then demanded loudly, "Where do we go from here?" As if that were not enough, the mischievous actor took a curtain call by himself.

The play failed to impress Philadelphia, the home of the Barrymores. It moved gloomily to New York (with Jack out of the cast!) for a two weeks' retrial, and stayed on for a triumphant seven months.

Two weeks after the New York opening, and on a windy February evening, Jack and Ethel came around the corner of the Garrick Theatre. Jack pointed to the marquee, and shouted, "Look! My God!"

Ethel looked. She saw her name shining for the first time in electric lights. She had suddenly become a star. When she excitedly thanked producer Frohman for this promotion, he replied, "I had nothing to do with it. The public did it."

"In that case," Ethel said, "I'll try to become reconciled."

That summer, while waiting for his second stage employment, Jack enjoyed the hospitality of Frank Case. Members of the Drew-Barrymore family often stayed at the Algonquin. Uncle John Drew was a resident of that hotel for nineteen winters, spending the hot summers at Kyalami, his Easthampton cottage. And at the Algonquin Aunt Dodo died.

Jack now had assumed many of the courtly mannerisms of his uncle, and much of his wardrobe as well. He was entering upon a "dressy" period, in imitation of his beau ideal, and whenever he needed replenishment of clothes would visit Kyalami. He would return to the Algonquin, not only with Drew suits but also with Drew luggage.

Jack was unusually destructive about clothing, particularly trousers and shirts. If Uncle Jack Drew happened to be out of town, Jack levied upon Frank Case for linen. It did not trouble the borrower in the least that Case was a much larger man than himself. Barrymore had a talent for pinning up sleeves, and making collars fit by shrewd adjustments of borrowed neckties.

One day Barrymore met Wilson Mizner, Paul Armstrong's play collaborator. Mizner, always on the lookout for philanthropists, asked Jack concerning the kind of man Frank Case was.

"He's great," said Jack.

"Describe him," said Mizner. "His character, I mean; his attitude toward the meek in pocketbook."

"His character?" asked Jack. "There are no adjectives available.

He's . . . he's . . ." At a loss for superlatives, Jack resorted to a Broadway phrase, "Why, he's the sort of man who'd give you his . . ." He paused, seemed to realize something amazingly co-incidental, pointed to his own bosom, then exclaimed, "My God! This *is* his shirt!"

Case became concerned about Jack's drinking, a matter subse-quently pondered by a multitude of men and women. Barrymore appeared one morning in the Algonquin restaurant, somewhat ear-lier than his usual noon, to request, "Waiter, will you create for me an absinthe frappé? On second thought, and I do have second thoughts when dying, prepare two."

Case overheard this order. He whispered to the waiter to delay the service of absinthe, then invited Barrymore to his own table. "Have a cup of coffee while they're mixing your drink," Case said. "It takes time to mix a real frappé."

Barrymore had three cups of coffee with Case, then, after the absinthe frappé arrived, found his stomach out of humor for worm-wood distillations.

The next day Barrymore encountered his host in the lobby. "That's a great idea of yours, Frank. Wonderful!"

"What's so wonderful?" Case asked.

Barrymore replied, "Coffee for breakfast!"

Like numerous other Algonquin guests of adolescent fame, Bar-rymore did not pay his bills on the barrel-head. Indeed, he was on a par in that respect with playwright Paul Armstrong. Jack frequently sat with the future author of *Alias Jimmy Valentine* at a table known for its chronic loss to the management.

One night Armstrong ordered an all-embracing dinner, and when it came time to sign the tab asked Frank Case for a pencil.

"Do you really *need* a pencil?"

"Yes." Armstrong received and waved the pencil. "And when they stop making these things, I'm ruined."

Case was passing through the main dining room on another eve-ning when Jack was entertaining Evelyn Nesbit with hearts of artichoke. Miss Nesbit, a Floradora girl, was about to become the eye-arresting attraction of *The Wild Rose,* as the protégée of archi-tect Stanford White.

Case pretended concern at Jack's lavish hospitality. He leaned over Barrymore's shoulder to inquire in a whisper, "Couldn't you have selected something less costly than hearts of artichoke?"

Jack seethed. He insisted that Miss Nesbit go with him at once to a restaurant that didn't quibble with guests. He hurried to his room, packed his John Drew trunk, had it brought to the sidewalk, then checked out of the Algonquin. No one at the desk remonstrated, or brought to his attention a long-standing bill.

It happened that delegates to a political convention had taken all hotel space in the White Light district. Barrymore and his girl, the trunk lashed to a cab, drove about mid-Manhattan for hours, seeking accommodations. Late that night Jack returned alone to the Algonquin, sent his trunk to his room, and, having no money with which to pay the hack driver, matter-of-factly signed Frank Case's name to a tab.

After Jack's second stage appearance in Sudermann's *Magda* (playing the part of Max) in Chicago, he became temporarily in funds. Upon his return to the Algonquin, he learned that there was such a device as a fountain pen.

Brandishing a fountain pen and a check book, he proudly commenced paying his bills. Then he began to run out of funds. Some Broadway economist recommended that he consult Frank Case about a reduction in room rent.

"I am promised a part in *Glad of It*," he informed Case, "but between now and then, I can't afford to pay you one cent more than twenty-five dollars a week."

"That's fine, Jack," Case replied. "You have named an interesting figure."

"Well, then," Jack said, "put me in a room that coincides with my dwindling financial status."

"Don't you like the room you are in?"

"I love it," Jack said. "I couldn't love a woman better." He patted a new mustache, an ornament supposed to look like John Drew's in miniature. Then he asked, "Are you implying that I can stay where I am for twenty-five a week?"

"If you wish. Certainly."

A tear came to the young man's eye. "I don't like to see you short-change yourself."

"Forget it, Jack. I want you to be happy here."

Jack started for the door. Then he turned to ask: "I said twenty-five a week. Right? And by the bye, what *have* I been paying for that room?"

"Two dollars and a half a day," said Case.

Barrymore again made for the door, expanding with gratitude. Then suddenly he became dubious, turned once more to the desk. "For the love of God!" he called out. "Two dollars and a half! Why, that's only seventeen-fifty a week! Or am I nuts?"

"Correct all the way around," said Case. "But you still can have the room for twenty-five a week if you insist."

After Jack had appeared in New York with moderate success as Corley in *Glad of It* at the Savoy Theatre, in December of 1903, the company moved to Brooklyn. Uncle Jack Drew and Case went over to that Borough to attend a matinee performance.

Jack did not see his uncle and his Algonquin host in the third row until it came time to dictate a stage letter. After the conclusion of it, and the actress-secretary had crossed to the exit, Barrymore suddenly spied Case and Uncle Jack. He called out to the departing actress: "One moment, please, Miss Twombly!" Then, as the mystified young woman turned, wondering what the devil was up, Barrymore beckoned. "I overlooked an important missive. Come back instanter, Miss Twombly, and sit down. We must get in immediate touch with Frank Scrooge Case." Then he dictated: "Dear Landlord: Not this week. Perchance not next week. But you shall be paid anon."

Case would not permit Jack to keep pets at his hotel, so Barrymore had to exercise his affection for animals by Sunday visits to the Central Park Zoo, where his father so often had taken him during childhood days.

"I had heard much of Jack's remarkable ways with animals," Case says, "so I went with him one afternoon. I found that Jack was more famous by far at the park than in the theatre. I was astounded when a big tigress recognized him. He went familiarly inside the railing that separated the public from the tiger-cage. He horrified me by thrusting a hand between the bars, stroking the big cat's head, pulling her ears, tickling her under the chin. A keeper said to me: " 'He's the only person in New York we allow inside this rail. Don't worry at all, mister. This cat is in love with him. Cries like a dame when he goes away.' "

In February 1904 Jack Barrymore appeared in the part of Charley Hine, wireless operator, in Richard Harding Davis's play, *The Dictator*. And although the role was a secondary one, and his behavior incorrigible at times, he really was taking his first slow yet significant strides toward the Temple. The high priest of comedy who conducted him thither was William Collier, his father's and his uncle's great friend.

3.

The Odyssey of a Spring Lamb

IT is a curious habit of most men to stay silent in regard to bene-factors who gave them a leg up in the days of their becoming. A successful man, whether he owns a tungsten mine or writes popular tunes, seldom volunteers a word of thanksgiving for the generosity of an ancient grubstaker or some friendly piano tuner of long ago. Perhaps it is to safeguard one's ego, this forgetfulness of Good Samaritans. Possibly an outspoken memorial for past favors would demolish a treasured American religion, that of the self-made man.

It is a satisfaction to record that Jack Barrymore proved an ex-ception to the rule of professional ingratitude. He may have been self-sufficient in many respects; he inherited a tradition, together with bodily endowments that earmarked him for success; yet he acknowledged that his career often had been accommodated by timely help. Perhaps it would come as a word cast by some intel-ligent person into the swift current of his mind, or as a talent-rousing direction by someone of cool discernment. Then again, it might be simply the love of a friend that uplifted him.

One of these early monitors of Barrymore's professional course was Willie Collier. This laugh-master's influence upon Jack's stage career as a comedian did not reach fruition until 1909, the year of *The Fortune Hunter*. Still, the four years of Jack's training under Collier became a solid education for him, as well as a boisterously gay Odyssey.

Collier had been a friend of the Drews and Barrymores since 1882, the year that found him a call-boy at Augustin Daly's Thea-tre, and the year in which Jack had been born.

Collier was the son of actor Edmund Kean Collier. He first went on the stage with Haverly's Juvenile Opera Company, playing in *H.M.S. Pinafore.* Then he returned briefly to school. The school meant nothing to Collier, and he meant nothing to the school. He jettisoned his primer to enlist as the youngest member of the Daly organization.

After Collier had left Daly's to become a comedy favorite with Weber and Fields, he went from his own dressing-room one night to pay a visit backstage at Daly's, where John Drew was to open in a play. Collier knocked at Drew's door, as he used to do when a call-boy, and sang out, "Fifteen minutes, Mr. Drew."

John Drew was greatly moved by this sentimental tribute. And when the Barrymore children began to grow their pinfeathers, Uncle Jack encouraged their liking for Collier.

"You'll learn a lot from him," Drew said. "He knows the theatre, every inch of it."

Collier also knew baseball and boxing. Lionel went to visit him for a week end at St. James on the north shore of Long Island, and stayed on at Willie's home for two years!

Collier's hobby was the St. James baseball team, on which he himself served as captain and pitcher. Lionel was a good third baseman; too good not to be fed and housed. The other members of Collier's team included some nimble burlesque-wheel artists, and there was plenty of beer for all.

Notwithstanding his strength and skill as an athlete, Lionel was so lazy that he earned the nickname "Turn-me-'round" Barrymore. Once, with a runner wide off first base, Lionel didn't throw the ball. Captain Collier upbraided him.

"But I didn't know there was a runner on first base," said Turn-me-'round.

Collier called the team into a quick huddle. "Listen," he said acidly, "we want no secrets in this ball club. The next time there is a runner on first base, I want you to tell Lionel."

The St. James team played against the nine of the King's Park Insane Asylum each year and then put on a theatrical entertainment for the inmates. During one of these games Collier pitched what he believed to be a strike. The umpire called it a ball. Collier began to argue with the umpire, a dignified but firmly resolved arbiter. The superintendent of the asylum interceded to admonish the angry Collier: "I would bow to the umpire's decision if I were you, Willie." Then he whispered, "You see, he's one of our inmates."

Each night Collier would entertain his team and an assortment of humorists in the billiard room of his home. Among these guests was John Kernell, the vaudevillian, whose stage partner and brother, Harry, used to say to him: "Lend me your face. I want to shake a girl."

Each morning John Kernell would set out in a carriage laden with cases of beer. He permitted the horse to go wherever it chose along the country roads, would toss the bottles out as they were emptied, then fall asleep. The horse usually brought him to the Collier diamond in time for the ball game, but if John didn't show up until after the day's activities, he could easily be found by following the trail of beer bottles.

By the time Jack Barrymore began to nibble at his theatrical inheritance, Collier was a star for Charles Frohman. John Drew, Ethel, and Lionel also were Frohman actors. So when it became necessary for Greengoose to go to work, the young man's availability was brought to the attention of the dubious Frohman.

He had seen Jack on the night he took the curtain call by himself in Philadelphia. Mr. Frohman admitted that the youngest Barrymore "might" have some hidden talent for comedy. Still, he wasn't too sanguine. The moon-gaping fellow seemed to have no ambitions other than sketching and staying up all night.

In January of 1904, after the midnight chimes of Trinity Church had rung in a new year to the tune of "Blue Bells of Scotland" and "Little Maggie May," Collier and Jack sat with Mr. Frohman at Shanley's. They were having lobster. When served, Jack saw that one of the lobster's claws was missing. He called the waiter's attention to this.

"I know," the waiter said, "but these here fellers is brought to us alive. They fight terrible. And sometimes they bite each other's claw off."

"Then take this crustacean back," Jack said, "and bring me the winner."

During the supper, Frohman said to Collier, "I have been reading several plays, but regret to say that I haven't found one that is meant for you."

Collier replied, "I just closed in a play that wasn't meant for me either."

"I do, however, have something that Richard Harding Davis

wrote with Robert Edeson in mind," Frohman said. "Suppose you take it home and read it."

Collier did so, and decided to open in this play, *The Dictator*. He suggested Jack for the part of a wireless operator in the first act. Frohman hesitated.

"Why overlook a horse of such good blood-lines?" Collier asked. "Anyway, Lionel took plenty of time coming into his own. And just think what he did to his Uncle Jack in *The Mummy and the Humming-Bird*."

Mr. Frohman winced at this reminder. Ethel had prevailed on him to cast Lionel for the part of an Italian organ-grinder in *The Mummy*. Lionel had been trying to get a New York job, at anything, for years. His sister frequently had pestered Mr. Frohman to employ her elder brother, but the producer always managed to change the subject. Finally, in Paris, and while Mr. Frohman was having a good time, Ethel put the annoying request once again. Mr. Frohman, anxious to safeguard the gaiety of his evening—for Ethel was charmingly tenacious—spluttered, "Oh, for God's sake, yes!" He allowed her to cable Lionel the news that he might have the part of an Italian organ-grinder in the play which was to star Uncle Jack.

Everyone had qualms about Lionel's assignment. Mr. Frohman, however, relied upon the great name of John Drew to divert public attention from the probable inadequacy of the nephew.

It might be well to keep in mind what Lionel did in secret preparation for this early test. It illustrates his resourcefulness, the kind of shrewd research that years afterward would turn the joint professional appearances of Jack and Lionel into classic theatrical duels between mighty individualists.

Lionel consulted George Barnum, who had played with Ethel in *Captain Jinks*. The young actor visited Barnum one night at his quarters in the Oriental Hotel. This rookery overlooked the Casino Roof.

When Lionel knocked at Barnum's door, the middle-aged actor, a Roman statue in a bathrobe, admitted Barrymore and heard his case. "My boy," said Barnum, "how fortunate that you should, of all nights, and in all places, come to me with your problem. I am the very man, appointed as it were by the gods, to advise and enlighten you in regard to this repulsive character. Sit down, my boy, have some beer, and let us explore your part."

For two and a half weeks Barnum rehearsed Lionel above the musical comedy din of the Casino Roof. Tutor and pupil would stay up all night, drink beer, and rehearse.

Lionel also consulted Ralph Delmore, an actor of Italian parentage, in regard to Sicilian accent. Delmore introduced Lionel to an organ-grinder. Thus fortified with such weapons as understanding of the part, Italian accent, and the technical management of the hand-organ, Lionel appeared at dress rehearsal to astound both Frohman and Uncle Jack. And on opening night, Lionel joined the choir of Drew-Barrymore immortals. It was his first great success.

When someone at The Players asked Uncle Jack how he was feeling, he replied, "I'm feeling quite well, thank you, considering that I'm merely playing second fiddle to my preposterous nephew."

When Willie Collier cited Lionel's unanticipated triumph in *The Mummy* as an argument for Mr. Frohman to give Jack employment, the impresario took the matter under advisement. Then Ethel appeared next day to make a Portian plea, and Mr. Frohman surrendered.

And now Collier's problems began, and were multiplied. His new protégé gave him little rest for the better part of the next four years. On the night of the out-of-town tryout of *The Dictator* in New Haven, Jack met some friends. They carried him into the theatre. "Call a mortician!" Collier cried out. "The cheapest one." Yet, once on-stage, Barrymore managed his part well. The wireless operator fortunately was characterized in the Davis work as a profound bottle-man.

When the play opened at the Criterion in New York, Jack wasn't there at all. Wally McCutcheon, the stage manager, stepped in as the wireless operator. Barrymore showed up as the audience was leaving the theatre. Collier was furious and Mr. Frohman less than happy when the truant appeared backstage.

"Well," asked Mr. Frohman, "where have *you* been?"

"At The Lambs," Jack said. "I took a few drinks there."

Collier snapped out, "A *few!*"

"Well, all I could get, I took."

After a long season in New York, *The Dictator* company went on the road. In Bangor, Maine, Jack didn't materialize for the matinee on Washington's birthday. When asked if he didn't know that a holiday always meant a matinee, Jack said, "I never knew till this instant that Washington's birthday was a holiday!"

Willie Collier was particularly insistent that his actors dress neatly. It galled him to see the weird things Barrymore did to stage costumes, especially the tropical white trousers of a wireless operator. Not only did Barrymore sometimes slip away from the theatre in pants belonging to the company, but often slept in them. Then again, he would stand in his bare feet on his make-up towel, and rub his hands on his trousers instead of employing the towel.

Once, in Chicago, Collier informed Jack that he would have to get some new white pants at his own expense or not be allowed to go on at all. It was winter, a season when white trousers were uncommon in the stores. It also was after business hours. Jack prevailed upon the manager of Marshall Field's personally to open the doors of that mercantile establishment. Together with a night watchman, they rummaged among last summer's stock for a pair of white trousers.

Jack neglected to try on the garment. When he came on-stage, Collier at once saw his predicament, tight pants. Willie departed from the lines of the play, a procedure often practiced by him to satisfy his own sense of waggery, and to sharpen the wits of his players as well.

"Won't you sit down?" Collier asked.

"No, thanks," the tight-trousered Jack replied. "I haven't time."

"Nonsense," said Collier. "Sit down. All the time in the world. Besides, you look tired, as if you'd been on a shopping tour."

"It wouldn't be polite," Jack said, "to sit in the presence of such a great man as yourself."

"But I insist on your sitting," Collier went on, "if only for a moment. Come, what is on your mind?"

"The survival of the fittest," said Barrymore.

"In that case," said Collier, "the last to survive will be a tailor. Do sit down, and we'll go into the matter scientifically."

"Very well then," said Jack. He sat, and the springing of trouser seams could be heard by everyone in the house.

Jack's tardiness and general misbehavior at last caused Collier to telegraph Mr. Frohman. He informed the producer that he was about to dismiss Barrymore from the company. Mr. Frohman wired back: "Don't fire him, Willie. It would break Ethel's heart."

Collier replied by Western Union: "If I keep him, it will break mine."

But Collier never fired Jack. "The trouble," he said, "was that I liked him too much. Otherwise, I might have disciplined him—or tried to. I didn't then realize that he was to become one of the really great actors, although he had the quickest of minds. He assimilated direction easily, especially in the art of timing. His memory was wonderful, yet no one ever caught him studying a part. I thought then that he would be a fine comedian, which, indeed, he did become. But I never in all my life saw a man get clothes so dirty so fast. After the fourth performance his white pants would be black. He could put on a brand-new suit today and look like a god, but tomorrow, in the same suit, he'd become Nat Wills, a tramp."

The Dictator proved so popular in America that in 1905 Mr. Frohman suggested that Collier take the company to England. Marie Tempest, another Frohman star, was at this time appearing most successfully at the Comedy Theatre, a London playhouse controlled by Frohman. It was the producer's novel intention that Collier and Miss Tempest make a trans-Atlantic interchange, each artist to appear for a four weeks' season at the other's stand. Instead of four weeks, Miss Tempest played for a year in New York, and Collier for more than a year in London.

On the opening night in London, and with much at stake for Collier, two of his actors put him in a fine predicament. Jack, of course, was the worse offender.

At the rise of the curtain on *The Dictator*, Collier, as Travers, is found in desperate need of a new name to cover his identity as a fugitive from the law. Ordinarily, in the play, one of his actors, in the role of Bowie, comes on-scene to sell his name to Travers for twenty-five thousand dollars. But tonight the actor appeared with alcoholic hauteur, and when Collier asked, "By the way, what is your name, the one I am to purchase?" he refused point-blank to tell it. Nor could Collier, as Travers, squeeze the name "Bowie" out of his suddenly obstinate actor. He wheedled him, but the actor refused any information. In fact he made an exit, leaving the firstnighters in ignorance of his identity. Finally Collier improvised, saying, "Of course I know his name. Knew it right along. Happened to meet his wife. She told me it was 'Bowie.' "

Hardly had Collier hauled himself out of this pit than Jack arrived on-stage to make matters worse, far worse.

The first entrance of the wireless operator was important for a proper understanding of the play. The business provided that Jack give Collier a wireless despatch written on two long sheets of paper. Collier would read the report aloud, thus advising the audience of the why, when, and wherefore of the action.

Jack appeared on cue, but had in his hand only a small fragment torn from a menu card, a triangle about the size of a Cape of Good Hope postage stamp. He offered this tiny absurdity to the astounded Collier with the usual dialogue, "Here, Chief, is the despatch."

Collier, his eye upon the scrap of paper, improvised, "But where is the real despatch? The longer one?"

Jack also improvised, "Here it is, sir. Or have your eyes gone back on you again?"

"Go to the wireless room," said the desperate Collier, "and bring the *first* despatch. There are two sheets of it. Remember? That's the one I want to read. Not a piece of confetti."

"But this *is* the first despatch," Jack insisted. "I took it down myself, word for word. Put on your bifocals."

Collier knew that the long, plot-point speech he was supposed to deliver hardly could be accepted by a London audience as being read from the menu-fragment.

"Look," he said, then added under his breath, "if you don't go for the prop, I'll break your leg!" Then, so that the audience might hear, "Someone is trying to double-cross us. Go back and look again. I'm sure you will find the genuine message."

"But I *know* this is the one, sir," Jack insisted. "It was sent by a well-known female impersonator."

"Then have her, or him, send us another."

"But," Jack said, "he, or she, can't. He, or it, just died." He wiped away a tear, and sniffled, "Are you going to the funeral?"

"No," said Collier. "How can I?"

"Why not, sir?"

"Because," said Collier, "I haven't got a black dress!" He barked, "Now go for the other message." He added under his breath, "It's a terrible thing to be stranded in London. Catch on?"

Jack went off-stage, leaving Collier to ad lib once again for almost half a minute. Then Barrymore re-appeared to present Collier with exactly the same triangular bit of paper!

"Sir, I have had this authenticated," and he held up the little scrap. "It was not written by the late female impersonator, but by the very clever fellow who engraves the Lord's Prayer on the heads of pins."

There was no other course for Collier than to take the miserable paper, hurriedly edit down his regular speech, and hope for the best. But Willie barely had reached the close of his abridged reading when the actor who hitherto had refused to give the name "Bowie," entered unexpectedly to shout: "I've decided to tell you my name. It's John P. Murphy!"

Collier brought his actors home to New York. He undertook a short season in another play, meanwhile advising his *Dictator* company to stand by for a San Francisco season, to be followed by a tour of Australia. He kept an eye on Jack, and when the time neared for the journey westward, went with Barrymore on a farewell tour of the Manhattan theatrical clubs. They came upon actor Richard Carle at the bar of The Friars. He was leaning on a cane, and watching the bartender polish a pyramid of glasses.

"It's my first day back at The Friars after a six months' unjust suspension," Carle announced. "Have a drink with me, gentlemen, to celebrate my formal reinstatement."

"Why did they suspend you, Mr. Carle?" Jack inquired.

Mr. Carle lifted his walking stick. "Because of a silly accident." He then demonstrated. "I was waving my stick idly over the flagons, like this . . ."

There was a shattering sound as he inadvertently swept the glassware from the bar. The miscellany of goblets crashed to the floor. The bartender shouted. The chairman of the house committee came on the run. The board of governors again suspended Mr. Carle from The Friars, this time for a solid year.

Collier and Barrymore strolled over to The Lambs to find Wilton Lackaye sitting glumly in the grill. He had been grievously misquoted in the public prints as to a remark made at a dinner attended by a religious group. The minister designated to preside at the dinner fell ill. Mr. Lackaye consented to take his place. Feeling that grace must be said before the meal, Mr. Lackaye mustered what was left of his religious training to announce: "There being no clergyman present, let us now thank God."

The reputation of Mr. Lackaye as a mordant fellow caused a reporter to represent him as having said, "Let us thank God that no clergyman is present."

Mr. Lackaye had not been working for quite some time. A sarcasm he had hurled in regard to a certain theatrical magnate's lack of culture brought about his unemployment. When asked, "Do you think So-and-so will ever produce *Les Misérables?*" he had replied, "Produce it! Hell, he can't even pronounce it!"

Today, as Collier entered The Lambs' grill, Lackaye leered, "How's the matinee idol?"

"Fine," Collier retorted. "How's the idle matinee?"

The night before Jack was to leave New York for San Francisco, he learned of the death of his old friend, Frank Butler. It somehow brought back to him the circumstances of his father's tragedy. Butler had been found in Central Park, calling out that he was Nebuchadnezzar of Babylon, and eating grass.

"The poor guy!" said Jack, turning on a man who laughed at this grotesquerie. "It was a symbol of his actual hunger. And if you don't shut up, I'll give you a symbol that even *you* can understand."

The morbid news of Butler's last hours sent Jack into a night of solitary wandering in the White Light district. He happened in at a tiny barroom operated by Billy LaHiff, next to the Gaiety Theatre at Broadway and Forty-Sixth Streeet.

Barrymore found a place at the foot of the bar, ate some rarebits from the free lunch, drank beer, and remained for hours. Finally he leaned over the bar and rested his head on his arm, as if drowsy.

Jack was leaning over in this fashion when a new friend entered his life. This was actor Jack Prescott, then playing in Rachel Crothers' *The Three of Us* at the Madison Square.

It was Prescott's custom, after the evening performance, first to drop in at the Fifth Avenue bar, then drink himself uptown, with appropriate stops at the Hoffman House, the Albermarle, and finally LaHiff's.

Prescott's favorite drink was a dash or two of absinthe in a whisky glass, with Bourbon on top of the stimulating foundation. Then, after Prescott had downed the masterpiece, the bartender would sprinkle a few drops of absinthe onto Prescott's hand. The actor thereupon would rub his palms together, sink his nose between them, and inhale like Muldoon.

Prescott was undergoing this ritual at LaHiff's on the night of Jack's solitary mourning for Butler. After the drink and the sprinkling of absinthe in Prescott's palm, the inhalation, the gargantuan sigh, Prescott called for an additional squirt of absinthe. With this he began anointing his eyebrows, and dabbing absinthe back of his ears

Barrymore, from the far end of the bar, and without lifting his head from his arm, said resonantly, "Christ! I never tried *that!*"

The Barrymore-Prescott friendship began so earnestly that Jack next night all but missed the train that was to take *The Dictator* company westward. The two Jacks had been many places and undergone many adventures, including fights at a tavern near Brooklyn Bridge, and a winefest at John Drew's Long Island cottage, Kyalami.

As Barrymore was hauled aboard the moving train, Collier said, "So nice of you to come."

Jack's only luggage, several fine shirts wrapped in an old newspaper, fell into the aisle. Collier studied the monograms on the garments, an embroidered "J. D." on each one, and easily deduced that John Drew's wardrobe closets at Kyalami again had been raided.

Collier indicated one of the "J. D.s," remarking, "Stands for 'John Doe,' eh?"

"No," Jack replied, "it stands for 'Just Drunk.' "

4.

With Mint Sauce

THE only letter of introduction that John Barrymore ever bothered to deliver was handed to Ashton Stevens in the editorial library of the San Francisco *Examiner* late one April night in 1906. Ethel had written Stevens to keep a monitory eye upon her twenty-four-year-old brother, and eventually see that he got aboard ship for Australia.

Mr. Stevens is a great-souled journalist who for these fifty years has assayed with searching brilliance the personalities and the products of our actors and playwrights. He has seen these darlings arrive and depart, mostly the latter, for stage fame seldom outlasts the butterfly. He evaluated Booth the younger and Modjeska at first hand, and appraised Forbes-Robertson long before a press agent gave that gentleman his hyphen. And although Mr. Stevens never coddled an inferior performance, he smeared no poison on his critical darts. He brought a gay creativeness to his task, a voice clearly heard, yet so unlike the iconoclastic snarls of those who grow violently wise after a last night's event. He became celebrated in the three cities of his critical ministrations, San Francisco, New York, and Chicago, as "the mercy killer."

He grew up in friendly intimacy among successive Drews and Barrymores. He has saved for us such utterances as Ethel's: "It doesn't take great demonstrations of sound to convey to an actor's mind that he is a success or a failure. There is no sound so terrible to an actor as silence." Or John Drew's: "An actor is exactly like a soldier. He has to be there, or be dead." Or Lionel's analysis, in 1904, of the Great Actor:

"The Great Actor always must act. He must make a ceremony of waking up in the morning. He must sit in his room and act so that his whole body vibrates to the thrill of it. Forever he must be a poseur. Every last second of his life must be pose and posture. He must be such a poseur as to be blinded against all rational points of view. He must live in roles and love them. He must be another fellow. Ridicule must pass him by. If by any chance it grazes him, the Great Actor must view it with pitying kindness. His last week's failure must be more than forgot—it never happened. Above all, the Great Actor must have no sense of humor. When he looks at himself in the mirror, he must do so through a telescope. And everything admirable that he reads or sees or hears must be his. Let the most profound, the most classic line fall from his lips, he must be unconscious of the fact that he is not the author of it."

Jack and Stevens, as we have said, came together at the *Examiner* at one o'clock that April morning. That is the hour, to quote Mr. Stevens, when actors and newspaper writers commence to live.

At the time of Barrymore's delivery of Ethel's letter of introduction to Stevens, the young actor was faultlessly attired in evening clothes. How he managed to acquire this finery remained a mystery.

He had been to a ball at the home of Senator Felton, and when Collier asked how he had managed to be a guest at that solon's mansion, Jack replied, "Because they didn't know me."

"The youngest of the Barrymores was sparklingly awake," says Ashton. "He pulled himself out of a big overcoat, and sprawled, a picture, in the nearest chair. His supper coat was double-breasted; mine was the same old single; his shirt buttons were three; mine the same old two. And where I wore shoe strings, he wore bows. Even our cigarettes were of different shades. Nevertheless, he treated me as an equal."

Mr. Stevens does an injustice to himself in demeaning his own attire. He has been a godsend to tailors and haberdashers. Indeed this dean of the inkpots is constantly being mistaken for a Vanderbilt or a steward of Belmont Park.

Stevens says that Jack sniffed the atmosphere of the newspaper shop and smiled. He described Jack's teeth as "deepwater gems, gleaming under a mustache larger than one of his eyebrows, but not quite as large as the two."

"I used to work in a shop like this," Barrymore said, "and draw big bug-house cartoons. I liked it—still like it—gives me nostalgia when I think of it. This acting is a new game. But that's superfluous, isn't it? I don't have to tell a critic that I'm new on the stage, do you think?"

Stevens told him that under any other name he might fool the best of them.

"Really?" Stevens remembers Jack as saying. "I fancied it was rather because the audience—that big funny thing, you know—believed that acting was rather natural to a Barrymore."

"Perhaps," said Stevens, "that's because the Barrymores are such natural actors."

"Undoubtedly," Jack said, "but don't overlook my good fortune in being the nephew of John Drew and the brother of Ethel and Lionel. It helps, fabulously."

He rose and looked around the room again. "Great, isn't it? I'd like to be back at it."

It occurred to Stevens that off the stage his visitor seemed of a smaller build than the Barrymore who played Collier's wireless operator. He was a bit less than five feet nine and a half inches in height, taller than Collier, but because of his admirably proportioned physique and his native skill in dressing for a part he seemed a person of superior stature when on-stage.

"What is it that makes you look so much taller on the stage?" Stevens asked.

Jack replied quickly, "Collier."

"And younger off the stage?" Stevens continued.

"Work," said Jack. "Work's the thing. Keep busy. You remember De Soto? A wonderful person, De Soto. He was always busy, always hunting for something. You couldn't kill him; he finally died of young age. I'm twenty-four, I think. What month is it?"

"April."

"And the year?"

"Nineteen hundred and six."

"Thanks. Then that makes me twenty-four. And work keeps me young. When I drew those bug-house cartoons in New York, I was supposed to be at the newspaper office at eight in the morning, and I never showed up later than three in the afternoon. The secret of youth is work. At least it seems that way to a person of my years. And no man is old nowadays until he is thirty."

When Stevens asked concerning young Barrymore's opinion of audiences, Jack replied:

"Audiences? No, the plural is impossible. Whether it be in Butte, Montana, or Broadway, it's an audience. The same great hulking monster with four thousand eyes and forty thousand teeth. I shouldn't be a bit surprised if some of those bug-house cartoons of mine were subtle impressions of an audience. What a wonderful monster it is, with a hide that might have been torn from a battle-ship, and warts on it like hills. And that monster unit with one great mind makes or breaks men like me. At least it gives or denies them the amusement of success."

Barrymore admitted that while some actors could "get away with almost any kind of part purely on the strength of that elusive and nebulous thing called personality," there had to be a seriousness of effort within a genuine artist. Of himself and his position in a family of actors, he said:

"The actorial family tree with its prestige, and a moderate share of the center of the stage, will, for a time, make the young actor a point of attraction. But he's got to make good later on. He's got to justify the tremendous start in his favor. And he's got to regard the thing seriously.

"Now, you take my brother, Lionel," he continued. "He's a wonder today, and one of these early tomorrows he will be great. He has not only the quality within, but the unconscious technique. Lionel is a paradox, in that he is both delineator and analyst. He's receptive, and he can impart. He doesn't depend on his personality. When he plays a part, he makes a character of it."

"But," Stevens said, "there's your Uncle Jack. Invariably he plays John Drew. Can you imagine him in a beard?"

"It would be worse than my worst cartoon," Jack said. "You don't know how good an actor is until you see him in a bad part. But you must remember this: while Uncle Jack does not run to a variety of facial make-up, which is frequently the resort of the poorest actor, he does give you the character the dramatist provided. And I'll be hanged, drawn, and quartered, if that character is invariably John Drew. Do you remember him in *The Second in Command?*"

"Yes," Stevens replied, "and I was dumfounded by the pathos he got into that scene where he was the only officer left behind."

"Well," Barrymore said, "that was only a touch of the character work he was putting in the part. His work is not like that of the painter that rushes you with sudden contrasts of white against black. John Drew's work has its gray, its gradations, its cumulations. That is character, great character. But I'll lay you anything you say that John Drew will be remembered only for having played the greatest Petruchio of his time."

Jack told Stevens that the Shakespearean "superstition" was hard to down. He thought that some of the Bard's works would last as long as the Bible. "Real literature," he said solemnly, "can be killed only when it is very young."

In recalling this and a hundred other visits with Barrymore, Stevens says, "I don't know when or where he got time for acquiring the knowledge he possessed. I never caught him reading. I wouldn't say that he was a student in the academic sense. Rather, I believe that he brushed against many things, in books or in life, and that the really good things somehow stuck to him."

That Jack's main ambition was to be a painter is substantiated by his first conversation with Stevens.

"Acting comes easy and pays well," he said, "that's the narcotic."

"Do you mean," Stevens inquired, "that you like the stage less, or the brush more?"

"Not taking the slightest suggestion from your tails-I-win-heads-you-lose interrogation," Jack replied, "I will say this: if I had to make my choice, I'd give up the stage."

How are we to understand the recurrent attempts of the Barrymore brothers to run away from Fame? Jack always responded to this question with a Pontius Pilate shrug. Lionel, as I write of this now, consented to be pinned down.

"Neither Jack nor myself preferred the stage. We both wanted to become painters. Yet it seemed that we had to be actors. It was as if our father had been a street cleaner, and had dropped dead near a fire hydrant, and we went out to pick up his shovel and broom to continue his work. Perhaps we didn't clean the corners well, but we did a better job at it than someone who never had been in the environment. What other thing could we have done better?"

Then Lionel told of one of his last conversations with Jack, disclosing what appears to me to be the most plausible explanation of the disinclination of the Barrymores to act.

"When well-meaning critics first began to compare Jack and myself to actors of other days, we felt uneasy. Hell! We were flabbergasted. To us, reared as we were among giants of the stage, those great names were sacred. We would exchange self-conscious glances, try to switch the subject, and, when by ourselves, would pretend that nobody had said a thing. We were even afraid that the ghosts of great actors had overheard the comparisons, and would haunt us.

"Well, Jack did become great. And one night last year, after our final radio broadcast together, and when Jack was near the end of everything, we made sure that no one was listening, even the ghosts, and spoke of the days when we cringed inside if anyone compared us to the great ones. Then I said:

"'Jack, you don't have to feel self-conscious now. No matter what has happened of recent years, you really did climb up among the stars. You were one of them.' He looked at me for a while, grinned, then said, 'This is a hell of a time to tell me!'"

Jack went with Stevens to the critic's quarters in the old Occidental Hotel, where Bret Harte had lived, and now where army and navy officers and several elderly ladies resided.

The elevator in this early San Francisco building enchanted Jack. It was operated by means of hand power, the cage being raised or lowered by Danny, a mild-mannered little Irishman, who tugged at the rope cable. But elevation was not this hoister's only duty. When elderly ladies entered the cage to come down to dinner, the little Irishman would check the descent at a place between floors. He would gravely and discreetly do maid service for the ladies, to the extent of hooking up their high-necked dinner gowns from behind, then resume the journey down the shaft.

On the night when Jack and Stevens arrived at the Occidental, three army officers entered the lift. As the army men were getting out at the second floor one of them made an allusion to the Victoria Cross.

Jack then said to Stevens, "I heard a great deal from my father about the Victoria Cross. I'd like to see one."

The next afternoon, when Jack and Stevens were leaving the Occidental, Danny stopped the lift at the place where he usually did maid service for the elderly women guests, then brought a small plain case from his coat pocket.

He opened the lid and handed the case to Jack.

"There, sir, is a V. C."

"Where did you get it?" asked the amazed Barrymore.

Danny answered, "I was to Khartum with Kitchener."

The little soldier received the case from Jack, restored it to his pocket matter-of-factly, then began hauling away at the rope cable.

On the occasion of Jack's next visit to the *Examiner* office, he found Mr. Stevens in something of an emotional dither. The Metropolitan Opera Company had arrived from New York for a three weeks' season in San Francisco. There also had come a twinkling telegram from Mr. Hearst, warning his western editor, Charles Michelson, not to count on the appearance of the stars at any theatrical benefit the *Examiner* might sponsor.

It seems there had recently been a benefit for some worthy cause in Manhattan, and Mr. Hearst's New York *American* had announced, as one of the money-raising attractions of that performance, the appearance of certain Metropolitan Opera Company principals. The opera management had abruptly frowned in a high-class sort of fashion, then sent a substantial check to the *American's* benefit fund, together with a note advising its editors that Metropolitan artists could not, under penalty of contractual breach, warble elsewhere than in their own nest.

Now, Charley the Mike was no music lover; he was not even a banjo player like his critic; or like his boss, who had once been the prize pupil of Banjoist Stevens.

Michelson felt it his duty to make Stevens feel it *his* duty to show the Metropolitan Opera people that when they gratuitously snubbed the young New York *American* they were not endearing themselves to the parent Hearst paper, the old San Francisco *Examiner*.

Michelson broadly implied that if any member of the Metropolitan Company so much as slid a bit off pitch, it would be just for Stevens to proclaim it the sourest kind of braying since the time when

Balaam's ass addressed that startled non-Israelitish prophet with words as well as music.

"I hope you see the light," said Editor Michelson.

This editor's figure of speech had more than casual significance. His brother Albert, head of the department of physics at the University of Chicago, was at this moment measuring the velocity of light, and next year would be the first American scientist to win the Nobel Prize for this achievement.

Mr. Stevens found himself in a less than pretty situation, ethically or otherwise. On this second night of its season the company had sung *Carmen* brilliantly, and Caruso had been in finest voice. There had been curtain calls in profusion, great applause, and cries of bravo and *bis!*

The editor leaned like a gargoyle over the critic's shoulder. He recoiled at Stevens' praise of Caruso's "amber note."

"Look here, Ashton," he intoned, "can't you calm it down a little? Can't you count Caruso's chins and in your own inimitable prose mourn the survival of the fattest?"

"Get away from my desk, Charley," Stevens said. "I'll grant you his chins, but, just the same, I'll grant Caruso his voice."

"But, Ashton," the editor pursued, "the Chief was embarrassed by the Metropolitan back in New York. Doesn't that mean anything to you?"

"He'd be more embarrassed if I tried to tell his San Francisco readers the greatest tenor in the world can't sing." Then Stevens added, "Never forget that W. R. is a better newspaper man than any he hires—and I'm not saying so because he's the best newspaper friend I have or ever hope to have. Now run along, Charley."

The editor tried a flanking maneuver. "Ashton, a critic's column is the matter of a mere day. It is read, then forgotten . . ."

"I'm getting a little mad," Stevens interrupted. "I'm getting a little mad," he repeated. "Please!"

"Stevens," Charley the Mike warned, "no notice is as good as a job. And a job—well, isn't a good job at good pay more important than . . ."

Stevens was on his feet. "Damn it!" he roared. "I've got three weeks of this Metropolitan season . . . I hope the God-damned opera house burns down!"

This expletive wish was perhaps the most remarkable father-to-the-thought since Old Testament days. For within a matter of hours the opera house *did* burn, together with many other buildings, in San Francisco's great disaster, the fire and earthquake of April 18 and 19, 1906.

The incendiary curse of Ashton Stevens, uttered at midnight, was regarded by Editor Michelson as a mere journalistic blowup. He saw in it no portentous implications. Notwithstanding his other talents, Mr. Michelson was not clairvoyant. Such irascible words as those used by Mr. Stevens were to be expected of hard-working newspaper men as they strained to meet deadlines. A nerve-frayed reporter might blurt out, "I hope your mother drops dead over the garbage pail!" or "I'll stick this scissors!" and then promptly receive absolution the moment the edition began to roll between the clamorous press cylinders.

Mr. Michelson shrugged, then sadly moved away from the critic's desk. The editor was entirely innocent of the prospect that the earth itself would take up his shrug at five-thirteen o'clock in the morning, and magnify it so many trillions of times that even his scientific brother couldn't measure its force.

As Stevens sat again in the dignity of his evening clothes and his critical candor, a messenger boy brought to his desk a note signed by Jack Barrymore. It was written on the back of a bill of fare:

Dear Rock of Ages: Meet me at The Oyster Loaf instantly for an emergency conference. Bring pocket-book and a modicum of advice for the lovelorn.

Stevens turned in his copy at twelve-thirty, then walked from the newspaper office to The Oyster Loaf. This was an all-night rendezvous for bookmakers, who formulated odds for next afternoon's horse races, and a meeting place for actors and newspaper men. The management made a specialty of fried oysters served inside hollow loaves of bread.

Barrymore was sharing a fry of oysters with Clarence Follis, a Golden Gate young blood, when Stevens entered. Jack had been to the opera, and was attired in white tie and tails.

"As you doubtless know, Ashton," he said, "I am sailing for Australia at high noon on the good ship *Moana*. Sounds like a cry of romancers, that name. Which reminds me: Do you happen to be in funds?"

Stevens explored his pockets to find little more than two opera house ticket stubs, a cigarette case, a bunch of keys, some matches, and a single silver dollar.

"The dollar is yours," he said. "Will it help?"

"I'm afraid not," Jack said. "You see, I encountered a charming young lady at the opera. Claims she is the fiancée of a collector of ancient Venetian glass. In fact I played footsie with her during Don José's first seduction by Carmen. The old boy sat the other side of her during Caruso's and my performance. Later he caught on, but not until we had arranged a tryst. Then he exchanged seats with the lady. I'm to visit her tonight after he has left her quarters."

"It sounds like true love," said Mr. Follis over an oyster. "Why do you need money?"

"For replacements, in case I break some glassware," said Barrymore. He shook his head sadly at Mr. Stevens' dollar. "No, I'd need at least fifty of these."

"Won't Collier advance it to you?" Stevens asked.

"Not one red cent," Jack replied. "Says I'm already overdrawn for six months' salary, if you call the few farthings he pays me a salary. How about the cashier's office at the *Examiner?*"

"Closed," Mr. Stevens replied, "but if you wait until morning, I'll try to borrow fifty from Mr. Bogart, our generous cashier."

Barrymore was deflated. "And I wrote on a piece of the program, 'Poison him if necessary. I'll be there,' and passed it behind the old glass-maniac's back, after he'd sat himself like a duenna between us. He's with her now, examining goblets or something, and I'm stuck with five and a half weeks at sea. God, what a prospect!"

"But," said Mr. Follis, a widely traveled young man, "there surely will be women on the ship."

"Bah!" Barrymore exclaimed. "A galaxy of seasick prudes!" He groaned, "Why did Collier have to think up Australia at a time like this?"

Mr. Follis left on a matter of his own, and Barrymore and Stevens remained at The Oyster Loaf until after three o'clock, discussing ways and means.

Finally Jack said he was going to the fifth floor of the St. Francis, to rouse Collier and make a man-to-man appeal. They walked to the hotel, and in parting Jack said, "Just in case, Ashton, I'll see you in the morning about that fifty from Mr. Bogart."

Willie Collier says that Jack did not wake him up, but something else did. He was hurled out of bed at five-thirteen and into his bathroom. The plaster fell from the walls. As soon as he could find a bathrobe and slippers, Collier went into Union Square, where opera singers and other guests of the hotel were spectators at a performance far mightier than anything concocted by Wagner.

"Jack didn't show up until ten o'clock," Collier says. "He was still dressed in his opera clothes. He was quite chipper. Seemed not at all upset by the now-raging fire, or the dynamiting of the buildings.

" 'What's up, Willie?' he asked casually. I was chattering with nervousness. 'Nothing's up at all. In fact everything is down. Half the town is burning, and the other half is being blown to pieces; but otherwise nothing is up.'

"I told him to go to his hotel, and put on some day-clothes instead of those opera togs. He agreed to do so, but pointed out the absurdity of my dressing-gown, and suggested that I do likewise. I told him I didn't have a cent, and had heard that the ship that was to take us to Australia had disappeared, maybe been sunk, with all our trunks and wardrobe and scenery of *The Dictator*.

" 'Don't worry,' he said. 'I raised two hundred dollars from a glass-blower's friend while you were sleeping.' "

Collier says that this unexpected news rocked him almost as severely as had the five-thirteen temblor. "Hand it over!" he shouted. But Jack was on his way to get his other clothing. He returned at about noon, Collier recalls, dressed in tweeds, and looking quite fit. When Collier asked for the two hundred dollars, Jack gave a start.

"My God, Willie! I left it in my dress suit!"

Collier was beside himself. "Go get it! Now!"

Jack obeyed, then came back in the afternoon to announce: "Do you know what happened, Willie? You'll get a laugh out of this. They've dynamited my room. The pants and my gold have gone up in flames and detonations."

"Good God!" Willie screamed. "Pants again! Always pants!"

Jack found out that the *Examiner's* staff had moved across the bay to publish emergency editions on the press of the Oakland *Tribune*, an afternoon newspaper. Jack properly deduced that his friend Stevens would be in Oakland, and finally managed, on the third day, to find Ashton, who said in reference to the disaster: "When God does such things, He has style."

Barrymore inquired if Mr. Bogart was available with the potential fifty dollars, but Stevens said he didn't think it the proper time to negotiate a loan. He asked Jack if he had been badly shaken during the first quake.

Jack winked. "Venetian glass fell all around us."

"Us?" asked Stevens. "Venetian glass?"

"I didn't stay at the St. Francis for long after you left. I kept my tryst with the charmer."

Some doubt was cast on Jack's story when a purposeful virago appeared in Oakland to accuse Jack of owing her fifty dollars as a social fee. Stevens by no means could reconcile this woman's status with that of a wealthy glass-collector's sweetheart or lover of the opera. He managed to whittle her claim down to five dollars, then prevailed upon the reluctant Mr. Bogart to underwrite it with a check.

In early press reports to the East, Barrymore's name had been listed among the missing. Regular telegraph facilities obviously were lacking, and personal messages banned. Jack didn't think his family would be at all worried about him, but Stevens disagreed. The critic prevailed upon Editor Michelson (their feud, as well as their office, having collapsed) to permit Jack to tag onto the close of a news service bulletin to New York a message to Ethel.

Jack wrote as dramatically as possible within the thirty words allotted him of how he had been thrown out of bed, had wandered dazedly to the street, where an Army sergeant put a shovel in his hand and made him work for twenty-four hours among the ruins of the city.

When Ethel read this message to John Drew, and asked, "Do you believe it?" Uncle Jack replied, "Every word. It took an act of God to get him out of bed, and the United States Army to put him to work."

In Oakland Jack shared a room at the Athenian Club with Bill Leech, publisher of the *Examiner*. The bar stayed open all day and all night during the fire and its aftermath. And here Collier found Jack, to announce that the company was setting out for British Columbia in a freighter.

At Vancouver, twelve days after the San Francisco fire, *The Dictator* company, minus scenery, wardrobe, trunks, and prompt-books, sailed for Australia.

Aboard ship, Collier began to rewrite the play from memory. Willie had Jack draw designs for new sets to be built when they reached Melbourne.

Neither Barrymore nor Collier enjoyed themselves in Australia. They found the nights all too quiet. In fact they were arrested one evening at nine o'clock for laughing too loudly on the streets of Melbourne.

"That's what ails our audiences," Collier whispered to Jack at the police station. "They're afraid to laugh after nine o'clock."

Collier decided to put on Augustus Thomas' play, *On the Quiet*. He and Jack visited the leading tailor of Melbourne for costumes, but encountered unforeseen trouble in that shop. The tailor flatly refused to make the suits as sketched by Jack and in accord with styles prevailing in America. Said it would hold his work up to ridicule. Only after Collier gave written assurance that the suits would be worn in comedy roles, and not on the streets, did the tailor consent to cut patterns from Jack's designs.

"Now look," Collier said to Jack one day, after Barrymore had reported late for rehearsal, "I've been crying 'wolf' long enough. The next time you are late or miss a performance, or do any of the terrible things that seem so dear to your nature, I'm going to abandon you in Australia."

Collier displayed an envelope containing tickets for the company's return to America. Then he added, "You see you are not in the U.S.A., where some soft-headed manager can rescue you, or you can make touches on Ashton Stevens. I have the tickets. And I'll not have one for you. Maybe your sister will send you the boat fare. I don't know. But I warn you, it will be an awful thing to be marooned among the kangaroos and boomerang-throwers."

From then on until the close of the Australian tour Barrymore appeared on time at the theatre. One morning he overslept, but hastily drew on a topcoat over his pajamas, and ran down the principal street of Melbourne to attend rehearsal.

A day or two before the voyage home to America, Collier said he wanted to have a "fatherly talk" with Jack. He pointed out that Barrymore had been with him, off and on, for almost four years, but instead of having a dime to show for this long employment was in debt to the company for five hundred dollars.

"I'll write off the debt," Collier continued, "and I'll show you how to make a stake during the five and a half weeks we are at sea."

"As a stoker?" Jack asked.

"I'm taking you to an art store," Collier said. "I want you to get materials for sketches. You can do them on the ship; then, after you arrive in New York, you can sell them. See?"

Jack promised to work painstakingly on the sketches. He kept his word, laboring earnestly over a dozen or so Shakespearean characters.

Weeks afterward, in New York, Collier found Jack at The Lambs. The young man said that he was broke.

"But what happened to those sketches you did aboard ship?" Collier asked. "You said they would sell."

"Good God!" Jack shouted. "I left them on the ship!"

5.

Exquisitely Velvet

IT is ever difficult to see her clearly, if at all, this imperishable lady at one's elbow. Perhaps we do not wish to glimpse the inscrutable one who pounces upon us to exercise a last option. And although some poets sing of her as beautiful beyond lilacs and roses, and say of her that she is a refuge for the sick of heart, my personal opinion is that Death is a great whore. She sleeps with everyone, promiscuously and obscenely, and everyone must sleep with her without willing it. Why lie?

Twice she has come close to me, and I am bound to report that I did not cry out either for forgiveness or for aid, although I believe entirely in Jehovah's existence and patient amiability. On the more recent occasion, with an automobile on my skull and gasoline drenching my body, I went into the dark with no prayer at all, but a fine peasant's curse for Death. And, after awakening in a hearse on the way to the morgue, I undertook no mock ritualisms to celebrate my physical salvation. This quality, my stubborn loyalty to life, became one of the first elements of my friendship with John Barrymore. He sent a note to the hospital:

No one who understands you in the least would have consigned your body to a hearse. It becomes the greatest *faux pas* since the naïve Trojans admitted a wooden Percheron within their gates.

The stimulus for this gratuitous intrusion on our story—Mr. Ben Hecht terms it a "bird call"—is the death of Alexander Woollcott, valiant trumpeter of all the Barrymores.

I knew this man of letters long; yet, strangely, I never knew him well until our visit during the last autumn of his life on his island in Lake Bomoseen, Vermont.

The Town Crier was sitting on a jetty as I boated in from Fair Haven. He waved, then called out, "Hello, Repulsive!" He seemed comparatively thin, and his heart was behaving like an old clockwork. The unseen harlot was at hand, as I now know, but Woollcott disregarded her solicitations. His mind was on the Barrymores. He loved them. He spoke of Ethel as having been the "most disturbing woman of her time."

"This shy, reserved, dignified beauty," he observed with firsthand authority, "had a more devastating effect than if she had been some glamorous adventuress. Without benefit of celluloidal circulation of her superb likeness, she influenced all the girls of America to copy her way of dress, her coiffure, her appealing manner. Her voice was very deep, and when a multitude of stage imitators tried to simulate Ethel's tones in the speech from the play *Sunday*, 'That's all there is—there isn't any more,' she did a thing entirely characteristic of the Barrymores. She deliberately pitched her voice one note higher, and left it there."

"Ashton Stevens," I said, "once called her 'Ethel Barrytone.' "

"Ashton could get away with that," Woollcott replied, "because Ethel knew that he loved her. Just as Charlie MacArthur, Hecht, and yourself could get away with calling Jack 'The Monster.' "

"Or your calling me 'Repulsive,' " I said.

"But that's different," Woollcott said. "You *are*." He sighed. "How unfortunate that Jack can't have a more suitable biographer than some noxious ex-police reporter. Of course any gold that I give you will be transmuted into tin foil—alchemy in reverse."

These belaborings by the eminent critic concealed as warm a heart as I ever encountered, notwithstanding the then present creaks in its mechanism. His sentimentality, as revealed in speaking of the Barrymores, seemed Dickensian. He told anecdotes on our way to the nearer of his two island houses, where he liked to play word games with guests. Some excellent pigeons, given him by playwright Edward Sheldon, were acquainting themselves with the new cote built to shelter them against the Vermont snows.

"Ethel once wired Frohman," the Town Crier said, "asking for new costumes. Frohman telegraphed her a laconic 'No,' to which she wired back 'Oh!' But we were speaking of Ethel's inward and outward beauty. Of course you can't comprehend this, because you've spent most of your life among corn-tassels or at police stations."

"Is that so?" I offered. "Then let me reveal to you that I have been secretly in love with Miss Barrymore for forty-three years."

He appraised me with owlish silence, then said, "One of us, eh? Well, it demonstrates that she stirred the emotions even of the lower classes. Do you know that practically all the staid gentlemen of London were about to jump out of windows for love of her? They would have, only the building ordinances over there precluded high enough edifices for such romantic demonstrations."

"But what does this have to do with Jack?"

"It has everything to do with Jack, you profound dullard! She mothered him. Led him by the hand from agency to agency after he had left Willie Collier's company. Paid his bills. Rescued him from love affairs, helped him escape to a summer resort in wintertime when he was wanted as a witness in the Thaw trial. Didn't complain when he stole her furniture or signed her name to telegrams sent to worried mothers of young ladies he was romancing and keeping up all night. Great Lord! She saw in him what no one else observed in advance—with the single exception of Edward Sheldon—that this apparently raffish clown had genius."

Woollcott then said with all gravity, "Whenever a Helen Hayes, an Alfred Lunt, or a Kate Cornell assumes first place on the stage, we could, or should, have seen in the years before their recognition the signs of ascendant personality. This was not so in Jack's case. Ethel foresaw, and never lost faith in Jack. And I wish to tell you now that my opinion of his character, divorced from all friendship, and founded upon long years of contemplation of life and letters, is this: When Barrymore sneered at and abused himself beyond the tolerance of the crowd, it was done not through weakness but strength, a defiance of God. And when you write of him, as I fear you shall, for heaven's sake remember one thing: you are not telling the story of a capon."

Barrymore was rehearsing the part of Nat Duncan in Winchell Smith's play, *The Fortune Hunter*, in 1909.

He spent the hot New York summer in the apartment of a friend. The friend returned from the country to find his mattress missing. Looked everywhere for it, and for Jack. Eventually a maid discovered the mattress on a fire escape. Barrymore had slept there during the sultry nights and not alone.

He then set up quarters on the top floor of Murray's Restaurant, installing there a piano upon which he could not play, and numerous *objets d'art* given him by Stanford White.

At about this time Barrymore disclosed to Ethel that he again was in love. In this instance she noticed but one discrepancy in her brother's usual romantic pattern. He displayed the same violent yearning as in other days, the same antipathy to food, and again asserted his life-long philosophy as contained in the one word, "Now." This time, however, he had fallen in love at long range. It was the single departure from his customary behaviorism when in love. Ordinarily he suffered, or enjoyed, these recurrent attacks at close quarters, oftentimes too close.

He confided to his sister that he now was in love with Miss Nora Bayes, singing star of musical comedies.

"But you've never met her," said Ethel.

"Did Dante meet Beatrice?" asked Jack. Then he groaned. "I think Nora Bayes the only woman in the world for me."

"You're not doing much thinking, Jake," Ethel said. "Besides, she's the romantic ideal of W. C. Fields."

"And who is he?" asked Jack.

"Mr. Fields," Ethel informed him, "happens to be a star comedian employed by Florenz Ziegfeld. You should at least know about *The Follies*. They were named after you."

"Will you accompany me to the theatre where this trivial mugger is performing? I shall study him for future reference."

Ethel sat with Greengoose while Mr. Fields juggled Indian clubs and otherwise displayed his remarkable talents. After the curtain had fallen, Ethel turned to Jack. "Well, Gus, what do you think?"

"Ethel," said Jack, "he's one of the greatest artists of all time.

I'm not in love with Miss Bayes now. Hell! I'm in love with W. C. Fields!"

Lionel returned from the studios of Paris soon after Louis Blériot, inventor of the monoplane, started his flight across the English Channel. The elder brother wanted to witness Jack's debut as a star in *The Fortune Hunter*. Lionel went with Kid McCoy to the Gaiety Theatre on the night of September 4. He had sent a red apple, to be placed together with similar tokens from Ethel and Uncle Jack on Barrymore's make-up table.

Lionel and McCoy could get no seats for *The Fortune Hunter* première. They stood during the performance. They saw Jack suddenly become a comedian of first rank. He gave a faultless and vital portrayal of his part. The theatre from now on would be enriched by his electric presence, and his fame would grow and endure for as long a time as his own volatile desires permitted.

Lionel and the pugilist went backstage to find a swarm of victory-inspired first-nighters crowding Jack's dressing-room. Kid McCoy was all for charging among them, but Lionel said, "No. Wait until they go. Even the catnip of hero worship loses its effect eventually."

Lionel and Kid McCoy eventually entered the now-cleared room. "Well, Jake," Lionel said, "it looks like you are hooked for good."

"What in hell has happened?" Jack asked. "Who am I?"

"It usually takes me two nights," Lionel replied, "to find out what occurred on the first. You'll live."

"But I'm scared stiff," Jack said. "Why didn't I give a stinking performance?"

"Because," said Lionel, "you couldn't."

"For God's sake!" said Jack, his face wet with what he called a Gethsemanic sweat. "Let's find some hole-in-the-wall that serves liquid dynamite."

The companions went to a small café on the East Side to stay up all night.

"In all the other arts," Jack said, "poor bastards starve, freeze, and strip their souls year after year. In this stage paradox, so-called success comes overnight. I'll tell you why I'm so scared. I heard thunder in the applause. A sign of storms to come."

Concerning Barrymore at this time, Booth Tarkington said:

"On a night in the first decade of the century Jack and I argued late at The Lambs. I think our subject must have been aesthetic, concerned with the nature of beauty; but the night wore on and we still talked, holding opposite views, though I don't know which was Jack's and which was mine, and I think that both of us at times became a little confused about that. Finally I grew solicitous on his account, as he had a matinee to play the next afternoon. I said he'd better be going home, and he amiably agreed but expressed some doubt of his ability to get there.

" 'Where are you living now?' I asked him.

"He looked at me for perhaps a full minute before he replied in a magnificent voice, 'On top of Murray's Roman Gardens!'

"He rolled the r's in the manner later familiar to radio listeners, and his superb eyes examined me to discover whether or not I felt the humor of his burlesquing, and also if I absorbed the complete nonsense of his living in an apartment so entitled. I did.

"We reached 'Murray's Roman Gardens,' a lively restaurant of that day, and, when we'd ascended to Jack's flat above it on the top floor, he asked me to look about the place and observe how it proved that he lived solely for beauty. I said he'd better get to bed, which seemed to hurt his feelings.

" 'No,' he insisted. 'Look at all these beautiful things that I keep about me, every one of them perfect! They'll help to educate you.' He pointed to a landscape painting above the mantelpiece. 'That, for instance. Give me your unenlightened opinion of it.'

" 'It's a daub,' I informed him. 'Entirely bad. Go to bed, Jack.'

" 'Observe the Persian rug upon which you are now standing,' he said. 'Have you no grasp of it?'

" 'None,' I replied. 'I think it's from an Atlantic City auction. You have a matinee tomorrow and what you need is sleep.'

" 'Observe that other rug, the one before the fireplace,' he commanded. 'Have you ever seen a white bear rug to compare with it?'

" 'It's sooty,' I told him. 'You ought to send it to the cleaner's.'

"Upon that, he seemed to despair of me; but he had a last card to play. On the grand piano stood an artificial plant easily divined to be the gift of some worshipful lady. It was a strange elaborate thing, a rosebush in flower, with leaves, blooming roses, and all exquisitely made of tinted velvets.

" 'What about that?' he asked, touching it with eloquent fingers. 'That reaches you, doesn't it?'

"I laughed disdainfully. 'Artificial, Jack. Velvet! Artificial leaves and flowers made of velvet. How painful!'

"He became intensely solemn, stood before the velvet plant and made a great slow gesture indicating that he now explained everything deepest within him. 'Velvet,' he said. 'Exquisitely velvet! Exquisitely artificial! *That* is the soul of John Barrymore!'

"Then, having achieved this climax of effect, he went to his bedroom door, bowed dismissingly and retired."

As a grace note, Booth Tarkington added:

"When he died it would have been many, many years since I'd seen him; but he was as vivid to me as he had been in the days when I met him daily. He's a grand memory!"

6.

The First Bus Accident

THERE was a rain effect in the fourth act of *The Fortune Hunter*. This stage rain exercised a sublime influence on Jack Barrymore, notwithstanding its commonplace origin in a perforated tin cloud, and its brief journey to the tarpaulins of the Gaiety Theatre.

A real rain stirs the emotions of almost everyone, it is said, a sort of mood music. It may bring even to a Bowery wanderer bold remembrance of a time of sheltered serenity, or to an old-maiden recluse in some shuttered brownstone house off Washington Square a dream of dress-uniforms and quadrilles.

Natural rain provoked in Barrymore either of two extremely opposite impulses: to go naked into the downpour, or else to draw the blinds, sit by a fireside and listen to the staccato serenade overhead and the contrapuntal crackling of hearth logs.

"It sounds like all the little beggars of the world," he once observed of the rain noise, "tapping their canes and crutches on the roof as they go out to ask for bread."

The stage shower, artificial though it was and arriving as it did on cue each night, became in Barrymore's fancy a symbol of his own loneliness of heart. His storybook mind ignored the fact that a Mr. John Thompson, and not St. Swithin, was the instigator of this stage rain. And while it was falling at each performance, Jack would think of a fireside. Then he began to associate the fireside with a dressing-gown and slippers, he said, and finally, in that connection, to think of taking a wife. Perhaps, had there been no iterative rain dreams, he might have postponed his introduction to wedlock in 1910.

One night after the tin cloud had run dry, Barrymore changed to evening clothes and left the theatre. He found a genuine rain driving down upon New York. This storm accentuated his desire for carpet-slippers. He wondered if it would not be better for him to go home and shut himself in than to attend a debutante's ball to which he had been invited.

The sound of carriage-starters' whistles rose above the rain beats and the traffic noises, the clompings of hack horses, the gongs of street cars. Barrymore found a hansom cab. While exploring his pockets for cigarettes, he came upon the invitation to the ball. He lighted a match to study the address.

The ball was being given for Katherine Corri Harris, a taffy-haired beauty with blue mirrors for eyes, and a charming little hesitancy, not quite a stammer, in her speech. Her parents occupied a comfortable place among those listed in *The Social Register*, the Koran of Newport and Fifth Avenue. The father and mother of this lovely person certainly didn't anticipate that a theatrical weasel would spring the golden trap they had baited for ermine.

It was prescribed that Katherine leave for Europe, a treatment frequently adopted by socialites to cool the love-fevers of their marriageable daughters. The Harris family might as well have saved themselves the expense. The girl soon returned to America. And in September, at the Church of St. Francis Xavier, the nineteen-year-old beauty married the twenty-eight-year-old victim of the rain.

"This event," Jack said, "was the first of my three and one-half marriages—all of them bus accidents."

After the wedding breakfast, the bridegroom announced that he had to "go on the road" with *The Fortune Hunter*. "It will only be for a year," he told his wife. "We'll be seeing each other at propitious moments."

The bride retired to Mamaroneck, to stay temporarily at the home of a relative, one of the few family members who cared to receive her as Mrs. Barrymore. Upon Jack's return to New York, the couple occupied quarters on the tenth floor of an apartment house on the east side of Gramercy Park. A balcony with a stone balustrade gave from their parlor. Jack would take a chair onto this ledge, sit, then lean back to look up at the gargoyle decorations of the cornice. Katherine had hysterics when her moody spouse teetered dangerously and made faces at the gargoyles.

The inexperienced girl tried hard not to quarrel with Barrymore But quarrel they did, frequently. It seems that it never was an easy matter for any of his wives to exist happily with him for long in wedlock. Perhaps the bottle may have been the chief cause of each domestic furor; yet in this respect we cannot wholly disregard the implications of Jack's own statement: "Unhappiness increased the drink, and drink increased the unhappiness."

It may be argued that as an extremist Barrymore either placed love too high or too low in his scale. Who can say? One of his associates believed that Barrymore sought the impossible when he demanded that a mate consist of, all in one, "saint, siren, mother, wife, and friend."

After Barrymore's first wife succumbed to the fiery Apollo of the stage, she confidently expected him to carry his theatrical embers into their private life. This he declined to do. It was his observation that even the greatest thoroughbreds didn't gallop when away from the race-course.

Elements other than drink increased the discord of Barrymore's first marriage. Katherine, young and blossoming, wished to exhibit her husband in public, to dance or dine with him where everyone might view her handsome prize. Jack wanted no self-display after theatre hours.

Between engagements, or on Sundays, he would appear in old clothes and with a beard-stubble, slouch about Gramercy Park, feed the pigeons there, or enjoy solitary strolls in side streets. He avoided off-stage applause. When he did seek company, he preferred the cubbyholes of Greenwich Village. He stayed up all night with newspaper men and down-at-the-heel artists. He sometimes forgot his marriage vows. He failed to advise Katherine as to where he was going or where he had been. He was not a man of explanations, nor a man to be explained. He simply *was*.

His favorite drinking companion, Jack Prescott, remembers an instance of amatory waywardness concerning Barrymore and a famous lady of the theatre. Shall we re-christen her "Roxana"? She was married to a comedian. Do you mind if we call him "Maximilian"? We do not wish our anecdote to be at loggerheads with the virtue-laden epitaphs chiseled beneath the real names of these once so lively folk. Roxana at forty stayed beautiful. She had a "crush" on Jack. He tried to dissuade her from anticipating an enduring liaison, for he was occupied with tutoring numerous younger students of biology. Out of generosity of heart, he permitted Roxana a few brief interludes. This proved a mistake, as he afterward admitted to his friend Prescott. Roxana importuned him to spend a night at her town house.

"What can I do about it?" Jack asked Prescott. "She is so damned polite, and always thanks me. Still, I don't want to waste a whole night. Besides, Maximilian lives on the premises, and I don't want him to catch me playing the registered-letter version of 'post-office.' "

One snowy afternoon Jack informed Prescott that he had agreed to stay the night at Roxana's house.

"She assures me," he sighed, "that Max's rooms are on the floor above hers, and that even if he does come home, he never bothers to look in on her. He might stop at the door, she admits, but only to call out, 'Hello, Roxy,' and then stagger upstairs."

At about midnight of that same evening, Prescott recalls, Jack rolled into the Players Club. He had no shoes on, and his socks were wet. He was sneezing and sniffling. He was madder than a defeated alderman. When asked how he had lost his shoes, and what had gone wrong, Barrymore gulped down a double brandy, peeled off his wet socks, then replied:

"I was relaxing when up the stairs came Maximilian. Roxana said for me not to become uneasy, but stay right where I was. She doubted if Max would even stop outside the door. I said to hell with all that. I dashed across the room to the clothes-closet."

He ordered another drink, sent an attendant to borrow some dry socks and bedroom slippers from a resident member of the club, then continued:

"Do you know how long I smothered among the silk petticoats in that closet? More than two hours, while that egotistical old bore gabbed and gabbed. Christ! I never was so mad in my life! He finally left, after Roxana practically made an affidavit that she had a vile headache. I refused to go back to sleep. The Twenty Mule Team Borax Company's stoutest animals couldn't have moved me in Roxana's direction. I dressed in the dark and sneaked out of the house. Well, I

began walking downtown in all the snow. I suddenly realized that
my feet were cold. I looked down to find that I was in my sock-
feet! I had forgotten my pumps! Give me another double brandy.
I think I have tuberculosis."

Prescott recalls one raw April morning when Jack and himself
were suffering from monumental hangovers. They had but a few
pennies left from the night before, merely enough to buy a newspaper, which Jack insisted upon purchasing.

"I didn't know that you cared what was happening in the world,"
Prescott remarked.

"I don't," Jack said, "nor what is happening in the next one.
merely want to tuck the paper inside my coat to keep me warm
until the saloons re-open."

While making a waistcoat of the newspaper, Jack happened to
read that the Federation of Churches had finished building a tabernacle and brought the Reverend Billy Sunday to New York to save
the black sheep of Manhattan.

"I hate to interrupt your reading," Prescott said, "but our credit
is fairly good at the King Edward Hotel. Let's promote a couple
of eye-openers from the bartender."

The friends went to the King Edward only to find that their
potential Samaritan was not on duty on Sunday mornings. They sat
down with the wild hope that someone might drop in, and out of
great generosity of heart ask them to have a drink.

The miracle happened. Actor Corse Payton entered the bar. This
gentleman publicized himself as "the world's best worst actor."

"Well, boys," Corse Payton said, "what are you going to have?"

His offer was taken up immediately. Payton was the kind of
buyer who, instead of ordering one drink, would say, "Bring two."
This habit was not offensive to the beneficiaries.

"I have just come from the Lexington Avenue Opera House," and
Payton smacked his lips over a Bourbon. "Rehearsal, you know.
Cold as a barn, no heat. I feel sorry for the wretched hams who
are now reciting in that clammy . . ." He broke off, his eye arrested by Barrymore's newspaper breastplate. "What's this?" Then
he read the headlines concerning the Reverend Billy Sunday's religious première at the new tabernacle. "Bring two more," Mr. Payton said to the bartender, "and, oh, yes, a telegraph blank and a
pencil."

A message to the Reverend Sunday was collaborated upon at the bar:

Dear Bill: If your tabernacle is as cold as my theatre, let's both go to hell. Regards,

Corse Payton.

Sometimes, after Barrymore's strayings, Katherine would be hopefully gay, as when Jack bought a small automobile, one of the open models then in fashion.

One day he parked Katherine and the automobile outside Tiffany's and went into that Fifth Avenue establishment to buy her a present. He saw Geraldine Farrar examining some jewels there. He shyly introduced himself to the Metropolitan Opera beauty.

"If you will do me a favor, Miss Farrar," Jack said, "I'll rear a stained-glass window to you in any cathedral of your choice. Of course you don't know me . . ."

"But I do know you," Miss Farrar interrupted graciously. "And I'll grant the favor, Mr. Barrymore. What is it?"

"My wife is outside waiting for me. If you'll only let me introduce you . . . well, it will make me seem mighty important. She adores you."

Miss Farrar went outside with Jack. Katherine was indeed impressed. Barrymore got into the car, preened his mustache proudly, then drove away, completely forgetting to buy the present for his wife.

Jack's mustache was one of his adornments that had attracted Katherine's eye when she first met him. She adored it. When it became necessary for Jack to play a smooth-face part on the stage, his wife grew quite sad. She wept over the news that the mustache must go. Jack was touched by her sorrow. He arranged for a barber carefully to remove the lip-fringe, then had it reassembled and mounted on chamois skin. He gave this trophy to Katherine. She hung it on the wall as if it had been something created by Leonardo.

Barrymore's first marriage always seemed vague in his own memory, as if he merely had dreamed it. It endured, actually, for seven years. Concerning this and other of his domestic alliances, Barrymore once said:

"They always ran about seven years, like a certain kind of skin rash. There was one exception. But let us not bother to analyze such bus accidents. Perhaps we can find a similarity between any of my marriages and that of the husband and wife who lived such un-utterably separate lives beneath one roof that they reminded each other chiefly of acquaintances during their schooldays. So opposite were their tastes, their leanings, their souls, that they might as well have been blind mutes, with a wall of perpetual snow rising be-tween them. On the woman's hastening to her husband's funeral, which she happened to remember in the midst of a shopping tour, and, oddly enough, while purchasing a pair of pink silk bloomers, the widow was ushered into a chapel filled with strangers. All of them strangers—even the corpse."

The nine successive roles that Barrymore portrayed following his success in *The Fortune Hunter* may be said to have found his tal-ents marking time. His popularity increased, largely because of the Villonesque legends that attached themselves to his personality, but the critics foresaw no artistic triumphs for the youngest of the Barrymores. He smelled more of alcohol than of fame during the six years antedating his mighty leap into serious dramatic art in 1916.

Perhaps it was because of his personal charm that managers put up with his idiosyncrasies. Perhaps it was because the impresarios had loved the Barrymores and the Drews. Perhaps anything. He survived demerits that, for any other actor, would have meant ex-pulsion from the stage.

Jack Prescott recalls a brush between Barrymore and Theodore Roberts during their appearance together in *Believe Me Xantippe*. Roberts, one of the finest character actors on the American stage, was an adroit trickster and "scene-stealer." Jack detested him but had a wary respect for his acting abilities. During one of the scenes in *Xantippe*, the large-bodied Roberts protected himself against Barrymore's counter-trickery by constantly jabbing Jack in the chest with his forefinger to keep him off balance.

Roberts had a prodigious reach. He made a pincushion of Jack's bosom. Barrymore, stumped, consulted Prescott. They settled upon a stratagem to cure the long-armed Roberts of his poking technique. Roberts strode into The Lambs after a performance one night to find Prescott there. The actor was pale and agitated.

"Do you know what your bastardly unethical pal did to me to-night?" he asked Prescott.

"Why, no, Theodore. What?"

Roberts said through his teeth: "Jack Barrymore tonight played the most unprofessional, low trick on me, the most foul business that ever occurred on the American stage. During my big scene, and when I reached out to touch his chest, as I usually do, he whipped off his hat. He hung it on my index finger! And the God-damned audience laughed like fools."

Florence Reed, star of *The Yellow Ticket*, rang down the curtain on Barrymore for doing something that she construed as a brandied insult. During her portrayal as the errant holder of a prostitute's permit, a most disturbing occurrence maddened her. Jack improvised that he was "getting fed up at seeing Miss Reed go about Russia with no adequate transportation." He emphasized these words by producing from his pocket a strip of Interborough Subway tickets!

Manager Al Woods sought to explain the ringing down of the curtain by telling the press that Jack had been stricken with gallstones! Within a few days Woods received a pair of topaz cufflinks and a note from Jack: "My gallstones. Thanks."

7.

Childe Harold in a Cupola

BARRYMORE was thirty-two, at the halfway house of his years, when in the spring of 1914 he undertook a Byronic flight to Italy. He was still married to Katherine. Certain intimates regarded Jack's domestic miseries as the provocation for his sudden journey abroad. Others held that a series of uninspiring theatrical roles had become intolerable.

We have had scant testimony from Barrymore himself as to what motivated the excursion of 1914. He was not the man to recall melancholy pretexts, had there been any. He seldom discussed the causes of his own personal misfortunes, although he often commented spicily upon their effects. He seemed to cherish only remembrances of pleasure.

When asked concerning the Katherine Harris period, he generalized: "Women bear up under the emotional hurlyburly much more successfully than we do. Certainly they can withstand more pain. They scream, or now and then reach for the poison bottle. Yet, if the world could hear the cyclonic yowlings that go on *inside* the frustrated male, the great din would rupture every eardrum within a thousand leagues."

Was he screaming inside himself in 1914? Who can say? It may have been that marital troubles caused him to leave the reminding scene. An examination of his subsequent domestic collapses discloses in each instance a fugue-like motif of flight. He would speak of "going somewhere else," then abruptly fly away, as if on the wings of his own words, to the sea or to foreign lands.

Whatever the cause of his hegira to Italy in 1914, the effect of that journey upon himself, and upon the theatre as well, would eventually be expressed in terms of meteors.

The importance of this Italian interval to his theatrical destiny was clearly recognized by Barrymore himself in later years. It was to hasten his emergence from a medieval-gothic pattern. He was then to rise like some inspired Florentine to become the torch and symbol of a renaissance of the American stage.

Let such opinionators as glimpsed him in the latter days of reckless self-caricature, or sniggered at the final radio exploitations of his name, first consider his mighty record among the Olympians before condemning him as a man, or belittling his genius. If, by any chance, you sneered at him toward the close of his tortured span, then you are the proper one to smirk at King Lear on the Heath.

"No one," Ashton Stevens said, in speaking of the decline of his great friend, "can run downhill as fast as a thoroughbred."

A human force, perhaps more stimulating to Barrymore's mind than the Italian environment itself, now began to rouse in his artistic consciousness the powers long hidden beneath superficial charms and headlong actions. He listened to wise words, and eventually acted upon them.

The person who spoke these words into Barrymore's inner ear was Edward Sheldon. Barrymore and the playwright had become friends as early as 1910. Now in Italy, four years afterward, and with reminders of man's artistic upsurge to be seen everywhere, the reunion of the two brilliant men became a fortunate circumstance.

Sheldon, a dramatic author of first rank, was four years younger than Barrymore. Now, at twenty-eight, the playwright was well on his own way to professional eminence. Like Barrymore, he had an uncommon physical presence. He was strong of body and of mind, courageous and generous in every way, a student and practitioner of the humanities. He differed from Barrymore in that he had spiritual balance and consistent professional purpose.

Sheldon had written *Salvation Nell* for Mrs. Fiske while yet an undergraduate at Harvard. That play had brought him immediate recognition. His successful drama, *Romance*, had reached the public the year before Barrymore bobbed up at the young author's Venetian quarters in April of 1914.

Sheldon's part in Barrymore's climb was clearly recognized by the discerning ones who witnessed Jack's exchange of sock for buskin. Yet, in deference to the unpretending nature of this Warwick, we set down Sheldon's reservations:

"Jack had his own great imagination. No one gave him that. He had his own theatrical genius. No one conferred that upon him. Persons outside made numerous suggestions to him, yet the man himself weighed them, and himself made brilliant acceptances or rejections. I always felt that Jack was completely responsible for his own career."

Still, we cannot overlook Sheldon's role in awakening Barrymore to his mission. Sheldon accelerated Jack's rise by rewriting speeches, scenes, or even entire plays for him, anonymously and without remuneration. He behaved with a generosity of spirit that set him amazingly apart from the Broadway world. He unbound Prometheus.

As long ago as *The Fortune Hunter*, this Harvard master of arts had advised Barrymore to undertake the playing of serious roles and therewith find recognition comparable to his powers. Now, in Italy, the author judiciously revived this suggestion.

Jack had certain pigeonholes in his mind, nooks in which he filed suggestions offered by intelligent persons. Friendly counsels in regard to matters of the heart, of course, never reached these pigeonholes; such advice sped with bullet-like velocity into one ear and out the other. Not so with artistic recommendations; they were received if valid, then pigeonholed. Sometimes they gathered dust, or seemed to have been entirely forgotten, but eventually they popped out, vital and fresh.

Barrymore was by birth and habit a procrastinator, a dreamer, yet when creative urgings finally stirred his will to action he would rise, as an extremist, to prodigious efforts, undergo drudgeries even, to achieve perfection in his art. Sheldon divined this slumbering quality in his friend well in advance of the time of renaissance.

Jack arrived in Venice soon after his incorrigibilities in *The Yellow Ticket*. There he found Sheldon spending a holiday. The men were mutually delighted by this reunion. They went for strolls late at night among the deserted squares and across the little bridges. They had long talks of a serious kind. They traveled the Grand Canal, discussed the poets and musicians and painters who had resided in the old palaces on each side of the romantic waterway. They listened to music. They studied architectural classics, sculptures, mosaics, and paintings. If Jack had had any confusions of mind, they now fell away.

Barrymore at length expressed a desire to visit Rome. He wanted Sheldon's company on the journey. The young dramatist didn't hesitate to interrupt his own plans. The friends went to the Italian capital. There they visited the churches and galleries, heard more music, sacred and profane, stood in the little cemetery where Keats' body and the heart of Shelley are buried, walked among terraced gardens, and in the moonlight recreated for themselves the Roman Empire from the shadows of ancient stones.

They enjoyed long drives among the outlying villages and towns. One night they heard singing. It seemed to come from the earth itself. They left their carriage at the roadside to enter a cellar-like place that proved to be an inn. In the candlelight they found a large Italian family seated at an old table upon which a supper of cheese and wine had been spread. The mouths of wine caves could be seen dimly in the background. A hunchback with a great key slung from a chain at his wrist moved about in this scene of medieval flavor. Jack was medieval. He felt perfectly at home. He at once became a part of the setting as naturally and forthrightly as if, on cue, he had entered into one of his own dreams.

The peasants at the table were momentarily startled by the advent of the strangers. Yet, after Jack had sat with charming familiarity among them, the moment of surprise and doubt magically vanished. They ate and drank with Jack as if he were an old and beloved friend. They accepted Sheldon as a favorite cousin. A little girl got up on the table to sing "Tripoli," with what Sheldon recalls "a voice like a slate pencil." Yet the song seemed entirely right and beautiful, and not at odds with the medieval spell.

Jack wandered off with the hunchback to explore the wine caves. He was gone for such a long time that the dramatist became concerned. The hunchback, he remembered suddenly, had looked like a cutthroat. Sheldon was about to undertake a tour of rescue among the bottled stalagmites of the caverns when he heard a loud duet.

One of the cave-mouths yawned with candlelight. Now Barrymore, an arm about the hunchback, and an old wine bottle in his other hand, returned to the party.

He entertained his friends with clown portrayals. He was magnificently gay. He made everyone happy. There were more songs and more bottles. When daylight came to the world outside the tavern, Jack left the Italians with protestations of eternal friendship. Nor did he, in spirit, lie when making such vows.

In a letter to Sheldon, twenty years afterward, and when again in Italy, Jack wrote:

Dear Ned:
I spent several days in Rome, where I attempted to make a pious pilgrimage to that marvelous inn where that charming child sang "Tripoli" to us for a solid ten minutes. I found various other *albergi*, but regret to say not that particular one. Perhaps after all it was the walled garden with the little green door that one finds only once. . . .

Barrymore one day informed Sheldon that the principal thing he had come to see in Rome was the Velazquez portrait of Pope Innocent X at the Doria Gallery. The gallery was closed at the time, but Sheldon arranged with the major-domo to open it.

Sheldon was examining one of the pictures when he heard a shout from an adjoining room. He hastened there to find Jack standing before the Spanish master's portrait of Pope Innocent.

"Look, Ned!" he cried. "It's Lionel!"

The two friends spent some days (particularly nights) in Florence. Here again Jack received stimuli that would, two years afterward, begin to bring renaissance instead of medievalism to him and his art.

Jack at length spoke of going to Paris. He thought it a good idea to spend his last Italian evening together with Sheldon in the cupola above the hotel roof while waiting for the sunrise. Sheldon was agreeable.

They found a trap door to the roof, and climbed out in their pajamas to negotiate the steep slates seven stories above the ground. They entered the cupola, and sat there until the sun came up to reveal the River Arno, the Ponte Vecchio, the Cathedral of Santa Maria del Fiore, the Uffizi Gallery, the palaces and gardens, the Santa Croce Church of the Franciscans in which was entombed the dust of Michelangelo, Galileo, Machiavelli. . . .

Under the sunlight and the blue sky of spring, holy bells and morning songs of peasants began to echo against the surrounding hills and across the green fields of Tuscany.

Barrymore, standing in his pajamas, said, "All this seems highly improbable."

The friends left the cupola and the rooftop. Sheldon made ready to return to Venice, and Jack to entrain for Paris. While Barrymore was hurling his things into a Gladstone bag, he discovered that he had lost his letter of credit. A virtuous and excited coachman appeared at the railway station later with the heartening announcement that he had found the letter on the floor of his cab.

"I'm glad to get it back," Barrymore told Sheldon. "You see, I want to buy some fox furs for Katherine."

This remark would seem to bear out an assumption that unhappiness in Jack's first marriage lacked any association of bitterness toward his wife. He was like that in subsequent rifts with his wives. After the immediate tumults of separation and divorce, the quarrels, the drawings-and-quarterings of the time of conflict, Jack would hold no lasting rancor. Even the pauperizing drains of alimony and lawyers' fees brought no martyr's whines from him.

"A man properly must pay the fiddler," he said. "In my case it so happened that a whole symphony orchestra often had to be subsidized."

Barrymore returned to America early in the summer of 1914 with a resolution to fix his attention upon the more serious aspects of the drama. Perhaps the gravity of war's announcement in July accentuated his purpose.

Sheldon also had arrived home from Europe's heightening storm. As he looked late each night across the iron-railed quietude of Gramercy Park, the playwright could see a light in the window of

Barrymore's apartment. He correctly assumed that his friend was pondering a farewell to inconsequential pursuits.

Sheldon was happy to learn that Producer Al Woods had cast Jack for the part of Chick Hewes in Willard Mack's melodrama, *Kick In*. Any other manager, as a victim of Jack's "gallstones," might have balked at this choice. But Woods had a brilliant instinct for casting; besides, he was a believer in "always taking a chance on a Barrymore."

Jack opened successfully in *Kick In*. During the run of that play he persistently sought, with the assistance of Sheldon, the kind of dramatic role that might place him solidly among the serious artists of the theatre. Such a play was found, Galsworthy's *Justice*. It was produced by John Williams, with Barrymore in the part of William Falder, a tragedy-marked bank clerk.

The amazement of the critics at Barrymore's immediate triumph as Falder is understandable. They were unprepared for the actor's sudden "size." At first Jack's triumph in *Justice* was regarded with the same incredulity as might have been aroused had "Honey Boy" Evans put off his burnt cork to sing *Faust* at the Metropolitan.

In the New Haven tryout of *Justice*, Jack pounded on the door of his stage prison with such fury that the bars gave way. This was the only scene that press agent A. Toxin Worm (can you imagine the kind of parents that perpetrated on a child such a label as this?) found interesting. Mr. Worm took it for granted that the bars were supposed to yield to the actor's frenzy.

Notwithstanding the vermifuge report of A. Toxin Worm, the bars of the prison scene were reinforced, and the play entered upon a memorable season in New York in 1916. The company then went on the road.

It was during this time that Katherine Harris Barrymore established residence in Santa Barbara to sue for divorce on the grounds of incompatibility. And it was in Santa Barbara that Jack and Sheldon discussed plans for still other ventures in the theatre.

Jack decided to give a party, a real one, in southern California. He enlisted his friends in a one-night production of *Pantaloon* at the Santa Barbara Country Club. Barrymore did the scenery, designed the costumes, bore the expense, and rehearsed the cast. Among the guests was Sir Herbert Beerbohm-Tree, celebrated English actor, and half-brother of Jack's friend Max Beerbohm.

During the performance of *Pantaloon* Jack's room at the club was given over to the ladies. Everyone else used Sheldon's room. It was a lively evening, with dancing in the patio. Sheldon became tired at dawn. He went to bed among high piles of bathrobes, towels, and other garments discarded by the actors. He awakened at nine o'clock in the morning to wonder what had become of Jack. He rose and went downstairs. There he found his friend sitting at the secretary's desk, his face on his arms, asleep.

"Come to bed, Jack," Sheldon said.

Barrymore opened his eyes. He grinned. "Let's go swimming instead."

From California, Jack continued on his tour with *Justice*. He took time out during Christmas week to go to St. Augustine, Florida, for some golf. Then, after the Galsworthy play had closed, Barrymore returned to New York. Sheldon now induced Jack to undertake his first straight romantic role, that of Peter Ibbetson.

The story of the *Peter Ibbetson* mission is one of faith, a white-robed quality of spirit that of late has been disowned. Several men and women joined to make *Peter Ibbetson* one of the theatre's outstanding co-operatives. The person who first took up its furtherance was an English actress, Miss Constance Collier.

The George du Maurier novel, published in 1891, had been extremely popular. Yet it was not dramatized until some years afterward, and then not actually produced until war had come to the wide world.

Miss Collier, one of Sir Herbert Tree's stars at His Majesty's Theatre, began her *Peter Ibbetson* crusade quite by chance and on a night when a Zeppelin air raid had come to London.

"I had taken a room in a hotel in Jermyn Street," she said, "because I was frightened at being alone in my home when the Zeps were coming over. This particular night, Sir Herbert Tree rang me to say that I must come down to supper at the Carlton immediately."

"But I'm in bed," Miss Collier informed the actor-manager.

"Then get right out of bed," Sir Herbert commanded. "There's a journalist over from Paris. It's terribly dull, so come down and do the talking for me."

Miss Collier says she found Tree sitting gloomily with John Raphael, the Parisian journalist.

"During the course of our conversation," Miss Collier recalls, "we started to discuss our favorite books. Tree was very rude and silent. He sat glowering at us. I thought Raphael a nice, charming man, very poor and sensitive."

Miss Collier happened to say that she always kept three books at her bedside, the Bible, Trelawny's *Recollections of Shelley and Byron*, and *Peter Ibbetson.*

Raphael replied quietly, "Well, twenty years ago I wrote a play about Peter Ibbetson. I have given it to every manager in London, but they all sent it back."

Sir Herbert Tree interrupted acidly, "Yes, I know. Everybody has a skeleton in his cupboard."

The poor author seemed uncomfortable. Miss Collier said, "Send it to me."

The actress knew little of Raphael or his possible talents as a dramatist. She was merely trying to keep Tree from seeming disagreeable.

About a month thereafter, as Miss Collier was asking for her key at the hotel desk, the clerk handed her a manuscript. There was a note from Raphael attached to it:

"It was just a charming gesture, I know. And I am being very conceited in taking you up on it."

Miss Collier couldn't sleep because the sirens had begun to howl. She took up the manuscript of the Raphael play. She read it twice through.

Miss Collier called up John Raphael next day. "You go back to Paris, and allow me to do this play on my own. I will do *Peter Ibbetson* if I never do another thing in my whole life."

The dubious Raphael went back to Paris, thinking that this would be the end of the episode. He had had twenty years of misfortune with the *Peter Ibbetson* play. He supposed the actress would do nothing further about it. Why should she?

"I didn't have a theatre," Miss Collier says, "nor did I have a penny in the bank. Only a faded script of a play. When I visited Tree, he seemed most annoyed. Said I had no judgment. But I was absolutely and utterly determined."

The Countess of Huntingdon telephoned Miss Collier to say: "I wish you would put on a performance for the war. The Base Hospital at Etaples. We shall have all sorts of turns, and you can organize the side shows."

"If you will give me your personal check for five hundred

pounds," Miss Collier replied, "I promise to make you ten times that amount."

The Countess was dismayed. "What on earth do you mean? I am not *giving* money away. I am asking you to *get* money for me."

"Very well then," said Miss Collier. "I can't do anything."

The Countess, however, sent Miss Collier a check for five hundred pounds on trust. The actress now solicited all the theatrical stars then in London:

"Will you do something for me? Will you take a part in a play without questioning the part, or even reading the script? We'll all meet on the stage, and I'll hand you the lines, and you will have to say them, whatever they are."

These stars never before had been asked to do such a thing. Yet they finally agreed to participate. They met with Miss Collier on the stage of a small variety theatre, where she distributed the various parts.

After a reading by the players, Miss Collier again went to Sir Herbert Tree. "I want you to lend me your theatre for the 14th of July."

Tree thought the fascinating Constance had lost her mind. "I am closing my theatre a week before that date," he muttered. "I don't care for this nonsense of yours to go on. The play is so bad, so stupid, so sentimental, that I am not going to allow you to do it in *my* theatre."

At length Sir Herbert yielded. He said, however, that he wouldn't permit his staff or box-office people to remain on duty.

"I don't care," Miss Collier told the celebrated actor-manager. "Just give me the bare walls of the theatre."

When rehearsals were begun, but one hundred pounds remained in the treasury for advertising and printing. There was no money left by the time the playbills had been posted. Notwithstanding the lack of widespread announcement a capacity audience attended the performance.

Tree was so amazed at this success that he wanted to lay aside his regular plans and keep *Peter Ibbetson* going. But most of the cast were engaged with other companies, and Miss Collier herself had a contractual obligation with the Shuberts in America.

Upon arriving in New York, Miss Collier took the manuscript of *Peter Ibbetson* to the Broadway theatrical managers. They were completely unmoved by reports of the success of the one performance in London. The fact that, in the play, Peter appeared three times at the same instant, stumped the impresarios.

"It's ridiculous," one of the managers said. "How can you have the same person three times on the stage at once?"

Miss Collier had a firm chin. She held this chin high. She decided to go where so many other artists had gone for guidance. She called upon her friend, Edward Sheldon. She gave him the manuscript to read.

Within a few days, Sheldon informed Miss Collier: "I will ask John Barrymore to play the part of Peter Ibbetson."

Had anyone other than Sheldon made this announcement, Miss Collier would have had doubts. It seemed incredible that Barrymore, now on a pedestal of popularity, would undertake the role.

What Miss Collier did not know at the time was that Sheldon had been writing a play, *The Lonely Heart,* for Barrymore, and that Jack had agreed to appear in it.

When Sheldon asked Barrymore to do *Peter Ibbetson* Jack looked at his friend in wonderment. "But I thought I was going to do *The Lonely Heart,* Ned?"

"My play is not unlike this one in certain respects," Sheldon replied, "the yearning of the dead to return to the ones they loved on earth."

"Well, then," said Jack, "let's do your play."

"No," Sheldon replied. "*Peter Ibbetson* will be a better part for you."

"Not only did Ned give up his own play," Jack afterward said, "but he sat down to rewrite whole scenes of *Ibbetson,* and, in fact, to compose the most powerful part of the play, the scene in prison. He asked for neither credit nor remuneration. There is no plaster to be discerned in this gentleman."

Constance and Jack went on a tour of the managers' offices. Miss Collier promoted money from Benjamin Guinness and from the Shuberts. But not enough. They visited Al Woods' office as a last hope.

Mr. Woods was most widely known for his production of bedroom farces. His press agent, poet Samuel Hoffenstein, called his employer "the Vulcan of the linens." On occasion, however, the large-hearted Woods came to taw with plays of merit and distinction.

"When Jack and I walked into Al Woods' office," Miss Collier recalls, "the manager said, 'I don't understand the play at all, sweetheart. There's a boy in it. Then we see him grow up. Then he is dead, but comes back just the same. It sounds nuts! But if Jack Barrymore plays it, then, sweetheart, that's all I have to know.' "

Mr. Woods was unable to promise more than twelve thousand dollars to back the play. But practical assistance was volunteered by many celebrated persons. Among them Florenz Ziegfeld offered to lend electrical equipment from *The Follies*, and Miss Maude Adams said she would supervise the lighting.

Now Jack confided in Sheldon a desire to have Lionel return to the theatre after a long absence. He recommended that his brother portray the wicked Colonel Ibbetson.

Lionel at this time was wholly content with his own manner of living. He had married. The only clouds that had darkened his peaceful retirement from the stage had been the death of his two infant daughters. The going away of his baby girls had caused him to withdraw into a private world of painting and music.

Lionel was then acting in motion pictures at the old Metro Studios in Sixty-First Street in New York. When done with the day's work he would go home to paint and etch, or to compose on the piano. He sometimes visited Jack. Occasionally he spent a night with Uncle Googan. Mr. and Mrs. Sidney Drew had successfully introduced a special kind of polite comedy to the motion-picture screen.

When Jack tried to persuade Lionel to play Colonel Ibbetson, his big brother shook his head. "I'm happy the way I am—a contented nonentity."

Jack enlisted Sheldon's help in furthering his difficult salesmanship. Lionel says this is what happened.

"I had some drinks one night as I listened to Ned's arguments. I loved Ned; we all did. So I thought I was merely being polite in not roaring my objections. Imagine, next morning, when I found out that I had promised to play Colonel Ibbetson! I wanted to kill myself. Good God! I was perfectly happy never to see the inside of a theatre. I was painting, doing a little music, and earning a living far away from audiences and rehearsals and the torture of travel from one hotel to another. I was like Cincinnatus leaving all the plows in the world. I really did want to blow out my brains— if I could have located them!"

The rehearsals for *Peter Ibbetson* were delightful sessions. True, the production money fell to a low mark, yet almost everyone had faith. John Barrymore had some misgivings as to playing the Peter Ibbetson role. He thought he might seem ridiculous when reciting lyrical words. He also viewed Peter's auburn wig with masculine suspicion. He depended upon a natty beard to offset the implications of the wavy, false headdress. He had planned to wear whiskers as a badge of fidelity to the Du Maurier illustrations of the *Peter Ibbetson* novel. However, the dandified muff did not altogether allay Barrymore's reservations as to the virility of the character.

On several occasions Jack threatened to quit the cast. He interrupted the rehearsal of a love scene with a howl: "This is nauseating! How can I bring myself to say such angel-cake speeches?"

Sheldon and Miss Collier patiently advised him not to worry about the love cries or the strawberry wig. Yet he never became entirely convinced that he was a romantic figure. Nor did he wish to be one. His own occasional remarks on this score plainly indicated that he had early fears of becoming known as a "pretty boy." Perhaps this is one reason underlying his preference off-stage for old clothes, ancient hats, and stubble on his chin.

Such carelessness seemed a perverse quality. Less favored figures spent hours before their mirrors, or at the barber's or the tailor's. But no matter how hard Barrymore tried to counterfeit the hobo styles, he fooled no one but himself. He had too much spirit, a too brisk carriage, and too much fire in his eyes to be mistaken for one of his Bowery models.

In writing the word "eyes," I was impelled to call Lionel by telephone to settle a point.

"I never seem to notice men's eyes," I informed him.

"My God!" he said. "Should you?"

"Only in a reportorial sense," I replied. "You see, I'm always getting mixed up when describing the color of eyes. I once wrote in a book that a fellow's eyes were black. I had worked for him for years. An outraged critic lambasted me, saying that the man's eyes were blue. I also had stated that a certain madam lived on one side of the street, whereas it was the other side of . . ."

"Tell me her name," Lionel interrupted, "and perhaps I can help you. What year was it?"

"No, I'm not needing the address for this book, or for anything else," I said. "What I want from you is some testimony about your brother's eyes. One of Jack's wives wrote that his eyes were 'grayish greenish hazel.' Ethel says they were deep blue. What color would you say they were, exactly?"

"Bloodshot," replied Lionel. "Go back to work."

There was but one drawback to Miss Collier's happiness at rehearsals. It was Lionel. He had left off sulking over his terrible decision to return to the theatre, but couldn't find out for himself what the Colonel was like, or even how he should look. Dress rehearsal was at hand, and Lionel didn't know his lines.

Miss Collier consulted Jack. "I am dreadfully worried about Lionel. We all love him, of course. But this is our great chance, Jack, and I wish you'd do something to stir him."

Jack spoke to Lionel about "getting into his part."

"I know what you mean, Jake," Lionel said. "I'm lousy. It's all a big mistake. God! I haven't the least idea what the character of the Colonel should be. And until I can characterize him in my own mind, I'll be no good."

"Well," Jack said, "the Colonel is a mean, lecherous old bastard, a roué . . ."

Lionel broke in with, "Who isn't? That's no special characterization. I wish I *had* killed myself after promising Ned."

Miss Collier interrupted the brotherly conference to announce: "Sir Herbert Tree has sent over some seats for his tonight's opening. As you know, he is to play *Colonel Newcome*, and I want you both to be my guests."

"But," Jack reminded Constance, "Lionel has to work tonight on his own part. He's going to make a Herculean effort to learn the lines in time for Sunday night's dress rehearsal. Remember?"

Miss Collier pondered this necessity, then said, "I am terribly concerned over your work, Lionel. But Tree will be offended if you don't attend his opening. Suppose you come with us, then toddle along home to study after paying your respects to Sir Herbie."

That evening Lionel groaned his way into his dinner jacket, snarled his way to the theatre, where he arrived earlier than the others, and growled his way through the reading of the program. When Constance and Jack appeared beside him, Lionel was surly and introspective. He was trying to decide upon some violent excuse for bowing out of the Colonel Ibbetson part entirely. Perhaps he should leap from the Brooklyn Bridge or sit on the tracks of the subway express train.

When the curtain rose, Lionel paid little attention. Then, as applause greeted Sir Herbert Tree's entrance, Lionel grudgingly looked toward the stage. His eyes opened wide. And now, to the embarrassed wonderment of Constance, he began to cackle.

"What's wrong, Lionel?" she whispered.

His neighbors looked at him reprovingly as he announced, "The hand of the Holy Ghost has descended upon my shoulder!"

What no one else knew at the time was that Lionel saw in Sir Herbert Tree's sideburned portrayal of the noble, pure-hearted Colonel Newcome the precise characterization for the vile Colonel Ibbetson.

Lionel left the theatre in a beatific condition of mind. He had several tall drinks, then went home. He didn't bother to read over his part. He retired to bed, to sleep happily, dreaming, as he recalls it, of pitching a no-hit, no-run game for the New York Giants against the Chicago Cubs. He rose early next day, skimmed over his part, and retained every line of it.

The Sunday evening dress rehearsal of *Peter Ibbetson* found the Republic Theatre filled with invited guests. Sir Herbert Tree went backstage. Jack asked him to pass judgment on his make-up as Peter. "The more I think about it," Jack confided in Sir Herbert, "the more I am worried about this beard. What do you think?"

"I see nothing wrong with it," replied Tree. "But I'll go out front and see how it seems from that vantage point."

After the first act, Sir Herbert again went to Jack's dressing-room. "Barrymore," he said, "I think you're on the right track about the beard. You look like a dentist."

Barrymore removed the beard at once. Then he went on, smooth-faced, for the next act. When he appeared, there was a gasp from the ladies in the audience. Barrymore now was convinced that he looked like "a pink marshmallow." As he retired to the wings, he tore off the wig. He hurled it at Miss Collier.

"What have you done to me?" he shouted. "Never before in my life have I been booed on the stage!"

The actress painstakingly convinced Jack that the great "Oh!" from the audience had been an exclamation of wonderment. She said that the ladies had been compelled to gasp at his beauty.

The dress rehearsal was a success in every way. Not only had Jack made a great impression, but Lionel had electrified everyone, particularly Constance Collier, by his sudden characterization of

Colonel Ibbetson. She of course did not know that Lionel had usurped Sir Herbert Tree's own portrayal of the good Colonel Newcome, and made from it a hideously nasty villain.

After the dress rehearsal Lionel found Sir Herbert studying him intently. Lionel asked Tree what he thought about the characterization of Colonel Ibbetson.

"The Colonel was magnificent," Tree replied. Then he said, "You know, as I sat watching the Colonel, I kept asking myself again and again, 'Tree, where have you seen this fellow before?'"

8.

The Reluctant Romanticist

BARRYMORE'S playing of the glittering Peter Ibbetson role established him as an enduring romanticist. Love letters and sentimental gifts came in with the tide. Yet he was so lacking in conceit that he could not regard himself as a ladies' man. He maintained that the label had been pasted on him when he was not looking.

He attributed the growing legend of his love life to circumstances other than publicity.

"I was working so assiduously," he said, "that a succession of heart flip-flops began to annoy me. Whenever I became excited, one of these harmless yet startling cardiac beats would make me jump, or call out like a moose. One evening, when enjoying the company of a lady, and with romance at its meridian, the heart went 'zoom.' I reacted with sudden bounds and cries. The lady mistook this for sheer ardor. She confided in some other lovely creature, and so help me God I had a similar experience with that one. The results of word-of-mouth advertising were incredible. Likewise the series of heart flutters. It got so that I was being exploited all over town like a patent medicine. Never could shake the reputation, even after the heart had returned to its former monastic serenity."

The New York première of *Peter Ibbetson* was a night of excitements and mishaps. The audience at the Republic Theatre became spontaneously alive and sympathetic as soon as the curtain ascended. The spiritual as well as the emotional appeal of the play took hold of the men and women out front. Everyone began sniffling or crying, the ushers even.

Jack as Peter and Miss Collier as the Duchess of Towers seemed the greatest lovers since Romeo and Juliet. So poignantly actual did the play become that even an exasperating mix-up of ropes, pulleys, and other rigging failed to spoil the illusion.

The lack of sufficient dress rehearsals had left the stagehands unfamiliar with the proper handling of the scenery. So when the rather intricate mechanics of the third act were undertaken, the laws of Sir Isaac Newton were demonstrated in terms of falling scenery, with a touch of Vesuvian earth-shakings.

The beginning of this act called for the scene in a wood to dissolve before the tear-dripping eyes of the spectators. In place of the glade, a magical opera house was conjured up in response to Peter's and the Duchess' wish to hear Patti sing *Mignon*.

Peter and the Duchess walked hand-in-hand toward the steps of the opera house, the music of *Mignon* coming over their pantomime. Then, to the amazement of the actors, the entire opera house began to topple. The scenery enveloped the romantic pair with canvas and dust! It became necessary to lower the curtain. The scene was rehung, and the beginning of the act repeated.

Barrymore's language, Miss Collier remembers, was "something awful." While his valet was dusting him, the actor revived oaths and threats unused since cutthroats sailed the Spanish Main. Yet, during this scene-setting intrusion, no one the other side of the curtain stirred. The audience sat like lotus-eaters, happy and anaesthetized.

Jack muttered to Miss Collier, "Thank God, the same railway accidents don't happen in the same place twice."

But they do. . . .

On the second night, and as the lovers began their walk toward the opera house, the same foul collapse reoccurred and at the same place. And once again the crew had to rehang the scenery. But at the third performance, the defect had been found.

The play became a great success, and its actors were acclaimed. Lionel, as well as Jack, took a great step forward in public esteem.

The scenes between Jack and Lionel were gritty actorial duels. When in the play Peter beat the Colonel with a club, the blows became brutally real. Lionel threatened to break his brother's jaw "if you do that again."

The brothers often revealed sibling envy of each other's abilities, and with reason.

Of their rivalry, Ben Hecht says: "It seems to me that the charm of these brothers as strong persons was that they were able to feel love and hate, and call each other a sonofabitch a hundred times over, and prove it, then end up unintimidated by the ogre each had unmasked, and be inclined to be overfond of him in fact, as a result of the battle, or of the exposure."

Lionel made few mistakes in his theatrical art, no matter how little he cared for it as a profession. He brought to *Peter Ibbetson* the same superb instincts for characterization as had unhorsed Uncle Jack Drew in *The Mummy*. For example, Lionel sang a long ballad that might have been an intrusive bore. He warbled this song slightly off pitch. To manage this kind of scene without falling into burlesque, in the opinion of experts, is one of the most difficult things to accomplish.

Jack had a real opponent in Lionel. He welcomed this opposition, for it gave him something vital to contend with, yet he never took his eye off this resourceful antagonist. Both men were strikingly honest and frank in private life, but when trying to take scenes from each other they surpassed the rogueries of purse-snatchers.

Among the numerous reports on John Barrymore's provocative medical history, there is to be found the following excerpt:

> Since the age of fourteen he has been more or less a chronic drinker. There was one period when he completely abstained from liquor for two years. Then, after taking one drink, he went back to his former habits again. . . .

The two-year period of sobriety occurred during the *Peter Ibbetson* time. Jack suddenly put aside the bottle but gave no reasons for so doing. Nor did he make a ceremony of the abstention.

Barrymore now directed his whole impetus toward the creative phases of the theatre, as distinct from its repetitious aspects. Perhaps his urge for creation entirely superseded for a too short time the self-destructive elements of his insurgent nature.

Miss Collier is one of three authorities to vouch for Jack's sobriety during the *Ibbetson* period. She maintains that even the rigors of the road, and with Jack growing more and more restless in his romantic part, did not cause him to drink. He became increasingly irritable, petulant, and unreasonably arrogant. Yet he did not resort to the flask.

He would take a sudden dislike to some member of the company. "Get rid of this damned idiot!" he would shout. Miss Collier knew that if she opposed Barrymore he would insist upon the dismissal. So, to protect a player from Jack's unfair rages, as well as not to disrupt her company, the actress-manager hit upon a clever method. If she saw Barrymore turn a malevolent eye upon any member of the company she would intervene at once.

"He is no good at all," she would tell Jack. "He can't act, and I'm going to get rid of him." She would pause to let this sink in, then add: "I don't care how poor his circumstances, or how hard it will be for him to get work. I have decided to give him notice."

Then Jack would invariably say, "Now look, you can't be as hard as all that! Have you no finer feelings? Give him another chance."

He would begin warmly to defend the person he had been glaring at only a little time before. Then he secretly would proceed to coach that amazed person theatrically. As Miss Collier fully anticipated, the star would put the actor under his own wing.

Jack's irritability increased as the tour of *Peter Ibbetson* lengthened. Perhaps his temperamental gales were compensations for the lack of alcoholic escape. He also grew restive when he no longer could be "creative" in finding new shadings for a part. He would snarl at those nearest him. He was genuinely fond of Constance Collier, and appreciated her gallantry and admired her skill as an artist. Yet he frequently provoked quarrels with her, as on the opening night of their Montreal appearance.

The Governor-General of Canada and a party of aristocratic men and women occupied the stage box. Word arrived backstage that Miss Collier and Mr. Barrymore were invited by the Governor-General to supper after the play.

After the rise of curtain some coughing began in the audience. Jack detested bronchial noises during a stage performance. He usually did something about it. He might reprimand the offenders, suggest picturesque clinical procedures, show an ironical concern for the ill health of the stricken ones, or else join in their hackings himself with thorough sarcasm. Tonight, however, his leading lady prevailed upon him to overlook the coughing and not offend the noble supper-party hosts.

Then something went wrong with a spotlight. Instead of illuminating the faces of Peter and the Duchess of Towers, it played upon their feet! Jack abruptly left Miss Collier during the love scene. There was a thud. He had knocked down the manipulator of the limelight. Then he returned to the stage in time to pick up his next cue and continue the scene.

No one could condone such an attack on a fellow workman, and this one in particular cost Barrymore several hundred dollars in damages. Yet strangely so, the stagehands loved the aggressive star, for he was as quick to fight their battles as he was to fight them if he thought they were falling down on a job. He was meticulous about "things going right" during a performance. Perhaps these men behind the scenes were loyal to Barrymore because he knew no class distinctions as subscribed to by other stars. At any rate, and with the exception of two or three exactions of damages and hospital bills, the stagehands forgave him for any upheaval.

Miss Collier was furious at having been deserted while Barrymore was punching the electrician. A quarrel was begun between acts. A violent one. The stage romanticists, however, did not reveal their anger to the audience. For the remainder of the play they smiled, mooned expertly, and the admiring spectators, particularly the Governor-General's party, thought them completely in love in fact as well as fiction. But after the curtain had come down for the last time they began again their loud wrangling.

The Barrymore-Collier battle reached new crescendos. The participants were so fiercely engaged as not to observe the guests of the Governor-General filing slowly through the pass-door. The party took up a position in the wings.

The visitors were amazed to see the lovers, who had been in each other's arms a few minutes before, now at each other's throat.

Jack's dressing-room was on the side opposite from where the shocked visitors were standing. He dashed toward it. Miss Collier pursued him. He entered his dressing-room, then slammed the door shut. Constance seized the knob and rattled it. She tried hard to open the door. He held it against her. The angry actress pushed and threatened.

Then the door flew open. Jack's eyes held flame. "You take one step into this room and I'll throw you out the window!"

"Very well," Constance called out, "do it!"

As Jack prepared to carry out his threat, he realized that the dressing-room was on the ground floor. It wouldn't be much of a fall for anyone. The same realization came to Miss Collier. They both began to laugh. The quarrel ended suddenly and humorously, as their squabbles always did.

Now Constance said, "Oh, my God! Those people were coming backstage."

They hastened out, but the stage was empty. Empty and dim, except for the lone pilot light. The Governor-General and the other gentlemen and their ladies had disappeared.

"I feel very repentant," Miss Collier said. "They surely must have overheard us."

"Oh, well," Jack shrugged, "let's have supper by ourselves. You will be my guest of honor."

Miss Collier was keenly worried about having offended the notables. She paid little attention to where Jack was taking her. They entered a hotel dining-room. There, to Constance's horror, sat the Governor-General and his party!

As Jack and Constance came into the room, conversation at the big table discreetly died. The gentlemen sat stiffly, as if suddenly embalmed. The ladies took on the appearance of waxen celebrities from Madame Tussaud's gallery.

Barrymore grandiosely escorted his lady to a small table not too far from that of the Governor-General's party. He ceremoniously planned a supper of cold fowl for Miss Collier, a meal which she didn't touch. He ordered a tureen of soup for himself. When it arrived he spooned it adroitly, smacked his lips, then said, "Constance, my dear, you rehearsed that scene for our next play so convincingly that for the moment even I was carried away. Usually it takes two or three stout temperance lectures to carry me away. You are so clever, so lovely."

The precise effect of Jack's remarks on the Governor-General's party was not immediately made known. A cloakroom woman, however, quoted somebody as having said that night: "Actors are quite mad, you know."

After the first week of the *Peter Ibbetson* tour, Actress-Manager Constance Collier found the company giving inexcusably bad performances. She couldn't understand this sudden inferiority. Jack was having a little trouble with his throat, but otherwise seemed fit.

"We would get on the train to go to the following town," Constance says, "and I would look after Jack, possibly give him an icebag for his throat, and see that he got to bed fairly early. Then I would go to my own drawing-room and we all would settle down for the night. When we arrived at the next town, we always rehearsed the company for the dimensions of a new stage. The members were doing so badly that I called them together and complained about their lack of enthusiasm. Then one actor reluctantly volunteered an explanation. It seems that after I had put Jack to bed, he would wait until all was quiet, then get up, wake some of the others, and play cards with them all night. The actors were devoted to Jack and hesitated to give him away, but they were utterly exhausted."

Barrymore frequently bought dogs for the fascinating manager while on this tour. She loved them. "I should have been a kennel maid," she said, "if I hadn't been an actress!"

One night a messenger arrived at the theatre with a litter of puppies on what seemed a white rug. It was a present from Barrymore. When Constance asked about the white rug on which the puppies lay, the messenger replied, "It's funny, but when Mr. Barrymore learned that the mother of these here puppies just died, he had us preserve her hide. It held up delivery a few days." He indicated the rug. "This is her!"

To relieve the dullness of one-night stands in the smaller towns, Jack and Constance began to collect glass. They both happened to set their minds upon yellow glass, nor would either one stir from this choice to take another color. This led to a rather intense rivalry, with some deceit added to the competition.

Immediately after their arrival at a hotel, they would pretend to go to their rooms for a rest. Alone in their respective quarters, they would at once telephone downstairs to find out the location of antique shops. Then Jack would call Constance. "I think I'll take a little nap. What are you going to do?" To this she would make some evasive reply, such as, "Oh, I don't know. Nothing special. Perhaps I'll go shopping for some gloves later on." They would hang up, then sneak out of the hotel in great haste to be first at the antique stores.

Quite often they would meet in the shops, one of them triumphant at having got there ahead of the other and bought up the best specimens of yellow glass.

Jack now made one of his great discoveries. This time he found out about the five-and-ten-cent stores. He suddenly went out of the yellow glass business. He interested Miss Collier in shopping among the counters of the five-and-ten, concentrating on the purchase of cookery gadgets. He set up a portable kitchen in his dressing-room. He disregarded the fact that the curtain soon would rise on a beautiful, romantic play, and that fumes of onions, garlic, and sizzling meat would spread over the place. Some of the theatres had little ventilation. The managers frequently objected, but the chef was a charmingly obstinate artist.

"Sit down, old man," he would say to a manager. "I'll cook you a filet with mushrooms and my own special Hellsafire Sauce."

Occasionally newspaper interviewers were amazed to find the romantic actor peeling potatoes or memorizing ten-cent store culinary formulas. But Jack was entirely serious about his cooking, as he was about anything—for a time.

There was one instance in which Barrymore did not come out on top when reprimanding a cougher. He was playing a love scene against a background of soft music. The theatre always was intensely silent during this episode. But tonight a man in the fourth or fifth row coughed.

Jack left off reading his lines. He glared at the offender. Then he returned to the scene. The man coughed again. Now Jack stepped back from Constance Collier and *really* glared at the man. He gazed so unblinkingly, so fiercely, that the man stirred, then got up from his seat. Slowly and clumsily he reached the aisle. His progress up the aisle was quite noisy from the thumping drag of his crutches.

The fact that he had embarrassed a cripple greatly upset Barrymore. He was remorseful and shaken. For a long time thereafter he did not pay attention to noises from the audience. At least he made certain not to single out a crippled person for his glares or his remarks.

Some weeks afterward, however, and in another city, he lost his temper entirely. It was at the end of the first act. At this point in the play Peter picked up the Duchess of Towers' bouquet. After looking at it tenderly for a long moment, he pressed the flowers to his lips. Then he murmured, "*L'amour.*" It was one of the most touching scenes in the play. It sent the ladies into near-swoons.

On this particular evening some girl in the gallery, hysterical with delight, giggled. Jack called out: "Damn it! If you think you can play this better than I can, come on down and do it."

He hurled the bouquet into the audience. It struck a woman in the face. The curtain fell. Barrymore stomped off-stage to his dressing-room to lock himself inside it.

Sounds of outrage came from the audience. Miss Collier was dismayed to hear high-pitched voices filtering through the curtain. The actors stood in their places on the stage as if paralyzed. Then the manager of the theatre, purple and blowing, charged round from the pass-door.

"I'll bring a damage suit against you!" he shouted at Miss Collier. "Barrymore has ruined the reputation of my theatre. I'll not. allow you to fulfill your engagement for the remainder of the week. My God! Nobody is safe with this man. I'll have him barred from every . . ."

He paused to regain his wind. The actress took this opportunity to beg the manager to allow the curtain to rise for the second act. He said no. The audience would throw things.

"They're sitting out there now, desperate and waiting," he said. "Peek out at 'em. You'll see. They're like a sheriff's posse."

Miss Collier did peer out to observe the audience waiting as if to exercise some terrible judgment. She finally persuaded the manager to allow the curtain to rise. He recommended that Miss Collier make a speech of apology and offer to return all box-office moneys to the patrons. She declined to do this.

"All right then," the manager warned, "but if you're killed, don't say I didn't tell you."

There had been half an hour's delay. Jack refused to come out of his dressing-room. No threats could move him. Finally Miss Collier informed him that he really had injured an inoffensive woman in the audience, and that the victim's eye had been bandaged.

"In that case," Barrymore said, "ring up the curtain."

The curtain rose for the second act. It seemed remarkable that so few persons had left the theatre or asked for their money back. There was the type of quietness that obtains before a prison riot. The slight plop of a moth against a spotlight slide sounded like a howitzer shell in the challenging silence.

Jack's entrance did not occur until halfway through the second act. Ordinarily, before this appearance of Peter, there were moments of laughter or hand-clappings. Tonight there was no laughter, no applause. Silence.

The cast was terrified. The suspense led Miss Collier to issue whispered instructions of an "abandon ship" nature. She admonished the crew to lower the curtain the moment the audience began to tear Jack apart.

The moment arrived, and Jack arrived with the moment. He entered with profound self-assurance. He was casual. He might have been on his way to a church, so poised was he. And now the presence that mysteriously was his on any stage, and always would be strangely his, spread its electric influence over the whole house.

He received the wildest sort of applause. Cheers even, and the waving of women's kerchiefs.

It is said that the manager of the theatre sank to his knees, either to pray or to keep from collapsing on his face. No one was sued. The play could have gone on for weeks to capacity business in that city.

Barrymore was tiring of his part. That was his destiny, to tire of parts.

"We got as far as Chicago," Constance Collier recalls. "Jack came into my dressing-room to announce restrainedly, 'I just can't go on.' It was a great, devastating blow to me, yet I understood. He was mentally and physically tired. He was strung up to a point where he couldn't go on. It is sad to think that such an outstanding success as *Peter Ibbetson* was suddenly taken away from us. Yet it really remained with me in spirit for always."

Of Barrymore's art, Miss Collier said: "He was the greatest of all the actors I ever saw, and I knew Irving and Tree and so many of the great ones. He had a wild soul, and no one could discipline him. Yet he was avid for criticism. He would say, 'Don't tell me if I am good. Tell me when you feel that I am bad, and where I am bad!' If I did have to criticize him severely, he would take it wonderfully well. But that is always the way with greatness. It is only the second-rate people who make things complicated and are difficult to handle. He had something in his eye, an almost mystic light, that only men of genius have."

9.

The Alchemist's Corner

BARRYMORE, in October of 1917, found sanctuary on the top floor of a century-old house off Washington Square. He chanced upon these garret quarters during the latter part of the *Peter Ibbetson* period. He began at once to transform the long-unoccupied attic into a studio which he called "the Alchemist's Corner." In providing atmosphere for this abode, he evidenced his last sustained expression of medievalism.

He admitted no women callers during his first two years of residence at Number 132 West Fourth Street. It was a place of solitude. He gave no parties. In this quiet environment Barrymore entertained few men other than Lionel and Edward Sheldon.

He embraced this off-stage loneliness, it seems, as an opportunity for self-evaluation, a quest for the verities. We can advance no detailed proof in support of this surmise other than to note that his nights in the hermitage presaged the days of artistic glory. We lack specific quotations from the man himself to define this exclusively as a time of monk-like prayers for revelation. In fact, his pertinent letters and conversations more often than not referred to the top floor of the house in West Fourth Street as "a home, the last one really I ever was to know."

That he did possess a deep spiritual consciousness was quite apparent to those who had access to his affectionate confidence. This spirituality somehow escaped the attention of the commentators. They seemed so engrossed with Barrymore's cape-and-sword externals as to make romanticism his whole legend. The public, of course, would be apathetic to the soul-contemplations of a matinee idol; just as lovers see in the moon's face a mirror of their desires, yet are unimpressed by the astronomical claim that it has another never-seen side away from the world. Hymns are endured on Sundays, love songs welcomed all the year.

That Barrymore was capable of platonic friendships with women is another facet that never sparkled in story or in print. Here we do have corroborating testimony. Perhaps one of his deepest friend-

ships of this nature was for the gentlewoman who became his landlady in West Fourth Street.

"I was rather a strange, lost creature in the days when we knew
one another," he wrote in 1926 to this friend and former benefactor,
"and you were unfailingly kind and sweet and wise."

This woman, Mrs. Juliette S. Nicholls, was slow to accept Barrymore as her first tenant in the house she had newly purchased. Mrs.
Nicholls had heard reports of his Bohemian antics. She did not care
to people the sedate, brown-painted, four-story dwelling with eccentric immoralists of the theatre.

Mrs. Nicholls had been living in comfortable retirement in France
for several years. A widow, she occupied a pleasant villa where, as
a woman of education and quiet habits, she hoped to continue
indefinitely to enjoy her books and flowers. The war, however, compelled her to close the villa and rearrange her finances. She purchased, through the medium of her bank, an income-bearing property off Washington Square.

An agent, whose name Jack insisted was "Pepe," listened to Barrymore's wants. "Find a hideaway somewhere in the Greenwich
Village area, a quiet place, the sort that would please a nun's grandfather. Top floor if possible."

Pepe discovered such an isolated place. He painstakingly convinced Mrs. Nicholls that Barrymore would behave like a gentleman within her walls. Furthermore, the actor offered to pay his rent
in advance until the next May first. This, the agent said, was solid
evidence against the lie that Jack never attended honorably to money
matters.

Mrs. Nicholls didn't see Barrymore for some months after the
lease was signed. He went on the road with the *Peter Ibbetson* company. After his return to New York he stayed out of sight for some
time, during which he communicated with Mrs. Nicholls by note.
She found his communiqués both charming and polite. He signed
himself "Top Floor."

When Barrymore finally paid a visit to Mrs. Nicholls in her
ground-floor apartment, she at once perceived the unaffected frank-
ness of his character. He had come down in person, he explained,
to ask if Mrs. Nicholls had any objection to his "fixing up the
place" at his own expense. Without knowing to what extremes Barrymore was planning to go, Mrs. Nicholls agreed.

Barrymore already had brought to his attic numerous treasures he and Sheldon had selected in Italy. He permitted a decorator to do the bedroom for him in the Victorian taste reminiscent of *Peter Ibbetson*. The walls of that room were covered with pink-striped paper. The baseboard and moldings were painted black. Square glass mirrors, framed in black, formed the doors. The bathroom walls were covered with glass squares, as was the outer side of the tub.

A flowered burgundy rug lay from wall to wall on the floor of the bedroom. The window drapes were of pale mauve taffeta edged with a white bead fringe. The curtains were of piped glass, with crystal drops back of them. Slender festoons of crystal edged the black moldings. A French fireplace of white marble with a grape-pattern relief faced the foot of a bed which Barrymore specified should be narrow and hard.

"A bed for one," he said, "a bed that implies celibacy for a change."

After the decorator had concluded this dream and had made ready to enjoy another vision in the large studio-chamber, Barrymore decided to intervene. He fashioned a bay window on the north side of the studio. He removed the panes from a small window at the left of the bay, replacing them with small squares of blue glass from Italy.

He stretched saffron chiffon over the wide skylight. He hung an elaborate lantern, a caravel under sail, from the skylight. He installed a white- and gray-veined mantelpiece. The fireplace grouping included a huge couch and a priedieu with stools. A Chinese hooked rug lay on the linoleum-block floor-covering in front of the Carrara hearth.

A music corner could be seen at the right as one entered the studio. A cover of embroidered gold brocade was flung over the baby grand piano. A bronze pheasant stood among the folds of this Empire period fabric. A tall candle-standard, an old Venetian mirror, a large antique globe, and a Lombardian chair completed this corner.

In one of his letters to Mrs. Nicholls, written in 1926, Barrymore said:

> I have recollections, some very happy ones, of a tall, pallid and very beautiful Madonna that I deserted in the eyrie that I occupied under your kindly and tolerant eye, and various other

things, notably a gold and red shrine with an old walnut piece under it, and what not besides?

After he had surfaced the walls with Chinese gold, Barrymore proceeded to do something quite characteristic. He lighted church candles and spent many hours smoke-smudging the walls and furniture. It was this "aging" of his retreat that caused him to refer to it as the Alchemist's Corner.

Now he turned his attention to the roof. Mrs. Nicholls was out of the city at the time, so Barrymore wrote to her:

> You have been so lenient in permitting me to exercise my fancy on the studio. Would you mind very much if I did a few ornamental things to the roof, at my own expense, of course? I'd like to build a little stairway to it, and place a few plants there, with perhaps a small pavilion in which I could sit when the locust blossoms come to the courtyards of Greenwich Village. It would be like living in Paris in the twelfth century.
>
> Yours entreatingly,
Top Floor.

Mrs. Nicholls, little knowing what her roof was in for, gave her consent. And now Barrymore became a landscape gardener and builder. He first of all hired an old carpenter to build a crooked, steep staircase to the roof. For a banister he mounted a thick hemp rope in rusty iron wall-clamps. He placed this on the left side of the crooked stair, saying that such a procedure held vital symbolism for all metaphysicians.

He purchased a graceful door of carved wood and hung it at the bottom of the crooked stairway leading to the roof.

Next he had the carpenter build a small structure at one side of the skylight. This was said by Barrymore to have been the first penthouse in New York.

The old workman had numerous worries. His rules, square, and level disappeared. When Barrymore volunteered that he had "stolen" these tools, the carpenter was entirely baffled. Then Barrymore explained: "I want you to build this cabin without benefit of rulers. I want everything crooked or off center, like a Nuremberg poet's home. Just guess your way along, old man, as we all do about most things."

Barrymore placed ships' models in this crooked little house, old navigation charts, a Franklin stove, and outside it the wheel from a wrecked schooner and a small ship's bell. On the fire walls he embedded shards of brightly colored glass to catch whatever sun New York permitted to shine.

Now he turned his attention to landscaping his roof. With customary disregard for consequences to the old roof beams, or a thought for proper drainage, he had thirty-five tons of topsoil brought from Long Island. It was lifted from the street in burlap sacks by means of a block-and-tackle over the cornice and distributed on the roofing tin.

The enthusiastic Jack planted cedars eight feet tall, as a hedge on the street side of the roof. Through this screen he could see, across the street, the façade of the Washington Square Methodist Episcopal Church. He also installed white wisterias, arbor vitae, cherry trees, and grape vines. He made a fountain, the overflow of which eventually seeped into the ceiling plaster of the Victorian bedroom and streaked the Chinese gold walls of the studio. He placed beehives beside the skylight. He fashioned little walks of broken flagstone. And now he was happy, alone, and in a world of his own making and of his own desire.

Mrs. Nicholls returned to find a horticultural frenzy atop her house. She was somewhat amazed, but did not complain. She could not, she says, for there was a startling yet weird beauty to Barrymore's creation, and the man himself seemed so childishly content as he fed the birds on his "estate."

Nor, after Barrymore had moved away and a subsequent tenant, artist Ben Ali Haggin, one morning found himself in bed with water from a spring rain pouring down upon him and the ceiling beams sagging dangerously, did this remarkably fine woman resent what Barrymore had done to her roof. It cost fifteen hundred dollars to remove the Long Island topsoil and reinforce the beams with steel girders. And she never billed Barrymore for having failed to devise a proper drainage system for the fountain or against the snows and rains.

Many letters from admirers came to the West Fourth Street house, Mrs. Nicholls recalls. Letters and flowers. Sometimes the hallway would be blocked by floral packages or potted plants. The potted plants Barrymore would place in the topsoil on the roof. He would send the other flowers to downtown hospitals.

He permitted letters to accumulate a week at a time. He never opened any of them. Some of these were bills, but they suffered the same consequence as their perfumed companions. Each Sunday afternoon Barrymore would appear on the mahogany stairway with wastebaskets of unopened mail. He would go to the basement, open the furnace, throw into it the heart messages and the duns, then either return to his Alchemist's Corner or stroll in Washington Square.

He permitted a cleaning woman to enter his quarters once a week, but gave stern instructions not to remove the cobwebs.

After the theatre he would go home, bolt the outer door to his apartment, stuff paper in the telephone bell, then enter the stairway well, lock the stairway door behind him, and retire to his cabin or sit among the shrubs and trees.

He was no pillar saint, ever, yet it seems that here on his rooftop he must have thought of life in its deepest expression within himself, and sensed that he was entering upon the most significant era of his artistic career.

I think Mrs. Nicholls knew him more objectively than most other women. His letters to her would seem to substantiate this claim. These communications were boyishly honest, as if he realized that he was writing freely to a dear and understanding friend.

When asked what she thought of Barrymore's innermost character at this time, apart from his elements as an artist, she said: "I think he was a confused child."

10.

The Road to Damascus

I SAT in Arthur Hopkins' managerial office at the Plymouth Theatre examining old pictures of Jack and inquiring into his prompt-books. Then Arthur and I went outside to the balcony to look down upon the stage where Barrymore had played *Redemption* twenty-five years before. Here also he had appeared in *The Jest* and *Richard III*.

The pilot light shone small in the down-distance, making the theatre seem darkly huge. Today's rehearsal long had been over; the stage, the back walls were bare, the seats empty—yet were they?

The clear small light standing like a votive lamp among cathedral shadows exercised an almost hypnotic power. Illusion was everywhere about the old playhouse, with a march-past of years long gone. One traveled back to the time when the slim, springing figure of the great young actor dominated this same stage, and the voice we knew so well sounded with rhythmic majesty.

It is wise not to try to thrust such moods on others, and stubbornly imply that here had occurred an era never again to be approximated. For each man carries within his own memory a special golden age. Then, when he becomes old enough to seem secure against rebuttal, he tends to make a shining legend of that time. He feels ordained to go up and down like some tireless evangelist seeking to enforce the gospels and the virtues of his own mental treasure upon younger men properly occupied with enjoying their present youth, which in its own ripening will have become a golden age for them one palsied day. Perhaps old men should be denied their clocks and calendars, their mirrors, and their writing tools.

Here in the still theatre, with the star-gleam of the distant stage light, the halo of dust about it, the smell that is the theatre and like no other smell, and the slow, chill updraft of air that comes from the great mouth of the proscenium arch, here one dreamed of days that were great with youth and circumstance.

"A man is not old," Barrymore once said, "until regrets take the place of dreams."

A police siren in West Forty-Fifth Street intruded on the spell. Hopkins chuckled, perhaps thinking of Jack's asides whenever traffic noises interrupted his scenes at the Plymouth. Once Barrymore had called out: "Mr. Hopkins! Why not give the rest of this performance at Grand Central Station?"

Somewhere in this balcony in the long ago, a man suddenly had burst out laughing during Barrymore's playing of *Richard III*. You may recall that Scene IV, Act V, opens on Bosworth Field, with Catesby's speech to Norfolk, suggesting rescue after Richard has been unhorsed in action. Then there is an alarum, and Richard clanks on-stage with his distraught cry: "A horse! A horse! My kingdom for a horse!"

On this particular night Barrymore hardly had delivered his penetrating vocals regarding the need of a charger than some gentleman in the balcony emitted the loudest guffaw since the days of Rabelais.

Barrymore, encased in black armor, raised his sword toward the balcony and, without departing one beat from the iambic pentameter of the Bard, called out: "Make haste, and saddle yonder braying ass!"

Barrymore's genius loses none of its luster by inviting attention to the group of men and women who undertook his artistic furtherance.

"There was an ambitious plan," said Alexander Woollcott, "not only to put the enormous Barrymore potentialities to work, but also to bring lasting prestige to the American stage. It was not an amateurish venture, like a church social. Everyone concerned in this labor of love was a successful person in his own professional right. Not one of them was looking for monetary return or self-aggrandizement."

Woollcott himself had been a participant in this quiet crusade. "I recall vividly," Woollcott said, "how my first knowledge came that such a partnership was in the wind. It was the sweltering spring night in 1917 when the Washington Square Players were presenting *Ghosts* at the Comedy and we were all moved to admiration by José Ruben's really extraordinary performance of the disintegrating Oswald. I remember Arthur Hopkins taking me aside and asking me, as one thinking out loud, on which actor it would be more interesting to build a repertory, this young Frenchman or John Barrymore who, the year before, had claimed his birthright by his performance in *Justice* and was then lolling in the charm of *Peter Ibbetson*. It is said that this is the only instance of Mr. Hopkins having asked anyone's advice in ten years.

"Probably he did not listen to my answer, and I myself forget what it was. Doubtless it was abstracted anyway, for at the time I was daily enlisting in the Army, the Navy, the United States Marine Corps, the Red Cross, or the Y.M.C.A., and was vaguely assuming that as soon as one of these handsome offers was accepted, the bereft drama in America would automatically suspend for the duration of hostilities."

Woollcott spent two years as an enlisted man in the A.E.F. He served for one year on the editorial council of *The Stars and Stripes*, then returned to his post as drama critic for the New York *Times*. He characterized himself as "a benign consultant for the Barrymore Board of Regents."

"It was a purely artistic plan for the betterment of the theatre," Woollcott continued, "just as the Provincetown movement gave Eugene O'Neill to the theatre everywhere."

The members of this "board" were Edward Sheldon, Constance Collier, Arthur Hopkins, Woollcott, Robert Edmond Jones, and Margaret Carrington.

"Barrymore," Woollcott added, "was a 'Sleeping Beauty.' Sheldon awakened him. The other experts came when the need for their services arose. What none of us reckoned with was that Jack never adhered for long to any plan. But suppose you wrestle with that perversity to your own satisfaction."

Woollcott agreed that few writers had taken pains to indicate the importance of Arthur Hopkins' wise and generous behavior toward Barrymore. Hopkins assuredly was in a position to see the man at his apogee. He produced four noteworthy plays for him, two of them by the Bard.

"Behind his scoffing and playful mask," Hopkins said, "John Barrymore unsuccessfully stifled deep artistic integrity and rich perception. For years he devoted himself to the masquerade, but his inconsequential amblings led him, greatly to his own surprise, to the road to Damascus. The revealing light into which he was drawn by Edward Sheldon was startling and uncomfortable. Here ridicule could not protect him. He had peeped over the rim of brittle externals and looked into inner and neglected richness that would not give him rest until it had found expression."

Then Hopkins spoke of the *Redemption* period: "There had been an unauthorized published statement that I was contemplating a production of Tolstoy's *The Living Corpse*. At that time Barrymore was in *Peter Ibbetson*. He came to see me, I am sure at the prompting of Sheldon, and told me he had wanted for some time to do the Tolstoy play. It was the first time we met. Somewhat doubtful of the persistence of his desire, I told him that if after the completion of the *Ibbetson* tour he was still of the same mind we would do the play. There was no further word between us until he returned from the road. At a luncheon we soon made plans for the Tolstoy play, and he told me of other plays he would like to do. I said we would do them, that we would stay at the Plymouth Theatre for three years, no matter how many plays we had to do."

Hopkins revealed that no written business agreements entered into this alliance. He continued:

"We dreamed of a great classical repertoire that would one day tour the world. And so, without the formality of contracts, we began. Neither of us thought of profits or legal obligations in connection with the dream. It was not that kind of dream. Either of us was as free to abandon the excursion as we had been to launch it. It was wholly a free-love association. The beauty of the offspring fully justified the old romantic belief in the blessings of irregularity.

"In beginning rehearsals of *The Living Corpse*, now *Redemption*, I came first to know the deeply earnest side of Barrymore. He was tireless in preparation. The myth of his laziness, frequently amusingly taunted by Uncle John Drew, had blown away. As though fearing to get too far from familiar shores on which he had long sported, he occasionally pulled himself up with a ribald interjection which seemed to be a kind of reassuring pulse-taking. Yes, he was still alive and swimming. He could always get back to the old scoffing safety.

"His rich imagination seemed to find its most arresting conjurings in ribaldry. There was constantly being unrolled before him a series of hilarious pictures, for which he knew the precise and shattering words. One realized that it was no easy task for a mind so engrossingly inhabited to avoid all pleasant wanderings and really confine itself to the painful creation of an entirely new picture, the picture of a proud, human soul in turmoil and death.

"In his immersion Barrymore was never drawn to the surface by an inflated ego. He was not burdened by vanity or the need of impressing others. It was less humility than concentration. Rehearsals for him were a ceaseless quest. This was not externalized by a conscious seeking for the impressive pose or the embroidered reading. He weaved himself into the complete texture, leaving no bright threads flying to emphasize his presence. He was the director's dream, an actor who asked no special emphasis.

"While *Redemption* was enthusiastically received, the reviews left the impression that it was enshrouded in Russian gloom and this gloom was reflected at the box office. For several weeks it looked as though the proud bark had grounded at its launching with the leaks working in reverse. There was not time to prepare a second production, and to halt the enterprise seemed fatal. So we hung on, praying, looking for the box-office tide that would free us. In the fifth week it came. Soon business climbed to capacity and remained there until the end of the run, twenty-five weeks later. The play could have run another year, but that was not our plan. We were building a repertoire."

Jack received word of Uncle Googan's death during the rehearsals of *Redemption*. Next to Mum Mum, Jack had loved Sidney Drew the most among his elders. Possibly Uncle Googan's death hastened Jack's return to the bottle, although he himself said, "A drinking man needs no excuse. If he did, Prohibition would provide every pretext in the book."

William Wellman, the now eminent Hollywood director, came upon Sidney Drew as the little man's smile was fading and his body withering.

Wellman had been invalided home from the Lafayette Flying Corps. He had been attached to the *Chat Noir Escadrille*. One of his comrades in France had been Sidney Drew, Jr. "Wild Bill" gained three official victories and a smashed-up body, returned to America with his medals, then disembarked in Boston. There he received a message from Sidney Drew. He called upon the once gay-spirited uncle of the Barrymores.

"Of course I have received word my son has been killed," Drew said, "but as a member of his outfit perhaps you could tell me more. . . ."

"He had plenty of guts," Wellman said. "It wasn't so easy for him to learn to fly. But once he got the hang of it, he quietly went to work."

"How did it . . . ?"

"On May 19 he fell in a hot combat against five Albatross. You can be proud of him."

"He was only twenty-six," said Drew. "I remember when Lionel, Jack, and I were in a hotel lobby years ago, and Sidney had come down from military school. All dressed up in his little uniform. A bellboy came up to him, thinking that Sidney was a bellhop from some other hotel, and asked what he meant by cutting in on business away from his home grounds. Then the two of them went outside. We followed after them, and I never was so happy in my life. Sidney had knocked the bellboy cold. No, I never was so happy in all . . ."

Drew suddenly excused himself. Then he turned to walk away, and he seemed to grow smaller and thinner and older. And it was not long until he died.

There was an influenza epidemic during the winter of *Redemption*. New York always manages to produce a marvelous collection of coughs in winter, but this year the city excelled itself with a million chorusing Camilles and their male counterparts.

As always, Jack resented bronchial excitations in the theatre. One night, while playing a scene with a "dying" fellow-actor, the coughing from the audience rose like the baying of asthmatic beagles. Fedor Vasilyevich Protosov's lines, pertaining to memories of friends of yore, were being delivered as he leaned above the dying man.

The speech ran something like this: "Do you remember dear Sergei? Dead. Do you remember poor Pedrovna? She too is gone . . ."

Then, without getting out of the scene, but improvising to the tune of the coughers, Barrymore asked, "But do you remember dear old Uncle Joe Seabrook? A stomach cough got him. What a fine old hacker *he* was. Just like the seals in this God-damn audience!"

Playwright Charles MacArthur says that Jack one night quaintly fortified himself against the coughing. At the crescendo of the raspings (MacArthur declares on his honor as a major in the Chemical Corps that it is true) Barrymore brought a five-pound seabass from beneath his raiment and flung it into the audience with: "Busy yourselves with *this*, you damned walruses, while the rest of us proceed with the libretto!"

One afternoon Arthur Hopkins asked Jack to attend a matinee at a near-by playhouse. As the houselights dimmed and the footlights came on and the curtain was about to rise, Hopkins whispered reverently, "This is the most impressive moment in the theatre."

To which Jack whispered back, "Shall we go now?"

At the close of *Redemption*, Jack said that he wanted Lionel to participate in the next play under the "plan." This met with the full approval of the Board of Strategy.

Lionel once again (from his own peculiar viewpoint) had suffered foul luck. He had made such a success as Colonel Ibbetson that playwright Augustus Thomas had thrown his hat into the air and howled: "Good God! He is magnificent! We must put him into *The Copperhead* at once!"

As Milt Shanks, the old soldier in *The Copperhead*, Lionel further distinguished himself.

Concerning Lionel's appearance in *The Jest*, Arthur Hopkins said: "Edward Sheldon had made a brilliant adaptation of the Sem Benelli tragedy, and Lionel, finishing a tour in *The Copperhead*, was to be free to join us. Jack's adoration of Lionel was the only form of worship I ever discovered in him. Lionel was the so-and-soest so-and-so that ever so-and-soed in the so-and-so theatre— What a so-and-so! When Lionel appeared for rehearsals he seemed a bent, shaky-voiced old man, anything but the blustering giant Neri he was to play. I was later to learn that he actually became the characters he played, and the present alarming version of Lionel was the Milt Shanks he had been so long playing. The death of Milt and the birth of Neri that followed in rehearsals was a transformation that would have saved Faust endless grief if he could have accomplished it without outside help. I was soon to see why Lionel was the so-and-soest so-and-so."

It looked as if Lionel never would be permitted to return to the status of "a contented nonentity." He moved into the house in West Fourth Street, occupying an apartment directly beneath Jack's Alchemist's Corner. The brothers practiced their scenes in the top-floor studio. One day an anvil chorus of blows next door interfered with the home rehearsal. Jack went to investigate. He found a plumber and a helper installing a bathtub and other fixtures in a house adjoining that of Mrs. Nicholls.

"Do you artisans *have* to make so much racket?" Jack asked the boss plumber. "A boiler-maker's tonsillectomy?"

Replied the boss, "This is a rush job, brother, and we got no rubber hammers."

"Your point is well taken," Barrymore conceded. Then he became slyly politic. "How much will you charge to lay off for a week?"

The boss showed no interest for the moment. "This is a rush job, like I said. And besides I don't get the idea."

"Would you and your colleague come to my quarters for a drink?" Jack asked. "We'll discuss a highly honest though profitable deal."

The boss and his helper exchanged glances. Then they hurled their wrenches and pipes to the floor. "Guess we could stand a little snort at that," the boss said. "But we gotta get right back on the job."

They had a drink or two in Jack's studio, inspected his mirrored tub somewhat dubiously, then settled down to some gin that had been manufactured on the Barrymore premises. It made them friendly and philosophic, and for a week thereafter they forgot about the rush job next door. They reported each morning, kept union hours, but at double pay, to listen to the brothers shout lines at each other.

The landlord of the adjoining building did not learn of the desertion until toward the end of the week. He almost lost his mind.

The Barrymore brothers shared a curious superstition. They believed that if they looked upon the Wrigley chewing-gum sign when it was aglow, they would give a terrible performance. This sign was atop the low and drab Putnam Building in Times Square, headquarters for managers of prize-fighters.

The brothers would walk uptown each evening from West Fourth Street at about the time when the dreaded advertisement began to express the virtues of chewing gum in terms of electrical cascades. If either of the brothers accidentally saw it, he would pretend not to have done so. If the other accused him of having glimpsed the incandescent bad omen, there would be loud denials. Sometimes the Barrymores would use their derby hats to shield their eyes as they passed the Putnam Building on their way to Forty-Fifth Street.

Uncle Jack Drew came in from Kyalami to attend a matinee with Frank Case soon after his nephews' play had become a great success.

Jack saw his uncle in the audience and let him know it by means of a departure from the lines. In the play Jack, as Giannetto, condemns Neri to a dungeon, the deepest, darkest pit. Today Jack said, "Take him to the dungeon, the deepest, darkest pit," then improvised, "No, wait! Not to the dungeon. Take him to Kyalami!"

This reference to John Drew's Easthampton cottage sent Uncle Jack into a tumult of laughter. The audience simply could not understand how the distinguished Mr. Drew, a model of gentlemanly behavior, could suddenly become so hysterically rude. Was he enviously trying to belittle his nephew's fame? Or had he carelessly been given the wood-alcohol bottle at a speakeasy?

"At the height of *The Jest* success," Arthur Hopkins recalls, "Jack decided he had to go to London. There was someone there he had to see. He urged that he knew it was an obscene thing to do, but his torn heart could only find needed healing in London. He said he hated to close a success so abruptly. I told him we could get along without him. I would put Gilda Varesi in the part.

"The idea of a woman for Giannetto was not original. Bernhardt had been a great success in the part in Paris. Rather bewildered by the idea of a successor, Jack was undeterred. He came into the theatre one afternoon while I was rehearsing Varesi. She was at her most eloquent. That night Jack told me he had changed his mind about leaving. He never went into details.

"Before the end of the run, Lionel was obliged to fulfill a previous contract. I substituted Alphonse Ethier, who quite successfully realized the pattern created by Lionel. It was painful for Jack to think of anyone attempting to wear Lionel's mantle. In unnoticed ways he goaded Ethier until the latter came to me one day. He was a genial old trouper who never looked upon the theatre as a place of loving kindness, but Jack had pushed him too far. Ethier was an old friend of mine and said if I wanted him to go on taking Jack's scorn he would try, but God! the bastard was hard to take. I told him he did not have to take anything, but surely he had been in the theatre long enough to protect himself.

" 'You mean you don't care if I go back at him?'

" 'Why should you pay any attention to what I care?' I asked.

" 'That's all I wanted to know.'

"It seems a few nights later Ethier pushed Jack into a corner and stagehands intervened. From then on Jack covered Ethier with his grace. On several occasions Jack had demonstrated that he had no stomach for showdowns. He assumed an air of pained surprise at being so misunderstood, but once corrected he stayed that way, never with apparent bitterness and certainly no sign of humiliation.

"In spite of the absence of Lionel *The Jest* played to capacity to the end, when it was taken off for the production of *Richard III*."

Perhaps no other actor of this century ever hurled himself with such tempestuous sincerity into a part as Barrymore did in undertaking the role of Gloucester. And, as if the demands on his mind and body were not enough, he entered upon a second marriage, the stormy results of which caused him to refer to it in after years in this fashion:

"When archaeologists discover the missing arms of Venus de Milo, they will find that she was wearing boxing-gloves."

II.

A Fig for Gloucester

ABLITHE and handsome poetess, whose quill-name was Michael Strange, became Barrymore's second wife. She had the face of a Romney portrait and the spirit of a U.S. Marine. Numerous heart experts have written a five-foot shelf of literature in behalf of this striking alliance. The principals themselves, Michael Strange in a memoir *Who Tells Me True*, and Barrymore in his poppings-off to the recording angels of Park Row, alternately evidenced their ardor and their disillusionment. They otherwise cried out their yearnings, she in her madrigals, and he in a series of Keatsian letters.

They dressed alike for a time, a symbol of their unity; yet it also might have been a precautionary vesture designed by one to prevent the ego of the other from drawing ahead by so much as a stitch, seam, or button.

Notwithstanding this love-in-uniform and the sounds and furies of the lovers' protestations, their passion occasionally merited a proscenium arch and footlights. Their fevered anxieties, unreasonable jealousies, trumped-up quarrels and giddy sufferings, mutual threats of suicide, unpredictable separations and wild reunions, all these perverse agonies of mind testified to the presence of an unendurable ecstasy. Perhaps the neo-Freudians have a proper label for such somersaults as these. The layman can only wonder at the spectacle, as if seeing Pegasus bob up at a Madison Square Garden rodeo with two cowboys in the saddle instead of one.

When an actor and a poetess begin to tear each other to emotional tatters, may we not presume it to be a type of flagellation designed to achieve the fantasy of a grand passion? There was a conflict, not of hearts but of prides. Soliloquies clashed with odes, and lawyers began to rub their palms together with glad expectancy.

One is never quite certain, when appraising the private lives of actors, as to where the realities cease and the simulations begin. These charming posture masters are not unlike convicts on parole:

their desire to go straight is admired and encouraged, but the police, nevertheless, look in on them from time to time.

A letter from Barrymore to Michael Strange some six years after their marriage may provide a clue as to his own status as actor-lover. This letter, it may be pertinent to remark, not only was composed after Barrymore had separated from Michael Strange but while he was most assiduously courting her successor. In it he discussed François Villon in a fashion that seemed to define his own views on romance.

The occasion for this letter was the submission of a scenario by Michael Strange to Barrymore during the early part of his motion picture career. He addressed his estranged wife as "Fig," a nickname they often employed interchangeably. In this letter the actor stated that he sought in his next motion picture "to do something totally different, that I have great sympathy with, can get much more fun out of, and I believe achieve a more significant result, and that is with the extraordinary figure of Villon, as a vehicle to burlesque the whole idea of romance."

He set down in this letter what may well have been the exact reflections of his own psychological image:

> He [Villon] was a creative artist, a poet, and everything happened in his *head*. When he is caught by Life in these movie situations, which always demand a rather asinine, heroic activity, he is frightfully up against it. Only by his amazing dexterity and imagination can he elude them, maintain a certain whimsical integrity, and prevent himself from looking like an ass, the audience being the only person he takes into his confidence. I think the picture of Villon skipping, bounding, and crawling on his stomach through a Gothic dimension of a dying chivalry and a brutal and slightly sacerdotal materialism till almost the very end, when he is forced, through the reality of suffering, his mother's death, etc., to a different attitude—always, however, flecked by a sort of pinched gaiety—is something that I can have genuine fun with and accomplish something real. . . .

Both Miss Strange and Barrymore were of dramatic fiber, stubbornly egotistically intense. They had such splendid ingredients of mind and body as to make one wonder why, in their possessing so much of life, they apparently never could possess each other.

The poetess, born Blanche Oelrichs of Newport's social caste, was denied such early contentions for bread and shelter as are presumed to bring profound rhythms to one's songs. She married a diplomat, Leonard M. Thomas, when she was but eighteen, had two children by him, and wrote poems of a Whitmanesque trend. These verses demonstrated a higher talent than Miss Strange's detractors conceded. If she had been less beautiful, less blue-booked, less vital, perhaps Michael Strange might have escaped critical envy and been forgiven for her abilities and her ambitions as well.

It is the recollection of the dark-haired poetess that she first met Barrymore at a party of the Theatre Guild Group. He then was playing in *Justice*. He had left Katherine Harris and was living at Edward Sheldon's apartment in Fifty-Fourth Street. That would have been late in 1916, or at the beginning of 1917.

Miss Strange wrote that Barrymore "looked elfin and forsaken" at that time. She added that he had "all the hypnotic magnetism of success . . . reinforcing his natural charm."

Her report on the courtship itself—there were at least three years of it—leaves confusing echoes, like a voice loosed in a rain barrel. The poetess mentions family opposition to her alliance with the actor. She says that Jack came to her parties, "a more or less silent, charming, and very decorative guest." She writes that she took Sir Herbert Tree and several friends to see Barrymore in *Peter Ibbetson*. She speaks of his playing in *The Jest*, and then discloses that she adapted *Redemption* from the Russian for him (a chronological slip, for *The Jest* followed *Redemption*) but without program credit.

Then she comes out of the bushes of schoolgirl trivialities to be her own forthright self and sound a plaint shared in by so many of Barrymore's loved ones: "How mortally depressing it often was to watch his deformation from art back into life."

Although Miss Strange is an unrepressed person, she does not choose to give us an insight into any epic clashes of personalities during the wooing period. This in contrast to her subsequent candor, her never self-sparing accounts of the marriage itself. Barrymore himself referred to prenuptial battles, but he oftentimes became an unreliable witness in respect to chronology. Perhaps he had in mind the nights of strife after the wedding aisle had been turned into a warpath.

Michael Strange, it seems, became the only one of his admirers to breach the walls of the sanctuary in West Fourth Street. Jack maintained that she accomplished this feat by means of sending him potted plants instead of cut flowers.

"I never cared to see flowers imprisoned in pots," he said. "It offended my own sense of freedom. Consequently, when potted plants arrived at the house, I would free them, like pigeons, on my roof. I began to notice that Blanche had exquisite taste in flowers, a taste that precisely suited my own predilections. I read into this the existence of other congenial qualities. God's wounds! I was hooked!"

His landlady, Mrs. Nicholls, recalls that such potted tokens did arrive with notes said by Barrymore to have been written by Miss Strange. He made an exception to his rule against opening mail and read these gracefully worded missives. The barrage of plants and notes had a siege-like quality. The successful campaign may have stimulated Barrymore's remark: "I never married any of my wives. They married me."

That Jack was in a taut state of nerves shortly before and for a long time after the marriage in August 1920 is amply attested by his contemporaries. He was working intensely. His theatrical labors taxed him. He also had done a few silent motion pictures, among which was *Dr. Jekyll and Mr. Hyde*. Besides, he had undertaken the task of reforming his voice to meet the classic demands of Shakespearean projection.

"We had been planning *Richard* for a year," Arthur Hopkins says, "as this was the great challenge to our enterprise. If we could successfully open the door to Shakespeare it meant that we might master *Hamlet* which from the first had been the crowning dream.

"Jack's chief handicap for the poetic classics was a furry voice. There was a rasp which one feared could only be removed by a surgical miracle. It was characteristic of Jack to know that he had to find a new voice. He never deceived himself about his handicaps, nor did he believe that by other compensations they could be got around.

"He had met Margaret Carrington, a retired opera singer, who had made a long study of voice production and the relation of words to meaning. She had deep reverence for the word. She had a quarrelsome ear that was easily outraged.

"Jack placed himself in her hands. She took him to her country place and kept him working for long, tedious hours. Exasperated by his vocal abominations, she frequently banished him to the garden to contemplate the violations. Her training was far from mechanical. Thought and soul had to find their way into vibrations of depth and beauty. It was beyond sound. It was communication of spirit."

There are two versions of Barrymore's going to Mrs. Carring-ton. Indeed, there are at least two versions about everything Jack did. On the one hand, we are told that Michael Strange, when vaca-tioning from Barrymore in Santa Barbara, solicited Mrs. Carring-ton to undertake the reshaping of Jack's elocutionary powers. The other version was given by Alexander Woollcott:

"John Drew was at The Lambs bar one day, talking to Patrick Francis Murphy, the head of Mark Cross. It was during the run of *The Jest*. Murphy at that time was the most admired after-dinner speaker in New York. His speeches always lasted exactly seven min-utes, no more, no less. They seemed alive and extemporaneous; no one then knew that he composed them carefully and rehearsed them to music.

" 'I wish something could be done for my nephew's diction and his voice,' Drew complained to the after-dinner orator. 'Jack speaks like a ruffian from Avenue A. It's a disgrace to the family. How he came by these shoddy accents, I cannot know. Probably sleeps among the barkers of Coney Island!' "

Murphy then advised Drew: "I think your nephew should consult Margaret Carrington. She is *my* teacher." Drew communicated this name to Jack. And Margaret Carrington became a new and valuable member of the Board of Strategy.

Barrymore remembered Mrs. Carrington with a schoolboy's awe, and once said of her:

"Through long and exhaustive study and practice, Mrs. Carring-ton had evolved an idea that was nothing short of tremendous. She had come to believe that it was possible to free the speaking voice to such an extent that one could hear, not the speaker's intention or his personality, but his inner essence, the self, the soul, speaking through him. Only a child or a saint or a genius could hold such a belief, and Mrs. Carrington was all of these."

Mrs. Carrington in 1941 began to write a series of essays on Barry-more, only one of which had been completed at the time of her death. It is an authoritative discussion by a great teacher of a great pupil. Mrs. Carrington represented Jack as having come to her home as a "tremulous, modest, and extremely shy person, as he was in his everyday life, to tell me that he was going to act Shakespeare, and that he was afraid of it."

Mrs. Carrington found it difficult to believe that the most popular actor in America could be afraid of anything. "Then with the devastating Barrymore charm, he made me understand that he was asking me to help him. I hesitated to undertake the responsibility of piercing the outer shell of a high-powered theatre personality with new ideas which might or might not help him in his first step in Shakespeare, especially as the play was announced to open in six weeks. His voice was tired, and in spite of its rare individual quality was of short range due to a complete lack of breath control."

Mrs. Carrington said that it is common knowledge among the coaches that a voice never before or since Barrymore's has been "built" in six weeks' time. She was amazed at his receptiveness, his agility of mind.

"I had worked for years," Mrs. Carrington continued, "on a kind of research in nature's laboratory on the spoken word in its relation to the speech of actors. After my first hour with Barrymore, I knew that here was an actor who was simple and obedient enough to understand what these principles would do. He responded to every nuance and implication of meaning in the text. Yet he worked incessantly on gaining the necessary breath control to suspend and sustain the long unbroken phrases of Shakespeare's verse. This was a veritable *tour de force* on his part in the use of his will and imagination, and in my experience has never been done by any other actor in so limited a time."

One day Jack was prevailed upon to have his hair cut, so that his Duke of Gloucester wig might fit properly. He usually patronized the Hotel Knickerbocker barber shop, where the scissors-men were familiar with his "quirk" of allowing no razor-edging of his neck or ear locks. Today he hurriedly found a chair in a nearer Broadway shop, sat in it, gave a few short instructions, then fell to mouthing his Margaret Carrington exercises.

The stout barber, who had the soft garrulity of a life insurance agent, tried to interest his customer in spring training news of the baseball clubs. Jack courteously indicated that he would appreciate "some silence, and very little of *that*."

He returned to his vowel-making, a circumstance which caused the barbers and manicurists to exchange glances. Was the gentleman a little nuts?

The stout barber endeavored to swerve Jack's mind from the antique hair-style. Barrymore held his exercises in abeyance. "If you please, don't edge my hair at all. I believe I told you when I came in that I didn't want a razor within a million miles of my neck."

"But the kinda way you ast me to cut it," the barber insisted, "is all out of style. Do you want it should look like a Dolly Varden?"

Jack was trying to focus on his elocutionary chore. "Styles don't bother me," he offered. "Just cut it as I asked."

The barber indicated with his comb a lathered customer in an adjoining chair. "I'll leave it up to Mr. Marcus here. He's with the Burns Brothers Coal concern. Let Mr. Marcus here take a gander at you and . . ."

Barrymore endeavored to keep an even temper. "I'm sure Mr. Marcus is a man of refined tastes, but if you don't mind . . ."

The barber broke in on this observation, as if trying to shame Barrymore into a modern haircut. "Yeah, I know, but is it treating them right to let your wife or girl see your hair grow neck-sloppy . . ."

"I haven't a wife, thank God!" Barrymore exclaimed. "I'm effeminate!"

This news disturbed the barber's moral sensibilities. He spoke with the sad modulations of a groaning sofa: "Of course you're only just kidding, Mister. But I'm not kidding when I claim you should ought to try a feather edge." His tones rose persuasively: "Just let me scrape off some of that there fuzz a little bit . . ."

The exasperated Barrymore sprang from the chair. He popped the barber on the chin. He sent him sprawling at the foot of Mr. Marcus' chair. Jack tore off the apron, snatched his coat from the rack, dropped a dollar on the cashier's counter, then hastened to the street, trying the while to apply the Margaret Carrington technique to his curses.

Some time after this outburst, Barrymore said to his attorney, "Why do I always get into trouble?"

He asked this question while his lawyer was drawing up a paper so that Jack might escape a court suit for damages by paying a hundred dollars to the stout barber.

In preparing to play the role of Gloucester in *Richard*, Barrymore insisted upon authenticity of costume. He found an armorer, an old German who did repair work for museums. This mail-maker fashioned for him two suits of plate-armor, one copper colored, the other black. The armorer's forge was in Newark, so Barrymore undertook as many as forty trips across the river for metallic fittings. This armor was not the customary, tinny plate to be found in theatrical warehouses or wardrobe rental establishments. It was heavy harness. Whenever Barrymore fell encased in it he suffered skull shocks and body bruises. His sword was designed from his own copy of a weapon of the War of the Roses period. The great blade had the austerity of a mendicant friar's crucifix. Barrymore corresponded voluminously with the authorities of the British Museum regarding both the armor and the sword. He superintended the making of his buskins and his robes of state.

In playing the deformed and lamed Gloucester, Barrymore glided across the stage like some unearthly spider. When asked how he managed such a "swift limp," and how he prevented the efforts of contortion from intruding upon the difficult speeches, he replied:

"I merely turned my right foot inward, pointing it toward the instep of my left foot. I let it stay in that position and then forgot all about it. I did not try to walk badly, I walked as *well* as I could. You will find, I think, that a cripple does not try to walk with a worse gait than he has to employ. He endeavors to walk as *well* as he can. That's the mistake Robert Mantell made, I believe; he consciously exaggerated, and thus made of the part a roaring caricature. This was true of Mansfield's Richard and in a lesser measure of Irving's. I once arrived late with Ethel at a London theatre, and in the darkness asked, 'Who in hell is doing all that groaning and snorting? Are we in the delivery room of a maternity hospital?' Ethel somewhat scornfully replied, 'A gentleman known as Sir Henry Irving is doing that snorting, and people pay to hear it!' I don't know how bad or good I was in *Richard*. I rather believe it was the first genuine acting I ever managed to achieve, and perhaps my own best. It was the first time I ever actually got *inside* the character I was playing. I mean I thought I *was* the character, and in my dreams I *knew* that I was he. As to comparing myself with other Gloucesters, I'd be afraid to have an opinion. What would it prove? Probably that I was bad, and that's one reason why I never could see myself in the mirror of another man's performance. Either I would crack the mirror, or the mirror would crack my own ego. A terrible prospect, eh? My father thought highly of Mansfield in the part, although I heard Mr. Jefferson say of Mansfield's Richard, 'It was not a performance, it was an impertinence.' On the other hand, Mr. Mansfield said of Mr. Jefferson's Bob Acres,

'He doesn't play the part, he assaults it.' So one actor's opinion of another is not to be relied upon, although I am inclined to agree with Mr. Jefferson, who held that 'all good actors are dead.' Perhaps we living actors should be allowed to say only this much: 'We're all hams. Only some of us don't know it.' "

The capacity of Barrymore for grueling work, and the scope of the repertoire planned for him was referred to by Arthur Hopkins:

"With the intensity required by *Richard*, constant playing would only have been possible if Jack had saved himself otherwise; but in his frantic pursuit of a new marriage he gave himself completely. The crash occurred. After four weeks he was obliged to close, and thus came an abrupt ending to his greatest triumph, and, as it developed, to our dream program. The plays we had planned following *Richard* were *Liliom*, *Cyrano*, *Richard II*, and *Hamlet*. Of these, after a long lapse, only *Hamlet* was done. We were in our third year at the Plymouth, and only three plays had been done. We could have gone on for ten years, or for that matter, as long as Jack lived."

Barrymore's voice teacher and Shakespearean coach, Mrs. Carrington, said in her unpublished memoir that the role of Richard was a challenge to Jack's mordant, rapier-like mentality. She called it a superhuman test of an actor's ability to play a villain such as Richard was and still project the beauty and significance of Shakespeare's text without falling into either the extreme of a theatric or a realistic interpretation. This role, she said, had numerous pitfalls for actors without creative or poetic imagination. Barrymore, she added, was no longer the young, handsome Giannetto of *The Jest*, but the living incarnation of Shakespeare's *Richard*.

In regard to one of the most puzzling problems Shakespearean actors have, the reading of asides and soliloquies, Mrs. Carrington said: "It might be defined as the difference between talking and thinking. The soliloquy must have only the sound of thought while dialogue is straightforward speech. But the real difficulty is that the audience is in on the soliloquy. How to bridge this seeming inconsistency depends on the actor's ability to project these two dimensions in sound. After Barrymore's scene with Lady Anne—whom he cajoles, and finally conquers her natural abhorrence of him, as evidenced by her accepting a ring and giving a half promise of surrender—he is left alone on the stage, and has to say: 'Was ever woman in this humor wooed? Was ever woman in this humor won?'

"To say the lines to himself lets the scene down. I suggested that Barrymore throw the speech right into the auditorium. The effect was startling and at this point in the play he got a tremendous reaction from the audience by prolonged applause. It took bold courage to step aside from tradition, and only an actor with Barrymore's natural theatre instincts could dare do it successfully."

It is said that Barrymore would leave the theatre after a performance, take the next train to Atlantic City where Michael Strange was temporarily residing, go without sleep, quarrel with his beloved, then catch a train back to New York in time to appear on-stage for the rise of curtain. The effect on Jack of this emotional depletion was catastrophic. Nor could these fiendish outbursts by the actor have done Miss Strange much good; yet her critics never have seemed eager to note her side of the matter. That she did have a "side" is obvious, for being married to Barrymore seemed to have been like setting up light-housekeeping inside the crater of Vesuvius.

At the close of *Richard*, the nerve-frazzled Barrymore had fears for the state of his sanity. He attributed some of his fogginess to the falls he had sustained when encased in armor. He retired to the health farm of his father's old friend, William Muldoon. The ex-wrestler, still erect and stalwart, had an establishment near White Plains where he bulldozed bankers, artists, lawyers and other sedentary drones back to physical fitness. Muldoon received Barrymore at the farm, pelted him with medicine balls, made him rise at six in the morning, sent him hiking cross-country, took away his gin and cigarettes, and generally abused him. He also demonstrated that the Muldoon memory had an elephantine quality by suddenly asking the panting actor one day in the gymnasium: "Still dream of monsters?"

Arthur Hopkins looked down at the vacant stage of the Plymouth last year, then spoke of the theatrical renaissance, and of Barrymore as its great exemplar.

"The enterprise had opened new and rich vistas, and, chief of all, a great actor had emerged. At all moments Barrymore was the artist. He created out of his own texture. He borrowed nothing. He copied nothing. His whole search was within himself. His wine was from his own vine. Whatever jewels adorned his final creation were brought from his own inner contact with the deep richness that is hidden in all men but found by so few. It is the finding that makes the true artist brother to all mankind. In revealing himself he reveals others to themselves. Hugo's 'Art is the only true democracy' might read 'Art is the only true brotherhood.' The artist cultivates our gardens and reveals to us blossomings of our own that had been hidden from us.

"As in other creative fields, the term artist is carelessly used in the theatre. There are more turners over of old, exhausted earth than breakers of untouched soil. It was Barrymore's complete devotion to creation that made him the true artist and, I believe, the only full grown theatre artist of our time. As applied to him the word towering had true meaning. He found the heights and there his banner will fly as long as there lives one whose shining eyes look up to it."

I telephoned Lionel recently to learn that he was busy rescuing a litter of kittens newly born inside the partition of his bedroom. He was tearing down the wall, for he likes cats beyond all other pets.

"I've been working all day getting at the kittens," he announced. "Had a hell of a time locating them. Used a physician's stethoscope to find the right place in the wall. What seems to be on your mind?"

"I was wondering," I replied, "if there couldn't have been a woman somewhere in all the world who might have loved Jack as he wished to be loved, and made herself gracefully subordinate to his career? As Cosima Wagner did, for example?"

"Perhaps," Lionel replied, "but you must remember that it took a Franz Liszt to create a Cosima Wagner. By the way, be sure to listen to Verdi's *Requiem* tomorrow afternoon on the radio."

12.

Trouble on Parnassus

BARRYMORE'S leave-taking of the Alchemist's Corner, where he had passed so many happy days, was for him a symbol of broken hopes. "I had put more into this eyrie," he said, "than mere sticks of furniture and pieces of glass. Everything about it had a meaning to me. I didn't want to leave. It was like saying good-by to one of my selves."

His good landlady, a witness to the romance of the actor and Michael Strange, rightly divined that the new wife would not for long be content in this sequestered, cobwebbed setting. Mrs. Nicholls, while on a vacation in France, wrote to Barrymore, inquiring if he meant to renew his lease at the West Fourth Street house. His reply, posted six weeks after his marriage to Michael Strange, clearly indicated his own desire to remain there:

> I sent you a cable the moment I got your sweet letter. But do you remember the story in the *Decameron* of the princess who was shipped to her prospective husband but—owing to her peculiarly stimulating type of façade—was inflicted with four hundred and twenty-three experiences before she finally arrived two years later, slightly bewildered, but apparently unimpaired?
>
> My poor cable of diminutive appreciation for such a sweet letter has disrupted all the trans-Atlantic telegraph companies, including the French. Apparently there is no record in their preposterous archives of such a place as Giverny. Poor old Vernon [his agent], after strangulating difficulties, has unearthed one in Eire, another near Vienna—but they couldn't take the responsibility of delivering it, and I must be mistaken in the name!
>
> You have picked out the place of my dreams, a spot so esoteric that even the geographicians and the police are in the dark about it. I shall probably move there at once! At any rate I will not move out of my top floor—unless I *must*—as I told you. I can see you tearing your hair and saying, 'My word, neither marriage, plague, nor earthquake can evict him! He is lashed to the house forever, unless death or fire intervene!' We

can go into it on your return, when you've had a good rest and feel strong.

Thanks a thousand times for your letter.

As always,

Top Floor.

Not long after writing this, Barrymore sublet his apartment, and went with his wife to live in Sixty-Seventh Street. Michael Strange says of this in her memoir:

"It was delightful to have some one in the 'home' at last whom the servants considered more temperamental than myself."

She added that Jack had a small room there, to which he could retire to draw. She observed that whenever he was at work on his sketches he "always seemed peaceful and happy, the reverse of the way he was when acting." The poetess confessed that Jack's attitude toward the theatre bewildered her. She frequently noted that his contacts with audiences "did not revive or elate him, but rather depressed him."

Jack seemed to have given up the theatre during the first year of this marriage. He bought a farmhouse near White Plains, and made a gift of this dwelling and its fifteen acres to his wife. She was expecting a baby in May of the next year.

In 1920 Jack made a motion picture, *Sherlock Holmes*, part of it in England. Roland Young played Dr. Watson in this picture, and Jack said of their association:

"When the modest, self-effacing Roland appeared on my horizon, I took a great liking to him; so much so that I began to feel sorry for him during our scenes together. For once in my life, I decided to be somewhat decent toward a colleague. I suggested a little stage-business now and then, so that such a charming, agreeable thespian might not be altogether lost in the shuffle. When I saw the completed film, I was flabbergasted, stunned, and almost became an atheist on the spot. That quiet, agreeable bastard had stolen, not one, but every damned scene! This consummate artist and myself have been close friends for years, but I wouldn't think of trusting him on any stage. He is such a splendid gentleman in real life, but what a cunning, larcenous demon when on the boards!"

Michael Strange wrote a play during her time of expectant motherhood. Her two-fold productivity enchanted Jack. Perhaps happiness, after all, lay waiting for them just around the bend of the road. In a manner of speaking, Barrymore behaved as if his wife were about to become the mother of twins, one of them physical, the other spiritual. He volunteered to appear in Michael's drama, *Clair de Lune*, a work suggested by Hugo's novel, *The Man Who Laughs*.

Arthur Hopkins could not share in Jack's enthusiasm over this play. Its production was undertaken by Alf Heyman of the Frohman offices. Jack played the role of the clown, Gwymplane. He persuaded Ethel Barrymore to appear as Queen Anne. His celebrated sister had just completed three seasons in one of her finest stage achievements, as Helen Haden in *Déclassée*.

Jack, Michael Strange says in her book, "behaved with a frenzy of generosity." He rehearsed the cast for long hours. He designed some of the scenery himself. The author of the play composed portions of the incidental music.

The critics of that day were a gifted group, zealous guardians of theatrical standards. Still, it seemed hardly fair for such distinguished artillery officers to have drawn up their heaviest guns to wing a butterfly. There are times, and this seemed one of them, when even the worthiest critics go beyond condemnation of the work itself to pounce upon the artist as if he were a forger, a cutthroat, a Benedict Arnold, even the anti-Christ. Mrs. Barrymore's play may not have merited a Nobel Prize, but the author was not a criminal.

Jack went into a three-alarm rage when the critics set fire to his wife's theatrical monument. According to Alexander Woollcott, the reviews so irked Barrymore that he had to be dissuaded forcibly from making a speech on the subject the second night.

"This," Woollcott said, "was a dissuasion which I have always regretted. Lionel and Ethel threatened to hurl their brother into the East River were he to upbraid the harried scribes from the stage."

Jack did relieve his feelings somewhat by writing the following letter, in which he singled out critics Woollcott and Heywood Broun, play reviewers, respectively, for the *Times* and the *Tribune*:

> Upon reading Tuesday those notices of *Clair de Lune* written by the gentlemen of the *Tribune* and of the *Times*, I became inclined to wonder if a malice so stark should be permitted to pass without comment, or such unauthenticity of statement to circulate without contradiction.

I am forced reluctantly to the conclusion that the gentleman of the *Tribune* is either jaded from forced attendance at the theatre throughout a long season, or that in his job he is, like Melisande, not happy.

As for the *Times* reviewer, one cannot help wondering, while reading his odd cacophony of words, if he has ever dualized those two functions—which the public daily expect of him as a critic—of thinking and writing at the same time.

Woollcott and Broun were then "told to stand in the corner" as follows:

In perusing these two strangely inaccurate reviews, one wonders if the dignity and beauty of honest labor should be froufroued away by these acidulated whirlwinds of lame invective, and if the time is not ripe for that laughter, which has been held rather long in one's sleeve, to appear upon one's face while asking one's self and the public in general if opinions of such sort are to be taken seriously, coming from those who have apparently neither the vitality to listen nor the knowledge to give the public—whose servants they are as much as we of the theatre—a sensible account of what is incumbent upon them to witness in a spirit of mental alertness and fair play.

Woollcott, speaking with what he called "kindly perspective," last year disagreed that the reviews of *Clair de Lune* had been unduly personal. He said that all the critics had "privately thought that the play would scarcely have been produced had it not been for the somewhat irrelevant circumstance of Michael Strange having married Barrymore." He denied, however, that the reviewers had elaborated in print upon this conjecture.

"In fact," he said, "they all described nervous circles around this central idea, dancing skittishly about it as though it had been a Maypole. All, that is, except one: Mr. James Whittaker, the same Mr. Whittaker, by the way, who married the fair Ina Claire secretly, and then one day suddenly announced their domestic status by means of a review in which he severely criticized Miss Claire's acting. Mr. Whittaker expressed the *Clair de Lune* excursion in these words: 'For the love of Mike.' "

In his *Confessions*, published in 1926, Barrymore attributed the failure of *Clair de Lune* to the fact that it "seemed entirely filled with dwarfs and Barrymores" to the audience's distraction from the play itself. Again, almost twenty years after the event, he maintained a gallant attitude toward his second wife's effort, holding himself responsible for the "gaudy trappings" that obscured the plot, adding that "a genuinely charming play became a Kansas outhouse, graced with chandeliers and a doorman from the Ritz."

Not long after *Clair de Lune* closed, Michael Strange gave birth to a girl. The child was christened Joan Strange Barrymore, but afterward officially called Diana. Jack nicknamed the baby "Trepiwee," or "Trepie," and for a time forgot his troubles and dissensions, private or public. He really had wished for a boy, but when asked concerning this, said, "I'm glad Trepie is a girl. If she were a boy, she'd inherit all my habits, and I wouldn't know how to combat them: I'd have such sympathy with them."

He had been planning to appear in a dramatization of *Monsieur Beaucaire*, by his friend Booth Tarkington. The author had wired him, "Of course I want you to do *Beaucaire*," but now, with fatherhood upon him, and delightfully so, Jack thought he should postpone further stage work, perhaps retire altogether from the wings. He eventually went with Michael for a voyage abroad.

When interviewed on the other side of the Atlantic, Jack was asked what he thought of Prohibition.

"Fortunately," he replied, "I don't think of it."

Michael Strange describes in her memoir the clashes that occurred during her European travels with Jack. There were quarrels, threats of suicide, noisy accusations of extra-marital romance. Barrymore afterward admitted to a major share of the provocations, and humorously recalled one of them as having been his drinking of the alcoholic fuel in Michael's curling-iron heater. Why he should have preferred such a violent and lowly grade of beverage in Paris, a city of wine, might have perplexed any woman.

After months of storms and rages, Jack one day appeared at Ethel's home at Mamaroneck. He seemed gaunt and stricken, Ethel says, not so much because of any specific physical ailment, but from long harassment of mind.

"I don't know what the hell to do," he said to his sister. "I'm a bit mixed up. I feel like a soufflé that has been out of the oven too long. Guess you'd better take me in."

Ethel, of course, "took him in." The next morning she put into his hand a small, inexpensive edition of *Hamlet*. "Jake," she said, "read the two soliloquies. You may enjoy them."

Barrymore was not a Shakespearean in the academic sense of the term. I do not know how many actors have been wholesale students of the Bard, but the general feeling persists that a person with the gift of portraying the great Will's characters must of necessity be such a scholar as to possess even an antiquarian knowledge of the source material for the masterworks of Stratford's first gentleman.

Garrick, as an upbuilder of Shakespearean enthusiasm, seems to have been in literary as well as dramatic tune with the finest lyre since the golden Greeks'. And if we may descend the stairs, several flights of them, at a swift downward bound, we find in our own time that numerous hams of our boardinghouse acquaintance actually were excellent analysts of the folios, no matter how wretchedly they carried the spears on-stage or how bombastically they hurled the labored line. Many non-Shakespearean actors are familiar with the Avon classics. Eddie Foy, of comedy a king, actually *knew* Shakespeare's works, majoring in the tragedies, and could recite, word for word, any of the longer speeches.

It is true that Jack had heard much of the Elizabethan text in his own richly endowed home. Likewise, he had seen numerous of the "greats" perform in the classic roles. But he himself pointed out that there was a difference between reading and viewing, and once told me that he never really had "perused the iambic perfections" until he played *Richard*.

Jack, during his later years, used to read aloud privately from various Shakespearean plays. There were two circumstances, two reasons actually, pertaining to these readings: first, my intention to keep him for a time off the streets and away from such Hollywood philanthropists as believed that fifths of straight brandy were a specific for his duodenal ulcers; and second, the exciting pleasure stirred by his first reading of several of Shakespeare's plays.

It so happened that neither of us had read *King Lear*. We had seen it, of course, yet neither had ever read it in toto.

"Cardinal," he said, "let us sit here in the Sistine Chapel of your home, before the auctioneer arrives with his gavel and his sheriff's authorization to sell you out, and see what *we* can exhume from King Lear's whiskered mind."

He was ill at this time, as one could plainly see, yet he acted that he was well. He put on his spectacles, a pair of ancient lenses borrowed from some woozy tourist at Earl Carroll's restaurant. One temple-bar was missing from the frame, but Jack had obstinately refused to consult an oculist or permit his friends to renew the mountings of these dilapidated windows.

"It has a lorgnette effect," he said. "Makes me feel like a dowager."

He seemed a bit "caved-in" this night, as I took *King Lear* down from the dusty shelf to give it to Barrymore. He snorted several times, a device used, I fully believe, to cover up his pain or deflect attention from his growing lapses of memory. I am confident that these tragi-comic snorts often were employed by him instead of groans.

He opened the volume, then began to read *Lear*. He entered the scenes without flourish or tumult. As he sat there, his jaws sagging at first, his hair stringing down in squaw-like disarray, his face stubbled with beard-hairs, and pale with loss of blood from a recent stomach hemorrhage, his heart heavy with long misfortune, he entered upon a performance and a transformation the like of which I never before had seen, and never again shall see.

A great majesty came upon him. Rather, it came from within him, for there always existed in his nature a latent dignity of mind behind the scoffing shelter of his public mien. One forgot the nondescript eyeglasses, the stringing-down hair, the slumped man on the couch. Indeed, his own ills, his own epic disasters of the last years may have enabled him the more readily to become Lear in immediate concept and projection. The tragic king now cried out in this room, and in Barrymore's reading one saw this old monarch wearing, not the customary crown of straw, but one of thorn.

When Ethel gave into her brother's hand the small, red-bound copy of *Hamlet*, he made one of his characteristic "discoveries." He reappeared to announce that he had read the two soliloquies. "They're pretty good," he said. "In fact, they're much better than some of Mum Mum's great friends seemed to think; that is, if we are to recall their renditions as conclusive evidence." Then he added slowly: "I think I'll run over to see my friend Margaret Carrington. I have an idea."

Ethel says, "That's the last I saw of Jack for about two months."

13.

Passport to Immortality

WHEN Barrymore set out from his sister's house that day in June 1922, he at last beheld the ramparts of Elsinore rising from the gray horizon banks. Sheet lightning, far off, reddened the clouds and the dust haze. Delayed thunderings rolled down like muffled flourishes of castle drums.

The two soliloquies possessed Barrymore. A voice clearly had challenged him from across three centuries. He accepted the challenge, and now his irresolutions fled. He would climb the highest of the magic mountains, the last great peak he was to scale in the fabulous domain of the theatre.

He announced to Arthur Hopkins his decision to draw on the black tights of the classic Scandinavian. He asked Hopkins to try to persuade Margaret Carrington again to assist in the Shakespearean ordeal. He did not go directly to her Connecticut farm to state his own case. Now, as often happened to him, he felt the need of an intercessor. A sudden shyness, the first cousin to self-consciousness, unsteadied him, a sort of off-stage fright. He always seemed to dread the asking of favors, although he would go far out of his way to grant one. He was abundantly bold in the larger battles, but childishly timid in the smaller ones. Perhaps, in this instance, as a prodigal son he feared a refusal by the remarkable woman who had led him to *Richard III* two years before this June.

The rejoicing Hopkins at once consulted Mrs. Carrington. Would she undertake a postgraduate session in behalf of her famous pupil? She would, but on these conditions: that there be no fixed date for the *Hamlet* première until she and Barrymore had worked together for a month, and that the play be produced when she herself felt confident that her charge was professionally and psychologically ready for the Danish assignment.

Hopkins readily consented to these stipulations. He then commissioned Robert Edmond Jones to "dream out the production." This master designer had originated the three former stage settings under the "plan." Jones had soul and size, and integrity comparable to Edward Sheldon's.

"No other artist," Hopkins said, "could have imbedded himself so deeply in our strivings, for Jones had dreams beyond any of us. At times his ideas frightened Jack, who in some ways was strangely tradition-bound. The simple, yearning backgrounds of *Redemption*, the decadent beauty of *The Jest*, the ruthless Tower of London scoffing down on *Richard's* futility had lifted all that took place into new theatre dimensions."

Jones executed for *Hamlet* an austere scenic scheme of a vast stairway with three platforms. A great arch, through which the sky might be seen, formed a soaring background. The fluidic lighting of this set complied with and accentuated the stark aspects of the tragic action. The ghost of Hamlet's father, for example, did not appear in the traditional, shadowy personification; his presence was indicated by a spectral play of light upon a wind-stirred background drapery.

"It is not nearly so important who plays Hamlet as it is who operates the lights," Barrymore maintained. "This virtuoso, half Edison and half Aladdin, hidden at his amazing console, should receive the loudest applause, command the largest salary, and merit the posthumous statue reared in the park, a sculpture such as critical pigeons always try their best to improve."

The late Percy Hammond, as eminent a critic as ever graced a modern aisle, once implied a wish to know how Barrymore prepared for *Hamlet*.

"Since John Barrymore is a mysterious and uncommunicative fellow," said Hammond, "we shall probably never know what exhausting hours of thought he spent in order to give his Hamlet to Broadway, if not the world. Other players have confessed the study by which their learning of *Hamlet* was achieved—the agonies of their research through the crypts of wisdom, the rigors of their long reflections. They have informed us how they resolved the chaos of the character into the luminous simplicities of their own impersonations. Sir Herbert Tree deliberated for eighteen months before he found out that Polonius' murder was a deed of wild hysteria, not, as Mr. Barrymore seemed to make it, a graceful, deliberate homicide. One's study of Sir Herbert's prompt-book makes one wish that the secretive Mr. Barrymore would publish some memoranda of his own arduous ponderings. Not that Mr. Barrymore's Hamlet needs a syllable of explanation, since it was so beautiful a picture, so clear an analysis, so untheatrical an impersonation, and so musical a rendering of Shake-

1. BARRYMORE'S FAVORITE PHOTOGRAPH OF HIMSELF

2. AS FRANCOIS VILLON IN *THE BELOVED ROGUE*

3. WITH DOLORES COSTELLO IN *THE SEA BEAST*

6. HAMLET

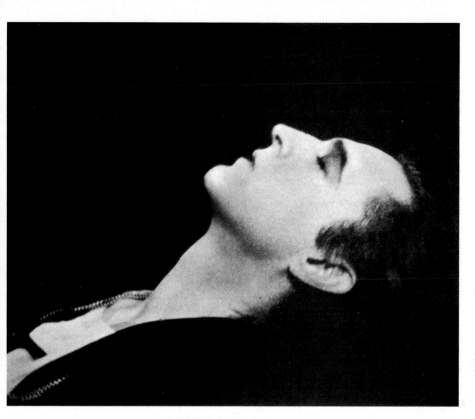

7. AS THE DEAD HAMLET

8. BARRYMORE AND GRETA GARBO IN *GRAND HOTEL*

9. IN *TWENTIETH CENTURY*

10. AS SVENGALI

11. AS LOUIS XV IN *MARIE ANTOINETTE*

12. JOHN AND ETHEL BARRYMORE IN *RASPUTIN AND THE EMPRESS*

13. WITH KATHARINE HEPBURN IN *A BILL OF DIVORCEMENT*

14. IN *TOPAZE*

15. IN *WHEN A MAN LOVES*

16. A SELF-PORTRAIT OF BARRYMORE AS KING LEAR

spearean song. But it would be enjoyable to read of his preparations
for the Great Accouchement."

As early as the *Peter Ibbetson* period, Percy Hammond recognized that "Barrymore, unlike the favorites who are actors by reputation only, makes an art of truths instead of a trade of mendacities."

If it were not for Margaret Carrington's unpublished memoir,
with lucid corroborations by Arthur Hopkins, perhaps we might
never learn how the problem was approached and resolved. Jack
himself was hazy in regard to useful reminiscence. Unlike other
practitioners of the tragic word, he never said, "When I played
Hamlet. . . ."

This quest for Shakespeare's Hamlet, as distinct from, say, Booth's
or Forbes-Robertson's, lasted for two and a half months among the
woods of the summer countryside. On the day when Barrymore
appeared at Mrs. Carrington's Connecticut farm, he brought with
him an armload of works having to do with the character and the
motivations of Hamlet. Mrs. Carrington suggested that these erudi-
tions be put away in a place where the silverfish might chew on them.

She chose for their only text the small Temple Edition of *Hamlet*
which sister Ethel had given Jack. It contained not many footnotes.

Jack detested footnotes of any caliber, and said of them: "It's
like having to run downstairs to answer the doorbell during the
first night of the honeymoon."

Mrs. Carrington announced that they would study the play exactly as they would a modern script never before performed. "I
think this accounted for his spontaneous reading and acting throughout the various scenes," she afterward wrote, "and helped to banish
any natural fear he might have had in appearing for the first time
in a part that has been the high spot in every actor's experience."

By means of her throwing out all previously conceived Hamlets,
Mrs. Carrington brought immediate response from Barrymore's
creative nature. He was relieved when the cargo of references went
by the board.

The student worked six to eight hours a day with Mrs. Carrington, as if for a master's degree. He underwent night sessions
of painstaking analysis and evaluation. Jack had agreed not to attempt to memorize the role until he had explored every shade of
meaning in the unfolding of the drama. He assigned himself to find
Hamlet, Shakespeare's Hamlet, and his own as well.

"This was our approach to the final interpretation of the play,"

Mrs. Carrington said. "Barrymore's diabolical sense of humor often distorted his performances in parts that did not call upon his highest histrionic powers. Yet this never occurred in his playing of Hamlet. Those who have not heard him in this play have not heard the greatest actor of our time."

As Arthur Hopkins has observed, Barrymore's genius came from within himself. So many men are tributaries, flowing into wider streams, the larger rivers in turn finding the great salt sea. Barrymore was a spring, a source. His own truths never with impunity could be walled-in or dammed.

When the *Hamlet* rehearsals began in September, Hopkins followed the directorial plan that had been so rewarding in *Richard*.

"All fustian and reverence were banished," he said, "previous interpretations were ignored. We began with our own conception, and developed it in all parts of the play. I doubt if Hamlet had ever been given a clearer course to sail. His bark was unencumbered by traditional barnacles that had long been accumulating. We spent no time charting the shoals. We struck at once for the deep, turbulent waters, with what seemed to us Shakespeare's clear intent as our compass. We made ourselves completely servants of the play, untempted by any beckoning to leave our personal and peculiar imprint on it."

The Jones background, Hopkins added, was eloquent and pliant in mood. The company was caught up by the inner intensity of the approach.

"The unfolding of the pattern," Hopkins said, "had the unbelievable authenticity of a witnessed miracle. One forgot Barrymore's beauty and grace, his wit and eloquence. The unseen and unheard was being communicated. The theatre has known few moments so startling as Jack's opening-night reading of his first soliloquy. The new prince was entering his kingdom."

The wearing of tights had been one of Barrymore's chief antipathies. This seems a curious aversion when we consider his superb physique.

"When I first got into these skin-fitting jollities," Barrymore said of his tights, "I felt as if I had put on the intimate wear of Peg Woffington. Good God! What an ass a grown male can become on occasion! I think I wore these dainties for the first time in *Panta-*

loon. I am not sure. No one is ever sure of anything in respect to tights."

He snorted like St. George's monstrous adversary, then continued: "When I had to play *The Jest* in these counterfeits of nudity, I decided to conquer them or be conquered. I spent at least three hours before a pier glass. True, I had to take a few drinks to brace myself. Then I began to stare at the asinine fellow in the mirror. I sneered at him, I reviled him, I questioned his authenticity in matters of romance. I walked, I turned this way and that, never taking my eyes from the fellow in the quicksilver. Finally I grew sick from the idiot-vision. Fortunately I hadn't taken enough alcohol to see *two* miserable, mincing scoundrels, else I should have died. Finally I got so tired of surveying myself, so sick, so damned fed up with tights that I no longer gave a damn how they looked, on me or on anyone else. I had 'em licked."

Jack borrowed a pair of underdrawers from Lionel to wear beneath the Hamlet tights. Not only did he regard his brother's shorts as a good-luck charm, but the garment was adroitly tailored so as not to form awkward creases on the thighs. When, toward the fiftieth performance of *Hamlet*, Barrymore's valet discreetly suggested a change of underpants, Jack bellowed: "Damn it, no! I opened in these drawers, and, by God! I'll close in them!"

What Jack did not know until long afterward was that the underwear originally had belonged to Kid McCoy. Lionel, one day at the gymnasium, had borrowed the apparel from the jaunty ex-pugilist to wear under the tights of Macbeth. By the time these drawers had done double duty in *Macbeth* and *Hamlet*, even a ragman would have refused to collect them for his heap.

"Do you believe," I asked Lionel one day, his own fiftieth anniversary on the stage, "do you really believe that Jack was on the level when he said that Hamlet was the easiest role he ever played?"

"Of course he was," replied the half-centuried stalwart. "You must take into account that when the Bard wrote *Hamlet* he had Jack in mind."

It was not always apparent whether Jack was elaborating or joking. His claim that Hamlet was an "easy" role brought a challenge, yet perhaps the reply was not wholly a jest.

"To begin with," he said, "not only does every actor play *Ham-*

let, provided he live long enough, but every member of the audience plays it, each in his own unyielding fashion. That's why we have so many thousands of essays, dissertations, comments, and multitudinous opinions, all of them sharply, yes, fiercely diverse, as to *how* the greatest character in all literature should be portrayed, and *who* did it best. The same is true of the simple, sane, charitable preachments and life of Our Lord. Yet a thousand religions and a hundred thousand sects have been squabbling unrighteously for almost two millenniums over matters that probably never were contained in the Messiah's texts."

One thing that enchanted Jack with the *Hamlet* play was the physical leeway it permitted the actor. "You can play it standing, sitting, lying down, or, if you insist, kneeling. You can have a hangover. You can be cold-sober. You can be hungry, overfed, or have just fought with your wife. It makes no difference as regards your stance or your mood. There are, within the precincts of this great role, a thousand Hamlets, any one of which will keep in step with your whim of the evening. Why, one night in London, after I had been overserved with Scotch at the home of—never mind her name —I got halfway through my 'To Be' soliloquy when it became expedient to heave-ho, and quickly. I sidled off to the nearest folds of the stage draperies and played storm-at-sea. I then resumed the soliloquy. After the performance one of the fine gentlemen who had sponsored me for membership in the Garrick Club confided: 'I say, Barrymore, that was the most daring and perhaps the most effective innovation ever offered. I refer to your deliberate pausing in the midst of the soliloquy to retire, almost, from the scene. May I congratulate you upon such imaginative business? You seemed quite distraught. But it was effective!' To which I replied: 'Yes, I felt slightly overcome myself.' "

Asked why, in the play, he alone of many notable Hamlets seemed so calm, almost joyously serene, upon seeing his father's ghost, Barrymore replied:

"The ghost, if I may be so impertinent as to have a personal opinion, actually is the God-damnedest bore since the ancient time when Job began to recite his catechism of clinical woes. Talks his head off. I am sure that Shakespeare modeled him after some unbearable bore back in Stratford, some town pest who got on everyone's nerves; the sort of stupid bastard whose wife was bound to cheat on him out of sheer ennui. But in the play, Hamlet is fond of the

old boy who was once his father, no matter what dull company
he might be at Billy LaHiff's Tavern. So I, as Hamlet, also must
be fond of him. The play, you know, rather depends on this bond
of sympathy to promote the revenge. Ergo, when the ghost of the
father appears, I am a bit startled, and for the moment confused,
yet I actually am glad to be with him once again. So I don't rant or
scream. I listen attentively to the old man, hear his gossip, then
engineer the appropriate murders. After the play I go at once to
LaHiff's or Dinty Moore's, where, as a civilian, I devoutly thank
God that the confounded old bore of a wraith cannot, in all like-
lihood, reappear at my elbow to cadge a drink."

Ethel Barrymore was playing the name role in Hauptmann's *Rose
Bernd* that November. The stage crew at the Longacre Theatre,
where she was appearing, worked hard to shift the sets so that
Ethel might be able to see at least a part of her brother's *Hamlet*
on the opening night at the Sam H. Harris Theatre. Ethel and the
cast subjected Hauptmann's work to an accelerated tempo. At
about ten-thirty the actress arrived in time to see Jack place a blade
in the gizzard of Polonius who was hiding behind the arras.

There had been another performance, however, the day before,
which Ethel considered the best ever given by Jack. It was at the
dress rehearsal. When Barrymore, coming late to the theatre, learned
that his sister was in the house and that if he took the necessary
time to make up she would be late for her own curtain, he persuaded Arthur Hopkins to allow him to play *Hamlet* in street
clothes. This was a somewhat incongruous circumstance, yet Hopkins himself afterward agreed with Ethel that Jack never had appeared to better artistic advantage. The discrepancy between his
modern tweeds and the ancient habiliments of the surrounding Danes
evaporated.

This was Ethel's great reward for having had the intuitive discernment to place the book in her brother's hands on that June day
when he had come to her Mamaroneck home with sighs of discontent and confusion.

There was a memorable night late in September of 1942 when
Ethel was playing in Philadelphia during her second season on the
road in *The Corn Is Green*. I had come down from seeing Woollcott for the last time, and from talking with Sheldon and with Hop-

kins. I was on my way west to see the great Barrymore pioneer, Ashton Stevens, in Chicago.

It was a miserable day, raining, and Ethel had a bad cold. Still, she never permitted herself to cough while on-stage, and I remembered that Woollcott had remarked the fantastic ability of all the Barrymores and Drews to perform against the odds of illness.

"They could be stricken with all manner of agues and infirmities," he said, "but once on-stage, their agility and their manner belied their ailments. John Drew was an example. He long had suffered from arthritis and could hardly walk. But in his last play, a revival of *Trelawney of the Wells*, the gallant old knight pranced onto the boards without a peep. Indeed, he was dying, and knew it, for when the cue line came: 'Shall I lead you to your box?' he replied: 'Yes, indeed. To a long, pine box.' I am convinced that when these people left their dressing-rooms to go to the footlights, another set of reflexes took charge of them."

"Why don't you call in a doctor?" I asked Ethel in Philadelphia.

"Because," she replied, "he would only tell me to go to bed." She looked out over the rooftops of her native Philadelphia, and said, as if to herself, "I love this old city, all of it."

"Because it is your birthplace?"

She turned from the window, and replied with great feeling: "It's the birthplace of our Nation." After a considerable silence, she said, "I have a special reason for wanting you to see the play tonight. I shall tell you what it is after the performance. Then you may tell Ashton. He will understand it thoroughly."

All during the play I felt that something unusual, something far beyond the drama itself, was occurring in the old Locust Street Theatre, with its tarnished gold ceiling and the decorations of angels and crusaders. The feeling persisted that I was not seeing Ethel on the stage, but Jack himself playing there. This was a ridiculous supposition, the illusion that Barrymore, then four months dead, was taking the role of the woman teacher of Welsh miners.

After the performance I went to Ethel's dressing-room to find her sipping hot tea. She was more than tired from the playing of her part and the repression of her coughs. She seemed to have that peculiar exhaustion one sees in a person who has roused from a mediumistic trance.

"Well," she said quietly, "how did it go?"

"I have not been drinking," I replied. "I have no temperature, so

I must attribute my reaction to some form of insanity. All the while tonight I felt that it was Jack, not you, who was playing the part. Shall we ring for the wagon?"

She smiled, although she was crying a little. "It *was* Jack," she said. "I played it tonight as he would have done it. Once in a while I do it that way—a secret memorial. I thought I'd let you know this, because you loved him too. He once did a *Hamlet* dress rehearsal especially for me." She rose, shrugged off her mood, then said, "Let's listen to the World Series together tomorrow afternoon over the radio."

In the days of theatrical uplift, say from the close of the First World War until the encroachment of talking motion pictures, Broadway was aware of its great people. An influential corps of journalists daily reported the scene. Some of the doughty fellows still remain on the desolate field, like old-soldier curators of Gettysburg's once busy terrain. Chroniclers Percy Hammond, Heywood Broun, Woollcott—yes, even the glib and often clever Alan Dale— have departed. Burns Mantle, dean of the New York gallery, recently has retired, but George Jean Nathan stays on and on, we are happy to note, and numerous younger guardsmen, from Gilbert Gabriel to Howard Barnes, keep their knowing eyes upon the dramatic remnants of the Big Town. One of the ablest of the younger crew, Richard Watts, Jr., has left Broadway to examine the international scene, yet sometimes writes in from China or from Russia to say that he never can forget Barrymore the artist, or Barrymore the man.

Watts and Broun were among the first to recognize the Freudian implications of Jack's Hamlet portrayal. They saw mirrored in the Barrymore interpretation such dark imageries as exist in every heart (except in yours and mine, of course) masterfully reflected by Barrymore's genius, and not at all offensive to public taste. The closet scene, for example, between Hamlet and the Queen-mother, might have proved a theatrical catastrophe had no Barrymore been its interpreter. It was played exactly as if it were a love scene.

Perhaps Barrymore did not actually insert these stark values into the play. Possibly he merely recognized, and then projected the suggestions which already were present, though long-hidden, in the tragedy. Still, one might turn psychologist long enough to wonder if the Barrymore lad's sex initiation, with the guidance of his father's paramour, were not the source of the now mature artist's daring conception of Hamlet as an incestuous prince.

There were a few dissenters who sought to cry down this portrait of a sane and human Hamlet, and who said, as did old Actor Quin of Garrick: "If he is right, then we are all wrong." But press and public acclaimed Barrymore as the "first Hamlet of our generation."

Of what did this man himself think during the hour of laurels? With the audience wildly applauding, and the curtain lowering, then rising again and again on the great new Hamlet, what was in Barrymore's own mind? Were we to believe him when he afterward said, "Fear was leaking out of every pore"? Had he again "heard thunder in the applause," as on the September night in 1909 when he suddenly became a comedy favorite in *The Fortune Hunter?*

Whatever he was or was not thinking of on this night of achievement, we can tell you what he did. He allowed no one inside his dressing-room other than a few immediate friends and relatives. He soon sent them away with promises to join them at a supper party to be given in his honor. Then he began to remove his stage garments. There was but one caller left in the room, Patrick Francis Murphy, the orator who had suggested Margaret Carrington as the one to remake Jack's voice for *Richard.*

"Well, Mr. Murphy," Jack asked, "how was my diction, my tone placement, and all the et ceteras of the evening's vocals?"

Mr. Murphy studied the question for some time, then solemnly replied, "It would have been perfect, Barrymore, entirely perfect, but for one thing which jarred me no end."

"Meaning what, Mr. Murphy?"

"The way you pronounced 'body.' You must correct the delivery of that word, Barrymore, then your performance will be flawless. You must under no condition allow the word 'body' to come out 'buddy.' "

After Mr. Murphy had bowed himself out of the flower-filled room, Jack picked up a red apple from the make-up shelf. It had been sent by Uncle Jack Drew.

"I sat there thinking for a long time while the theatre was being emptied," Barrymore said. "I remember thinking about Uncle Jack. He was getting old, about seventy, and he had arthritis. His liquor and he were beginning to quarrel with each other. . . . I still felt scared from the night's work. I tried to focus my thoughts on the red apple. I reflected upon what a great old warrior Uncle Jack was. Not long before this I had been up with him all night at The Lambs and The Players. He was game. He was meticulously dressed in evening clothes. Not a speck of dust on him, not a wrinkle in his garb. But his jaw would drop down, and my job was to tuck it back in place from time to time. He was always so spruce and neat, you know, and would have been shocked to learn that his jaw ever drooped in public. . . . The noises outside the dressing-room had begun to fade, like the footfalls in an apartment house corridor, the going-away footfalls after the lady has been. You listen to the clanging of the elevator door, the whir of cables on their spools, then a fainter clang from downstairs. Then you wonder why in hell you hadn't spent the last three hours reading a book instead."

Barrymore, now in his street clothes, went to a telephone to call his old friend Frank Case at the Algonquin Hotel.

"Hello, Frank," Jack said over the telephone. "Is the kitchen still open?"

"Why, sure, Jack," replied Case. "But I thought you were going to the big dinner? I was on the way there myself when your call came in. Where are you?"

"Stay right where you are, Frank. I'm coming over."

Case says that when Jack called upon him and Mrs. Case in their rooms he ordered a glass of milk and some finnan haddie. "We talked until morning," Case continued, "and never once, even remotely, did Jack refer to *Hamlet* or to theatrical matters. It was as if the night of his greatest triumph had never been."

"Good God!" Jack suddenly exclaimed. "I promised to be at some damned supper party!"

"I don't think that need worry you now," Case replied. "It's after five o'clock."

"That's perfectly fine," Jack said. He sighed, then added, "And I want to tell you, Frank, that I never enjoyed a finnan haddie so much in all my life."

All that week and the next the celebrity-seekers tried to produce Barrymore at their parties and their salons. So far as is known, the only social gathering he attended was at the house of agent Elisabeth Marbury, to whose supper party he brought a small cold roast chicken. He ate this from the piano instead of partaking of Miss Marbury's excellent buffet supper.

One Sunday night, soon after *Hamlet* opened, there was mild excitement at the place where Jack used to live during a time of lonely happiness, the home of Mrs. Nicholls in West Fourth Street. The janitor heard a noise that came from the basement. He went there to investigate. Perhaps a prowler had forced his way into the premises. He flashed on the electric light to see a man asleep on the cement floor near the furnace. The janitor was undecided whether to call for the police or simply rouse the intruder, then eject him.

The man's hat concealed the upper part of his face. There was a one or two day growth of beard on his chin. His clothing was rumpled. He smelled of liquor.

The janitor somehow sensed that this slumped-over figure was not entirely unfamiliar. He leaned over to remove the hat. Then he recognized Barrymore. He was amazed to find the great theatrical hero sleeping in the basement. He touched Barrymore, who didn't rouse at first. Then he shook him awake. Jack looked up at the janitor, somewhat confused.

"Can I do something for you, Mr. Barrymore?" the janitor asked. "Should I tell Mrs. Nicholls you're here?"

Barrymore shook his head. "No. Please don't bother her."

"But she ain't seen you for more'n two years. Don't you want we should do something? What's wrong with you, Mr. Barrymore? Something wrong?"

"No," said Barrymore, "I just thought I'd come home."

Much has been said concerning Jack's playing of Hamlet for one hundred and one consecutive performances on Broadway. This exceeded the younger Booth's all-time record by the margin of one appearance. It has been offered, quite erroneously I believe, that Jack had some egotistical reason for wishing to surpass the Booth record. It was so unlike Jack to be conceited about anything, he cared so little for evidence of his own deeds, that we should look for a more convincing motivation.

The real solution, I think, was supplied by Frank Case, and lay within the sometimes perverse humors of the actor's nature. Case says that Jack was tiring of *Hamlet,* as he invariably wearied of all theatrical iteration, at about the sixtieth performance. Hopkins himself confirms Case's statement by revealing that Jack was talking increasingly of "quitting this damned nonsense."

"I was in Jack's dressing-room one day," Case said, "when a deputation of old gentlemen, not one of them under seventy, called. Jack was most courteous, recognizing most of them by name as retired actors, playwrights, and theatrical personages. Their spokesman shook his white locks, then began to address Jack:

" 'We are all proud of your vast success,' and the old boy gave a William Jennings Bryan flourish of the arm. 'We know that, should you choose to do so, you could continue on as Hamlet for years. But we are here to urge you to close your Broadway run at ninety-nine performances.' "

Jack was enchanted by the request, Case recollects. "May I ask," Barrymore inquired of the patriarchal delegates, "why you fix such an arbitrary number as ninety-nine?"

"In memory of the great master," said the old boy. The other old boys nodded impressively.

"Who in hell is the great master?" asked Jack. "Shakespeare?"

"Not Shakespeare," the spokesman replied. "Booth. We do not think you would want to destroy the record of the great Edwin Booth."

"What was the master's Broadway record?" asked Jack, who never kept track of matters numerical.

"Booth played on this street for exactly one hundred performances in succession."

"Gentlemen," Barrymore replied, "I think it about time that you stop living in the past. That's what is wrong with the world. It is run by a lot of persons who keep bitching up the present by applying only the rules of a dead past. I am compelled to inform you that I shall play Hamlet for exactly one hundred and one times. And when you see the master, give him my regards. I knew him when I was a little boy, and he'll laugh like the devil when you tell him that you saw me."

Barrymore did play the Hamlet role for one hundred and one times. Then he abruptly threw Lionel's drawers into a corner of the dressing-room. Instead of returning to the theatre the next afternoon for the matinee, he called upon Feodor Chaliapin, the great Russian basso. They ate and drank until evening. Chaliapin was to sing that night, and Jack asked him (by means of an interpreter who, Barrymore said, was a burlesque actor) how he could drink and eat so much and remain fit for a performance.

"I thought for a moment," Jack said, "that the lusty Feodor

would explode. He laughed until the dishes on the speakeasy tables rocked. Then he began to yell in Russian. When this earthquake had died down, I asked our linguist from the burlesque wheels, 'What in hell did Feodor say?' To which the interpreter replied solemnly, 'He says he can eat and drink like a big horse before singing, because he is such a God-damned fine actor!' And, by gosh! he could, and did. We had many fine times together in New York, and again in London and Paris."

Jack did not say good-by to *Hamlet* permanently. He toured as the Dane for a brief season of nine weeks the following year. Concerning this campaign, Hopkins said somewhat sadly: "The largest theatres were inadequate. In Cleveland his last classical appearance in America was made, and there passed from us the theatre's richest gift."

It was during this tour, in Boston, that Jack met the aging portraitist, John Singer Sargent. The artist had sketched Ethel during her early London days, and Jack hoped that he would do even more for him—perhaps paint his portrait. Sargent, however, at sixty-seven, had put away his brushes for all time. He visited Jack's dressing-room, and showed considerable interest in Barrymore's skill at making-up, complimenting the actor on the deft manner with which he accentuated the frown lines and the highlights of the cheekbones.

Barrymore did not come out with a bold request that Sargent paint his portrait; that would have been against the promptings of his own shy nature in such matters. Sargent, however, seemed to read the thought in the actor's mind, for he volunteered: "If I were now in oils, I might venture to suggest that you sit for me."

Jack leaped at this, as a salmon to a fly. "It would be the greatest moment in my life," he said, "just to watch you at work."

Sargent finally arranged to do a crayon sketch, nothing more, of Barrymore's head and face. He would not undertake an oil painting. "Besides," Jack remembered him as saying, "you would be a difficult subject for any artist not in his best stride. Your features are too regular. There is, you know, a bit of the caricature in every great portrait."

The sketch, made and presented by Sargent to Jack, would seem to bear out the artist's contention in respect to the features of the sitter. The sketch, although highly prized by Jack, lacked distinction. It had a collar-advertisement quality, a pretty-boy aura.

Jack at one time intended to present this full-face sketch of himself to The Garrick Club. A sheriff, however, impounded it in behalf of Barrymore's great-hearted persecutors during his dark days.
It now hangs in the San Diego Museum.

In regard to Jack's tiring of *Hamlet*, Arthur Hopkins commented:
"As invariably happened, his first performance was his best. It was
as though all his forces, summoned for one supreme flight, could
never quite be evoked again. It was not from indifference, for at
times when he tried the hardest, he was at his worst, notably when
he gave a performance for the members of the Moscow Art Theatre. I have always felt that his realization of this hastened the termination of his stage career. At his least inspired he was unforgettable, and without question the great artist of his time. Did his
mastery of *Hamlet* plunge him into the Alexandrian dilemma? I have
often thought so. After *Hamlet*—what?"

After a series of hit-and-miss attempts to mend his domestic life,
Jack went to Europe. He and Michael Strange were alternately together and apart. Once he stormed out of their quarters in Paris
to go alone to Switzerland, where he climbed Mont Blanc. From
St. Moritz he wrote an impassioned love letter to Michael. He was
unhappy with her or away from her, it seemed.

He finally decided to become an actor-manager and himself put
on *Hamlet* in London. He had retained about twenty-five thousand
dollars from his recent theatrical proceeds, and put this amount into
the London venture.

Constance Collier, forever grateful to him for his help in the
Peter Ibbetson dream, now offered to try to interest London managers in the Barrymore *Hamlet*. This was a difficult task, one that
required many months of diplomatic persistence.

"Jack was living at the old Whistler house in London," Miss Collier said. "He seemed comparatively happy in the environment, but
had intermittent periods of dejection."

They went, week after week, to the managers, in the endeavor to
hire a theatre. "Just as success seemed near," said Constance, "Jack
would spoil everything by putting on a tough voice. The manager
would be shocked. 'How can you expect in England,' an impresario
would ask, 'the home of Shakespeare, a man to be any good with a
voice like that?'"

Constance frequently upbraided Jack for "putting on that voice."

But he did it to shock the conservative managers. When autumn came, Jack seemed depressed by his failure to interest the English managers in his *Hamlet.* Miss Collier tried to divert him from his tendency to drink. She encouraged his eating of candy as a substitute for alcohol.

"We often went to the theatre together," Constance Collier remembers. "He would never sit in the stalls, but somewhere in the back of the dress circle, or the gallery, or pit. We would go to a candy store and buy little bags of various kinds of sweets. He would have a different-colored bag in every pocket, and we would sit in the pit and eat candy and watch the show. He wouldn't go in the stalls, in case he wanted to leave in the middle of a play, which he frequently did."

She told of how he liked to wander in the London fogs.

"He loved the fogs," she said, "and felt they were full of romance and adventure. Whenever there was a real fog, Jack was in his element. He became most poetic. In spite of his brilliant wit, there was something very childish about Jack. I still can see him huddled up in his overcoat, with his collar turned up and his hat pulled down over his brow as he tramped along in the heavy fog by the railings of Hyde Park.

"There was something childish in the droop of his shoulders, like a little lost boy. I remember once in my apartment at the top of Baker Street that Jack and I talked for a long time, ending in an argument of some sort, and he dashed out of the door, saying he had finished with me, and wasn't going to speak to me again, that I was the most aggressive, offensive person he knew.

"While we had been dining a heavy fog had come up, practically pitch-black. I was sorry about the quarrel and hurt with Jack, and made up my mind not to speak to him again; but I should have known how anxious he was about *Hamlet,* and what a strain he was under, and that he hated to be thwarted.

"However, I went to bed and must have slept but a little while when the doorbell rang. I slipped into a dressing-gown and opened the door, and there stood Jack, great fog rings round his eyes, looking humble and small.

"He said how sorry he was, and that he had been walking round and round the block for hours. He couldn't find his way home, as the fog was so thick, and what was he to do?

"Of course I took him in, and made him a bed on the dining-room sofa. He locked himself in and didn't wake for thirty-six hours, much to the amazement of my English parlor maid, whose habit it was to clean the dining-room every morning. Nothing waked Jack up, and as he had locked the door the maid was fully convinced that he had committed suicide. However, he emerged two days after, bright as a button, gay as a bird, and ate an enormous meal, winning the hysterical maid over with his charm, as he could win anybody if he put himself to it."

Barrymore returned to America that autumn. Here he obtained some additional backing and then went again to London, to live at Number 2 Cheyne Walk, Chelsea. He and the faithful Constance Collier started off once more in search of a theatre for *Hamlet*. It had become an obsession with him now, the giving of this play in England. Constance Collier thinks he was so stubbornly set upon this venture because of the opposition he had met.

"I now persuaded Jack to let me do most of the negotiations," she said. "I talked to Mr. Frederick Harrison, lessee and manager of the Haymarket Theatre, and fortunately I got the contracts drawn up before Jack met that very conservative and dignified gentleman. Mr. Harrison had a production coming on, but there was an intervening period of six weeks, and he was glad to get his rent paid."

Miss Collier, on January 24, 1925, took Barrymore to Number 91, Bishopsgate, the offices of Foss Productions, Ltd., controllers of the Haymarket. This was the theatre in the foyer of which his own father long ago had found the stage-name, Maurice Barrymore, in an old playbill, and afterward where he had appeared as an actor.

Constance introduced Jack to the reserved Mr. Harrison. "Jack started conversing very well," says she, "but gradually sank into that tough voice. Mr. Harrison's face was a study; but it was too late, the Haymarket directors already had put their names to the contract! The manager must have suffered tremendously meanwhile, but on the first night Jack's exquisite diction and lovely voice absolutely overwhelmed the English audience."

Michael Strange attended the London debut of her husband at the Haymarket. Her escort was George Bernard Shaw. The eminent Irishman next day composed and sent to Barrymore a long letter attacking him, not as an actor, but as a person who dared to alter the play as written. This oft-quoted Philippic for a time nettled

Jack. It was a minority report, but such a solid Shavian uppercut that Barrymore called it "A haymaker at the Haymarket."

Shaw said that the American had saved "say an hour and a half of Shakespeare by the cutting, and filled it up with an interpolated drama of your own dumb show." He added that this "was a pretty daring thing to do." The paragraph that gave Jack the largest saddle-sore was the following:

"Shakespeare, with all his shortcomings, was a very great play-wright, and the actor who undertakes to improve his plays undertakes thereby to excel to an extraordinary degree in two professions, in both of which the highest success is rare. Shakespeare, himself, though by no means a modest man, did not pretend to be able to play as well as write it; he was content to do a recitation in the dark as the Ghost. But you have ventured not only to act *Hamlet*, but to discard about a third of Shakespeare's script, and substitute stuff of your own, and that, too, without the help of dialogue."

Opinions vary as to the Shaw letter. Constance Collier thinks that the fluent vegetarian was more grievously offended by Jack's introduction of the *Oedipus Rex* flavoring into the classic pudding than he was by the omission of certain textual matters. Lionel has an opposite view; he believes that Shaw was entirely justified in demanding that the "word" never be deleted by the "actor." Lionel points out that Shaw in no wise attacked Jack's ability as a player; and, to the contrary, thought him glamorously magnificent.

"Neither Shaw nor myself," Lionel added, "ever regarded Jack as Shakespeare's equal at pushing the quill."

Constance Collier, who played the Queen in this London *Hamlet*, says that the first night at the Haymarket was an incredible success, Shaw or no Shaw. She embellished her eyewitness statement by saying:

"Our six weeks were soon over, with standing room only for every performance. Then, for the following six weeks, Jack had to pay the entire cast of Mr. Harrison's incoming play; but at that we could only continue on for the additional six weeks, as otherwise the option on the new play would have lapsed to the loss of the Haymarket management, so our run had to be curtailed!"

When asked, years afterward, to compare his own reactions on the night of the London première of *Hamlet* with those of his New York debut, Jack replied:

"All opening nights found me, when the curtain fell, empty in-

side the skull, the chest, the shoes, even. Sometimes, when Lionel
or Uncle Jack was there to hold my hand or fill up my glass, it
was not as unbearable, the loneliness I mean, as it otherwise proved.
All I remember of the London mood and the activities of the first
evening is that I waited until the theatre had become dark and
empty. Then I walked out on the stage, stood there, alone, looking
toward the black vacuum of pit and stalls, and I knew what the
Viscount St. Alban meant when he said that the poets had made
Fame a monster. Then I went to my house in Cheyne Walk, found
a bottle of beer, and decided there and then that I would quit the
theatre as soon as I could do so. I might have quit it that same night,
had it not been for the sake of Winston Churchill. He was so fond
of our family, such a great friend, that I didn't want to let him
down. A note from him next day brightened matters considerably,
and our visits together made the *Hamlet* labors endurable for the
remainder of what the gods humorously have called my acting
career."

All the young and aspiring actors in London, Miss Collier recalls,
tried to get into the *Hamlet* company. It wasn't the money they
wanted, it was a desire to act with Barrymore. The part of Laertes
required several changes of personnel. Miss Collier tells us why.

"Boys used to come in, proud and happy to have been chosen for
the role. Little did they know what was in store for them. When it
came time for the graveyard scene, Jack would fight violently.
While in Ophelia's grave with her unfortunate brother, the young
and enthusiastic actor who had lately told me how proud he was
to receive the great honor of being allowed to play with Jack, was
led to the slaughter! He would come from the encounter dripping
with blood! These successive young men would bear it patiently for
a time, quite bewildered as to what had happened to them, thinking
it was their own clumsiness, that the blows they had received were
accidental. But not at all: Jack fought Laertes with the greatest
realism, as if he were attacking a true opponent. He actually hated
the actors who played the part. In the end each Laertes had to give
up and send in his notice and retire—covered with scars. Then another bright, young-faced actor, full of enthusiasm, would take his
place!"

Constance Collier says that at the close of the London season
numerous offers came to Barrymore to take the *Hamlet* company
to Berlin and then to Paris. He declined to do this.

"By this time," Miss Collier says, "that strange resentment of any part Jack played too long had overtaken him. He hated the very sight of the stage and the sound of the lines he had to speak. He gave so much of himself to every performance that each one seemed a chip off his life. He was really obsessed when on the stage, where not a bit of the off-stage Jack existed! Acting had the most extraordinary physical effect on him."

In connection with this "physical effect," one of his leading ladies said: "I have known him to be only half awake at times. I have gone to his dressing-room to shake him from sleep. He would drink brandy and champagne, then stumble to the wings and onto the stage, where he suddenly would become vital and strong, as if nothing on earth was the matter with him. His voice would ring clear; then, at the end of the scene, he would come off the stage, and sink into the same' apathy as before. His diction would be stumbling and muffled, his steps uncertain!"

Is this a corroboration of Woollcott's theory that "another set of reflexes" possessed and sustained the Barrymores on-stage?

When Jack closed as Hamlet in London, he quit the theatre itself. He arrived home in America on what he called a "cloud of glory," with a valet, Blaney, and a small white-nosed monkey, Clementine. Blaney had been Sir Herbert Tree's dresser, and Clementine was the gift of actress Gladys Cooper, leading lady for Sir Gerald du Maurier.

Barrymore's leave-taking of the stage seemed to him a natural, almost a casual matter. Many persons deplored his retirement, but Alexander Woollcott was not among them.

The plump oracle of Lake Bomoseen, when sounded on this subject, became vehement:

"Why in hell shouldn't he have quit? Must the monstrous demand be heeded that a delicate instrument do *Hamlet* every night, merely because there is a public for it? After all, he couldn't keep up with the population. If he kept on playing *Hamlet* for fifty years, and in a hundred Yale Bowls at a time, he couldn't show *Hamlet* to all the population that keeps pouring from the human assembly line. It's ridiculous to cite public clamor as a reason for Jack's having stayed on in *Hamlet,* or in anything else of great artistic size. He amply rounded out his destiny in art as well as in life."

CANTO THREE

Golden Siesta

I.

Ale and Roses

THE great ex-Hamlet sat in a speakeasy off Times Square late on a spring day in 1925. His companion of the afternoon was Marshall Neilan, a Hollywood director, himself a fellow of epic attitudes.

They were renewing an old acquaintanceship. It had begun in 1910, at a time when Jack played a season with the stock company at the Belasco Theatre in Los Angeles. Master Neilan, known in the City of the Angels as "Mickey," used to play children's roles on the Belasco stage, usually depicting polite little boys. He was the sort of tad that everyone wanted to pet—the first time.

Peck's Bad Boy was a cream puff compared to the cherub-featured Master Neilan. Jack called him "Mercury." The young Irishman earned this special nickname by smuggling drinks into the actor's dressing-room against the rules of a temperate house manager.

There was a bar in the Belasco building, to be sure, but Barrymore was known in that cubby as an "eighty-six." An "eighty-six," in the patois of western dispensers, means: "Don't serve him." So Mercury had to range as far as the Van Nuys Saloon to procure stimulants for his hero during a performance.

Neilan, eleven years afterward, became enfranchised with Barrymore in motion pictures. We hitherto have avoided extensive references to Jack's cinematic experiments, out of respect for Shakespeare and Ella Wheeler Wilcox. The picture upon which we shall now drape a hasty festoon was undertaken at the close of *Clair de Lune*, and after the birth of Jack's daughter.

This screenplay, *The Lotus Eater*, became Barrymore's fifteenth essay before the lenses of the silent cameras. None of these whimsies, with the possible exception of *Dr. Jekyll and Mr. Hyde,* had contributed ten cents' worth to his own or the public's cultural advancement, although critic Heywood Broun remarked that Jack's face "usually entered a scene like an exquisite paper-knife."

The company was formed by Frank J. Godsol, Neilan, and Barrymore. The business manager was Major Bowes, who still regards the experience as nothing short of black malaria. An astute Mr. Baxter assisted Major Bowes as financial chaperon to *The Lotus Eater.*

The picture was begun at the Biograph studios in the Bronx, with Neilan directing it. Jack would frequently announce that he was going out for an hour to call upon his infant daughter. He usually was absent for three days at a time.

The company eventually entrained for Palm Beach, Florida, at the busiest phase of that resort's social season. Lobby antics soon made it expedient for the star and the director to transport their celluloid, their tripods, and their cast to Miami Beach.

Barrymore scoffed at Neilan's preposterous habit of trying to snatch at a little sleep. Jack would ring Mickey's telephone at all hours, disguising his voice and assuming the names of famous Floridian vacationists. Sometimes he even would impersonate ladies over the telephone, and make provocative suggestions to the director.

One morning, early, Neilan's telephone roused him from sleep. A dignified voice asked: "Is this Mr. Neilan?"

"For God's sake!" Neilan roared. "Go to bed, you silly, no-good bastard! We have to get up in a couple of hours, damn it!"

Before Mickey could hang up, the dignified voice said: "This is William Jennings Bryan. Am I speaking to Marshall Neilan?"

"Go to hell!" Neilan said, hooking the receiver.

The telephone once more began to ring as Neilan turned over on his pillow. He angrily picked up the instrument to be informed by the hotel operator: "Mr. Bryan is on the line again. Says he was cut off."

"Tell that Barrymore bastard to lay off this funny business!" Neilan said. "I'm getting sore."

"But this call is from outside the hotel," the operator intoned. "What shall I tell Mr. B.?"

"Tell him to go to hell! That's what you tell him. He's drunk again. Just silence my telephone till six o'clock, will you? I'm dying."

Later that morning, Neilan went downstairs to find Barrymore at breakfast with Major Bowes. Jack was having some bloater, the odor of which the Major did not enjoy. Barrymore usually ordered bloater for breakfast to divert the Major from business discussions. Jack appeared not to understand why Neilan refused to speak to him this morning. The actor, Neilan thought, seemed extraordinarily sober and serene after an all-night romp. He certainly had great vitality and recuperative powers.

The next Sunday afternoon Barrymore and Neilan attended a tea, to which various notables had been invited. While the director was fortifying his tea with something from a flask, a woman of obvious distinction singled him out to inquire: "Mr. Neilan, would you mind explaining to me what prompted you to be so insulting to my father last Friday night?"

Neilan passed the flask to Barrymore, then asked of the lady: "Your father?"

"Yes," she replied frostily, "William Jennings Bryan happens to be my father!"

Mr. Bryan's daughter Ruth let it be known to Mr. Neilan that her father was unaccustomed to the epithets of motion-picture directors. It seems that her papa, the great Commoner, had composed a scenario, and had telephoned Neilan in the hope of interesting him in its purchase.

On that spring afternoon in 1925 when Barrymore and Neilan were sitting in the speakeasy, Jack revealed these three things: he had astounded his London audience upon taking his last curtain call as Hamlet with a saxophone tucked beneath one arm; he had entered into a separation agreement with Michael Strange; and had signed a contract with the Warner Brothers to go to California to appear in three "super" motion pictures.

It was growing late. The friends, now more than mellow, went outside to find a hansom cab drawn up at the curb. The driver had left his post, perhaps for midnight refreshment at one of the many speakeasies in the row of old houses. An elderly woman was selling roses near the cab.

Barrymore bought her entire stock. Then he happened to observe that the hansom-cab horse was looking at him with a speculative air. This was a swayback gray mare, gaunt and ready for the glue factory.

The gray mare seemed low in mind, as though she had been a

mule's mother and could not live down the disgrace. She regarded Barrymore with no little suspicion at first, or perhaps she merely had forgotten how to be a coquette. He held the roses against her nostrils, and spoke to her with a "Here, Emma, my love."

She explored a blossom with her lip, then risked a mouthful. There was a certain delicacy about the old girl, as if she had known better times; perhaps she once had been the toast of the horses of the Seventh Cavalry. She began to nibble at the bouquet. Her bridle-bits set up a jingle as she munched the faded roses, stems and all. Emma apparently had endured so many weary years at her rheumatic labors on the pavements of New York that even the thorns did not disturb her ancient palate.

After Emma had downed the roses, she turned her sad eyes again on her benefactor as if to thank him. He kissed her on the nose. She rubbed her muzzle against his shoulder. He loudly claimed that he had fallen in love with her. Emma seemed to regard these protestations with the calm and philosophic air of one who had learned that Times Square vows do not last beyond the night on which they are uttered.

Nevertheless, Emma appeared somewhat romantic for the moment, with one rose-petal still clinging to her lip. Jack kissed her again, and the petal changed over from her face to his, like one of those transfer-pictures with which children used to play.

"We must get Emma some refreshment of a liquid character," the actor announced to Mickey.

He applied at the barred peephole of the speakeasy and was admitted inside. He persuaded a cynical attendant to fill a champagne bucket with ale. The attendant cautioned Barrymore against attracting the attention of Prohibition enforcement officers, particularly "Pussyfoot" Johnson, by engaging in any silly antics. He promised to be discreet. He said the ale was for his invalid father, bedridden in a near-by apartment.

Jack returned to the curb to hold the bucket to Emma's lips. She quaffed appreciatively, with a smooth, almost noiseless suction. Several pedestrians now had gathered at the curb. A mounted policeman cantered onto the scene and called out: "Hey, what's going on here?"

"I'm a member of the humane society, officer," Barrymore said over the bucket. "This animal is suffering from malnutrition. Would you kindly summon a veterinarian?"

The policeman leaned down. "Don't give me that, Jack," he said. "I'm gonna ride around the block, and when I get back, you'll be gone." To the spectators, he said, "Break it up, now! Mr. Barrymore is through with his free act."

The officer galloped off. The gray mare now looked after the policeman's horse. She seemed to have taken on a vital personality. The ale had brought delusions of youth. Her ladylike manners vanished. She whinnied lewdly, and otherwise cavorted like a wanton.

"Well, I'll be damned!" Jack said. He turned to address the spectators: "That's a New York dame for you. You give them flowers, supply them with liquor, then they dust you off!"

He walked to the back of the cab, sat down in the gutter, a high rear wheel between his knees, then began to strum the spokes as if the wheel were a harp. He improvised a lyric to a melody that Neilan, a musician, says belonged in the main to Felix Mendelssohn:

> Oh, faithless love!
> Oh, faithless love!
> I brought thee roses and nut-brown ale.
> Oh, faithless love!
> Oh, faithless love!
> I've lost thee to a quadruped male. . . .

Now the police officer again cantered onto the scene to threaten: "Barrymore, if you don't get away from here, I'll telephone your sister!"

Barrymore and his second wife, Michael Strange, entered a final separation agreement on May 23, 1925, in New York City. Other papers of this character previously had been drawn, one formulated in October 1922, and another in Paris in March 1924, but the Barrymores had become "reconciled" before the notarial seals were dry.

There had been a renunciation of guardianship by Barrymore in respect to his daughter as early as June 16, 1921, a mere month after the birth of the child. There is no explanation offered for this extraordinary waiver of the father's statutory rights other than the record that Barrymore himself, and not his wife, requested it by means of a telegram addressed to Henry Root Stern, attorney for both husband and wife. There is an implication that Jack wished legally to assure his wife that he would at no time interpose himself between mother and child, no matter what might arise to plague the parents.

The separation of May 1925 took on the aspect of finality. There suddenly was no bitterness. Instead, we find that both Barrymore and Michael Strange entered into the friendliest of relationships. Their egos no longer were in competition. The emotional causes of torment had vanished. Their occasional correspondence, in which they continued to address each other as "Fig," revealed polite and calm attitudes on both sides. It seemed as if they understood each other better, and were more interested in the other's success now, than when in wedlock.

Jack frequently wrote to inquire about the welfare of his daughter. Not long after the separation, she became known as Diana instead of Joan, but his letters and telegrams usually referred to her by the pet names "Trepie," "The Rabbit," and "Binky." His communications also showed concern about Michael Strange's intermittent undertakings as an actress. In 1927, when both Percy Hammond and Alexander Woollcott wrote favorably of her appearance with Margaret Anglin in Sophocles' *Electra,* Jack telegraphed her:

DEAR FIG: HAVE JUST READ TWO SPLENDID NOTICES BY HAMMOND AND WOOLLCOTT THAT WERE SENT TO ME FROM NEW YORK OF YOUR PERFORMANCE IN ELECTRA. I NEVER SEE PAPERS, SO DID NOT KNOW OF EVENT. SINCEREST CONGRATULATIONS, DEAR FIG. I THINK IT IS MAGNIFICENT.

When Michael sent Diana's photograph to Barrymore as a Christmas present in this same year, he telegraphed his thanks, and included the hope that the play was "going fine." He also sent a wire to Diana:

DEAREST TREPIE, MERRY CHRISTMAS. I LOVED YOUR PHOTOGRAPH. EVER SO MUCH LOVE. YOUR OWN FATHER.

The separation agreement provided that Jack pay $18,000 a year for the maintenance of Michael Strange and their daughter. He was to keep up the premiums on a life insurance policy, at $1,500 a year, with Diana as the beneficiary. He also gave to Michael the White Plains house and its furnishings. He afterward wrote to her in regard to a few articles:

The only things I would like in the way of furniture are the three little chairs of black and rose petit point, the piece of red velvet with a gold fringe, the small stool, and the funny little breakfast table with the sort of linoleum screen in the back, that is up at White Plains. I have no use for anything else, and want to thank you a thousand times for your kindness in enumerating the things to me.

Barrymore, however, had many pieces of furniture in storage, some of which had been at the Alchemist's Corner in West Fourth Street. These things were scattered among seven warehouses or homes of persons who had borrowed them. They required the capacity of a freight car after they had been assembled painstakingly for transportation to California.

In regard to alimony in general—and he paid several hundreds of thousands of dollars of it, including lawyers' charges—Jack once said: "Alimony is the most exorbitant of all stud-fees, and the worst feature of it is that you pay it retroactively."

Barrymore had made one picture for the Warner Brothers, *Beau Brummell*, the year before his London *Hamlet*. Now he was entering, in 1925, upon a contract that (bearing in mind it was during the silent-picture era) seemed extraordinary in terms of salary and conditions. It consisted of nine pages. It stated that Barrymore should work seven weeks on each "photoplay," and receive $76,250 a picture. "Overtime" was to be at the rate of $7,625 a week. He was granted the then unusual privilege of approving or disapproving the stories, and of being the only actor starred in his productions, unless he himself approved a "co-star." The publicity was to be in keeping with Barrymore's "standing, reputation, and prestige."

An examination of the first draft of this document discloses that Jack had penciled-in numerous shrewd amendments and notations, an indication that he could focus his mind intently and analytically upon matters of moment when he wished to do so.

His mind was alert and clear as he set out for the West. It may be important here to remark that one of Barrymore's attorneys afterward recalled distinctly that Jack had had fleeting lapses of memory of recent happenings during the days when the separation papers were being drawn. In the light of much later events, it is believed that this was a foreshadowing circumstance of the time when his power to recollect the newer yesterdays would become an unsilvered mirror.

He quickly regained his physical bounce and agility of mind, however, once he boarded the train with his valet Blaney and his monkey Clementine. The gentlemen in Hollywood were paying the traveling expenses for Barrymore and his companions. More, they would foot his bills for a four-room suite at the Ambassador Hotel in Los Angeles, provide for all his meals, and supply an automobile and a chauffeur for his use as well.

He was in a high-sky mood all the way to California. He amazed his valet by holding grave conversations with the monkey, warning her against the pitfalls of Hollywood. Clementine, perhaps, was the best loved of the multitude of pets Jack was to have in the western citadel. He often held her in his arms; he supervised her feeding. He wrote engaging reports as to her health and "education" to Gladys Cooper.

Blaney did not like Clementine at all. The valet's former employer, Sir Herbert Tree, had had several eccentricities, to be sure, but Sir Herbert never had requested his man to superintend a monkey's business in the W. C. Not once!

Blaney was a short, thick-through man of much dignity. He was fussy in a staid sort of fashion, and he was greatly liked by Jack, who said of him: "He's the kind of person you don't know is around, and speaks only when he's spoken to. In fact, he's rather like myself, only a little different."

Jack, Blaney, and Clementine took up quarters in what was known as "Siesta 9, 10, 11, 12" at the Ambassador. This was an upstairs suite in a detached bungalow of the hotel. There was a private entrance and stairs from the lawn. It comprised a large living-room, a bedroom for Jack, a second bedroom, and another chamber which Barrymore used as a combination "museum" and office. Here he hung his mounted fish-trophies and maps of his voyages. In this fourth room he also installed a large, ornamented cage for Clementine. The monkey detested the cage, for she had to stay in it when Jack was away from home. During the day Clementine was tied by means of a long leash to an outdoor balcony, where she quarreled with the blackbirds.

There were large closets in each room. The one that interested Jack most had a stout lock. The key to this was the only one that he did not constantly lose. In this closet, piled to the ceiling, were burlap-wrapped bundles, containing exactly what you think, booze.

Barrymore began at once to redecorate his suite. He covered the walls with blue damask. He placed valances and curtains of this material at all the windows. He removed the hotel furniture. He selected chairs, divans, and beds, period pieces of attractive design, from the Warner Brothers' property warehouse, and oriental rugs. As Jack grew used to these things, he decided to buy them.

He kept fresh flowers in all four rooms. He had most of his meals served there for himself and his friends. He rarely went out socially. He seemed happy again, and free.

Lionel was a frequent visitor to this suite, where the brothers would sit up all night, playing the phonograph, and reminiscing.

The initial commitment under Barrymore's new contract was *The Sea Beast*, a story based on Herman Melville's *Moby Dick*. Jack himself had chosen that story, although the studio had hoped that he would first make *Don Juan*.

During the formulation of his earlier pictures Barrymore entered into each production with the same great care and industry that had possessed him during his best theatrical days. He took advantage of the privileges permitted him under the terms of his contract to see to it that his stories were superior to the child-mind tales sometimes regarded as proper amusement for motion-picture patrons. He even participated in the supervision of sets and costumes.

What he did not know at first, and what many other Hollywood invaders have to learn, if not to like, was that a motion picture never is the work of one man. It is the collaboration of many persons concerned with the writing of it, the acting in it, the direction, the photography, the editing, and the distribution. One person may be able to spoil a motion picture, and this frequently happens somewhere along the line, but it takes many persons to make the production a good one.

On the face of this system, it would seem that here is a democracy-in-little, a form of government both practical and satisfying. It would be so, no doubt, except for the same element that sometimes plagues the larger democracies—greedy, self-centered human beings.

Here, also, in the motion-picture commonwealth, there are to be found too many doubters, procrastinators, credit-grabbers, prize-seekers, vainglorious politicians, opportunists, and dunderheads.

There are also the well-intentioned artists who suddenly have come out of the worlds of their own creation—the novel, the play, the sonata—in which worlds they had been self-appointed and supreme. They now find themselves abruptly demoted to subordinate roles, as employees. They become either artistically flabby or wildly resentful.

It took some years before Barrymore became artistically flabby. The man himself stayed peculiarly and definitely himself. His indomitable spirit, wit, and great sense of self-criticism made of him a one-man Alamo. In this connection, Richard Watts, Jr. gives us perhaps the best synthesis of Jack's elements as a personality:

> In some paradoxical fashion, the very manner in which Barrymore seemed almost to revel in his disintegration convinced people who had never seen him in *Hamlet* and *The Jest* that he must have been among the giants. For even when he showed signs of physical and spiritual collapse he did not enter into any kind of ordinary decline. Everything he did was in an epic way, and, even when he appeared to be making an embarrassing clown of himself, he did so on a grand and wholesale scale, coming apart with boisterous gargantuan humor and a sardonic air of self-criticism.
>
> For, be it noted among the characteristic traits of John Barrymore was a keen and invariably witty critical sense. He could afford to laugh at the world because he could always laugh at himself. A genuine sense of humor, which is considerably rarer in this country than we sometimes think, has a dangerous way of interfering with practical achievement, but, developed in a man in hearty proportions, it can give him a wonderful savor and raciness. These John Barrymore possessed magnificently. He either succeeded or failed on a grand scale.

During the making of *The Sea Beast* Barrymore occupied what he regarded as an Olympian position. He was to be permitted, among other things, to choose his leading lady. There was, to be sure, no lady in the Melville tale of *Moby Dick*, not even a woman. The studio was somewhat alarmed over the box-office aspects of a picture that had, as its principals, Mr. Barrymore as Captain Ahab, and a mere whale. So the Warner Brothers assigned a bright and extraordinarily clever young woman, Bess Meredyth, to devise a scenario that would include a leading lady in the photoplay.

Barrymore, of course, wanted to "sit in" on the writing of the story. Fortunately, Bess Meredyth knew how to deal with this situation. She was entirely aware of Jack's great artistry and charm. She knew that he was well worth heeding in respect to suggestions as to characterization of the figures in the scenario. She also soon learned that, in regard to problems of plot and story construction, Jack had the playwriting abilities of Lefty Louie.

Bessie knew that Jack had two other amiable weaknesses: cold

boiled potatoes and deep-sea fishing. She kept a bowl of boiled potatoes in the icebox of her home on Crescent Heights Boulevard.
She encouraged him in his fishing when they went to Catalina
Island to look for locations for the shooting of the picture. These
pursuits kept him busy while Bessie was writing the script.

One evening Jack came from the studio to the Meredyth home
to announce excitedly that he not only had found a leading lady
for *The Sea Beast*, but "had laid eyes upon the most preposterously
lovely creature in all the world."

Under these circumstances a male host would have asked Jack:
"Are you sick?" As a woman, and a very lovely one, too, Miss
Meredyth inquired instantly: "What is her name?"

Barrymore didn't seem to hear the question at all. He took on a
glassy-eyed expression as he began to report what seemed to have
been a momentous experience. "She walked into the studio like a
charming child. Slender and shy and golden-haired. Never saw such
radiance. My God! I knew that she was the one I had been waiting
for. Waiting all my life, just for her."

"What is her name?" repeated Bessie.

"I thought I would drop dead on the spot," Barrymore said
dreamily. Then his manner changed. He angrily began to shout at
Miss Meredyth, as if she were objecting to the signing of his love-
light to a motion-picture contract. "By God!" he roared. "Nobody
is going to talk *me* out of making her into an actress, a great one,
too. Nobody is going to palm off some highly publicized wench on
me. To hell with all the big names. This lovely girl plays opposite
me in *The Sea Beast*, or I quit!"

"You are quite right about that, Jack," said Bessie, her tongue in
her cheek. "Don't give in on it." He nodded, as if he had won a
point. She then asked, "Did you talk it over with her father?"

"It wasn't her father," Jack said. "Her mother was with her.
Mrs. Costello, a fine but wary guardian."

"Oh," said Bessie, "is the daughter, by any chance, related to
Maurice Costello, the actor?"

"In a way," Jack said. "He's her father."

Bessie, a well-informed Hollywoodian, had heard that Helene and
Dolores Costello, the two daughters of Maurice Costello, the former
motion-picture star, recently had arrived for screen tests at the
Warner studios. They had been traveling with George White's
Scandals, as members of the chorus, when a Warner scout had seen

them in Chicago and sent their photographs to the West Coast. One of the daughters, Dolores Costello, had been signed to play the part of a maid.

"Maid parts, hell!" Jack said. "Can you imagine them casting an angel to wear a cap and apron and carry around a dinky little tray? I suppose they'd hire Lord Nelson to run a coal barge. I'm doubling her salary at once. I think I'll triple it."

Miss Meredyth restrained her understandable amazement that a little-known girl was about to become a Cinderella because of Barrymore's having chanced to see her. Still, such things did happen in Hollywood. Bessie assumed that it was Dolores who had caught Jack's eye and heart, for she was blond, and he had spoken of golden hair. Helene was darker than her sister.

"It's Dolores, I suppose?" said Bessie, to make sure. "Have you eaten? Do you want a cold potato and a glass of beer?"

He brushed aside the delicatessen part of the question. Then, as if uttering a benediction, he said, "Dolores. Her name is Dolores. And I'm going to quadruple her salary. I shall not eat nor sleep till I see her again." He paused reverently, then said, "But I'll have just one short drink to tide me over till tomorrow."

2.

So This Is Paradise

EXACTLY what was said about it in the Costello household never has been disclosed, but Jack was less than a welcome suitor in the eyes of the mother and father of the girl who now occupied his dreams.

Barrymore, playing love scenes on the motion-picture stages with Dolores, was sly enough to insist that these photographic moments be repeated more times than were at all necessary. The burning emphasis of his love managed to enhance the mood of the scenario, a result that does not always obtain, either on the stage or in the films.

Indeed, Jack himself maintained that actors in love usually play unconvincing performances opposite each other. "The trouble with impassioned wretches of the theatre," he said, "is that their pale faces and throbbing temples mislead an audience to believe that ptomaine poisoning has just set in, and that the next line will be: 'Is there a physician in the house?'"

His love-making in *The Sea Beast* refuted his own theories in respect to professional romantics. Dolores' part was not pitched in a major key, yet her actual love for Jack was so like the bright spring—and it was her own springtime of beauty and of life—that the role seemed important beyond its genuine dimensions. They won each other, and *The Sea Beast* won the love of the world.

He seemed young and he looked young, yet Jack was forty-three years old when he met Dolores. She was in her twenties. Barrymore said that it was her naturalness, her childlikeness, that appealed so strongly to his heart. She seemed to fill his need for expressing paternal as well as romantic love.

He was incredibly happy when with her, but the fact that he was expected to be secretive about the romance annoyed him. There was the technical obstacle of his marriage tie to Michael Strange. They had been legally separated but not divorced. The studio was guarding against scandalous implications being read into publicity touching upon the eminent actor and the young actress.

During the time when Jack, as Captain Ahab, was making the whaling scenes, the studio asked him to attend a party at the home of actress Marion Davies. He did not like parties, especially when he could not appear at them with Dolores, but the Warner Brothers had been so lenient with him in all other respects that when it was explained that his appearance at this costume fiesta would be helpful to the publicity of his picture, he said he would make an exception. He decided to attend the party with Mickey Neilan.

Neilan called at the Ambassador bungalow to find Jack away from home. Mickey waited for two hours, then went to the party. He saw there all the Hollywood crowned heads, in costume. Rudolph Valentino, in a *Monsieur Beaucaire* creation of powdered wig and satin breeches, seemed the foremost attraction. His only competitor, a man with a putty nose, ragged beard, and in hobo's clothing, was amusing the guests when Neilan arrived late and without Barrymore.

The tramp, after a time, became less amusing. He was trying realistically to borrow money from the guests. His stories of hardship were so gloomy that a plainclothes member of the police force, guarding the cloak-rooms, quietly drew the tramp aside to make sure that he was a bona fide member of the film colony and had been invited to the party. A group of suspicious gentlemen looked on as the detective unfroçked the hobo, who was revealed to be Mr. Barrymore.

The morning after the Davies' soirée Jack was to be at the San Pedro waterfront at seven o'clock for the shooting of scenes aboard the whaler. Six hundred "extras" had been hired for this sequence. The studio deputized an assistant director to call at Jack's hotel-bungalow at five-thirty in the morning, to see that he reach "location" in time for his day's work. It would be a needless expense to the studio if he were to be late, with so many "extras" being paid by the hour.

Barrymore was not at home when the assistant director called there. Valet Blaney said that his employer was still at the Davies' party. But when the assistant director looked for him there he had gone.

The company waited at San Pedro for Jack to appear. The production manager himself arrived on the scene at ten o'clock. He was grim, as well as a little upset in the stomach. Nothing makes a producer so ill as the sight of idle players on an active payroll.

The director was pacing the deck of the whaler, chewing the shooting-script. The photographers were studying the sun and the clouds. The "extras" were whiling away their time near the foremast. Some of them were talking among themselves, others lay stretched out upon the deck, sleeping.

Toward noon, or eight bells aboard the whaler, one of the sleepers awakened, yawned, then asked distinctly: "Well, when do we start?"

It was Barrymore, still dressed in the hobo costume worn at the party. He had come directly from the Davies' home to the whaling vessel at San Pedro, boarded the craft, then fallen asleep.

When *The Sea Beast* was completed, Barrymore began a second picture under his Warner Brothers' contract, *Don Juan*. Mary Astor, the leading lady for that photoplay, had been chosen and approved by Jack before he had met Dolores. The studio refused to make a change in its plan, although Barrymore tried to place Dolores in the cast.

Early in October of 1925, when Jack was calling on Miss Astor at her home in Temple Hill Drive, he met two persons who were to become closely associated with him during the ten best years of his Hollywood career. They were Mr. and Mrs. Henry Hotchener. The Hotcheners had retired, so to speak, to develop a real estate site north of Franklin Boulevard in Hollywood. Mrs. Hotchener, among her many other gifts, had a surpassing flair for art and architecture. She designed a group of Moorish-style houses for the Temple Park development, and her husband proceeded to build them.

Mrs. Hotchener, a native Californian, was born Marie Barnard, the daughter of Judge Allyn M. Barnard, a pioneer. She was graduated from Mills College, Oakland, and when but a girl attracted the interest of the famous Adelina Patti. The great diva heard Marie sing in San Francisco, and recommended that she study for the opera. Marie toured as soprano soloist with John Philip Sousa's band, then became a soloist with the Boston Symphony Orchestra.

She later studied music in Europe. She sang leading operatic roles, sometimes with composer Puccini conducting the orchestra, in Italian, French, and German centers. Suddenly she renounced a distinguished operatic career, declining, among other engagements, an invitation from Frau Cosima Wagner to appear at the festival at Bayreuth. The young Californian now turned her whole interest to the study of the deeper phases of philosophy, psychology, theosophy, and abnormal psychic phenomena. She attended psychotherapeutic experiments by scientists Bernheim, Liébault, and Charcot at their clinics in Nancy, and the Salpetrière in Paris.

Voyaging to India to study the ancient wisdom, Marie met Annie Besant, president of the Theosophical Society. She became Mrs. Besant's official deputy and traveling companion on world-wide journeyings. She served as editor of Annie Besant's magazine. Mrs. Besant called her "Helios," because of her brilliant, sun-like character. Helios became noted as a lecturer on the spiritual training of the personality, the ideals of the future race, the brotherhood of religions and peoples.

She married Henry Hotchener in California in 1916. The two were sympathetically unified in their outlooks and purposes. They continued their spiritual objectives during their world-wide travels, and during their subsequent years of association with Barrymore.

Henry Hotchener, a person of experience in both business and cultural pursuits, was a calm-mannered gentleman whose pleasant exterior, when scratched too rudely, disclosed steel beneath the surface. Several long-time exploiters of Barrymore's money-ignorance and carefree ways were to learn that Jack's new friend and counselor was a Marshal Foch, traveling incognito. He introduced a new word into the Barrymore lexicon, the word "no."

Hotchener had attended the College of the City of New York, then studied law at both Georgetown University and the University of Southern California. An expert court reporter as a young man, he also had served as secretary to Daniel Guggenheim, President of the American Smelting and Refining Company, and head of the vast Guggenheim family enterprises. Afterward Hotchener became general manager of a realty enterprise of Maximilian Morgenthau, uncle of the present Secretary of the Treasury.

Hotchener became deeply interested in after-death phenomena and oriental philosophy. He visited India in 1912, and there met Annie Besant and C. W. Leadbeater, authorities on these subjects. He served them both as a collaborating amanuensis.

Both Helios and Henry had lived much in India. This fact alone would explain why Barrymore, upon meeting the Hotcheners at the home of Mary Astor, at once was drawn to them. His father had been born in India, and Jack always had been interested in that land of ancient culture. Furthermore, there lay deep within his nature a poetic mysticism that only his closest friends might discern beneath the robust wildness that made up his public legend.

There were two things on Jack's mind—other than Dolores—the night he met the Hotcheners. One was India and the latest news on reincarnation. The other was a materialistic problem expressed by his question: "Hotchener, do you know anything at all about the damned income tax?"

Hotchener knew a great deal about the income tax. He volunteered to examine Jack's return, a matter into which the governmental sleuths had entered with no sense of humor whatsoever. The Bureau of Internal Revenue, it seemed, wanted something more businesslike from Taxpayer Barrymore than a series of explanations drawn from *Alice in Wonderland*.

Jack invited the Hotcheners to lunch at his Ambassador bungalow the next day. Henry found Barrymore's income tax the least garbled of the actor's business affairs. Jack didn't even know the name of the manager of the New York Bank that was receiving his money. His huge pay checks were being sent by the Warner Brothers directly to his New York attorney. His two alimony obligations and other current fixed dues were being paid out of this account. He hadn't the slightest idea as to how much money he had in the bank. He never kept statements or memoranda from business firms. When Hotchener finally had the papers forwarded from New York to California, he pointed out that Jack had more than a hundred thousand dollars in his checking-account, and was receiving no interest on this sum.

One day in March 1926, and when the income tax bogey man again was sitting at Barrymore's door, it dawned on Jack that Henry was doing an enormous service for him, free.

"Hank, for the love of God," he cried, "take over! Manage me."

3.

Such Stuff As Dreams Are Made On

BARRYMORE now decided to re-examine his life as objectively as possible, to consider thoughtfully how much happiness might still be his. He felt a need for arriving at what were for him important estimations. There was no Alchemist's Corner in which he might immure himself, so he turned his eyes to the sea as a place for meditation.

On week ends, during the making of his motion pictures in California, he had gone on occasional fishing trips off Catalina Island. He was an excellent sailor. He had greatly benefited by these brief holidays at sea.

For the first time in his life he now enjoyed financial elbow-room for the carrying into execution of his grand plans. He wanted very much to own a yacht, not as an evidence of growing wealth, nor for the sake of luxurious ease, but for the adventurous escape from a convention-bound world. Meantime he decided to charter a power boat. He would have preferred finding a seaworthy schooner, but he did not have enough time in which to take a long voyage under sail. He was to appear soon in a camera version of *Manon Lescaut*, eventually entitled *When a Man Loves*. He chartered an eighty-foot cabin cruiser from producer Hal Roach, together with its captain and a crew of five men. This was a diesel-powered craft, equipped with a launch and a dinghy for fishing. The vessel was four years old, trim and fast.

Barrymore now professed a foreboding that, were he to win a final freedom from Michael Strange by divorce, then marry Dolores, their love somehow might languish. He said he actually was afraid of marriage, believing that for him a dark spell lay upon the institution. He wished to go to some remote place to think things out, appraise himself in relation to his great new love, and at the same time decide how best to ward off the antagonism of Dolores' parents.

Jack sailed away aboard *The Gypsy* upon what he termed "a quest for myself." He steered a coastwise course for the southern tip of the Mexican peninsula of Lower California.

During this sea voyage he began a "log," to which he confided his innermost musings. Three years afterward, in 1929, he made further handwritten entries in the same ledger, when on a cruise on his own yacht, *The Mariner.* So far as is known, these two diaries are the only ones Jack ever wrote.

It was unlike him to make a personal record. And until some months after he had died no one other than the Hotcheners knew of its existence. On May 1, 1939, Barrymore designated Hotchener as his literary executor. Jack entrusted the sea log solely to him for publication, together with such other confidential documents as his manager might care to entrust to a biographer upon the actor's death.

The Hotcheners were in intimate, detailed knowledge of Barrymore's activities during the ten years after their first meeting in 1925. Hotchener himself kept a daily diary in shorthand, thus gaining a Boswellian position in respect to Jack's Hollywood sojourn. Hotchener has given us full access to these diaries and papers.

The sea log permits one to look inside Barrymore the man. It is perhaps the most important and authentic record of Barrymore's emotions that we ever shall be given. There is no hearsay about it, no outside opinions, for now the witness himself takes the stand in his own behalf.

The mood of Barrymore's sea log is one of great yearning. We find in it a variety of expression. There are sometimes heard the childlike tones of a callow serenader, and suddenly again there rise up the passional echoings of a splendid harpist. At times there come from the closely written lines such cries as seldom are voiced except in the love letters of the immortals.

The log is shot with wit and artistic observation, with a sportsman's notes showing both enthusiasm and love of adventure; but the over-all mood is one of ecstatic yearning. Barrymore was alone on the sea, tired after long-lasting confusions, yet enraptured. He wanted to take an invoice of himself and his destiny. He brought chaplets of amaranth to his soul's desire.

The first section of the handwritten log contains the voyager's thoughts and fancies from Sunday, December 27, 1925, to January 19, 1926. Dolores saw him off on *The Gypsy* at late evening from the Wilmington breakwater. He stood at the stern rail holding Clementine, the small monkey, in one arm, and waving good-by with the other. Blaney, the valet, was below deck, stowing his employer's personal belongings. The night was fair with an off-shore breeze and a bright moon.

Barrymore promised himself not to drink any hard liquor while on this voyage. He apparently wanted to have a clear head for his ponderings. He swiftly returned to his old-time activity of muscle and of brain. The sea cleansed him of the past.

On the first three pages of his sea log are to be found Barrymore's pen-and-ink sketches of the skipper and the crew members, with the captions: "Cap," "Mac," "Hill," "Harold," "Bill," and "Bruno." A small sketch of a cat accompanies the first entry in the log. The cat, it is obvious from the text, was his symbol for Dolores. He had various nicknames for her, such as "Small Cat," "Catkiwee," "Winkie," and "Egg." The first entry, rather schoolboyish to be sure, is cast in the third person, under the dateline of Sunday, December 27, 1925:

> Got away ten p.m. from Wilmington. "Winkie" saw him off. Only she is the very dearest smallest cat, and he is crazy about her, and hopes and truly believes they will be the very happiest things, if they have *any* sense at all! Wrote that small thing the longest letter, and went to bed after looking at its own curled up picture, and after praying that they both may be happy together for always.

The Gypsy put in at San Diego early next morning. Jack was up at six-thirty, he writes, then went ashore for a weather report and to obtain necessary letters to Mexican officials. He received,

while ashore, a telegram from Dolores, which made him extremely
happy. He shopped, motored across the Mexican border to Tia Juana,
where he obtained a shooting-permit. Of this dust-ridden Mexican
town, he writes in the diary:

> Amused by Tia Juana. Looks like movie mining camp when
> King Baggot was a devastating juvenile. Had glass of honest-
> to-God-beer. Liked it, but more than ever convinced wagon
> is proper plateau from which to view the surrounding world!!
> Hope to God it keeps up! Thought of telephoning "Wink,"
> but realized how mean that damned instrument is, and that she
> would probably be surrounded and unable to talk as she would
> wish. Cap got harpoon and small spear-heads for what might
> turn up. Got away about two p.m., made Ensenada eight-
> thirty p.m. Boat going finely, weather perfect, wonderful sun-
> sets. Everything divine. Wrote "small egg" long letter, last
> for some time. Went to bed nine o'clock.

The next morning he was awakened by the Ensenada port-doctor
and a customs-house official. Jack writes that the only formalities,
other than the recording of the numbers on the guns, consisted of
his giving the officials each a pack of cigarettes and a drink. He then
went ashore with Cap, and says:

> Posted a letter and sent long wire to "Wink," which I
> hope to Christ she gets! Sat in the sun, while the officials
> mañanad themselves on the most costive typewriters I have
> ever heard. Went to American Consulate. Person in charge
> pleasant and reminiscent of a vital poultice! Met a Capt. Han-
> sen who is returning to Cape St. Lucas. Bought seven cases of
> beer for crew. Came aboard, got away from charming-looking
> harbor, about one-thirty. Headed for Leammon's lagoon, as
> neard St. Quentin no good for fishing. Passed Island of Todos
> Santos two-thirty p.m. Coastline Lower California extremely
> beautiful, wonderful sunset, marvelous moon. Wishing ter-
> ribly "small cat" was along. Definitely made up mind she will
> be some day soon. Best plan to meet South probably.
> Early to bed reading *Jack Ballister's Fortunes*, Howard Pyle.
> Realized what an unusually excessive objectivist he is in his
> writings. Presume this is inevitable, as his genius is that of the
> illustrator.
> Always think of the dear "small egg" last thing before going
> to sleep.

He says he lay in his cabin late on a cloudy, rainy morning, with the cruiser keeled over in the wind, and bound for Cerros Island. The swell was too heavy for the boat to make Leammon's Lagoon. He finally awakened, examined his guns, then studied Cerros Island through his binoculars. The craft dropped anchor at three-thirty in the afternoon off-shore near some springs.

During his romance with Dolores, Jack had made another of his remarkable "discoveries." This time it was the brilliant planet Venus. Dolores and he knew it as "our star." It seemed to them as if they owned it, as, indeed, they did. He writes of their "star" under the dateline of December 30:

> Came back to boat as our own star came out in beautiful absinthe-green sky, piled up with purple clouds. Wish that "small thing" was here in her tiny white pants, but she will be. Very glad came down this time for future trips.
>
> Sailors caught ten pound "bonito," trolling, and several sand-bass off side of boat at anchor. Dived, talked with Cap for about an hour and went out on deck. Glorious night, sky cloudless, with thousands of very bright stars, moon full and brilliant, shining on still, black, gleaming water, like lacquer.
>
> Read delightful book, *History of English Literature* by Edward Albert, of Watson's College, Edinburgh, a most engagingly written textbook, a miracle of concise compiling.
>
> Found two enchanting things in it, that fluttered "Winkie's" wing through my mind—the last two lines of one of the speeches in Marlowe's *Dr. Faustus* about Helen of Troy:

> > *Oh, thou art fairer than the evening air,*
> > *Clad in the beauty of a thousand stars.*

And an adorable lyric of Ben Jonson's:

> *Have you seen but a bright lillie grow,*
> > *Before rude hands have touch'd it?*
> *Have you mark'd but the fall of the snow*
> > *Before the soyle hath smutch'd it?*
> *Have you felt the wooll of the bever?*
> > *Or swan's down ever?*
> *Or have smelt the bud of the brier?*
> > *Or the nard on the fire?*
> *Or have tasted the bag of the bee?*
> *O so white! O so soft! O so sweet is she!*

It is called *The Triumph* and is so exquisite it *must* have been made into a song. I must get it, and Winkie can sing it to me, like a small fat blue robin!

The moon is looking down from a mackerel sky that has just come up, meaning rain tomorrow. It doesn't seem to matter. It is so peaceful, this life, and every pore of this aged and angular person is drinking in rest, thank Heaven! and I am fanned by dear thoughts of her, so am not lonely. Only I shall be glad when Clementine can get out on deck in the sun.

She is at present "enjoying" the dubious freedom of the well-appointed bathroom. She gets more affectionate and companionable all the time, and has developed a passion for pomegranates which is going to be difficult to allay, I imagine, on this particular trip!

The clock has just struck eleven, which is ungodly dissipation. I meant to go to bed much earlier, but the habits of a crimson past must be *bent* gradually, I suppose! Only he kisses his dear small "Wink" good night and closes this very journal for the day.

It seems a little odd keeping it. I know *one* reason why I do. The others are vague!!

During the last hours of the year 1925 Jack wrote variously of sports, of birds, and of the beautiful sky:

Had marvelous day. *Gypsy* went into Leammon's Lagoon. Got stuck in shallow water. Lagoon is as yet very imperfectly charted. Missed channel, bright sun making it impossible to see any variation in water. Let her "lay," which she proceeded to do—on her side—as the tide went out, till deck was finally at an angle of forty-five degrees.

As Cap went back for skiff to cross deep wide stream, sat down in reeds and waited for him and realized what a heavenly time I was having. As I lay there, big blue and big gray herons circled over my head, terribly close, with their strange cry, and many curlews with their fantastically long beaks, and snipe without end.

The sky was wonderful, bright-chocolate color and bright-silver, with a long low rainbow, distinct and beautiful, on one side; on the other, brilliant cerulean blue, with heavy spattered clouds, through which shone bright rays onto the horizon, like celestial searchlights.

Now Barrymore gives us his views on the subject of holidays. He closes the entry with a sudden, characteristic departure from the dramatic, as if he had just finished acting a scene. The anti-climax is so amusing that we take the liberty of italicizing the last sentence.

Got home at dusk, to find big boat absolutely on her *ear*. Walking the deck was like an Alpine ascension. Speared a shark on the way in while walking in shallow water. Terribly hungry, ate dinner of lamb sandwiches and coffee, as Chef couldn't get into icebox on account of list. Sitting on floor, using wing of table off which to eat. Cleaned guns, talked to Captain till eleven-thirty p.m., then went to bed after playing phonograph and hearing radio. Got Warner Bros. station on range, with preposterous chance of getting something out of the air from "Winkie." Thought of her so hard on this New Year.

I must say sailors are amazing, and their point of view is peculiarly akin to my own. New Year's Eve meant nothing whatever in their lives. Any more than it does in mine. I have always been subconsciously embarrassed by the "function" of Christmas and New Years. The spirit of "loving kindness," that is presumed to come to a head like a boil once a year, when it has been magnificently concealed up to that moment!

The fact is that I hope to enter something different than what hitherto has come into my own life. And the hope that I can bring something different into the life of another human being makes this particular "New Year" significant; but it would be the same in the middle of the year, or in the middle of eternity —if that can have a middle!

I wonder if there is any more pathetic evidence of the fatuity and childishness of mankind than the "New Year's Resolution"? The definite point people have elected to start over and over again, to inhibit or "arrange" their innate desires and weaknesses. Only he will go to his bed with his nose pressed tightly in his dear baby's neck, which is more fragrant than philosophy!! *Must get up for geese at 3:30 a.m.*

The New Year found a happy man writing and sketching in his sea log after a day of healthful sport. As can be seen in his entries, he rose early each morning, and life was good, and the heart full.

Friday, January first, 1926: Got off at four a.m. in dinghy, trailing skiff. Moon and stars still up. Lovely time of morning. Landed with skiff. Dawn came up beautifully about five. Couldn't get near geese. Struck by thought, as sat in water, abortively stalking these shy and elusive bloody birds, how God-givenly sensible it was to not have brought any other man along. It works out perfectly this way, as it rings the Cap *in* on the sport, and keeps his interest alive, and creates a similar objective between the man running the boat and the man he's running it for!

Came back to *Gypsy* at ten a.m. Got stuck again about one p.m. Nothing to do but wait till tide gets us off. Saw huge turtle, went out and speared it, proving efficacy of small harpoon-like device. Pierced shell and held turtle for twenty minutes while getting it to boat.

Made some very good shots with Mauser 30. Crazy about her, very powerful, beautiful mechanism. German sailors on board handled it like Pygmalion did Galatea, before she came to! Shot some ducks from boat. Took dinghy after geese. Nothing doing. Sky dark with them, but too far away.

Great possibilities in this lagoon. Coming here again, spend more time, build blinds, etc. Beautiful electric storm came up. Sky wonderful, looked like painting by Lucifer. Crabbed, spending night on island, as intended doing. Bed awfully early.

He writes in his diary frequently of sleeping well, as if that were some phenomenon. He usually did sleep well when at sea. On land, where he so often neglected slumber, it was his strange practice to close all the windows and doors and draw the curtains when he finally had gone to his bedroom. How he managed to keep healthy with no fresh air in the room seemed amazing.

In contrast to his land habits, he slept when on the water with the ports wide open and the sea breeze blowing across his bunk. Perhaps, at sea, there was no psychological need for him to shut out the world.

After another discussion of his indulgence in sleep at sea, he continues with his entry of January 2:

Getting to look more brown and human. Not going to shave till Cape St. Lucas, much to delight of Captain, who won't either!!! Clementine on deck every day now, crazy about it. Took some motion pictures of her with new camera.

Thought how heavenly it would be if "Wink" was along. Have an idea she might like putting on rubber boots and crawling after game. If that ever comes off, and it *must*, it will be simply wonderful and unforgettable and eminently *sane!*

He writes that he had decided to leave for Turtle Bay after seeing a school of whales spouting and sounding in the neck of the lagoon. He wanted to follow them out to deep water. His motion picture, *The Sea Beast*, had turned his interest toward whales, and it was his ambition to harpoon one. In fact, he had tried to persuade the studio to permit him, during the filming of the picture, to have a duel with a real whale instead of with the massive rubber fac-simile used in the production.

The studio heads had two reasons for denying him this bit of realism: it would have been unduly expensive to locate a real whale, and, even if that were practical, they did not wish to endanger the life of a box-office attraction. As it was, Barrymore fre-quently took risks during his motion-picture career. He refused to permit "doubles," or stunt-actors, to take his place in action scenes. He had several deep scars and evidences of old fractures because of this adventurous quirk.

From the deck of *The Gypsy* Barrymore shot at one of the whales, a huge, black bull, but missed. He added:

> Will harpoon one if possible at Magdalena Bay. January is best season, and tackle should be there. Came very close to boat, most exciting looking beasts.

Dolores occupied his mind, even when whales attracted his im-mediate vision. This is indicated by a paragraph which follows a description of the playing of the sea monsters.

> Hope there is a wire from "Winkface" at Magdalena Bay. I wonder if I made it clear enough to her surely to wire there? We'll see!!!!

The Gypsy nosed into Turtle Bay at about nine o'clock in the evening. Barrymore found the bay a beautiful body of water. He inspected some bass that his valet Blaney had caught with a hand line, then went to his cabin to write:

> Gorgeous night, never saw our own star so bright, made sil-ver track on water, just like moon. Played radio till about eleven, went to bed.

The next morning, Sunday, Barrymore went on deck to find several Mexicans aboard. In years to come he would have a great affection for the Mexican people and they for him. Long before the time when it became both fashionable and highly expedient to praise these neighbors to the south, Barrymore grew to love them for themselves, to admire their native generosity, and to respect their pride. He writes of his first contact with them:

Several Mexicans on deck, simple, smiling folk. The more I see of these people, the better I like them. They gave Cap huge sackful of crawfish for nothing, and cut up turtles. Interesting operation; watched it so I could do it myself on trip with "small egg."

The Gypsy got under weigh, bound for Magdalena, shortly after noon with a brisk wind and a small quartering sea. The cabin cruiser that same afternoon dropped anchor near the coastline, after some houses were sighted. Barrymore went ashore in the dinghy to get some wine with which to cook the turtle. But the cantina was closed. He does not name the small coast colony, but writes of it:

Funny little community of about six huts; must be gay as the devil as a steady diet! Took moving pictures of pelicans, tame as possible, did everything but come on board to get fish. Pulled out about two p.m. Dined on turtle, fried, tasted like rabbit, very good.

At night pretty rough, about a hundred small squid flew on deck, some going as high as pilot-house. One I was holding, small one, bit me hard. Can imagine what honest to God devil-fish must be like. Largest about four or five inches. Tried to keep them alive for movie-camera, but they died in bucket.

The vessel had an all-night and all-day run, putting into Magdalena Bay late the next afternoon. Here was another small community. The diary continues:

Saw whale being cut up beside big boat. Officials out of Gilbert and Sullivan came on board. Usual drink, bunk, and cigars. Left like two Spanish grandees in preposterous little rowboat with two large flags.

Went ashore to wireless. No message from "Wink." Disappointed, but blame it on mean weather conditions, or on difficulty she might have had in sending it. Feel strangely secure about that dear own "egg." Sent her wireless and wrote letter at night. Wireless government operator on board, *bel-homme*, with oily black mustache and meticulous English, very exhausting to listen to, as every word was like having a child, but he seemed so pleased with it one had to let him go!

Reading Pepys *Diary*. Not particularly pleased with it, although expected to be. Ran across delightful line in another book, a quotation from Renan. He says: "The man who has time enough to keep a private diary has never understood the immensity of the Universe." Am inclined to agree with him, except in special instances!

The devastating Mexican wireless operator, with the military hat, said that on the night of December thirty-first there was a dance, a fiesta at the school-house, at which thirty "charming girls" participated. I'd love to have seen them! There are about eighteen houses, but the owners do what they can to help the census, one lady having twenty sons! One would like to know the husband's point of view, if he has any left?! Bed early, nine o'clock.

Jack hired a guide, took him on board and sailed some twenty miles farther down the coast, where they went deer stalking. Jack said that his gun was "tricky as the devil, and so sensitive it explodes like Alice Ben Bolt if one *coughs* at it."

The cruiser got under weigh in the afternoon, bound for Cape St. Lucas. Jack became a book critic for the night:

Read book by one Ronald Firbank of whom I have never heard. Got it in hectic quest for "reading matter" day before leaving Los Angeles. It is called *The Flower beneath the Foot*, and has as a frontispiece a portrait sophomorically done after the archaic manner of St. Laura. The first couple of lines, when judged by the sort of railway-station perusal one inflicts on a volume in a book-shop, with a taxi cab and its mounting clock waiting outside, seemed amusing if ultra-sophisticated. But I was completely unprepared for the epicene riot, the super-civilized, arrant merry-go-round of all-around-sportingness, this Beardsleyesque duck indulges in! Some of it genuinely funny, but the whole book becomes illuminating as to the casual and apparently accepted method of treating the modern point of view by, I should imagine, a virtuoso! Orange taffeta dressing-gown, Lido, Taormina—the whole works!

It makes one feel blazingly and happily relaxed in the atmosphere of normality—fish, guns, California, et al.—after the pale, liver-colored but pungent memories of Paris, Venice, God knows when, Deauville, Chamonix . . . when one in the desperation of loneliness climbed Mt. Blanc, with a taciturn and preposterous little person, whose passion was mountain peaks, which he collected with his large nose pointed consistently to the ground, the rocks, and the snow; till the summit, when, after a short rest, he went down again the same way! Amazing! Exhausted as I was, and bewildered by my own trance-like pilgrimage, with an aspirin tablet rattling 'round in my stomach, and nothing else, I could still realize the beauty of a dimension that I was never to see again, and knew it!

But this small, archaic, black-avised ass, with his Alpine button for which he risked his amoeba-like life, scaled one blazing pinnacle of beauty after another, where the sun rises underneath one and casts gigantic shadows of celestial purple up over the eye-splitting brilliance of the snow, like giant diamonds gone mad, or on a bat with the spectrum!

Reading that exotic pustule of a book, on this open swinging sea, brought back the pathetic jackass-years of absurdity in Europe, of my trying to make a life with B. or her with me! This West of hicks and sunsets, if properly used, may be a spiritual bath that will mean never living against one's own center again!

Barrymore was up early the next day, looking at the Cape St. Lucas coastline. He took photographs of it and of the lighthouse, which he said looked "like a single, inconsequential hair on the jagged scalp of infinity!"

The arrival of the officials after the boat lay at anchor in the little roadstead was referred to by Jack as the "advent of the Bab Ballad outfit" from San José del Cabo. He supplied them with tequilla and other "absurdities." He continues:

Went on shore in extraordinary primitive dugout boat "manned" by same type of childish opera bouffe crew as have already encountered. Entirely unprepared for positive enchantment of place itself. Rode official's horse. Buttercup-colored, like D'Artagnan's, with large retention of early beauty. In the town itself one saw the most decorative, provocative, enchanting little damned horses I have ever looked at, bred here.

Bowled over completely by town itself and everything to do with it. All of which is possibly affected by the fact that there was a wireless from my beloved "Cat." Perfectly amazing what a difference it made. Must be horribly young somewhere inside. Really unbelievable reaction, having been thinking *so* much about her, and if I would hear from her or not. Went about town with young American in the tomato-canning business, met in wireless office.

Slipped the Governor-General in charge two bucks, which he deprecated, but *took,* to be sure to get dear "Wink's" telegrams.

George Tomato, on hearing my name, after having asked it point-blank, slightly impressed although greatly bewildered by my peculiar exterior—khaki pants full of old fish and older gravy, and Nat Wills beard—took me to his house and introduced me to his wife, a native of the place itself.

Of his visits to the little Mexican town, he writes in his sea log:

Can imagine nothing more divine than being here with "Wink." She would adore it. There was a dance tonight, which, needless to say, we passed up! Mounted Rosinante, and ambled at peace with the world toward the setting sun and the beach.

Our purchases: five boxes of fresh tomatoes, an indigenous cheese, some jerked venison, and several bottles of oddities to drink, on pack-mules trailing behind.

Finally arrived at beach. Loaded purchases, assisted by jumblese crew in dug-out boat. Went back to Cape St. Lucas. Dined ashore with Captain. Paid "visit" to house of his Mexican friends, presided over by piratical patriarch of eighty, husky, brown, huge white-haired old beggar, with an eye like a gimlet, great charm and no more (I find it difficult to spell "conscience!") conscience (?) than a snake has hips! Large, high, bare room; three daughters of varying ages, typical lasses of the *Estados Unidos Mexicanos!* Pale, liver-colored, mauve-powdered, stealthily poised, with an occasional provocative glimpse of gold tooth. Beer and "Damiana" wine. Sat and rocked, not understanding a word of the glutinous and occasionally musical Spanish.

On board and in bed about ten. Read "Winkie's" telegram again—copy of which I got at house—and put in my pocket like a squirrel does a nut!

On January 7 Jack wrote in his diary that if Dolores had been with him "this would have been the most utterly and entirely glorious day I have ever had in my life. As it is," he continued, "with the thought of her coming like a scented wind every now and again through the stark and baking sunlight, and the diamond-like Pandora's casket of a sea, that might and does conceal almost anything, it is the most divine day I think I've ever had anyway."

He writes at some length of his deep-sea fishing, and has numerous comments of a technical nature. He was thrilled by many exciting strikes, but the sharks usually got his fish. On the way back to the boat from the early morning's sport, the launch came among a school of whales, of which he writes:

We had brought, by the Grace of God, the moving-picture camera. Directly in front of us whales were spouting, many of them, and showing occasional black domes above the water. At last, not over a hundred yards in front of us, a whale shot up straight out of the sea, and flopped on its back with a gigantic burst of spray—then right back to wave its long black, shiny flukes in the air. Over and over again this happened as we crept nearer, if a launch can creep! The Cap taking pictures all the time. In the midst of this performance, which seemed especially staged for us, wham! I got the biggest strike I've ever had in my life—*fishing!* It was like a beatific three-ringed circus on the most marvelous day. I'll never forget it.

The artist in him responded to the panorama of rocks and sea:

The cove we are anchored in is peaceful and silent, with strange, fantastic, jagged rocks rearing out of the sea like gnomes' castles, one sinuous, slender one, like a cyclops' forefinger, with a pelican's nest perched rakishly on the top of it. The very end of California, bleak and beautiful, like a swordpoint breaking through the scabbard of the hills in back.

The diarist suddenly checked his poetic gallop with a Barry-morean halter of self-criticism to remark:

Nota bene! As an evidence that I am getting either very pure or very dull, I forgot entirely to remark that the whales mentioned were in amorous dalliance when photographed (if anything so enviably and titanically active comes under the head of dalliance!) but be that as it may, we eavesdropped, and I trust, for the stimulus of one's old age, recorded the largest mammals *in flagrante delicto!* A memorable day!

On Friday, January 8, there is this brief exuberance:

O day of days! O song of songs! O Jesus, Mary and Joseph, and all points going south! Today I caught my first unbelievable Marlin swordfish, landing him in thirty minutes. Weight one hundred and eighty-five pounds. Seven and one-half feet long, seventeen inches deep, measured properly.

He sketched this fish and others of his acquaintance. His diary also contains drawings of various tackles used by him during his catches. He described a dolphin, as an artist might see it, in terms of color and drama:

The most beautiful sea-denizen that swims, I imagine, bright gold, silver, Prussian blue. Looks like an iridescent mermaid in the water, and like some fallen angel when it gets in the boat. Color fades terribly quickly.

The Barrymore log, after numerous entries concerned with deep-sea fishing and descriptions of enjoyable visits ashore, now suddenly sounds a cry so poignantly lyrical as to leave no doubt of the man's soul-hunger, his need of a great and abiding love. There is a relatively large blank space left on the page for a sketch that never was drawn. Perhaps he could not make one that could match his emotions of the night. The entry itself is set apart, as if to sanctify it, or to emphasize an apostrophe to his and Dolores' star.

Early to bed, looking at the billions of stars that make the strange soft black sky look almost over-dressed to anyone who has had the damnable misfortune to have lived in sophisticated communities. Every evening I look at the fat, lovely, healthy, ever-young, ever-bright, ever-poised beacon of a star that is the symbol of "Winkie's" and my life together, and, like the Angelus, say a gay, lifting, happy, husky, tiny spout of a prayer to it. It is as if the bottom of my soul, that has had so damned much happen above it, were stirring awake and saying, "Hello," like a child at something.

What in the name of God I have been doing in this maelstrom of fourteen years I cannot imagine. It has been like some strange form of bombastic levitation. I seem finally to have been permitted to be loosened, and light on the sand, instead of on a spike! like Sindbad dropped from the Roc!

I haven't had sufficient rest yet, *surcease*, as it were, to know quite what the Hell it's all about. That, I imagine will come, now that my "Plantagenet nose," as Mrs. Pat Campbell called it, isn't at some whirling grindstone, furiously working inwards, backwards, and counter-clockwise by some absurdity of my own. And I can peacefully *sweat* or get cold in some normal ether, instead of in the radiations of my own fevers! *brain*-fevers, coming from concentrating all my undeniably great potential energies upon some figment, self-astigmatized, through no fault, God knows, of the object in view.

Perhaps in time, as by the grace of God I am settled in my *labors*, I will again become a human being, and clasp hands, and amalgamate myself into the person I *was—cum* the experience and bus accidents—fourteen or fifteen years ago.

Maybe some lobsters have escaped from the lobster-pot with scratches that heal, with their actual organs unimpaired! Impervious or crustacean, I don't know which, but something,

something terribly young, terribly strong and vital, and fairly lost as yet, is inside. It is looking at and snorting tiny, whimsical, and frightfully needful exhortations to that big evening star, that I've never noticed before till this time in my life! After August the twelfth—some time after, really! It only seemed to start to get big, not so very long ago!

4.

At Hamlet's Hideaway

BARRYMORE'S sea log finds him in excellent spirits the day after he had inveighed against the "maelstrom," the fourteen years of his two marriages. Perhaps, having set down a synthesis of his past confusions of heart and mind, he gained a degree of self-absolution.

He now writes as though he were breathing more freely, seeing more clearly, partaking more joyously of the passing moment than ever before.

He has preposterous daydreams, which he records as simple realities. Among them was a plan to purchase the craggy tip of the Lower California peninsula, and build thereon a "strange, castle-like place on the highest rock." He sketches this fabulous eyrie on a full page of the diary, in the manner of Doré, with soaring bridges and towers against the wide sky. He writes of it with a self-assurance that might stagger anyone unfamiliar with his capacity to dream:

It would be a perfectly feasible feat in engineering, I imagine, and would most certainly invest existence with a blessed isolation that not even Wrigley could impair! The sun would rise on one side of one, be in front all day, and set on the other side without one's having to turn around at all! And directly below would be jumping all the most worthwhile fish in the sea; and in the back, low rows of mountains, green and mauve, and the cup-like valley below, and the big circling eagles, if they *are* eagles. I think they must be. They have gay, yet sinister, crested heads; and above one, out to sea, hundreds of beautiful things called "Marlin Spikes" that fly like monoplanes in squadrons high in the air.

After he had had lunch ashore, overlooking "the most buyable cove in all this world," he wandered about the village, which he describes:

> A heavenly little community, filled with sunlight, low, inconsequential houses, "lowing kine," friendly dogs, and children, dressed alike—the dogs and the children—something round the neck principally! Things to eat drying in the sun. Fascinating cheese machines. Little pigs and big pigs peering casually from the front doors. A steer's head being barbecued in the earth, one or two of the same tiny patrician ponies, with beautiful arrangements of leather on perfect saddles. The horses are always better dressed than the people.

He held fast to his intention not to drink any whisky, but thought he might risk sampling some "wine of the country from an amazing bottle, a Cervantes five-gallon receptacle." He sketched this on a diary page, and wrote that the wine "had a primitive taste, like port and claret, mixed with a not unpleasant nuance of *hide* about it, like *Yerbe Mate* has." He bought four deerskins, one of them all white:

> The lovely white one is for "Winkie." It looks like her somehow. "O! so white, O! so soft, O! so sweet is she!" She can have some tiny moccasins made out of it, and gloves, and maybe a charming little waistcoat with little brass buttons!

He decided to stay at the cantina until time to go out of doors to see his and Dolores' star rising in the twilight, in "a green sky with a lovely, sullen, dusky horizon, like an angry Cuban debutante, umber and black roses." He returned to the cantina to sketch a full-length figure of a Mexican with a huge sombrero, a machete blade, serape and other accouterments. He captioned this drawing: "Undulating Louis, the Human Snake." Jack writes of this fellow:

> The proportions of the machete on the gentleman's [undulating Louie's] right buttock are correct in this accompanying sketch. It is that which first drew my attention to him. It appears on inquiry that he needs one that size "in the Hills!" I also liked the little gadget hanging down back of his chapeau. The blanket slung over his shoulder was half vermilion and emerald-green. When he rides, it is put back of the saddle over

the haunches of the pony and is very smart. The shirt he had on was entirely incredible, a vivid, bluish, excessively hot *purple*—hot and thick. When the sun hit it, it jarred the landscape like a seismic disturbance. His neck-handkerchief, by some oversight, was neutral; but the *pièce de résistance* of his façade for futurism—or for honest to God painting, if it comes to that—was that his hair and sprouting beard were violent orange red! Next to his brownish green skin, and with rather pale eyes, he would have been terrific to paint as Sigismondo Malatesta.

While I was sitting there in the cool, soul-resting, diffused light that seems peculiarly the property of bars, watching one set of extraordinary banditti playing pool at a tiny table and another set playing stud-poker for cigarettes as chips, two peacocks, lovely ones, wandered in through the door, walked sedately about, secure in their beauty, like movie stars, and wandered out again!

That Sunday afternoon as he sat with the five-gallon bottle and his sketch book in the cantina his eye was alert for local characters:

The Piratical Patriarch came in with a square, iron-clamped box full of silver, which he placed back of the bar and permitted drinks to be bought him! He really is an extraordinary old duck. His native charm would be in no way diminished while he was removing one's right eye!! He called for *"musica,"* as I was a new guest that must be clamped by every attention onto his clientele. A slightly wheezy gramophone played "I'm tired of everything *but* yew," and "Pal of my childhood days," which reminded me of my "Winkie," and the last shots of *The Sea Beast*, and I wished so that "Cat" was sitting on my lap like a sailor's sweetheart in that very bar, hearing those funny tunes, listening to the click of the pool-balls, the clack of the poker players, and that redheaded guy's shirt. And looking at the peacocks strutting about, throwing off marvelous reflections when the sun hit them.

I declined the Patriarch's invitation to join the family circle, which were seated just across the sward (there is no street here—perhaps that is why it's so delightful), and wandered out with my deerskins into the gathering twilight.

The Cap, who was planted midst a bevy of exotic and slightly vintage beauties, offered to accompany me, but I said I didn't need him. I wanted to be alone anyway.

Our own, the big star, I believe it is Venus, was out in the green sky, and I thought how much I loved being alone, and how happy I was that way. It's probably a reaction from the sense of freedom I feel always now. I wondered what "Winkie" did with her own self that very day, it being Sunday, as I sat on the beach *and* the deerskins in the twilight waiting for the skiff to take me back to the boat.

He says that he had a lazy charming day on Monday, January 11, doing little of anything other than making entries and sketching in the sea log. Clementine assisted him, he playfully suggests, in the writing:

Clementine put her long, little, black, leathery forefinger in the ink and showed me how to write! I'm afraid it will take her some time. She is at the moment flirting with me shamelessly from the bathtub spigots where she is tied for the night.

As I am blissfully in bed after a lazy day in the sun, as I write this at seven p.m., the bathroom door is open to keep her company. She is leaping about, " 'avink a rare romp!" as Blaney would say, occasionally pausing to stand on her head to look roguishly between her hind legs with her tail straight up in the air! She is far more charming than anyone I know, except "Wink." There is something about them that is vaguely alike. The reassuring thing about Clementine is that one knows *definitely* that she is fond of one, as she proves it so extraordinarily and unequivocally! She clutches one with her little black hands and buries her little white soft nose like a pussy-willow in one's neck and won't let go.

It is too divine being in bed tonight seemingly a million miles away from everything, at seven p.m., thrice blessedly alone. There is a large fat first edition of Boswell's *Life of Johnson* next to me on the bed in the original binding with little urns on the cover (absurdly typical of the period) on which is resting an open can of tobacco and a fishing-hook. While outside, through the porthole, there is heard the intermittent lap of the waves on the beach, like lace in the utter stillness, punctuated by little happy grunts from Clementine, who is going to sleep with her finger in her mouth.

He was eating, sleeping, and exercising with regularity, proof of itself that Barrymore was a "new man." He seldom had done any one of these three healthful ritualisms for long at a time, else he probably would have lived to be one hundred and ten years old. Some days he fished early and late, as on January 12, of which,

following an expert's discussion of lures and other tackle suitable
for Mexican waters, he writes:

> Had gargantuan luncheon, as did Clementine, who was on
> my right. It's a wonder we didn't both bust. We fell into a
> heavy slumber afterwards. Went out again later about four,
> took some movies and photographs with Graflex of these mar-
> velous rocks, that are unforgettable in their stark, immediate
> beauty.
>
> Put out a lure with no particular ambition or intention, more
> occupied in watching a Fifth Symphony sunset of blood and
> amber, with gigantic rays bursting up fanlike almost to the
> middle of the sky. If Lucifer fell into the sea when he was
> bounced by the Regular Party Machine, the sea must have
> looked very much as it did tonight!
>
> Got a mammoth strike rounding the rocks on the way home.
> Played him in the dusk, but he tore loose the jig I was using, a
> makeshift combination of rags and feathers, that thank God I
> lost in a few minutes. I should have known better than troll
> again at that hour; but the Cap, who is jejune, said, in the voice
> the Pudding used to Alice, "Go ahead." So against my better
> judgment I did, and, Wham! almost at once, almost to a cer-
> tainty a shark, and at that hour. I played the bastard till seven
> o'clock and cut him loose when I felt the double line on the
> reel, particularly as there were hints from the gallant Captain,
> whose soul at the moment was with a succulent dish called
> *Chepine*, a fish-chowder one of the sailors made for supper to-
> night.

Barrymore had let his beard grow, but the Captain, he points out,
had gone back on his promise not to shave. The reason for the skipper's fastidiousness, Jack thought, was that the boat was in a port
where there were several señoritas.

Barrymore speculated upon the hold the sea has on some men,
writing in the diary:

> "Bruno," one of the crew, has made the most magnificent
> line-dryer which we needed badly. I gave him a dollar and a
> half in real money. He will probably get boiled on it. I was
> thinking what a terribly odd life a sailor has anyway, a life
> divided into four-hour "watches," occasional shore-leave, when
> they get a bun which is quickly cured, and other things that
> aren't. Perhaps it is something in the actual element itself that
> lassoes certain natives and never lets them go. It is pretty

damned attractive and mysterious and terrifying at that, and I presume it's feminine.

There is a sketch of a cat in the margin of a page, an indication that Dolores was much on his mind. On the next page he has a drawing of the cook, Mac, of whom he says:

> Mac is the tallest person I've almost ever seen, strangely reminiscent of *Long John Silver's* younger brother, with a dash of *Noah Claypole!* Incidentally he is an *excellent* cook. He drapes his slim and sinuous person, half in the galley and half in the "saloon," while I eat. We talk about food, and various matters, some approaching profundity, some not coming within a mile of it! He is a cheery and equable elongation, pallid, chinless, and very nice indeed. He started to grow a mustache but thought better of it, why, I cannot imagine!—has gone ashore for the evening, (I have never written a sentence more like Henry James!) leaving me—(Good God I'm still *at it*) with a glass of anisette, *excellent* too, at my elbow, and this manuscript! which I hope I am writing in English.
>
> One of the sailors caught a diverting looking fish today over the side. It has a bright yellow tail and spots all over it. It is called the Quarantine Fish. I think it is a dramatic critic, except that it has no horn glasses.

Now Barrymore decided to lift anchor and proceed to San José del Cabo. He was becoming restless with no word from Dolores. It occurred to him to return to Hollywood by way of train, to be with her sooner than if he went by boat.

He writes that he also missed Lionel. He had declared in a previous entry how glad he was that no other man was with him on the voyage. But now he reverses that stand:

> Must wire Lionel. Have been thinking about him a lot. Wish he could have come. He is the only person except "Winkie" I would love to be here.

When *The Gypsy* arrived at San José del Cabo, Barrymore shaved off his beard and put on a necktie:

> It is positively Mexican in its color composition. Yellow, blue, and red in broad stripes. It is only a coat of tan and a general rakish demeanor supplemented by a yachting cap, à la Admiral Webb! that enables one to get away with it! Felt horribly respectable and uncomfortable and like a character part!

He "dressed up" in honor of Dolores. If there were a telegram or a letter from her awaiting him at the port, he wanted to make the day seem a gala one. That night he wrote in the sea log:

Got in the dug-out and "beached" through the surf. Went to the town elegantly in a Ford, with a gear shift that enables it to go through the sand, although I always thought they could go through plague, fire, sudden death, lava, and New Jersey, anyway! Went to the Post Office on a chance—a fatuous one I imagined—of getting letters from "Wink."

A chinless, ocher misanthrope was looking out from the "bars," painted like iron and made of wood. It was like a movie set, as are all the "Executive" offices, to keep the *"Publico"* in its proper bloody place, and add to the dignity and significance of the Civic Authority, eight pesos a year, all the year round.

On being questioned by Cap in varicose Spanish as to whether there were any letters for Señor Juan Barreemorey? the gamboge dental-filling unraveled himself like an anemic bloodworm, doddered to a pile of fusty envelopes, came back swooning, shook his head, then collapsed. Suddenly he came out of his coma with a galvanic spasm, and, clutching a piece of gray toilet paper, and a pencil that looked like Marshall P. Wilder's thumb, he shoved them toward us and loosed a series of guttural sighs, like a wet bladder being stepped on by a horse. He evidently said in Spanish: "Give it to me straight, I'm sinking."

I wrote my name, more legibly than I've ever done it before in my life. He got up again with a quick, or fairly quick glance of bilious resentment, and weaved toward another pile of mail, which he went through like a souse goes through the Stations of the Cross. He pulled two letters out of it, like Herman the Great did rabbits out of a cuspidor.

I damn near dropped dead! There were actually two letters from my own beloved, tiny brown "Egg," covered from cheek to jowl with stamps.

I took them out in the sun, and sat on the curbstone and devoured them. I never loved anything so much as those very dear letters and those little yellow rose leaves that fluttered out of one of them in the wind. I dove after them like one of the Karno brothers. Six horses, tethered in the alleged shed, died of blood pressure and heart disease. They hadn't seen anything as quick in that town since they were foaled.

The two letters from Dolores filled him with pleasant excitement and yearning. He decided to curtail his voyage. He wired his adored one that he was leaving by train on Wednesday, January 20. There were only two trains a week. He would catch the first one.

He went into the "baking sunlight," where he met Blaney and an English engineer "doing the town." The three retired to a cantina, to talk about London and of Dan Leno, the famous comedian. Barrymore said that "it was great fun and pleasantly incongruous to have such a discussion in that tropical setting." He ordered six cases of beer for the crew. He had a nap, and woke up back at the mooring at Cape St. Lucas.

The next day he wanted to be alone on the craggy coastline. He writes:

In the afternoon, after lunch, I had almost the most divine time I've had here yet. I fixed up a Leger casting-rod, and had the skiff drop me at the little beach among the rocks. I went on shore alone, and wandered about those rocks out of a lost world, and those heavenly, sandy, isolated stretches as the sun was setting. I climbed 'way up on the rocks and took some movies of the surf breaking into a little jagged Mephistophelian cove.

It seemed like Hamlet's "hideaway"! It is the most utterly fascinating, untouched, loneliest, loveliest place I have ever been. One could sit there for hours and smoke and do nothing but watch the sea and the birds and the marvelous vital sky changing. I felt somehow today it was a place I was certain to come back to, many times in my life.

When I got back to the boat it was dark, and there were little, deep-yellow lights on the top of the hill where the cross is. It seems there is no church here, but a priest who was passing through years before put a cross on the top of the rocky hill, and some saints in niches, and said: "That is your Church."

I must say it sounds more attractive than any church I can imagine. The great cross against the sky, and those small lovely saints, to whom the people here burn candles, "when they want anything," as I was naïvely told! Or "when they've gotten what they want, they light their candles, to sort of fulfill their obligations."

One or the other must have happened, as the little beacons were going tonight in the darkness. I must go up there before I leave.

After lunch next day, Barrymore, Blaney, and Cap "paid a pilgrimage" to the cross on the hill. Of this excursion, Jack writes:

It reminded me of the first day up Mt. Blanc. The view as one gradually got to the top was enchantment. I wish we had gone earlier to have gotten better photographs. The small shrine was pathetic and most charming. Against the rock there was a little paper picture of some small person, who looks exactly like "Innocence" or "The Little Sister" in Currier & Ives. It was surrounded by tiny angels. In front of this were mounds of candle-grease, and the primitive grotto is smoked black with the flames of many offerings.

Any penitent or suppliant who climbs up that "bally 'ill," as Blaney called it, ought to get what he came and candled for, God knows!

There was a new moon as we rowed home to the boat, with our fat star above it, and another one for good luck, twinkling 'way in the opposite part of the sky. I made the very same wish I have for ages, ever since "Winkie" and I had our moon-time. Read Boswell's *Johnson* and went to bed and slept divinely.

There now was but "one day and a half" left of Barrymore's time of solitude off the coast of Lower California.

I have had, really, a more divine time than I have ever had before in my life. I wanted a rest, and to get away from people, and maybe catch a fish or two. I was perfectly contented to catch *at* one. I found the most cyclonically engaging country, splendid weather, lots of fishing under peculiarly ideal conditions, and got a Marlin the second day down here.

He now narrates an adventure which might have cost him his life. He speaks of his danger, as he always did of any personal risk, with a tongue-in-cheek style.

This afternoon went on to the point. Heavy surf, difficult to land, took cameras. Wanted to get back into those delightful caves, but surf too peculiar. It came from two ways at once and would have swamped skiff. Difficult enough as it was.

Decided to climb over high rocks and get to caves that way. Had, on the whole, what would come under the head of a diverting experience. Got three-quarters of the way up with heavy Graflex camera tied around neck, hanging down back, weighing needless to say a ton by that time. "Bruno," the German sailor, who, it turned out later, used to be a "steeple-jack," gave out, not being on *his* vacation, and went back, and he cameraless!

Got to a place about ninety feet up (like Mt. Blanc the first day). It seemed impossible to go either one way or the other, up or back. Being there with that damned camera getting leadier and leadier, and the left leg going gradually from bad news to worse, from varicose to locomotor. Realized what a fix I was in. Bruno had left and couldn't help if he were *there*.

The pieces of rock I tried tentatively broke off like plaster; the entire damned thing being formed of some kind of sandy granite, and as old as the hills first formed by volcanic eruptions from the sea.

And here was I, photographer, "sportsman," and blazing jackass, spread like some heraldic lizard on the lonesomest rock in the Pacific Ocean, with nothing between me and dissolulution, in an extremely unpleasant and jellified form, but a gradually atrophying big toe. One thought of prayer came, one must confess, but one also retained—I am enchanted to say, now that I am *seated* once again—some sense of proportion, however desperate the situation.

I couldn't expect any reasonable God to imagine I had any respect for His sense of fitness, if I flung Him a strangled prayer under such conditions, having been in the habit of doing so, so very *little*. I *have* done it, and always tried to be fairly on the level in the performance.

I don't remember ever quite indulging in that deliciously naïve rhapsody of Louis XI's "Just *one* more *little* murder, dear, dear God—and we'll call it square!" Meanwhile, as I was beginning to sink, something had to be done. I noticed a tiny jutting edge of that filthy fakey rock—that looked as solid as the one Peter built his church on—and that fell to smithereens the moment one actually depended on it, about level with my waist.

If I could get poor old George Toe into *that*, I'd be nearer by a couple of feet to a beautiful saddle-like resting place that would either be the last thing I would objectively see on this odd planet, or a memory transcribed in this nautical *Book of Hours*.

I placed the sweating palms and the prehensile fingers on the bland and bulbous forehead of that poxed and passive peak, and heaved. The only thing in God's world that stood at that moment between Papa and Infinity was that *one* effort, and it had to be done. I remember distinctly, as I was doing it, being rather grateful that I was far less like a human being at that moment than I was like a monkey with a dash of octopus—otherwise I never would have survived.

I got, not the toe, but the *knee* in that blessed but painfully temporary sanctuary, and hung. Something, rock or sweat, I don't know which, *gave* slightly, and one felt a sensation not so much of fright as extraordinary lightness and breathlessness —like levitation. It may indeed be the acme of fright, if such a sensation can apparently make clearer the scintillant facets of one's bean and body. It seemed as if every pore of the about-to-be-smashed system was working by itself, like a colored retreat (not caring a damn).

Precisely what muscles and movements *made* that ledge—I naturally cannot tell, nor could I were I as imaginative an anatomist as Leonardo da Vinci. All I know is that there I was, safe for the moment, with that damned camera, like an albatross, the symbol of a preposterous but plausible profession, heavy, heavy, around my neck.

At that moment, be it observed, I thanked in as deprecatory a fashion as possible a Higher Force. As Rupert Hughes said about the piece of "business" in *The Sea Beast*, "From one gentleman to another!"

In a situation of this character, one is two-minded. One immediately unslung the Incubus, 3¼ x 4¼, and went instantly into the business of resting. The sun was low. One wondered how in Hell one was *ever* going to get *down*. The way one *came* seemed damnably unsavory. On the other hand, the drunken Jacob's ladder to the cave on the opposite side was gray, forbidding and, although it looked easier and the rocks more trustworthy, had an unmistakable air, a positive *scent* of Death about it.

It looked exactly like the inverted tooth, magnified to demon proportions, with which the Madman created the denouement in Edgar Allan Poe's "Berenice." True however to the instincts of an erstwhile newspaper man, I stood up, by that time inured to acrobatics, on the knife-blade of Chaos, and took some photographs of it. Inasmuch as it had pretty nearly put me on the blink, it seemed reasonable that the camera should be utilized before we both were amalgamated into one unctuous mass of ground glass and movie actor at the memorable (for twenty minutes: the first edition headline: "Distinguished Tragedian falls to Death while Walking Cliff in Drunken Stupor!") juncture of some Mexican crevasse.

Meanwhile, to add to the "gaiety of nations" (I never knew till last night, by the way, reading Boswell, where that particular expression originated) it was getting much rougher below. I put the black things one tears out (when one remembers it!) after a picture is taken, in a niche in the rocks—more out of bravado combating nausea than anything else, and scratched with my fishing knife a "J" for jackass as deeply as I could in the scabrous rock. I then prepared—without gusto—to descend.

Bruno had evolved the idea of throwing me a leaded line, by means of which I could unburden myself of the child, "Graflex." After repeated effort, all well-meant, he finally scraped the cerebellum with one desperate heave, on which the jaded incumbent lashed B. G., or Bastard Graflex, and lowered it down, cursing softly and enviously the while.

Then there was some haggard shouting anent throwing me up a rope; but I made a mental reservation that this would not only be slightly degrading but it would also be unfeasible. So I decided nobly to come down as I came up, minus S. O. B. Graflex, the which I proceeded to do *at once*. If I'd waited one more second, the nobility would have been cold, and I would have descended cavewards. Where, how, in the name of Heaven I could have gotten away that night is a question, as it was far too rough to land any boat, a trifle which I forgot to mention.

When I went casting the day I saw Hamlet's soliloquy-parlor, I was imbued with a terrific desire to bathe in those enormous breakers, and could scarcely credit the Cap who said, "The sharks did everything but lay eggs right on that there beach."

When we climbed up to the cross that day, we had the glasses, and directly below us at the very edge of the breakers on that same beach, one could see with the naked eye dark shapes moving, and with the glasses they were seen to be large, healthy sharks.

Anyway, that's that. It's taken a deal of footage in the telling. It will be amusing to read maybe in the years, as a photograph however badly taken and exposed, of certain sensation. It will also be bound to be relaxing to read any literary endeavor of one's own when one isn't used to the medium. It will be a little, I imagine, like "Lasca, down by the Rio Grande," recited after dinner at an otherwise inoffensive party, by the younger son, who is a champion quoit thrower.

Jack was up early the morning after his adventure to have a last day of fishing. His dinghy was swamped in a swirl of surf, and he had to swim in from forty yards off-shore. He had his camera and a pair of large field glasses lashed to his neck. The beach shelved precipitously. Barrymore's burden and the undertow threatened to take him under, but a wave fortuitously carried him ashore. He reached safety, he says, "looking like a slightly mad bug collector." He went to bed to "sleep like a stunned sow," and next day unlashed and laid away his rods and reels. He was going home to Dolores. The cruiser put in at Mazatlán the following morning, where he called at the American Consulate, then visited the bar of the Hotel Belman.

It should be kept in mind that this was during Prohibition days in the United States. When a thirsty wanderer from the North entered a legal bar for a legal refreshment, it became an experience.

I wandered entirely unprepared into what seemed a vision of the past—a high, cool, scrupulous bar, presided over by angels in white, *real* bartenders with linen coats, affable exterior, everything. Two excellent English cock-fighting prints on the wall and the inevitable stoutish nude lady stepping over a brook, whose name used to be legion in the old days.

I stood hat in hand in the sanctified twilight of that spacious and cleanly haven, like a good Catholic would in a cathedral on his return from arid and heathen ports; and, after the proper genuflexion, ordered a glass of beer. It was hotter than blazes outside, real tropical, depleting heat. Here, within that exquisitely appointed grot, all was peace and zephyrous coolness. The beer arrived—*draft* beer—in a tall, thin, clean crystal of Grecian proportions, with a creamy bead on it.

I tasted it, dear reader, black or white. It was heaven. It was liquid manna. It had the frou-frou of ambrosia, the tender unctuousness of a melted pearl. The planets seemed to pause a moment in their circling to breathe a benediction on that Mexican's brewer's head. One felt some great rubato, sweet yet vibrant, in the celestial orchestra of the revolving spheres. It was like a slight ecstatic sigh from the left lung of the Cosmos. Then the universe went on its wonted way again. Hot Dog! But that *was* a glass of beer!

There is a small envelope pinned to the sea-log page in which Barrymore told of his pilgrimage up the rocky hill where the great cross stood against the southern sky. The envelope contains a thin paper. Inside its folds there is a cluster of dry petals. On the paper there is written in Barrymore's hand:

"Flowers I picked for 'Winkie' on the way to the Cross."

5.

All This World for Juliet

WHEN he returned from his sea solitude in January 1926, Jack was reminded in many quiet ways that Dolores' mother was a conventional person. He seemed pained at this, thinking that the ardor of his suit should cancel out all parental qualms.

Mrs. Costello was a sweet-tempered woman, widely admired. Her first duty and desire was to safeguard her daughters. She did this with firmness and agility. She was, of course, mindful that Dolores had come abruptly into a career. She also could see that Barrymore and her older daughter were completely in love. But until Mrs. Costello could hear the word "marriage" spoken she would visé no passports.

Jack liked Mrs. Mae Costello sincerely. He called her "Mamma," but that didn't lessen her watchfulness. She insisted that Dolores be chaperoned whenever Barrymore called at their small home in Ivar Avenue, toward the Hollywood hills. This supervision drove the enamored actor almost out of his wits.

Notwithstanding his high regard for Mrs. Costello, Jack once said naïvely to his business-manager, "Why is it that such a lovely girl as Dolores has to have a mother?"

He employed various stratagems to be near her. He acquired an easel, canvas, brushes, paint tubes, then took his paraphernalia to the Costello home. He began one of his few portraits in oil. Jack readily admitted that the completed picture of Dolores was not the work of a Fra Lippi. But he afterward said that his own thoughts at the time had been somewhat similar to those of the troubled Florentine when that impassioned friar was contemplating the abduction of Lucrezia Buti from the convent.

Barrymore had come back from the sea with a great dream. He would buy a yacht. Dolores and he would sail in it away from a world of prosaic conventions. Everything would work out simply. He was certain of that. It never occurred to him to reflect that his grandiose projects hatched out with the infrequency of porcelain eggs.

He consulted his friend, Douglas Fairbanks, as to enlisting the advice of an expert on sailing vessels. Fairbanks recommended P. H. L. ("Doc") Wilson. Barrymore and Doc traveled to Oakland. There in the harbor they found a craft to Jack's liking.

She was the gaff-rigged schooner *The Mariner*, and belonged to sportsman L. A. Norris. This Gloucester type schooner was ninety-three feet over-all, with a twenty-three foot beam, and a fraction more than eleven feet draft. She weighed a little less than ninety-five gross tons. *The Mariner* had two masts and a sail area of four thousand six hundred square feet. Her keel had been laid down at an Essex, Massachusetts, yard in 1922. She was sleek and white. She had won a San Francisco to Tahiti yacht race in record time. *The Mariner* was seaworthy though sensitive, and quick on the helm.

Jack immediately began to convert the schooner into a cruising-yacht. Although he preferred sail, he wanted *The Mariner* to be comfortable and entirely safe for Dolores. He had three double state-rooms built, a large saloon aft, and a galley. Space was made for an engine room below, and an Atlas Imperial Diesel installed. *The Mariner*, if becalmed, could make eight and a half knots by means of power from the auxiliary.

The purchase of the yacht and its alterations stood Barrymore $110,000. He had not asked Mrs. Costello whether or not she would permit Dolores to sail with him to far places—or even to near ones. He seldom looked before he leaped. Indeed, he seldom looked *after* he had done so. Dolores' mother informed the pained dreamer that her daughter might not so much as step aboard the yacht without a chaperon, the chaperon to be herself, Mrs. Costello.

The Mariner sailed down from Oakland to San Pedro in February. The yacht remained at her mooring to be outfitted. Jack had hopes that Mrs. Costello would relent. She would not.

Meantime *The Sea Beast* had its première. Barrymore already had completed two pictures under the Warner Brothers' contract, the second one being *Don Juan*. He was to make a third, the pictureplay drawn from *Manon Lescaut* and called *When a Man Loves*. Dolores again would be his leading lady. He looked forward to holding her repeatedly in his arms during the love scenes.

He decided about this time that he would make no more pictures for the Warner Brothers after the completion of his third assignment. He was attracted by the prestige of United Artists, a com-

pany graced by Mary Pickford, Douglas Fairbanks, and Charlie
Chaplin. If he joined this constellation, he planned to take Dolores
into that same galaxy as soon as possible. Jack would make of
Dolores a great actress. It all seemed simple and logical and appropriate.

Joseph M. Schenck, head of United Artists, one evening called on
Barrymore at the Ambassador. Before he left the hotel, Schenck put
in his pocket a contract with Barrymore. It provided that Jack make
two pictures for United Artists and share in the "profits." Barrymore
consulted no one, but signed the paper.

He soon was to learn that he needed advice in such matters. There
was no time-clause in the new contract. In fact, it took him two
years to complete two pictures. After the fixed studio charges and
expenses had been subtracted from the "budget" there *were* no
profits for Jack other than his original price of $100,000 for each
picture. Under the Warner Brothers' contract Jack had made two
pictures within seven months, and had worked not more than seven
weeks on either one.

Notwithstanding the impressive figure of $100,000 a picture un-
der the terms of his new pact, what really happened was that Jack
earned less than $2,000 for each work-week, as against more than
$10,000 a work-week under the Warner Brothers' arrangement.
Also, the Warner Brothers had been paying his hotel and transportation bills, whether he worked or not. This cost the studio $1,500
a month. There were no provisions for Barrymore's maintenance
set down in the new contract. Besides, Jack would have little time
to go fishing or cruising once he took up quarters at the United
Artists Studios.

When Henry Hotchener officially became Jack's manager, and
afterward pointed out to Mr. Schenck that Barrymore had not
realized a profit beyond his salary, the producer signed the actor
for a third picture at $150,000, with a time limit and many other
concessions. There would be no hotel bills paid by the studio, notwithstanding.

In April Hotchener had the Bank of Italy (afterward the Bank
of America) make Barrymore a member of the advisory board, of
which Jack's manager then was chairman. This greatly amused the
actor. His name, in gold letters, appeared on the front door of the
bank; but he had the good sense never to attend a meeting of
the board.

"It's a wonder to me," he said, "that when the public finds *my* name on the door there is not an immediate run on the bank."

In May work was begun on the third of the Warner Brothers' Barrymore pictures, *When a Man Loves*. Between "shots" Jack spent his time (Dolores in a canvas-back chair beside him on the set) designing silverware for *The Mariner*, selecting linens, curtains, and planning other decorations for the yacht. He used his family crest, his father's, on lamp-shades for the staterooms and the main saloon; it was an azure serpent—he called it a "snake regnant"—on a yellow field. His owner's pennant also bore this device. The silverware was charged with this design, as was the stationery.

On May 14, 1926, *The Mariner* was made ready for a final inspection. Jack and his manager drove down to San Pedro harbor that evening. He looked the craft over from a rowboat, then went aboard. Barrymore and Hotchener sat in the owner's stateroom until far into the night, and discussed plans for the actor's future.

It was clear to Hotchener during this and other conferences that Jack was undergoing a great conflict of mind. He loved Dolores beyond anything. Yet somehow the thought of marriage horrified him. He said of it:

"I have had such foul luck with the institution. I don't know what might happen if, this time, everything is spoiled. Have you not noticed that the musical composers had the honesty to write their wedding marches in the same tempo as the dirges?"

He determined somehow to take Dolores with him on a long voyage. He would show her the places where he had been six months before. She would see the villages of the Southern California peninsula, the simple folk there, the smart little horses, the sea-world of fish, Hamlet's hideaway. Together they would ascend to the primitive shrine with the great cross above it on the high rocks.

He confidently gave orders to provision the yacht for a long cruise.

Doc Wilson was serving as *The Mariner's* skipper this year. He had a crew of seven men. Among them was Otto Matthies, the mate, a deep-sea sailor. Otto was to obtain his master's papers and captain the yacht for ten years.

Otto now was thirty-seven years old. a man of muscle and unflurried mind. He had been a roistering fellow in his time, but upon experiencing a series of psychic manifestations he suddenly left off drinking, smoking, and swearing. Otto told Barrymore that he had seen a "blinding light," such as that which assailed Saul of Tarsus, whenever he departed one whit from the truth.

Jack remarked that Otto several times had been able to predict the hazards of uncharted reefs, foul weather, or other navigational threats several days in advance of *The Mariner's* log.

With Dolores and the proposed journey on his mind, Barrymore decided to send East for certain of his properties for installation on the yacht. In a letter to his beloved friend, Mrs. Nicholls of the Alchemist's Corner, he wrote in part:

> I have invested in a schooner, having, after much travail and repeated bus accidents, arrived at the age and state of common sense. It seemed a happier plan to invest in the broad acreage of the Pacific, where one can wander about under the sun and sky, and fish, than to get a house which I would furiously fix up and be lonesome as the devil in it, particularly as it would have no understanding person on the first floor when it got too much for one.
>
> The schooner has a huge cabin like an old 1840 boat's, and all the heavenly things I had in the sea captain's cabin on the roof would be divine in it. . . . Is there any way I could get those things, or are they also in the "hands of the Philistines"? . . . The most wonderful accident that ever happened to me was my coming out to this God-given, vital, youthful, sunny place. At times I feel older and more aloof than St. Joseph of Arimathea, but it doesn't last long. In fact, it's over almost instantly.

Jack finally had to choose the alternative of setting out on his voyage without Dolores, or taking her mother with them. He prevailed upon Hotchener temporarily to leave Helios, who was not a good sailor, and "come along to divert Mrs. Costello."

The manager brought aboard, among other things, some five thousand letters from motion-picture "fans" and two pill-boxes containing a remedy for seasickness.

On June first, Dolores, Jack, Mrs. Costello, and Hotchener sailed on the first cruise of *The Mariner* under its new registry. The early course was set for Catalina, San Clemente, and other ports in adjacent waters. The yacht was under full spread of canvas. She heeled over beautifully on a long tack in a moderate breeze. A ground swell gave the craft a camel-bounce that presently caused Mrs. Costello to retire to her stateroom.

It must be admitted that Jack was improperly stimulated by Mrs. Costello's indisposition. He went below to advise Henry of the news. Hotchener already was aware of the lady's discomfort. Barrymore found his manager at the door of Mrs. Costello's cabin. The manager was holding a pill-box in his hand.

"What are you doing here?" asked Jack.

Henry indicated the small package. "I thought I'd better offer Mrs. Costello this Mothersill's Remedy. I have another box. Helios gave me two packages of it in case I got . . ."

Jack interrupted by taking his manager's arm. He guided him toward Hotchener's quarters. "No," Barrymore said, as they moved away from Mrs. Costello's stateroom, "you'll give her none of that remedy whatsoever. After all, you are *not* a physician." There was mischief in Jack's eye. "I'll thank you not to practice medicine on this craft."

They went inside Hotchener's cabin. There Barrymore noticed the mail sacks. "What's all this?" he inquired. "Are you also the postmaster of Los Angeles?"

"It's your fan mail," his manager replied. "I intend to reply to all these letters. Builds up a larger public for your pictures."

"Listen," Barrymore said, "don't you know the *real* way to handle fan mail?"

"No."

"Then I'll demonstrate." He called for Otto, the mate. The several mail sacks were taken on deck. Jack pitched them overboard.

"There," he cried, "it will be taken care of efficiently by David Jones." He thrust his left hand in his pocket, a characteristic pose, snorted, then said to his manager: "Now, Hank, go read a book, or look out a porthole. Dolores and I at last can have the after-deck to ourselves."

Mrs. Costello became more seasick with each chime of the ship's bell. After three days of it, even Jack grew genuinely worried. Dolores insisted that they put back to San Pedro. Barrymore yielded, but it meant that the cruise was another one of his "porcelain eggs."

"My God!" Jack said. "I shall never again celebrate Mother's Day."

In his desire to make an acknowledged actress of Dolores, Jack "threw" many scenes to her during the filming of *When a Man Loves*. Ethel Barrymore, on a visit to her brother, sat in a projection room with scenarist Bess Meredyth to look at the "rough cut" of the photoplay. Ethel was amazed at the spectacle of an accomplished actor deliberately "tossing away" his scenes. She thought it a sin against art. She was not altogether unprepared to see her brother lose all sense of proportion in respect to the private phases of his love. That had happened to him many times. But Ethel *did* expect "a Barrymore to live up to tradition in regard to art."

Barrymore was immune to criticism. He committed another headlong act. He wrote an unethical telegram to his future employer, Joseph M. Schenck. In the telegram he informed the head of the United Artists that he was going to advise Dolores to quit Warner Brothers. She had a contract with them and was about to renew it. Jack recommended to Schenck that he help Dolores "jump the league."

Schenck in New York handled the message as if it were a bomb. It was an explosive piece of business, this plan of Jack's, one which Barrymore, with customary heedlessness, had thought entirely logical, desirable, and matter-of-course.

In Hollywood, with its all-year-round Christmas tree heavily laden with treasure, the producers maintained a defensive watchfulness of the movements of everyone. They had appointed Will Hays, former Postmaster General, to keep a super-eye on all matters having to do with censorship, morals of the members within the industry, and codes of competitive business practice.

The telegram which Jack so complacently wrote out was entrusted by him to a bellboy. Within twenty minutes thereafter Barrymore's telephone began to ring. He was in trouble, and was profanely informed to that effect by a friend.

"Are you nuts?" this friend shouted over the telephone. "The telegram you just wrote to Schenck will blow you out of the water!"

Jack could not understand why such a simple wire should blow him out of the water. He summoned Hotchener from sleep for an emergency consultation. The manager went to the Ambassador at once to hear his charge ask: "Now why would a little message like this get me into trouble? I simply wanted Dolores to work beside me."

Hotchener tried to explain the sanctity of contracts. But Barrymore remained mystified. The next day the Hays office telephoned Jack, advising him to confine himself to acting and to minding his own business.

In June Barrymore became excited over the annual yacht race to Honolulu. He spent a week recruiting a Corinthian (amateur) crew. The fastest privately owned Pacific coast sailing vessels were entered in this deep-sea regatta. Barrymore took his monkey Clementine along. She became seasick, but recovered the second day out.

There was little wind during the early days of the race. The vessels drifted idly apart. *The Mariner* was becalmed. There was no wireless aboard, hence no news from Barrymore's yacht. There was some anxiety on the part of Jack's friends, especially Dolores, when the boat became long overdue at Honolulu.

Jack himself was not drinking during this cruise, but insisted that his colleagues enjoy themselves with gin or the other liquid delicacies he had brought aboard.

During the doldrums the running lights of a tanker were sighted one night. *The Mariner* signaled the vessel by means of flashlights. She approached, hove to, then an officer from the bridge-wing megaphoned to Jack: "Are you in distress?"

"Hell, yes!" roared Jack, who needed no megaphone at any time. "Plenty of distress!"

"What is it? Do you need water?"

"*Water!*" Jack shouted. "God, no! We need *booze!*"

The need somehow was supplied. The tanker resumed its voyage, and her captain sent a wireless message to San Francisco, where the ship-news reporters learned that Barrymore and his Corinthians were safe. The logbook of *The Mariner* notes that severe weather afterward beset the yacht. A spinnaker was ripped and then mended. Jack described this repair, in a log remark, as having been effected "by the members of the ladies' sewing circle."

Jack left *The Mariner* at Honolulu to be met by director Alan Crosland, according to plan, to prepare Barrymore's first picture for United Artists. Crosland was to direct it from a scenario based on the life of François Villon, the picture to be called *The Beloved Rogue*.

In the welcoming party, besides Crosland, was assistant director Gordon Hollingshead, a close pal of Jack's. He had been on all the Barrymore pictures since the making of *The Sea Beast*.

"I am not drinking at the moment," Jack informed Holly as he stepped ashore at Honolulu. "But I want you to attend to the needs of my crew. I also am not interested in strange women, as I am in love. But my crew has its own pressing needs." He gestured impres-

sively and roared: "Hence, my good Holly, will you do the following things in the order of their utterance: find the best bootlegger
in all Hawaii, engage a cozy hook-shop for my loyal crew, hire a
Polynesian orchestra to play at all hours, day and night, then for
God's sake get me a place to sleep at the Moana Hotel."

"Fine," said Holly. "I suppose you have the money for all this?"
Barrymore came up for air. "Money? There is such a thing, I suppose. Let's see." He turned one pocket of his old khaki trousers inside out. There was a hole in it. He now did the same with another
pocket. There was only a five-cent piece in it.

"Holly," and he raised a brow, "wire the generous Joe Schenck
for what is known in the idiom as two grand."

The "two grand" arrived with incredible speed in the form of a
cable. As for the hotel, Holly had arranged for the Prince of Wales
suite. Barrymore looked at it and said, "Not quite what we need."
A two-story bungalow, similar to his quarters at the Ambassador,
was found.

"Who occupies the first floor?" Barrymore inquired.

"No one," Holly said. "Vacant."

"Hire it also," Barrymore said. "That will be our saloon."

When the bootlegger arrived Barrymore said to him, "You will
install a keg of your potent beverage, *Okolehao*. And when it runs
dry, and if you do not have another keg on the scene instantly,
you will get no more of our business."

Now the orchestra arrived, a large one with ukuleles and steel
guitars. Barrymore divided it into three "shifts," each one to play
for eight hours.

That night at a dinner of welcome, Barrymore asked Holly to
advise the toastmaster not to call upon him for a speech. After a
dull session of oratory, the toastmaster did call upon Barrymore,
who rose to say:

"Speech-making is exactly like child-birth. You are so God-
damned glad to get it over with."

Barrymore, Crosland, Hollingshead, and a writer returned to the
American mainland on the *S.S. City of Los Angeles*. Jack still was
partaking only of soft drinks. This may partly explain the ginger-
ale vagueness of the scenario of *The Beloved Rogue*.

During Jack's absence from the mainland, Helios Hotchener had
his rooms at the Ambassador thoroughly cleaned and re-arranged.
His valet Blaney had become homesick for England and had gone

abroad to see his family. The housekeeper, Anna, had been told by Barrymore not to disturb anything, "not even a cockroach." She had taken this command literally. Jack's quarters looked like the city of Rome the week after King Alaric arrived there at the head of the Visigoths. When Barrymore came back from Honolulu and found his rooms clean and his socks darned, he seemed amazed and gratified.

The writing of the Villon story dragged. Barrymore's own ideas as to plot did not speed the composition. Among the several Hollywood authors who struggled with the scenario was one man who lived in constant horror of Jack's literary eccentricities. This writer belonged to a school of authors known in cinematic circles as "breast-beaters." The "breast-beater" is one who shows himself to greater advantage in the oral telling of a proposed scene than he does at the typewriter.

The "breast-beating" overawed the producer of *The Beloved Rogue*, yet he wondered why nothing practical came out on the author's machine. The actors finally got within range of the camera on August 27.

Douglas Fairbanks, Sr. gave Jack the use of his own dressing-room. This studio bungalow had the combined auras of a Turkish bath, the gymnasium of the New York Athletic Club, and the country place of Charles Atlas. It was tiled, had shower stalls, bar bells, rubbing tables, wrestling mats, exercise bars, and many other muscular appurtenances. When Jack entered this temple of sinews, he glanced about, then asked, "Yes, but where do you keep cracked ice for a drink?"

Fairbanks, a teetotaler, was a little confused by his friend's implied criticism of the establishment.

During *The Beloved Rogue*, Jack came across an old friend in need of a job. The studio officials wanted no part of this particular "extra." But Jack insisted that he be hired. Barrymore again delayed activities on the picture to ponder a sequence in which his friend might appear to advantage. The friend timidly suggested that he was "great at acting with a duck." Barrymore decreed that a duck must be "written" into the scenario. The breast-beater refused flatly to "write for a duck." Director Crosland made a long speech against all ducks.

The assistant director, however, sympathized with Barrymore's duck problem. Hollingshead advised Jack to make use of the services of a bright young gag writer, Bryan Foy. Holly assured him that Brynie could "handle the duck situation."

"Is this young man," Barrymore asked, "by any chance related to my father's great friend, Eddie Foy?"

"His son," replied Holly. "I went to school with Bryan Foy in New Rochelle."

"Get him!" Barrymore shouted. "The Foys grew up among ducks!"

An attempt was made to explain to Jack that Brynie was "on his way out." He had been hired for *The Beloved Rogue* as a gag man but "had not delivered," and had been sitting out his contract for the last eleven weeks. He was to be fired as soon as his three months' term as a gag man expired. All he did, Barrymore was told, was to read sports pages. Besides, young Foy had just been married, and had taken two days off for a honeymoon without asking permission.

Under the Hollywood caste system, Foy had not been permitted to attend the story conferences or visit the sets of *The Beloved Rogue*. He was an untouchable.

On his way from the story conference, Barrymore stopped at Foy's desk to ask, "Can you think of anything funny to do with a duck?"

"Well, there are lots of things you can do with a duck, but maybe if I were allowed to see the script I could help out."

Brynie now buckled down to the "duck request" with a "what-have-I-got-to-lose" psychology. He was not permitted to deliver his suggestion at the story conference personally. A secretary, holding the Foy memorandum as though it were something in need of antitoxin serum, laid it on the producer's desk, then fled. The producer was unable to understand what the Foy scribbling was about. Director Crosland bluntly said the effort stank. The author-in-chief beat his breast sadly and murmured, "Mediocre! Mediocre!" Against this landslide of opinion Barrymore himself wasn't sure, but insisted that the scene be tried out with the benefit of camera lenses.

The scene was shot. Foy slipped into the background of the stage to find out that the routine he had written was being done upside down and backwards.

As Barrymore came off the set he saw Foy and asked, "How was it?" Foy looked at him gravely. "No good." Barrymore became interested. "What's the matter with it?"

"Well," Foy said, "when you see the 'rushes' of it tomorrow, you'll find that it was no good."

Barrymore, worried, went to his dressing-room (which by now had an icebox among the gym-traps).

An hour afterward, while Foy again was sitting out his contract in the corner of the office, a studio spokesman informed Foy that he should not have worried Mr. Barrymore, and that he had done a most unethical thing.

The next day Brynie established himself outside the door of the projection room. Inside that chamber the work of the day before, the duck sequence, was being viewed and analyzed by the star and the general staff. Barrymore, followed by the studio bigwigs, came out of this Black Hole of Calcutta.

"You were dead right, Brynie," said Barrymore. "What shall I do about it now?"

The director and other officials endeavored to pry Foy away from Jack, so that Brynie couldn't do anything further along unethical lines. They failed in this attempt.

"If I were allowed to see you at work," said Foy, "and make any suggestions where they might count, and we could get rid of some of these brass hats and breast-beaters, I might tell you."

"Come to my dressing-room, sir," said Barrymore. "It is full of turning poles, bust developers, and other athletic knick-knacks, but we *may* find a drink."

"I really should go home early," said Foy, in the actor's dressing-room. "I'm just married."

"In that case," said Barrymore, an absinthe bottle in hand, "this can't do you the least harm."

After four absinthes, Foy said, "You're a damned fool not to pay more attention to the brains that are to be found in the lower brackets."

Barrymore looked at him appraisingly. "You know something? Your father and mine were great friends. In fact, I am told that your father almost married my mother. And if this had happened, what in God's name would have become of all of us?"

"I don't know what would have become of *us*," said Foy, "but I know what will become of you, if you don't listen to some people who can straighten out simple things like your duck."

A worried courier now poked his head in the doorway to announce that Mr. Barrymore was wanted on the set.

Foy dismissed the courier, then said to Barrymore: "I don't think you want to go back to the set today. Think of what our possible relationship might have been—what we have been saved. We should celebrate it."

"You're right," said Barrymore. "We shall repair to the Ambassador Hotel instantly."

Foy found the bathtub in Barrymore's suite piled high with champagne bottles, and the closets full of various liquors.

Three days afterward, when they had come back to the Ambassador from places which neither man remembered clearly, Foy thought it time to go home to his wife. He was delighted to learn that somewhere he had bought a gift for her, a replica of Christopher Columbus's flagship, the *Santa Maria*. The miniature caravel under his arm, Brynie made a hasty inspection of Barrymore, dead asleep on the couch.

When Brynie and the *Santa Maria* arrived at the Foy home, the ship was put to immediate use, sailing against his head. He spent the night on the couch in the living-room.

The next day at the studio a policeman was in the act of barring Foy from the gate when Barrymore drove up in his Lincoln roadster. The actor got out as chipper as you please. He took Foy by the arm. He then declined to return to work unless his friend was admitted to the studio and to the set as well.

To the perplexed studio authorities, Barrymore said, "You do not realize that, by insulting my friend, you are insulting someone of whom I can say, to quote John Bradford: 'There, but for the grace of God, go I.' But of course you cannot understand. Out of the way, please!"

At the preview of *The Beloved Rogue*, Barrymore heard that a two-reel comedy was to precede the showing of his picture. He said that the "two-reeler" would interfere with the mood of his own feature-length photoplay. The studio heads became frantic, especially when Jack indicated Foy and said, "I'll withdraw the picture unless my friend, and almost-brother, thinks otherwise."

The breast-beater and the studio authorities gingerly awaited

Foy's verdict. He managed to keep them in suspense, but finally said, "The picture should be shown." To Barrymore, Foy added, "It's quite likely that this work, when released to the public, frequently will be accompanied by two-reelers. If it is not good enough to outshine them, you should know it now."

Barrymore turned to his anxious employers to say, "Show the picture."

Bryan Foy since that time has become a successful producer of motion pictures. He never is impressed by breast-beaters. He still reads the sports pages, talks to anyone, and now has in his home models of all three of Christopher Columbus's ships.

That Barrymore now was "settled" in his California environment, and, above other things, unwilling to leave his loved one, is evidenced by an exchange of cablegrams and letters concerning a return to *Hamlet.*

In December of 1926 the Foss Productions, for whom he had done *Hamlet* in London, cabled Barrymore. William Foss offered him the use of His Majesty's Theatre for two months. It was suggested that Jack do *Richard* the first month, and *Hamlet* the second.

William Foss also advised the actor that he had acquired the rights to a play based upon the Paolo and Francesca legend. Would Barrymore be interested in doing it, then make a photoplay of it in London?

No. Jack was not interested in leaving either Dolores or California. However, he wrote to Foss:

> The fact of actually getting a letter from me will probably establish in your astounded cosmos the basis of an aneurism that might cut short a brilliant managerial career. I have thought of your letters with sporadic frequency, usually before I get up in the morning, each time accruing more and more of a Gethsemanic sweat. I consider it disgraceful, my not having answered you earlier, but by saying so I am merely amplifying my autobiography, which as a phrase is redundant, but which as a fact I have a vague feeling you will understand.
>
> I have been so saturated in cinematic labor (I use the word "saturated" in the broader sense of benignant actuality) that I have literally had time for no mental reactions away from this line of endeavor. . . . Heaven alone knows when the vicissitudes of a precarious profession shall land me on your shores again. . . .

The "autobiography" mentioned in the letter to Mr. Foss pertained to a series of articles ghost-written by Karl Schmidt. Schmidt also had written (in Jack's name) the Barrymore *Confessions*, which appeared in magazine and also in book form. Schmidt was a stout and learned fellow with Websterian eyebrows. Jack and Lionel both were fond of him. He reminded them in many ways of their old friend Frank Butler.

Many commercial offers now came to Barrymore. Among them, a knitting-mills company wished to name a bathing suit after him. To this request, he replied that he "never bathed." Also, without his personal sanction, a malt-drink company advertised him as "taking and enjoying" the pap-like product. Barrymore's manager demanded a retraction. When asked if he "ever had tried this malt drink," Jack replied, "Yes, and it turned to suède in my stomach."

He never before had paid attention to the sending of photographs of himself to newspapers or magazines. But he now took a sudden interest in such publicity whenever it included pictures of Dolores. When he learned that *Vanity Fair* was publishing in its next issue two photographs of him, he sent that magazine two pictures in which Dolores appeared at his side. To induce Editor Frank Crowninshield to believe these pictures more desirable than the ones already in hand, Barrymore made out that he was dissatisfied with the photographs sent by the publicity department of the studio. He wrote to Crowninshield:

> The pictures the estimable Warners sent you of the younger *Don Juan* looked a little like Frederick Warde, made up for James G. Blaine, Sr. In other words, it struck me—and we movie actors still retain our facial apprehensions long after every other function has gone back on us—as a trifle too authentic. . . . The girl playing opposite me is Dolores Costello. These photographs have appeared nowhere as yet.

Barrymore was not a dependable correspondent. Now, with Dolores and California at hand, he did even less personal penmanship than before. His manager had to see to it that Jack didn't throw away unopened letters from friends or members of his family. One such letter arrived from Ethel's daughter, Ethel Colt, of whom Jack was particularly fond. He telegraphed his sister that he had "opened Chi Chi's letter through some amazing gymnastic of the Holy Ghost." He then wired "Chi Chi" that her letter had made him "feel more like King Lear than Huckleberry Finn; which is the role one always attempts to assume in this particular community."

Barrymore carelessly put off replying to a letter from John Drew. He finally telegraphed Drew in December of 1926:

> DEAR UNCLE JAKE, PLEASE FORGIVE MY NOT ANSWERING YOUR LETTER SOONER. I HAVE BEEN ABSOLUTELY UP TO MY NECK IN CELLULOID. THE PICTURE IS JUST FINISHED AND HAS REQUIRED INTENSIVE LABOR ON THE PART OF NEPOSITY, WHO, IN SPITE OF HIS CREAKING FUNCTIONS, DEPICTS THROUGH JUDICIOUS GAUZES A BRIGHT LAD OF EIGHTEEN. AM WRITING YOU FULLY. I MEAN IN FULL. AM GETTING MORE CALIFORNIAN EVERY DAY, AND AM AFRAID AM ABOUT TO GROW A BEARD AND TAKE UP HORSEBACK RIDING. EVER SO MUCH LOVE.
>
>   GREENGOOSE.

For Christmas Jack bought gifts for the Costellos, jewelry for Dolores, books for Helene. But he did not stay home for the holidays. He suddenly left aboard *The Mariner* with Karl Schmidt for a long cruise in Mexican waters. He did not return until February 16 of the next year.

We know that Jack did not pay much attention to holidays. Still, he would not have left Dolores for such a long time and during a season which she naturally associated with happy thoughts, had he found no reason for so doing.

We feel it permissible to say that he was undergoing another one of his frequent conflicts of mind. He still had not brought himself to believe that he should obtain a final freedom from Michael Strange, and risk toppling his present romance by daring to enter for a third time into matrimony.

There was still another hazard than his belief in the "bad luck" of marrying. It was his own doubt as to his ability to quit drinking. He discussed this phase of his life at length with Hotchener before sailing away with Schmidt.

"I'll probably drink a lot on this voyage," he said. "I'm tired of the waiting, the silly mix-up of it all. Drink has been one of my two great weaknesses. I have tried, since meeting Dolores, to overcome the booze. Really I have. I do not want to hurt the one person I love more than I ever have loved anyone else, for she seems to adore me so trustingly."

He did abstain from drink for several weeks in 1926, the year then ending, and again in 1927. During these intervals he would be in excellent health, a bright mood, and would vow never to drink again. His periods of sobriety temporarily restored an equability of temperament and general joyousness. He would volunteer that it was "easy to stay on the wagon." He worked hard, helped to design all his sets as well as the costumes for the leading players, and otherwise participated in phases of production beyond the terms of his contract, and well beyond the powers of almost any other actor of his time.

Then some bottle-companion would come along, or some worry arise, such as a feeling of frustration at not being able to see Dolores privately. He would lapse into old habits. Each "fall" would make him morose and desperate. His nerves and emotions were delicately adjusted. It did not take much in the way of an irksome situation to disturb his equilibrium.

Sometimes he was haunted by the fear that his mind was doomed to impairment. One afternoon an actor was introduced to Barrymore in the dressing-room. Jack was in a black mood, and not at particular pains to be gracious. Also he was highly suspicious of strangers. When the visitor had the bad taste to inquire: "Mr. Barrymore, is it true that your father died at an institution for the insane?" Jack rose slowly, his face pale, his eyes turning green. Then he said in a slow, agonized tone: "I am now going to kill you, you miserable, low, stupid son of a bitch!"

The visitor was most fortunate in reaching the door.

That same afternoon Jack received a smile from Dolores. Suddenly all was sunshine, bright California sunshine, once again. A kiss from her made him forget all the woes that had been his. Her love seemed a promise of happiness unending.

O so white! O so soft! O so sweet is she!

6.

Gemini Ascending

JACK took an astrological calendar with him on his present voyage. For some time he had become increasingly confident that
the energies of the stars affected earthly beings. When friends
expressed skepticism, he would reply, "Yes, I know. But it works
in my case."

He once told Lionel, "Today, according to my horoscope, is an
auspicious one." To which Lionel shot back, "Is today also auspicious for the undertaker?"

During a winter cruise of 1926–1927, Jack underwent an experience which strengthened his belief in the stars. He had asked
Helios Hotchener to mark on the astrological calendar any days of
special import to his voyage. He would be too absent-minded himself to remember which days were either "good" or "bad."

Helios had been a student of astrology for many years while in
India. Barrymore regarded her as a woman of profound intuitional
faculties, one whose abilities in no way resembled the fortune-
telling shenanigans of Atlantic City crystal-gazers. He referred to
Helios Hotchener as his "Court Astrologer."

Barrymore, inspecting his calendar for the winter cruise, remarked that Helios had drawn a circle with red crayon about one
of the dates. She warned him to guard against accidents that day.
Upon Barrymore's return to San Pedro on February 6, 1927, the
Hotcheners asked him if anything of moment had happened.

"Happened?" he said. "I damned near lost my life; that's what
happened. We were moored off the Mexican coast," he continued,
"on the January day marked with a red ring on my astrological
calendar. I decided to stay in my bunk. I tried to read a book, but
grew restless toward noon. I said, to hell with the aspects! I selected
a shotgun, then went ashore, alone, in the dinghy. I thought I'd
bring down a few game-birds inland among some scrubby woods I
had seen through the glasses. I was almost formally discreet in handling the gun, so careful with it that I did not pay much attention to
anything else. I didn't particularly notice where I was walking

288

among the low trees of a marsh. I suddenly began to sink in some kind of quagmire or quicksand.

"I fired all the shells of the gun's magazine," he went on, "a signal to *The Mariner*. No one aboard construed the shots as other than those of a stewed sportsman. I kept sinking, spiritually as well as bodily. I was in the quagmire up to my waist. Now I distinctly saw my dead father's face rising before me. I could envision him as clearly as ever I had seen him in my boyhood. I had been getting desperately numb and full of futility until I saw my father's face. He turned his eyes toward an overhanging scrub, which, in the surprising suddenness of everything, I had not noticed until now.

"With great effort, I managed to draw a branch within reach of my fingers, using the stock of my gun as a 'fetcher.' I barely caught hold of the branch. I now was down to my chest in the death-trap. It looked as if the branch might break. Fortunately it was green and tough. I must have fought for five minutes to work free of that hell-hole. And all the while my father's face stayed before me. My God! When I finally got out of this trap, all wet and dazed, I staggered to a solid place, and lay down exhausted. The vision of my father left as soon as I had extricated myself. I was impressed and thoroughly scared."

From this time on Jack would not begin a motion picture, or even an important scene, without first conferring with his Court Astrologer. Barrymore believed that the contract he had entered into with Schenck turned out rather badly for him because the actor had not consulted his *Astrological Bulletina* instead of the label on a bottle of Prohibition gin.

The producers for a time did not know why Barrymore so often "stalled" while awaiting a "propitious moment" for the signing of a contract or the shooting of a sequence. When on the set Jack's manager carried in his pocket a detailed astrological list of the aspects of each hour pertaining to the actor. If Barrymore suddenly wished to know what influences were at work, he would call out, "Hank, the W. C." Hotchener would retire to the washroom secretly to consult the astral memorandum, then return to the set to nod or to shake his head.

Assistant director Gordon Hollingshead, whose business it was, among other things, to arrange the time-tables for the taking of scenes, was in Barrymore's astrological confidence. Holly believed in humoring his friend. The assistant director would receive instructions from the actor, then manage to accelerate or delay the shooting of various portions of the script, as the heavens might recommend. For example, Barrymore wanted all battle scenes to be photographed under the sign of Mars. In like manner, the love scenes were taken under the zodiacal influence of Venus.

Jack also demanded that Holly find places in all his pictures for a troupe of dwarfs and "old-timers." He said that these familiar though somewhat wizened pals "brought good luck." Besides, he was at ease when among friends. He had all sorts of friends, such as the dwarfs Johnny George and Little Angelo, the former major league baseball player Mike Donlin, Jack Dempsey, Miss Tiny Jones, Winston Churchill, and Einstein. It pleased him when any of these faces could be seen on his set or in his dressing-room.

Barrymore was capable of such immediate attunement to anyone's lifework, whether that of a dwarf newsboy or a scientist, as to seem a colleague. Einstein, for example, said after a visit with him: "Several mathematicians understand my theories, but of all persons it is an actor, John Barrymore, who *discusses* them the most intelligently." Similarly, Dr. David Starr Jordan, president emeritus of Leland Stanford University, corresponded familiarly with Barrymore. Their friendship arose from their mutual fondness for monkeys and apes. At a later time Barrymore impressed Dr. Gustav Eckstein, celebrated physiologist and author, as "the most remarkable man I have met!" Dr. Eckstein kept numerous pet canaries in his laboratory, and each one would answer by name.

Barrymore just as easily, and just as sincerely, kept in touch with the wanderings of "Gentleman Jack" the hobo, or the enterprises of pugilist Jack Dempsey. On the night of the Dempsey-Tunney fight at Philadelphia, Barrymore received an immediate wire from the defeated champion:

DEAR JACK. I FORGOT TO DUCK.

Whatever influence the stars may or may not have exercised on Barrymore's career is not a matter for a biographer to set down with pretended authority. But we do know that he had an inborn trend toward mysticism, that he had read the Chaldean books, and that he had come to believe that "the stars impel."

As an example of the sort of happenings that reaffirmed this belief in the stars, we cite an incident that occurred in 1932. On the evening before the fifth day of production of a picture for David O. Selznick, he was warned against driving his own motor car to the R. K. O. studio. He mentioned this warning to me during a discussion of dialogue for the photoplay.

Barrymore stayed up all that night; then, in the morning, failed to look at his astrological guide. He started off in his automobile from his Tower Road home. The wheels went off the narrow surfacing. The car turned over. Barrymore lay beneath it, half conscious. He suffered a fractured hip. The picture was delayed for two weeks. Jack never drove an automobile again—with one hilarious exception in 1936, an event to be described in proper sequence, if the author meanwhile does not collapse, or run out of ink.

One of the reasons why Barrymore regarded his Court Astrologer as an oracle was that Helios had made an arresting correction in respect to the zodiacal sign under which Jack supposedly had been born. Professional astrologers in New York understandably had accepted his birth date as February 15, 1882, the one given in the encyclopedias. They variously cast his horoscope under the signs of Virgo, Scorpio, and Sagittarius.

"The horoscopes concocted by the wise men of the East," he said, "somehow seem wide of the mark. I agree that I possess the virtues of a gangster, as indicated by Scorpio, and the domestic constancy of a dove, as intimated by Virgo, but things don't seem to work out in accord with other aspects of these celestial monitors. Why?"

Helios informed Barrymore that the events of his life clearly indicated to her that a mistake had been made in the published date of his birth. He characteristically knew little about the authenticity of this anniversary reminder. He never observed the day with ceremony. "I am always thirty-seven years old," he said, "a permanent thirty-seven, according to studio publicists." His family members themselves were unused to bothering with dates other than those which defined their theatrical seasons. They somehow had come to accept February 15 as the day of Jack's debut.

Helios had said to Barrymore that he definitely was a "Gemini person"; that he *must* have been born when Gemini was ascending on February 14. Llewellyn George, an authority on the astral science and long-time editor of *The Astrological Bulletina*, subsequently supported Helios' deductions. He reached his conclusions after a diligent mathematical estimation of dates and facts supplied in regard to Jack's career. A search of the records in Philadelphia disclosed, officially and terrestrially, that Jack had been born on February 14, 1882, under the name of John Sidney Blythe. A new horoscope was drawn for him in consonance with that date.

Barrymore returned to Hollywood from his winter cruise to insist that Helios read the stars with regard to himself and Dolores. Would they find lasting happiness together?

In reply, Helios said, "Please ask someone else about an interpretation of the stars concerning your marriage."

"What?" Jack called out. "Did you say *marriage?*"

"I am so fond of you both," Helios went on, "that I fear the stars would only answer me through my wishful hope for your happiness."

Jack sought information. "But you used the word marriage!"

"Ask someone else this time," Helios repeated.

He became both petulant and suspicious when Helios refused to "investigate so far ahead." He risked saying that the stars "might be slipping up in this instance."

Producer Schenck, during Barrymore's absence on the cruise, had had a bungalow built for the actor on the United Artists lot. Jack placed in it some of the furniture and pictures that once had decorated the Alchemist's Corner in New York. He removed one of the windows and put in its place a cage for Clementine.

"You know, Hank," Jack said to his manager, "there's an old superstition among actors that if you put personal things in your dressing-room, you'll have bad luck!"

Not long after this, on May 18, 1927, according to the Hotchener record, Mrs. Costello took Jack to task for having visited Dolores without the mother's consent. She advised him that this must not occur again. The melancholy wooer temporarily turned his energies toward work at the studio. He began to make tests for *The Tempest*, although the picture itself was not to be commenced until the next October.

Some days afterward Barrymore learned of the illness of John Drew. He left Hollywood on June 3 to be with his uncle at the Dante Sanitarium in San Francisco. The elderly actor had been appearing on tour in the all-star revival of *Trelawney of the Wells*, playing the part of Sir William Gower. While in Vancouver, B. C., Drew's arthritis severely troubled him. On May 31, in Portland, he became quite ill. He was taken to the San Francisco sanitarium,

where it was determined that he was stricken with the further com-
plications of rheumatic fever and septic poisoning.

Jack remained with his uncle for three days, then returned to
Hollywood to do a *Hamlet* reading over the radio. This was the
"O! what a rogue and peasant slave am I" soliloquy, his favorite
speech of all Shakespeare.

On June 27 Barrymore's friend Jack Prescott (of the "absinthe-
anointed eyebrows") arrived in Hollywood. Together with Lionel
they journeyed to San Francisco, word having reached them that
Drew had suffered a relapse. Lionel interrupted the making of a
motion-picture version of *Rain* to be with his uncle. Drew's daughter Bee, and his son-in-law, Jack Devereaux, also were at the bedside of the great actor.

Drew had jokes for these worried visitors, notwithstanding his
pain. When the ambulance siren sounded beneath his window, the
grand old actor turned his eyes toward Jack: "Let's all go to the
fire."

Drew's condition improved somewhat. Lionel returned to work.
His younger brother, however, had a presentiment that his uncle
was "about to bow out," so Jack stayed on in San Francisco. Prescott says that whenever Barrymore left the sanitarium he gave instructions as to where he could be reached immediately.

During this three weeks' stay in San Francisco, and when not
with his uncle, Barrymore prowled the waterfront or went among
antique shops. He bought old picture-frames to be sent to Hollywood. He frequented the Chinese theatre with writer Gouverneur
Morris, the Press Club with the newspaper men, Idwal Jones of
the *Examiner*, and William Chandler of the *Chronicle*.

Idwal Jones says they went to a film exchange one afternoon to
see *Chang*. "Barrymore was entranced by the monkey in the picture, and remarked, 'The monkey is a better actor than anybody
in Hollywood.'"

Jones also reports that Barrymore paid frequent visits to the Bohemian Club, and to the Family Club where there was a good bar.
In Room 8 of this club, he would sit up late with journalist Edward
L. O'Day and Larry Harris, the jute magnate and originator of the
remark regarding the San Francisco fire: "The damnedest, finest
ruins."

"Jack was particularly fond of George Sterling," Idwal Jones recalls. "Sterling was the last of the demi-gods of San Francisco in its

Bohemian heyday. He had the profile of a Dante, a bleak New
England voice, like a seagull's. He never drank whisky without
sugaring it, a weakness that Barrymore deplored but overlooked.
These two tramped all over North Beach, the Italian quarter, at
night in the fog, talking. One of the reasons Barrymore liked San
Francisco and its people was that they didn't talk shop to him. They
talked San Francisco."

Sterling took Jack to Bigin's, an Italian place, hangout of Bohemians, and, says Jones, "in the manner of Pickwick, introduced
Barrymore to all Sterling's friends, pals, hangers-on, taxi-men, bar-
keeps, masseurs, politicians, waiters, and the rest."

Barrymore and Prescott, during John Drew's illness in San Francisco, often visited a café known as "The Lost Crosses." This gin-
fogged rendezvous had a small floor space where waterfront dandies
danced as if on pogo sticks with their gillies.

The friends took their own Prohibition liquor to "The Lost
Crosses," as was the custom. One night, while they were drinking
and dining near the kitchen door, a huge fellow appeared suddenly
at Barrymore's and Prescott's table, and seized their half-emptied
glasses.

"What the hell!" Jack shouted. "You're taking my life's blood!"

"Pipe down, Jack," Prescott cautioned his friend, then whispered, "I don't know, but I think this joint is being knocked off."

Prescott barely had uttered this conjecture when the same fellow
who had grabbed their glasses leaped onto a piano bench to call
out: "Ladies and gentlemen, you will all remain seated right where
you are. This is a Federal raid!"

"Good God!" Barrymore said. "Here we are, sitting in probably
the lowest dump in San Francisco—regardless of its religious nomen-
clature—and Uncle Jack is dying at the hospital. I trust that Ethel
won't read of it in the newspapers."

"I don't believe there is a soul here who knows you," Prescott
said, "or even cares who you are."

"Perhaps you're right," said Jack. "Let's feign innocence."

"But," Prescott continued, "in case we *are* led out of here in
chains, remember one thing: your name is not Barrymore, but
Blythe."

Jack brightened. "I'd forgotten all about that."

They sat for some time, Prescott reassuring Barrymore that no
one in the place knew him. Suddenly the same bulking fellow who

had announced the raid, again stood up on the piano bench to call out in a senatorial voice: "It's all right, Mr. Barrymore! You and your friend can leave now!"

As Jack started out across the dance floor everyone began to applaud. He turned, made an elaborate bow, then said, "Thanks. That is more applause than I have had since *Hamlet,* and much more welcome."

On the night of July 8 Jack was enjoying a boxing match. An usher went to his seat to relay the message that Mr. Drew was in a coma, dying. Barrymore remained at his uncle's side all that night.

Early in the morning Mr. Drew roused from the coma to recognize his nephew. The last thing he said to Jack was a cheery: "Stake the nurses! Stake the nurses!"

Upon his return from San Francisco, Jack learned that his yacht, *The Mariner,* had begun to show signs of dry rot. As sometimes happens to a converted sailing vessel, the installation of power had permitted sea damage to penetrate the yacht's wooden skin. Jack wished to preserve *The Mariner,* mainly because of sentimental reasons. He decided that every effort, no matter how expensive, be made to counteract the dry rot. He was assured that the condition could be corrected.

Barrymore sailed on *The Mariner* to San Diego the latter part of July. The Costellos and Prescott traveled there by rail. Then the party motored across the Mexican border to Tia Juana. Jack became morose over some real or fancied frustration concerning his romance, and returned alone to *The Mariner,* then sailed for home.

To shake off his dark mood, a state of mind he himself described as "the bad Jack," Barrymore went with Prescott for long motorcar rides in the Hollywood hills. One day they found themselves near a reservoir.

"We were gabbing about this and that," Prescott recalls, "and finally we turned the car around and started down the mountain. The wall of the mountain was on one side, and a sheer drop of many hundreds of feet on the other side of this narrow road. Without any apparent reason, the brakes of the car went haywire. The automobile started downhill like a greased pig. Jack could not get it under control.

"There was one hairpin turn after another," Prescott continues. "We were both badly frightened. Now Jack whispered to me:

'Well, fellow, as we are a couple of renegade religionists, now is the time for us to do our stuff. If you can think of a couple of Hail Marys and an Our Father, or even if you have to do some ad libbing, I shall join you, because this may be the finish for both of us.' We commenced saying 'Hail Mary,' and staggering through 'Our Father.' We eventually reached the bottom of the precipitous drive. The car came to a stop. We got out, a couple of badly shaken fellows. Then Jack, with that merry twinkle and that quizzical little look, shook himself for a moment, and said in a whisper, 'It worked!' "

In September 1927 Dolores' father obtained an uncontested divorce. The papers had been filed in June of that year, charging incompatability. Dolores Costello now leased a new home for her mother, Helene, and herself at No. 1388 Schuyler Road, Beverly Hills. Barrymore began to visit Dolores more frequently than when her father had been on the premises. Mr. Costello had not regarded Jack as the village paragon.

The housekeeping activities of the Costellos in their new and splendid abode revived in Jack a longing for a place to live other than in a hotel. One morning in September he telephoned Hotchener: "Clementine spoke to me in my dreams last night. She wants a home in the country, where she can play."

Jack's manager inquired: "Is it to be a bachelor's house, or a—?"

Barrymore interrupted him: "A house for two, meaning Clementine and myself, of course. The imp has persuaded me that a reconnaisance in Beverly Hills is indicated. All the swells live there. Why should Clementine reside in a lower social environment?"

Manager Hotchener, upon calling at Jack's hotel, suggested that property owners might "raise the price" when it became known that Barrymore was house hunting.

"We'll fix that," the actor said.

Jack turned, while speaking, to open a chest of drawers. Hotchener naturally thought that he was looking for a bottle. The manager was hardly prepared for what followed. Barrymore wheeled about suddenly, to present a face of horrible contours. Fangs protruded from his lips. Talon-like nails curled from his fingers. He was wearing part of the make-up once used by him in *Dr. Jekyll and Mr. Hyde*.

After Hotchener's pulse again became normal, Jack drew on a

wig and a battered hat. "I don't think the real estate harpies will mistake Mr. Hyde for a man of means," he said.

They set out among the hills north of Beverly. Clementine, after becoming somewhat accustomed to Mr. Hyde's demoniacal phiz, went along.

Jack now remembered having visited a five-room Spanish type dwelling, a hilltop home belonging to King Vidor, the Hollywood director. He had seen a "For Sale" sign there. Jack didn't remember the address. They cruised among the hills for more than two hours. Jack finally located the Vidor house on a private drive off Tower Road.

"That's the place," he said. "Buy it instantly!"

Hotchener decided against stopping to inspect the estate at close range. As Mr. Hyde the actor might invite a shot from the house. Barrymore agreed to crouch low in the car while his manager consulted the agent on the premises, some thirty yards from the road. The prospective buyer and the broker, after a tour of inspection, stood in the Spanish garden to "talk terms." The agent for the owner placed a "fancy price" on the property, almost $60,000.

The agent caught a glimpse of the crouching Mr. Hyde. The hat and wig and one malevolent eye could be seen above the door-level of the automobile. The broker squinted apprehensively.

"A friend," Hotchener explained. The manager touched his forehead momentarily. "A somewhat peculiar fellow. You see, I take care of him."

The agent nodded a little dubiously, then began to explain why such a handsome price had been assigned to the property. "This beautiful place has many advantages. Large acreage, permitting no end of improvements . . ."

"No, no!" Hotchener interrupted. "We don't wish to make any improvements. We lead simple lives."

The agent removed a thousand dollars from the asking-price. Clementine now crawled outside Barrymore's car. She was getting mixed up with her leash. Her jabberings caught the ear of the broker. At this distance he could not be sure whether or not he saw long claws on the hand that reached over the side of the car to seize the little monkey.

Hotchener again explained, nodding toward the automobile, "Have to humor him with pets."

"I see," the agent said worriedly, then returned to his salesmanship. "Think of the beauties of this location. You have an excellent view of the sea, the mountains. At night, millions of lights of Los Angeles twinkling like a jewelry store. You can have, as you see, an extensive tennis court."

"We don't play tennis."

"But," and the agent took another thousand dollars from the price, "that space easily can be turned into a swimming pool."

"Unfortunately, we don't swim."

"Well," and the agent removed a third thousand dollars, "you can have extensive walks, gardens, fountains, even an orchard."

"We have been told," said Hotchener, "that unless one expends a great deal of money on it this is not a favorable district for citrus culture. Also, to bring trees and other supplies up this steep hill and from such a distance would be rather expensive." He nodded toward the automobile, where Mr. Hyde's unwholesome grin now could be seen even at thirty yards. "You see, we entertain *very* seldom. Except for the physicians."

The grimace of Mr. Hyde may have unsettled the agent's judgment. At any rate he now took off three thousand dollars at one slice.

"We do not feel justified," Hotchener told him, "in investing such a great sum. You have been very kind. Good day."

Mr. Hyde could be seen kissing the monkey. "Wait!" the agent said. "How about $52,000?"

The purchaser proposed to pay $50,000, no more. The agent cast another glance toward Mr. Hyde, then surrendered. A deposit was given, and the deal closed.

Several days afterward Jack visited his new home. King Vidor now found out that Barrymore had been the real purchaser of the property. Vidor took the matter good-naturedly, but admitted that Barrymore had saved himself at least $10,000 by wearing Mr. Hyde's fangs, talons, and wig.

As soon as the Vidors had vacated the premises that December, Jack began to redecorate the house. That he intended it for a bachelor's home was indicated by the type of furniture he installed and the changes he made without regard to feminine taste. In the beginning there had been two master bedrooms. Jack brought his books out of storage and converted one of these rooms into a library, with shelves built and carved by a cabinet-maker.

Barrymore did not move into this house until the following year. Meantime he was making *The Tempest*, a story of the Russian revolution, for United Artists.

Toward the close of December 1927 Jack frequently drove from the studio to the Costello home in Schuyler Road to have dinner there. Dolores had done so well as an actress at the Warners' studio that she decided to buy the house in which she and her mother and sister were residing.

Jack's interests now were divided among Dolores, the house renovations in Tower Road, and *The Tempest*. He called almost daily at the home of his beloved. Sometimes he would leave the studio to go shopping with her, choosing window-drapes and furniture for his "bachelor home." He still held to a belief that somehow a wedding would shatter his romance. Besides, there was the fact of his not having been completely freed by Blanche (Michael Strange).

Early in February Jack caught a bad cold. Mrs. Costello put him to bed at her home and attended him with motherly solicitude. This would seem an indication that she really was fond of him, however strict she was in a conventional sense.

At about this time Jack hired a Japanese gardener, C. Nishimura. Nishimura had extraordinary botanical knowledge, and, to quote Jack, "power over plants." He was a quiet, noncommercial little fellow. Had it not been for the business ability of his son, Mark Nishimura, he would have failed at his own private floral enterprises. Both father and son served Barrymore for years.

The elder Nishi enchanted Jack with horticultural marvels. One day he placed rose bushes where Barrymore would be certain to see them. Each plant showed both red and white roses blooming simultaneously.

During March of that year Dolores and her mother left for a holiday in Havana. Jack, one night when lonesome, had a long conversation with his manager about "quitting drink." He said that his first contact with liquor had occurred when he was five years old. He remembered that he had drunk the "residue" from glasses at his boyhood home in Philadelphia, having slipped downstairs in his nightclothes after some dinner guests had gone to Mum Mum's theatre, and before the servants cleared away the table. He added that the servants had laughed at his behavior after seeing him "a bit high." This, of course, may have been one of his fictions. Jack's medical reports, as drawn from his own testimony, place the time of his first "serious" drinking at the age of fifteen, during the year when Mum Mum died.

He now said that if he could turn himself toward some great theatrical enterprise, hurl all his energies into rehearsals and dramatic production, the effort might keep him from drinking. With this in mind, he discussed plans to give *Hamlet* in the open-air Hollywood Bowl.

Jack took Hotchener to the vacant Bowl one evening. The actor stood in the moonlight on the bare stage. He asked his manager to sit in the farthest row of empty seats, high on the hillside. He wished to determine if his voice would "carry" to the limits of a stadium which could seat more than twenty thousand persons. Then Barrymore began the "O! what a rogue and peasant slave am I" soliloquy. His voice sounded clear and resonant in the night air.

Dolores and her mother returned to Beverly Hills to learn that Jack had reserved the Hollywood Bowl for the week beginning September 24. He said that he also intended to do *Hamlet* at the Greek Theatre of the University of California at Berkeley.

Now Jack again asked Helios Hotchener to reveal what the stars foretold for Dolores and himself, and what Helios herself as a friend thought of the romance.

"You will marry her," said his Court Astrologer. "Of that I am confident."

"But Blanche will never divorce me," Jack said with some alarm. "I'm sure she won't."

"Why not go East to see her?" asked Helios. "I feel that she will receive you sympathetically."

Jack next day consulted the head of the United Artists art department, William Cameron Menzies. He asked Menzies to inspect the Tower Road property, and to supervise the designing of a six-room addition, with servants' quarters. "Just in case I want to have a larger house," he said. Plans for the enlargement were drawn by architect Paul Crawley.

Ghost writer Karl Schmidt now arrived in Hollywood. Jack began again to drink. The journey East to see Michael Strange seemed on his mind. He made some "retakes" for *The Tempest*, discussed doing *Hamlet* in the Bowl, then left Los Angeles by train with Schmidt on April 5, 1928. He told no one other than the Costellos and the Hotcheners of his plan to see his second wife. He informed questioners that he was going East to purchase "some special things" for his Tower Road house. He added under his breath, "To purchase freedom, if I can."

He returned to Los Angeles the morning of May 2. An inflammation of the eyes had been troubling him during the train ride. He consulted Dr. A. C. Macleish, then went to the studio. Early in the afternoon he drove with his manager to the Tower Road house.

Here two kinds of alterations were simultaneously in progress. The changes ordered for the "bachelor's quarters" were not yet completed, but work on enlarging the house "just in case" had been begun in accordance with the designs of artist Menzies. This material confusion seemed a symbol of Jack's mental conflict.

"How did you come out with Michael Strange?" his manager asked.

"Just fine," Jack said. He changed the subject, then drove away to Dolores' home. He stayed as a guest of Mrs. Costello until May 6, when he packed a small bag and left for his Tower Road house, to sleep his first night there "officially."

Dolores and Helios had arranged flowers in every room of the "bachelor's quarters." The sun was still shining when Jack arrived in the early evening. The place seemed joyous. Barrymore appeared entirely content. He talked chiefly of two things, his love for Dolores, and the doing of *Hamlet* in the Hollywood Bowl.

But not many days afterward when Jack called at the Hotcheners' house, he appeared to have something on his mind. He revealed sheepishly that while in New York he had "not directly broached the matter of a divorce." He said he had wanted to mention it to his second wife, but added: "Blanche was so very friendly that I simply could not speak of a divorce. We had a really happy visit together. I couldn't put the question. She was pleasant and attractive. In fact, we both recognized that we were much nicer people when apart than we had been together. How could I tell her that I now wanted to marry someone else?"

"Well," his manager said, "you went on a six-thousand mile errand that you did not accomplish. I advise you *right now* to telephone Michael Strange long distance, and ask her for a divorce."

Jack winced. "I'll do it in a day or two." He paused. "I must wait for a propitious moment."

A few days afterward Jack stood on the hillside at Tower Road. He was pale and furious. He held a Hollywood "gossip" column in his hands. It had been sent to him by Mrs. Costello. Otherwise he probably would not have read it. He gave the column to his manager. It was an "exposé" of Jack's secret romance. The article hinted at "more of the same" in a forthcoming issue. Such publicity as this obviously did no one any pleasant service.

"I was waiting for a propitious moment to telephone Blanche about a divorce," Jack said to his manager. "It seems now that the moment has arrived."

He talked to Michael Strange for half an hour. He was amazed to find her both gracious and sympathetic. She was willing to divorce him, but insisted that the proceedings be brought in New York City.

The actor paused in the divorce plans only long enough to sign a contract with Warner Brothers. This was for a million dollars, Barrymore to make five pictures within two years from the date of signature.

On June 22, Barrymore and his manager left Los Angeles on "The Chief." Jack had been abstaining from liquor since May 2. Aboard the eastbound train Jack found actor George Jessel. They spent most of their travel time together playing dominoes, sipping gingerale, and discussing love.

Upon his arrival in New York, Jack stayed as much as possible away from Broadway. He spent the first evening with his great friend Edward Sheldon. Later on that same night he discussed terms of the divorce settlement with attorney Henry Root Stern.

Toward the end of June Jack went to Mamaroneck to see Ethel and her family. He told his sister that he was keeping "out of sight" as much as possible, as no one other than the parties immediately concerned knew of his divorce plans.

On June 29 the divorce proceedings were held in a conference room at the Bar Association Building. No members of the press were present. Nor were the newspapers likely to be interested in the domestic rifts of the litigants under their names of Mrs. Blanche M. L. Blythe and John Blythe.

The divorce, it was explained to Jack, would be granted, and the papers sealed, once he had gone through with some minor formalities. One of these had to do with the filing of an affidavit by someone who had known his father, and who would attest to Maurice having been an American citizen, and not a subject of the King of England.

"I know the King's son very well," Jack said to his manager.

It was thought best not to disturb His Royal Highness with such matters. It also was believed expedient, in the interests of secrecy and until the divorce would become official, to seek out some tactful friend for the procurement of the affidavit.

It was arranged for Barrymore to obtain the document from his father's and his own good friend, the former postmaster of New York, Thomas Patten, now in retirement in Los Angeles.

Barrymore, with his new freedom almost at hand, left New York on July 1, 1928.

He stopped over in Chicago to telephone the news to Dolores. Then he resumed the summer-hot journey toward the West, still not drinking anything but ginger-ale, and playing dominoes with his manager, and thinking and talking of Dolores.

7.

Fifty Keys and a Trunk

IT would be five more months until their marriage, and still another month before they set out together on their wedding trip to the enchanted isles.

These months of waiting accentuated the contrasting humors of the mercurial actor, whose today's elations became tomorrow's broodings. He grew impatient over the first month of snail's pace legal technicalities required for the divorce decree. When the final papers reached him, he became suddenly gay and affable.

Then, one day soon afterward, he chanced to overhear the remark of a fellow actor that New York divorces "were no good in California." There was no basis whatsoever for such a claim, yet Barrymore didn't investigate its lack of validity. He plunged forthwith into a dark frenzy, and stayed in that condition of mind for weeks. He became suspicious of almost everyone.

He now began to imagine that Dolores was flirting. Jack had no reasonable ground for this belief; Dolores had nodded in response to a greeting by an old friend of the family's, a mere smiling civility. Jack became furious. The fact that everyone, women and men alike, turned to look at the beautiful, blond creature, aroused in Barrymore the thought that he was about to lose her. It was natural for Dolores to smile; it was characteristic of him to demand all her smiles for himself alone.

In this state of mind, he stood late in July within the unfinished walls of the new house he was building for his and Dolores' occupancy. He cried out above the noise of saws and hammers and planes that he had been "disillusioned."

He sulked for days. He refused to discuss the script of *Eternal Love*, the forthcoming picture he was called upon to do under the United Artists' contract. It would be his third and last photoplay for that studio. It would be his own final silent motion picture as well.

Sound now had begun to reach the screen. Even the prospect of undertaking his first talking motion picture at Warners did not immediately interest Barrymore. The important thing to him was that Dolores had flirted.

Jack waived all plans for the playing of *Hamlet* in the Hollywood Bowl. Other, simpler duties likewise were slighted. He was reminded, for example, that he had received ten thousand dollars to serve as a judge in a beauty contest sponsored by a soap company. All he had been asked to do to earn the large fee was to appraise the photographs of some thirty young women, then choose from among them "the most beautiful debutante, the most beautiful college girl, the most beautiful young matron." He refused even to glance at these photographs. The soap company was in a lather at the delay. He didn't care. Dolores had flirted!

He decided to sail alone on *The Mariner* to Ensenada. He was gone during the first seven days in August.

Upon his return home Barrymore telephoned long distance to Edward Sheldon. His friend may have counseled him against behaving like an ass. Sheldon does not say. At any rate, Jack felt somewhat better next day. He spent this morning at his gardener's nursery in Glendale. In the afternoon he conferred with director Ernst Lubitsch concerning a trip to Canada for location shots for the making of *Eternal Love*.

He still would not visit Dolores. She had flirted. He went to Lionel's house in Roxbury Drive to spend the night with his brother. They sat up until dawn listening to phonograph recordings of Brahms' works.

Next day Jack found a new and more reasonable cause for brooding. He had been persuaded after long argument to give away his monkey Clementine. She had become jealous of Barrymore, because of his love for Dolores.

Jack took Clementine to the Luna Park Zoo, held her for a long time, made certain that she would be well cared for, then started away from her cage.

"I wish to God I never had looked back at her," he afterward said. "She was holding out her little hands to me through the wirework of her cage. I sat in my car, heavy-hearted. I didn't dare drive for several minutes. It was the nastiest trick I ever played on anyone."

The sun began to shine again on August 13. Jack reported to his manager that there had been a reconciliation with Dolores. He announced also that he wanted "instantly" to buy the four acres to the north of his estate, and higher up the mountain, because the new house was so close to the property line of his own three and one-half acres.

Jack called the new structure "The Marriage House." It was connected with the original Vidor hacienda by means of a long, cloisterlike pergola. He came to know the older house as "Liberty Hall."

The Marriage House had six rooms, Liberty Hall five. It was not foreseen by anyone at this time that Barrymore's establishment one day would comprise sixteen separate structures, fifty-five rooms in which furniture stood, storerooms, a projection room, dressingrooms, a large aviary, a rathskeller, six pools, a bowling green, a skeet range, several fountains, and a totem pole, upon the topmost figure of which a fern grew incongruously, like the hair of Signor Arturo Toscanini dyed green.

He was gone for six weeks, at Banff and Lake Louise, Canada, on location for *Eternal Love*. He did not drink during that time, although exposed to the good and legal bottles of the Dominion. Upon his return, toward the middle of September, he found the Marriage House nearing completion.

Barrymore was sleeping in Liberty Hall, attended by one manservant, Clito, a Filipino. Jack would rise early each day to watch the builders at work on the Marriage House.

"The place is beginning to look like Angkor Wat," he said.

One day in October, while inspecting the large bedroom which he was to occupy with Dolores, he turned to the builder, Emmet

D. Camomile, to exclaim: "My God! I've forgotten to include in the plans the most important place of all. A hideaway!"

"Do you want to look at the blueprints?" Camomile asked. "We'd like to start plastering tomorrow."

"Never mind the blueprints," Jack said. He moved to a balcony outside the bedroom, then pointed to a tower directly above the boudoir. "That's the very place for it. Can you build a room in the tower, with a trap door, and a ladder that I can pull in after me?"

Camomile thought it possible to do this. The hideaway was built, a low-ceiling eyrie that became hot from the midday sun beating upon the roof tiles. Notwithstanding the heat and lack of head room, it was a place for privacy.

Four matters now perplexed Jack early in November. He became worried about the dry-rot signs appearing in *The Mariner's* hull. Next, he wondered, "What age should I concede when I apply for a marriage license?" Then his eyes began to trouble him after a gypsum snow-scene during the final work on *Eternal Love*. And, not the least of his problems, a clergyman friend, whom he had asked to perform the marriage ceremony, refused to officiate because Barrymore was a divorced person.

The first three problems were resolved in order. The underwriters examined *The Mariner* and pronounced her safe for the honeymoon voyage. Jack himself settled upon "thirty-seven as my perennial age" for the marriage license, instead of his actual forty-six years. Next, Dr. Macleish treated his eyes successfully. The fourth of his present worries, however, stumped him. His clergyman friend declined to perform the ceremony.

Jack had not been drinking for two months. As an heroic measure, however, and when the clergyman called upon him in Liberty Hall, Barrymore opened a bottle. They both partook liberally. A second bottle swayed the clergyman's body but not his mind. He would not speak the necessary words at Barrymore's wedding.

Jack and his manager went next day on a tour of parsonages. They finally prevailed upon the Reverend Theodore Abel, a Unitarian minister, to undertake the marriage service. On November 20, Jack, Dolores, Helene, and Hotchener drove to the Los Angeles license bureau, where the actor and his fiancée signed the formal papers.

Reporters arrived to ask Jack when and where he had obtained a divorce. He declined to reveal this information. He went from the bureau to a jeweler's to buy a wedding ring and numerous other presents for Dolores. Then he visited a tailoring establishment for a last fitting of the suit in which he was to be married.

On the morning of November 24, 1928, Jack drove to the courthouse to pick up his license. He was gay. He returned to Tower Road, dressed himself in his new suit, then, in the early afternoon, drove to Schuyler Road to marry Dolores in her home.

The bride at this time was making a picture at the Warner Brothers' Sunset Boulevard studio. Jack himself was deep in plans for his first talking picture on the same lot. They drove each day to and from work, talking of where they would go for a wedding trip, and when.

Otto Matthies now was captain of the Barrymore yacht. He conferred with his newly married employer as to the cruise, and finally it was agreed that Otto sail *The Mariner* to Balboa, Canal Zone. The Barrymores would take the Panama-Pacific liner *Virginia* to that port, then go aboard their own yacht for the long-delayed voyage without a chaperon.

At noon, December 29, 1928, a radiant Dolores appeared in her husband's library to say, "Mamma just phoned to remind us that we ought to pack our trunks and get them down to the steamer. We don't want to have a last-minute rush."

"That's a good idea, darling," said Jack. "Suppose you get your things ready first."

The *Virginia* was to sail from Wilmington, a port some thirty-five miles distant from the Barrymore house, at midnight next day.

"I'd offer to help you," Jack continued, "only Lionel is coming over with a story he's been writing. Thinks we can use it for my first talkie. I'd like to get that settled before I leave."

Lionel arrived, and the brothers talked about painting, music, and anything but business. Lionel finally left toward one o'clock in the morning. Dolores wakened long enough to ask, "Was everything all right? Did you get finished?"

"No," her husband replied, "Lionel hasn't done the end of his story yet, and it looks as if the Warners will insist on their own story, *General Crack*. They want to build the sets while we are away."

"I mean," said Dolores, "did you get your *packing* finished?"

"Oh, that!" snorted Jack. "Don't worry about it, darling. It only takes *me* a few minutes to pack. Done it all my life."

The first thing Dolores asked the next morning was, "Now you'll pack early, won't you, dear? The baggage man will be here at four o'clock."

"You may be sure of it, Winkie. But first I want to run down the hill to see Hank. I've thought of so many things that ought to be done around the place while we're away."

"Well, so long as you get packed."

"Packing is second nature with me," he said.

Jack went to the office he had built for Hotchener over a new garage. It had in it, among other things, a couch he had "borrowed" from Ethel some ten years before.

Today he signed some checks, one for $3,500 pocket money for the honeymoon trip, and many others for current bills, including $361 for the month's long-distance telephone calls. Then he fell asleep on the couch.

At four o'clock there was a knock on the office door. Barrymore's drayman friend, Dave Connor, came inside to announce: "Mrs. Barrymore told me to get your trunk. I've got her things already loaded on the truck for Wilmington, and I'm telling you her baggage looks swell."

"My God!" Barrymore said, rising from the couch. "I'd forgotten all about packing. Get my trunk for me, Dave, will you? You brought it from the Ambassador when I moved in."

"You mean the busted one?" Dave said. "The old busted one, with the top loose, and the handle knocked off, that you said you was going to have fixed?"

"It's a big, sturdy theatrical trunk," Barrymore said defensively. "And I'll thank you not to slander it. Bring it down here. No, that way I'd have to carry the things down here to put in it. Just take it to my bedroom."

"Where'll I find the trunk?" Dave asked.

"You brought it here. Go find it, instantly."

Barrymore and Hotchener went to the house. Presently Dave staggered in with a huge trunk, a box so old, so mildewed and buffeted, that it might well have been the original patent model. It bore dog-eared hotel and theatre stickers, remnants of customs stamps, the tarnished initials "J. D."

Hotchener noticed the lettering. Barrymore read his mind. "Belonged to Uncle Jack Drew," explained the actor. "Borrowed it from him. Carried it around with me since *The Fortune Hunter*. Practically set up light housekeeping in it."

Barrymore patted the ancient flanks of the trunk and fiddled with the corroded, greenish brass lock. "Damn it!" he said. "It's locked! And Blaney has put the key somewhere. And Blaney's in England. Think we could shoot him an emergency cable?"

"I ought to get started for Wilmington," said Connor. "I've had nothing to eat since breakfast, and we got to make the steamer before they quit loading."

"I'll find the key, don't worry," Barrymore said. "I'll empty all the drawers on the floor. It'll save time anyway."

He began to empty drawers. He finally cried out exultantly. There clattered from one of the drawers of a chifforobe, in which his dress-shirts had been, a huge bunch of keys. These were of various sizes and shapes, and strung on a long rusty chain that had left marks on some of the white shirts.

Barrymore happily picked up the keys. "What'd I tell you? Now we're ready for any ordeal."

"But," asked Hotchener, "can you pick out the right key to this trunk?"

"Instantly," said Barrymore.

He began to examine the fifty or more keys with great interest. There were several hotel keys among them, as indicated by their tags. It was well known that Barrymore never bothered to return a key to a hotel desk.

"Can I help you find it, Mr. Barrymore?" the worried drayman inquired. "It's getting awful late."

"No, thanks," Jack said. "I'll find it instantly. These keys are all old friends of mine. It's like a class reunion."

He was examining the keys reminiscently. A brass key, larger than the others, caused him to lift his brows.

"Now what do you think of *that*?" he cried. He showed the big key to Hotchener. "Do you have the least idea how it got here?"

Hotchener was looking at his watch. He glanced at the key in Barrymore's hand. "No. Do you?"

"Can you imagine?" Jack said. "It's the key to Whistler's house in London. Historic! Ought to be enshrined alongside the *Magna Carta*." He paused, then said aggrievedly, "When I checked out of the great artist's abode, the agent kept asking me what had become of the key. How in hell was I to know what had become of it? You'd have thought I had stolen it for a souvenir. This proves my innocence."

Clito, the Filipino servant, opened the door. Barrymore dropped the keys. He sprang to the pile of clothing on the floor. He picked up two pairs of long underwear, as if to simulate packing.

When he saw it was only the servant at the door, he sighed. "I thought it was Mrs. Barrymore."

Barrymore dispensed with the long underwear, and again took up the keys. He selected a slightly bent one.

"You see!" he cried. "Life can become very simple." Then he tried to turn the key. It snapped off in the lock. He stared at the piece of metal in his hand. Then he said slowly: "Gentlemen, there comes a tide in the affairs of bastards when no amount of cursing will suffice. Let us merely observe a moment of silence, like a deaf-mute who has just hit his fingers with a hammer."

Barrymore turned to Hotchener. "Hank, get a locksmith instantly."

"I'll drive down to Beverly," said Connor, "where I know one is."

Clito again entered the room to say, "Missus wants to know if trunk packed, and tell you dress for dinner to go home of Missus' mother."

"Clito," said Jack, "tell Mrs. Barrymore that if she will only look to the road, she will see the baggage-truck speeding on its way. I shall be with her instantly."

While waiting for the locksmith, Barrymore had a drink. Then his eye lighted upon a decrepit pair of khaki trousers among the heap of clothing on the floor. He picked them up, fondled them.

"These fishing pants," he extolled, "surely must be taken along. Don't laugh. This garment is a bit soiled, and the seams giving way at vital junctures, but these pants are *pants!* Had 'em for years. Had 'em on *The Gypsy* and aboard *The Mariner* during the Honolulu race."

Dave Connor and the locksmith, a scholarly appearing man with a satchel like a lung-doctor's, arrived in the bedroom at almost six o'clock. The key specialist opened the trunk with such speed that Jack said to him: "Sir, you are one locksmith that Love dare not laugh at."

Jack maneuvered the warped and creaking lid. Then he dived

into the ancient depths with a loud cry. He came up with a small weapon, then turned to the group. "Know what this is?"

"I only know I'm hungry and it's late," said Connor.

"I've been looking high and low for this precious relic," Jack said. "It's Hamlet's dagger! What archeologists we have become this day!"

Clito again poked his head in the doorway. "Missus says what's making Mr. B. late as usual?"

"Tell her I'll be with her as soon as I put on my necktie," Barrymore said. Then he sniffed the moldy interior of the trunk, and cried, "I have not been as thrilled since the first time I stepped inside the Louvre."

"Jack," said Hotchener, "do you think it's right to take this old wreck of a trunk on a honeymoon trip?"

Barrymore stiffened. "What do you mean 'old'? There's a lot of honeymooning possible in this trunk yet."

"I was only wondering," Hotchener said, "what people will think, or perhaps say, when it is placed beside the shiny new luggage Dolores has packed for the honeymoon."

"If you are hinting at a December and May alliance," said Jack, "you are wide of the mark. I see no symbolism at all in the juxtaposition of the trunks. This one has many treasured associations."

"But, Jack," Hotchener persisted, "how many honeymoons does this trunk represent?"

"Both of 'em. Why?"

"What do you suppose Dolores will think when she sees it alongside her *first* honeymoon luggage?"

"She won't think a thing of it. She's a great sport."

"Then," said Hotchener, "do you yourself regard it as a symbol of happiness in regard to marriage?"

Barrymore opened his eyes wide. "Get another trunk! Instantly!"

Hotchener consulted his watch. "I don't know how we'll do it. It's past six o'clock. The shops are closed."

"Well, *try!*" said Jack. "We've got to have a new trunk."

Hotchener got the Hollywood Luggage Shop on the telephone.

Barrymore prevailed upon the "boss" to remain open until he could come down to the luggage shop. He set out in his roadster with Hotchener, calling out to Connor in passing: "Wait here for me. I'll be back instantly."

At the luggage shop Barrymore selected a large trunk, then with his manager's assistance carried the trunk to the roadster. It would not fit in the rumble seat. Hotchener took the wheel. Jack stood up in the rumble seat, steadying the trunk on the swift return ride to Tower Road.

Mrs. Costello said good-by to her daughter and her son-in-law that night in the flower-filled sitting-room of the Barrymore suite aboard the *Virginia*. Mrs. Costello was weeping. Jack put his arms about her, kissed her, then said: "Don't worry, Mamma. I'll be sure to cable you every day. And I'll take good care of Dolores, always."

8.

The Enchanted Isles

THE MARINER took aboard the last of her stores at San Pedro on Saturday morning, December 15, put the gangway ashore, then underwent a compass adjustment in the outer harbor. At noon the breakwater light was abeam hard by, then the yacht sailed southward for a rendezvous with the Barrymores at Balboa in the Canal Zone.

January 4 found the yacht at quarantine anchorage off Balboa. A pilot came aboard to take her into the harbor. There *The Mariner* dropped anchor and also made fast a stern line to a mooring-buoy.

First Mate Henry Kruse, a fellow after Barrymore's own point of view, entered in the ship's logbook this comment on Sunday, January 6, 1929:

> Cook and steward went to church. Cook recovering at nightfall, but steward still benumbed by divine services.

Next day all hands turned to, scrubbing the decks and sides, setting up forestays and mainrigging, putting up awnings, and polishing the bright-work. The honeymooners, arriving at Balboa on the *Virginia*, were due aboard *The Mariner* at noon.

It now was discovered that *The Mariner's* main tank had rotted through at the bottom, and was shipping bilge-water and oil. This meant a delay in port until the tank could be cleaned and cemented. The Barrymores did not go aboard their yacht for the next two days.

What Jack and Dolores did meantime to occupy themselves is told in Barrymore's diary. This latter section of the actor's sea log was kept in the same ledger used by him aboard *The Gypsy* during his winter "voyage of yearning," 1925–1926, almost three years before the honeymoon. The second part of Jack's memoir often fails to specify the days to which the entries refer. The dates, however, are fixed by cross-checking the actor's own record against the ship's log kept by First Mate Kruse.

This sequel differs in mood from the earlier Barrymore outpourings. Then his soul had cried out for possession of his far-off loved one. He had sought to express his own innermost meanings, as in a *Ballade Pathétique*. Now Dolores was physically here in his arms, and without anyone to say no to his passion. The time of introspection and of emotional civil war seemingly had ended. It was as if a third symphonic movement, jubilant and festive, were being played within the man's heart. Indeed, Barrymore's whole life seems to have been a variegated symphony, and, to some degree, an unfinished one.

Dolores and he, Jack's diary states, had enjoyed themselves while on the steamer. They had white wine, legally, and "wandered about the ship, arm-in-arm, with complete disregard for anyone else."

At Balboa, and while the yacht's tanks were undergoing repair, they were entertained by an old friend of Jack's father. Mason Mitchell, a white-haired gentleman, arranged for permits for the Barrymores to hunt and remove fauna from the Galapagos.

"Went with Winkie and Mitchell," the diary reads, "to a dinner place, Mrs. Bryan's. She keeps birds, and how! The birds all seem to know her, and adore her. We ordered ten pairs to take home."

Barrymore now spent more than a hundred dollars on a detailed cable to his business manager, directing him to build an aviary "instantly" at Tower Road. Hotchener was advised to remove the tile roof from the trophy room, then construct the aviary as a second story, with heating apparatus for tropical birds.

Barrymore's diary says that Dolores and he "had an amusing time in Panama all around," and adds:

Everywhere we went to have a drink, dinner, or buy a toothbrush, we collected a crowd of varying proportions, depending on the length of the drink. Tonight we had dinner on a little balcony above a funny old hotel with a bar overlooking the Prado. A crowd gathered like the mob scene in *Leah the Forsaken*. Winkie and myself were in a state of complete well-being with the world, with cocktails, wine, beer, etc., and got into our open-faced hack, which was waiting, and drove away waving like Napoleon the Third and the Empress Eugénie, amid the cheers of the enraptured multitude.

The Barrymores boarded *The Mariner* for the first time as husband and wife late in the afternoon of January 9. Jack writes that they were "seen off by a large crowd of amiable well-wishers of various colors."

The yacht put in among the islands of Bahia Honda, Colombia, two days afterward. Jack wrote of this excursion:

The most beautiful Islands we had ever seen, charming natives living in unbelievable primitiveness, with funny little paper altars in their sugar-cane storerooms, dirt floors, thatched roofs, babies on the floor wrapped up, chickens and pigs next to them, countless very thin dogs, and rather fat ducks that the dogs look at with a terrifying fixity but never go near. Winkie and I had a bath in an amazingly beautiful mountain stream with a deep cool nook in it. The hot sun beat through the leaves of gigantic mahogany trees. *Trout* eight inches long in this stream. As a matter of fact this was on the mainland; the islands were near it in a lovely bay. Caught big cavallos (pompano) weighing thirty pounds. Shot one alligator which promptly sank. "Up in three days," they said. We couldn't wait.

Barrymore admired Dolores for her readiness to try her hand at shooting or deep-sea fishing, although she had been reared as a "delicate flower in a mother's hothouse." He tells of her "palship" and her "adaptability" while they were out shooting curlews.

Winkie made a perfect shot with the Parker 28 I had given her. First time she ever had a shotgun in her hand. Otto and I almost fell off the boat. Landed on a beautiful white sandy beach on heavenly island called Afuerta, next to a larger one called Asuera. We think seriously of buying it. It sounds fantastic at first blush, but isn't, considering how we like to live.

The most memorable thing we encountered was our alligator-guide's appearance. He had on a splendid homemade shirt and a funny little hat that defies description. It looked like a child's work-basket perched on the top of his raven locks. God alone knows how he kept it on! The arresting part of his get-up were his pants. He was as swell as the devil as to hat and shirt, but every time he bent over, well, the seat of his breeches was in shreds!

There was more "tank" trouble aboard *The Mariner*. The yacht lay at anchor for four days instead of proceeding to Cocos Island, the next port of call.

Jack's lack of time-sense when he was "away from the world" was indicated by his having forgotten to cable his worried mother-in-law, in accord with his promise. Dolores assumed that Jack had sent word to Mrs. Costello. Barrymore had promised his wife to do so "instantly." Their cruise was forty-three days old before Jack cabled:

DOLORES IS WONDERFUL.

The Cocos Island interlude is described in Jack's diary:

Got away for Cocos Island. Think more seriously than ever of buying islands here. There is *everything* here any human being could wish. Got to Cocos Island the next evening too late to get a really good peek at it. Seen in the morning it was beautiful beyond words.

We took the small boat and went slowly around the island, or rather the northeast side of it, and were knocked completely out by its loveliness. Enormous high banks covered with brilliant green moss-like ivy, surmounted by every possible type of graceful feathery tree, and every few hundred yards slim cascades of water falling down three or more hundred feet like smoky silver ribbons of mist into the sea.

The whole thing is unbelievable and intensely "operatic." It is like Chateaubriand's *Atala* with Doré at his best. I don't suppose there is any place quite like it in the world. It was a beautiful day, calm sea, porpoises leaping all around us, almost touching the boat, thousands of birds, frigate-birds and boobys, flying around us absolutely fearlessly, almost lighting on us to satisfy their curiosity.

It was sometimes impossible to fish as the birds would swoop to pick up the lure then carry it up in the air and fight among themselves over it. One got hooked this way and we had to pull him into the boat and unhook him. He lay with his huge wings outstretched in the bottom of the boat, looking at us with a baleful eye. Then when he thought he could make it, clambered with beak and claw to the gunwale, deliberately threw up over the side, and flew slowly away.

Below us in the clear water we could see the snow-white sand flecked with large coral rock; and fish such as never were, things of gleaming and sombre fire, every color imaginable, radiating beauty as if lit from within. All sizes, all shapes, with copper-colored sharks with silver lines on the outside of their fins, and all living amicably together.

On Sunday, January 13, Barrymore was up earlier than Dolores. He went in the launch with Captain Otto to do some harpooning among great swarms of sharks. He wrote in the diary that night:

We started by going after an enormous manta ray or devil-fish. Otto harpooned him with great dexterity with regular whaling harpoon. The line attached to the empty gasoline drum went overboard when the ray made for the open sea after being struck. It was fascinating to watch that huge thing swimming powerfully enough to drag the heavy drum under water.

Otto lanced him, but Charlie Ray appeared so healthy and so dangerous—he was a whopper—that Otto said, "Shoot him." I had brought the heavy Manlicher rifle along. I pumped about seven shots into him before hitting a vital spot. It was like operating on something when one knows nothing about its organs. It did no good at all to hit him in the head. There is a spot about eighteen inches square half-way between his stumpy tail, like an elephant's, and his humped back, where he carries everything he has of internal importance.

Dolores had come on deck to watch this battle. She called out to Jack to "go after a fifteen-foot shark that had been coquetting with her as she leaned over the rail." The diary continues:

So we piled into the little boat again, after Otto had harpooned the shark from the deck of the big boat, still using the gasoline drum idea. The "idea," by the way, missed me about two inches as it whizzed past at about forty miles an hour. The shark bent three harpoons before one finally stuck, and here is a remarkable thing: we had a big piece of the ray on a shark-hook for bait, and after the shark was harpooned I shot him through the side of the head a little off-center; he tore the harpoon out, and, with the blood streaming from him like black smoke in the water, went quite casually to that bait again and swallowed it!

Otto harpooned him again. Whiz went the gasoline drum after the shark, and we after the gasoline drum! Winkie was "excited but controlled" like Mrs. Martin Johnson. She is really grand at what is for her a totally new dimension. She doesn't seem to be a damned bit afraid of anything.

Anyway we got up to the shark, which had bent two lances all out of shape. I shot him gleefully and without the compunction I had felt about the ray. We photographed him and cut his jaws out, then sent him on his way bottomwards where he belongs. Earlier we had hung him up by his tail, and quantities of feathers came out of his mouth from his stomach, proving he feeds on resting birds. The shark's length was exactly fourteen feet, ten inches. He must have weighed almost two thousand pounds. The ray, by the way, was seventeen feet across from fluke to fluke.

It was a fairly eventful first morning in a new spot. It even almost satisfied Winkie.

They went bathing the next day under a waterfall, and saw carved upon the rocks surrounding it the names of "pirates and privateersmen and of their ships."

"We filled the water tanks," the diary continues, "by the simple device of first filling the dories with a hose from a waterfall that fell into the sea. We towed them to the boat with the launch, as we knew that Galapagos and fresh water meant nothing to each other."

He daydreamed of living with Dolores on this island. In his mind's eye he already could see a house built for them here. He wrote as if it were already a reality:

I carved Winkie's initials and mine on a beautiful cocoanut tree in a grove, with a cat under it (I mean a *carved* cat) as I know the "small egg" and I will come to this divine place again. It is, after all, only a short jaunt from our dear bamboo house with the big veranda facing the sunset at Afuerta Island.

The Mariner's windlass brought in forty-five fathoms of chain, the crew stowed anchor, then on January 20 the Barrymores sailed for Tower Island in the Galapagos. Light variable southerly winds, accompanied by a steadily increasing sea swell, were followed by delaying weather. The diary continues:

> Arrived off Tower Island at night. First morning view very different from Cocos. Couldn't imagine greater contrast. From Paradise straight to the outposts of Hades! Tower Island is flat, bleak, dusty gray, dead as a deserted out-house doornail. Bad breeze from shore, didn't land. Turned tail and fled straight to Tagos Cove, Albermarle, passing Bidlos. Crossed Equator. Tagos Cove much more interesting. Saw our first sea-lizard squatting in archaic majesty on a surf-beaten lava rock as we rowed slowly in the skiff near the shore. He was unbelievably exciting to see. Straight from the Dead Past, the veritable model of all the beasts one drew on slates in the Convent of Notre Dame in Philadelphia instead of the more baleful arithmetic. He looked whimsical and delightful.

The Mariner's windlass broke while heaving anchor in Tagos Cove. The hook fouled under the ledge of a shelf not indicated on the chart. The anchor and sails now would have to be hoisted by hand.

The honeymooners happily explored the island, fished, photographed birds, sea-lions and huge lizards. Jack, of course, liked these reptiles. He says in his diary entry of January 25:

> Lunched on the rocks in a little cove, among the iguanas, whole families of them, tame and pleasant as possible. Cannot see them as hideous monsters in the sense Darwin describes them. They seem like animated cartoons by Winsor McKay. Also flightless cormorant on nest with young. Her husband did everything but butt us off the rocks like a goat! Absolutely fearless.
>
> We sat there in the sands with the waves lapping on the beach, the sea-lions nosing around the launch. The marine iguanas, with flocks of eight and nine young ones, let us scratch them on their stomachs, their preposterous antedeluvian profiles turned toward the blazing sky. The almost extinct cormorant, with its brilliant milky green eye, made occasional gurgling noises at us; its white fuzzy infant uttering shrill musical squeaks on that utterly uninhabited sunlit strand. With a bottle of cold (authentic) German beer in one hand, and a large turkey leg in the other, there seemed no such place as Hollywood, and in the bright lexicon of youth no such word as "Camera." It will sink into one's memory never to be really erased!

Something in Jack's character, all his life, responded to monsters and to scenes of desolation. He had an eye for the stark manifestations as well as for the handsome displays of nature. He writes of Seymore Island:

> Winkie and I went ahead as Otto tied the boat just over the sand dune at the top of the beach. Here was a field of red clay, looking like the lost world of Conan Doyle. To make the analogy complete, there, smack in front of us, silent, enormous, watchful, red like the clay hummock he crouched on, we saw our first land iguana. I made futuristic and strangled gestures to Winkie, who was just behind me, looking the other way. When she saw it she almost dropped with the thrill of it.
>
> We stood watching it for minutes, then looked about to see countless other ones lying under trees, eating, waddling about, all silent, always silent. I chased one and finally grabbed it by the tail. They can run like the devil, in spite of the scientists.

There came to me as I caught it a delightful passage in Darwin, where he had done the same thing to a burrowing one:

> I watched one for a long time, till half its body was buried; I then walked up and pulled it by the tail; at this it was greatly astonished, and soon shuffled up to see what was the matter; and then stared me in the face, as much as to say, "What made you pull my tail?"

When one has always visualized Charles Darwin as a venerable, bald and bearded person, with fame and with honors, this is pleasant reading from a young man of twenty-six, as he then was.

On February 2 *The Mariner* arrived at Chatham Island, where there were coffee and sugar plantations. Barrymore engaged a young native from Guayaquil, Ecuador, who spoke French, to act as their guide to the inland plantation of Señor Cobos and Jesus de Alvarado. The diary continues:

> Jesus Alvarado met us at dock, and we rode to the ranch, straight up, and upon an extremely good road. *Bueno Camino*, made of round boulders of equal size, covered with red earth. Alvarado was a distinguished-looking type about forty, fine Spanish head. We were met on the way by Señor Cobos, his brother-in-law. Apparently they run the ranch between them. Señor Cobos spoke beautiful French. He was educated in Paris.

My rusty French of fiacres and corner cafés and railway journeys must have amused him; but his manners, like those of everyone else we have met on these islands, were perfect.

The ranch itself is utterly feudal. The big cement house of the owners overlooks the palm leaf huts of the workmen and women and countless children. These huts are below the big house. The ranch is surrounded by those deep green hills, the sun glinting everywhere, in the distance.

The oxen come in in the evening, and the children wash under the pump in the meadow, and the old women draw water. An occasional cowboy rides up on a little horse, and looks like a chessman. The riders have amazing serapes, with bottles and gourds for coffee slung over their shoulders. They wander into the store next to and below the big house where the meat and coffee are drying on the roof. Then they wander away again, while we sit on the balcony in the setting sun, eating sliced pineapple and drinking cognac and *maiza water*. It all seems essentially medieval.

Dolores and Jack left the Galapagos on February 6, bound for Guayaquil. Although near the equator, the nights were cool; the crew had been sleeping on deck. There was a fine breeze, so Captain Otto stopped the engine and the yacht proceeded under sail. Next day the wind freshened and a sea began running. A backstay was carried away and a staysail torn while being lowered. The wind began to die down toward the evening of February 8 and the sea to flatten out. The engine again was started that night, and on the morning of the 9th the Barrymores arrived at Guayaquil, Ecuador.

We picked up a pilot at Puna, a flat, muddy, unprepossessing place which we were told was the "summer resort" of the wealthy residents of Guayaquil. Guayaquil has fine *marina*, or long quay, and new government buildings, little hills near the shore with houses clustered upon them, the whole effect Mediterranean.

Went ashore. Same scenes were repeated by populace as in Panama, if anything more so. Wandered about for a couple of days, met a great many people. Every morning there would be a "deputation" of citizens outside the door. They would come in while we were in every possible state of undress. It didn't matter. They sat down, having brought us the strangest array of presents.

One woman in the hotel gave me a beautiful iguana, very

tame. Countless people offered to sell us everything from their houses to their kidneys!

The Barrymores decided to go to Quito, the capital of Ecuador, where Jack made three excellent water-color sketches of Indians. He writes of this visit:

> We arrived in town looking like the Chief of Police in a St. Patrick's Day parade! The papers had evidently printed the fact of our coming. The crowd at the hotel in Quito was really terrifying in its dimensions. They had been waiting there for five hours.
>
> Winkie and I had to go out on the balcony before they would go away. It may sound amusing, but it was pretty dreadful. The same thing happened whenever we went out. The only time one felt fairly comfortable was when one was double-locked in the bathroom!

The Barrymores returned to Guayaquil, then sailed from that port on February 20, homeward bound. Jack writes this postscript to his sea log:

> Came nearly forgetting the last night in Guayaquil, possibly because it flies from the memory like a released pigeon. While we were in Quito the people who own the motion-picture house at Guayaquil decided the opportunity too good to lose, so they tried to get *The Tempest*, and, failing that, got *Beau Brummell*, and decreed a program "gala night for D. C. and J. B. who will positively appear in person!"
>
> There was nothing else to do, other than offending everyone mortally by stealing away like the Arabs in the night—a difficult job anyway, on account of ship's papers, port doctor, etc. One cannot sneak out of a port. Too damn many people have to say, "All right, you can go" first!
>
> So we dined happily alone in Albert Gildred's flat, one of the cleanest, most restful and charming places in Ecuador, I imagine. We then went to *Il Teatro*, all dressed up, Winkie in blue and silver, with her little silver Hellstern shoes, she looking about sixteen. The old man felt about eighty, with nine more wrinkles in the corrugated brow, as, in a moment of expansion—though I cannot be positive—after dinner, I decided to make a speech in Spanish! God help me!
>
> Gildred wrote it, and I learnt it—or thought I did till every time I tried to say it. I don't know a damn word of Spanish, and could only memorize it by the look of the words, like an

astigmatized parrot! I remember the first word after *amigos* was *agradezco!* My father was born at the fort of *Agra* in India during the Mutiny, and I had seen a *desk*, so that was how that one penetrated and stuck!

We got to the theatre, and it wasn't packed, it was positively stuffed to bursting. It was an old-fashioned theatre, 1860, with a tier of boxes running all around back of the orchestra seats, filled with the beauty and fashion of Guayaquil "dressed to kill"—an unfortunate phrase, I thought, perspiring over the oncoming speech.

This speech was flowery, and here lay madness, rather long! I gave up trying to remember it. I sat in a state of expectant coma at the foot of the scaffold, till the picture was over and the awful moment arrived.

I've seen a lot of long pictures, but I know till the day I die I'll never see one half as long as *El Hermoso Brummell!*

It was almost over at last, and we picked our way in the suffocating twilight through the pulsating miasma of the very warm standees to the backstage of the theatre in the dark. We stood there like two respectable bourgeois in the French Revolution, before they faced the howling convention.

It was over. They were waiting. We went on the stage. I was so nervous I didn't realize the lights weren't up till they suddenly sprang to life and hit us in the stomach. While the audience were applauding, someone brought a huge basket of flowers on for Winkie. I had a quick strangled peek at the house. The top gallery near the roof was jammed with what seemed coal-black people. The audience got lighter by gradations of galleries as they neared the ground floor.

The hideous moment had come. I raised my hand for silence, much as a man might have done from the electric chair to the official to turn the current on! There was silence, dead, clammy silence for what seemed minutes. Then like a galvanized horse, I stepped forward, dragging Winkie in my wake, and yelled "*Amigos!*" and stopped dead.

I don't know about one's past life appearing in lightning kaleidoscope to drowning people. I have never drowned—entirely—but I saw myself as a little boy fishing happily at North Long Branch, New Jersey. Then, in a flood of boiling consciousness, one came to.

I had a side glance at Winkie in blue and silver, very straight, like a condemned patriot against a wall, with her eyes starting out of her head. Then, in a voice of thunder, I spat out that speech with gestures, conviction, unction, nuance, stomach-tones, whimsy, and pathos. Then I ducked like a streak of greased Spanish lightning, pushing Winkie ahead, and grabbing that basket of flowers in our flight. I didn't want any excuse for going back there again!

We dove into the alley and met Gildred, who had written the speech. He was triumphant but very weak, and quite a good deal older looking. "God!" he said. "It was great, that long pause, to get their attention! Just listen to them!"

I looked at Winkie, and she at me! "Yes," I said, "that's all training! Where do you suppose we can get something to drink?"

As we drove back to the hotel with the moon shining above the deserted streets, Winkie yawned and said, "Well, I presume that's *one* way of spending a honeymoon."

9.

The Ungrateful Maloney

THE Tower Road estate underwent growing pains during the almost three-months-long wedding cruise of its master. The "bachelor house" already had lost its identity by the time Dolores and Jack arrived home March 17, 1929. They found work still in progress on the house and grounds. Crews were bringing hundreds of tons of topsoil to the rocky slopes, planting numerous trees and shrubs, among them a dwarf Japanese cedar that cost eleven hundred dollars, and an olive tree from Palestine, said to be a hundred years old. New water mains were being laid, and power lines brought from considerable distance to supply electricity for the several structures and for the heating of the new aviary.

This aviary, atop the trophy room west of the Marriage House, now occupied Jack's closest attention. He was reluctant to turn his thoughts from the unfinished bird home long enough to confer with producers in regard to his first talking motion picture, *General Crack.*

It was pointed out to him that he was being paid $30,000 a week (including a profit-sharing bonus) for this studio work. He should not view such matters casually. Indeed, he was warned, other motion-picture stars that very minute were quaking in their buskins because voice had come to the screen. Many of them would die professionally, as in a purge of royalists during a revolution.

Already the thin voice of Douglas Fairbanks, Sr. was disillusioning a public that somehow had associated his athletic virilities with the larynx of a Cossack basso profundo. And the hitherto enormously popular John Gilbert, Greta Garbo's co-star, and Barrymore's near neighbor on the hill, was suddenly deserted to sit out his fabulous contract, partly because of the chickadee sound-recordings of his voice.

"From Garbo to Limbo," Barrymore observed. "Thistle down versus the cyclone."

"But," a producer inquired, "do you consider your first attempt at the talkies of secondary importance?"

"Not secondary," said Jack. "I consider it of *tertiary* importance."

Barrymore had brought back from his cruise a cargo of skins of fish and reptiles, and of birds. These were mounted, then placed in the trophy room. His iguanas had died en route. They were entrusted to the taxidermist.

The ten pairs of live birds purchased from Mrs. Bryan had been but a beginning. The Audubon-minded actor brought up from Wilmington harbor a truck-load of crates and boxes in which his numerous tropical birds would be confined until the aviary could be completed. Jack cabled Mrs. Bryan to send him more birds:

ONE BLUE-CROWNED MOTMOT, TWO SMALL TOUCANS. PLEASE DO NOT CLIP WINGS ANY MORE, AS WISH THEM TO FLY IF POSSIBLE. TWO OROPENDULARS, ONE CRIMSON-BACK TANAGER, ONE BLUE TANAGER. THREE PAIRS HONEY-CREEPERS, AND ONE OR TWO TROGONS. PLEASE TELEGRAPH ME NAME OF BOAT AND DATE ARRIVAL SAN PEDRO WHEN BIRDS ARE SHIPPED.

He obtained feathered rarities from other dealers. Receipted bills from Horne's, the wild animal and bird importers of Los Angeles, tell of Jack's purchases of Australian green parakeets, broad-tailed wydahs, red-billed Chinese magpies, berbets, bleeding-heart doves, pearl-necked doves, gallinules, black-headed nuns, white-headed nuns, and strawberry, saffron, and fire finches. Six birds of paradise cost him $1,900. Canaries, weavers, crested Yucatan jays, and a choir of seldom-captured jungle warblers were brought to the great aviary.

By day Jack supervised every decorative detail of the bird haven, designing the mural jungle scapes. By night he pored over the available authorities on bird life, tropical bird books in particular.

He learned from experience that the carnivorous birds, however beautiful, devoured their smaller, herbivorous companions. He arranged for a partition to separate the two groups.

Barrymore telegraphed to John Wanamaker's in New York for a catalogue of cemetery furniture. He selected from it two iron chairs which he himself painted green. He placed these chairs, as well as a granite bench (reminiscent of the Tomb of the Capulets of his Philadelphia boyhood) inside the aviary.

To keep his birds from flying against the clear glass and injuring themselves, he made foliage designs on the panes, the lattice-work and wire mesh. He set artificial as well as stunted live trees inside the aviary; he installed bird baths, fountains, and devised cotes for nesting. The floor was platted with tough Korean grass instead of gravel, turf which could be raked without being uprooted. Remembering his experience with drainage at the roof garden of the Alchemist's Corner years ago, he now saw to it that troughs, vents, and leaders were properly fashioned to keep water from seeping into the trophy room.

Outside the aviary he built attractive entrances to the place of the birds: rock steps, winding paths, with small pools along the walks and fish in them.

Ordinarily Jack was a heavy smoker. While at home reading, or on hunting or fishing expeditions, he usually sucked at a pipe. At other times he consumed long cigarettes, one after another, constantly. But when in his aviary, where he often stayed for hours, he used no tobacco. He would sit on the cemetery chairs, immobile, for long periods. This seemed a contradictory circumstance, his not moving, when one considers how restless he was by nature. He had, however, in his paradoxical make-up a vein of stoicism.

It was amazing to see Barrymore's birds yield so soon to the charm, understanding, or whatever power he seemed so definitely to possess when in contact with them.

Perhaps his unrestrained naturalness with animals and birds partly explained the bond between him and them. Again it might have been his patience with dumb creatures. Strange dogs singled him out wherever he went. Unlike most other persons, he permitted them to lick his face. And now he allowed the birds to feed from his own lips. He would hold mealy-worms there for the birds to fly down and peck them from his mouth. He didn't mind when they lime-streaked his clothes or hair.

Barrymore decided to build a squab house so that Dolores might have young pigeons for the table. After it had been constructed, and the squabs introduced, Jack made pets of them. He would not let them be killed.

He now had several servants, none of whom coveted the task of cleaning the aviary and squab house, or of feeding the many birds, turtles, fish, numerous dogs, cats, a pair of mouse deer, and other pets. It came to Barrymore's attention that one of the workmen employed by builder Camomile, a Mr. Alexander, had taken an interest in the ornithological aspects of the estate. Jack hired this man, and thereafter referred to him as "Alexander the Small."

An "office" was provided for Alexander the Small, a catacomb in the basement of the Marriage House. The office was hollowed out of the side of the hill, two stories underneath Jack's own hide-out in the tower.

In his cave-like "office," Alexander the Small stored various kinds of animal and bird food in bins and dented tin cans. He cut up meat for the dogs, liver for the cats, presided over cross-fertilization of mealy-worms, kept tins of sunflower seed; and whenever he went into his office, a congress of dogs, cats, ducks, and pigeons gathered noisily outside the screen door. When Alexander emerged with his various diets, there would be a noisy parade trailing behind him as he went on his rounds.

One day when Barrymore was strolling outside this subterranean office of Alexander the Small, he heard voices of servants.

"It ain't safe," one of the servants was saying.

"What ain't safe?" another voice asked.

"Why," said the first voice, "I mean the worm business ain't safe. The way Mr. Barrymore holds them in his mouth for the birds to come down and pick out."

"You mean it ain't safe for Mr. Barrymore? Like germs or something?"

"Hell no! I mean safe for the birds. That's just what I mean. Get me?"

"No," the second voice said, "I don't know just what you mean, unlest it's not human on worms or looks kinda nuts."

"Lookit," the first voice said. "I mean it's the booze on Mr.

Barrymore's breath. It gets the worms drunky when he holds them on his lip. Then the birds eat the drunky worms, and then they get booze in their own system. Get me? The birds get dullened in their system."

There was a pause, then the second voice said, "By God, you're right! I noticed how some of the birds flies sideways after he feeds 'em off of his lip."

Barrymore said that he promptly went on the wagon—for twenty-four hours.

Now Alexander the Small was required to add another sort of provender to his stores: stale meat, in fact over-stale meat. Mr. Barrymore had bought Maloney, and Maloney was partial to carrion.

This king vulture at once became Jack's bosom friend. Indeed, had it not been for a social error on Maloney's part long after his and Barrymore's introduction to each other, it is possible that the king vulture might have occupied a lasting place in Jack's affections, perhaps an even higher one than had the beloved Clementine.

Notwithstanding Maloney's rancid fare, Jack insisted that his large vulture "had a breath like a kitten's." This testimony lacked corroboration; no one other than Jack would risk coming within reach of Maloney's beak, a straight, fierce thing with a hook at the end of it.

Maloney wore a long thin chain on one leg. He had a naked head, eyes like a pawnbroker's, a fine, downy ruff of bluish gray, into which he sank his baldness at times for warmth while sitting in an attitude of torpid malevolence. He had black quills and tail, was white underneath, and somehow reminded one of a cynical mortician. Maloney was voiceless, except for hoarse hisses and lewd snortings.

Jack's scavenger friend would perch on his knee, to the horror of Lionel, and hiss.

"Good God!" Lionel once said. "He'll have your eye out one of these days."

"Maloney is happy whenever he hisses," Jack said to his disgusted brother. "He doesn't understand the theatrical implications of a hiss. Means nothing personal."

The goose-sized bird would preen Barrymore's mustache lovingly, and even caress Jack's hair and eyebrows with his rapacious beak. This sort of thing drove Lionel out of his wits.

"God Almighty!" Lionel would say. "Get rid of that stinking bird."

"Vultures are most tidy about their persons," Jack said. "They wash and preen their plumage, and take hours at their toilets."

"Toilets is right," said Lionel. "They *are* toilets!"

Maloney ate so much that it sometimes was difficult for Alexander the Small to find enough aged meat to satisfy the vulture. So Jack frequently picked up tidbits from trash cans to take home to his friend.

One evening, and at a time when Barrymore was making $30,000 a week, the actor was strolling in town, his chauffeur following slowly after him in a limousine. On this night Jack was dressed rather shabbily. He had spent the afternoon in his aviary. Feathers and lime clung to his garments. His coat collar was turned up, for the night air was chill. He wore an old Homburg pulled low over his eyes, and was unshaven.

Jack saw a trash can near the curb. He immediately thought of Maloney. He found a stick, lifted the lid of the can, then began to explore it. He discovered a piece of old meat, put it in his pocket, and again began poking inside the can with the stick when a well-groomed gentleman of middle years and plentiful belly passed the absorbed searcher.

The gentleman looked with casual interest at the frowsy, unshaven antiquarian, who was muttering happily as he located another piece of high meat that would suit the low standards of Maloney. The stranger halted, presumably debated with himself, then reached beneath his smart topcoat, to bring a ten-cent piece into the light of a street lamp. He held the coin gingerly toward the explorer of trash cans, as if not wishing philanthropy to exceed the bounds of sanitary precaution.

"Here, my man," said the generous stranger. "Here you are. But be sure to spend it only for food."

Jack looked up. He took the dime. Then, as the stranger stepped back quickly from the good deed, Barrymore touched the brim of his Homburg in a kind of salute.

"God bless you, sir!" said Jack throatily.

"It was Maloney's damned ingratitude," said Jack, "that brought us to the parting of the ways. I had been sick with influenza, and I refused to go to the hospital. My nurses objected when I kept

Maloney, his chain tied to a water faucet, in the bathroom. But I loved him. It made me feel better whenever I saw him and heard him hissing for my speedy recovery—or, so I interpreted his hissing at the time.

"Then, one day," Jack went on, "I had one hell of a relapse. And although I was only semi-conscious, and had no actual proof of what occurred to Maloney, I believe that one of the nurses, who had been nipped by him, saw to it that the chain was unfastened and the bathroom window opened.

"When I roused from my fevered state," Jack continued, "I asked where Maloney was. I received evasive answers. I was sad as I looked out of my window. I was weak as the devil, but I started straight up in my bed. There, soaring in slow circles in the sky, definitely waiting for me to knock off, was Maloney!

"The ungrateful bastard! Predicting my death, anticipating it, wishing it! That's why he had been hissing so happily in the bathroom. Well, I recovered just to spite him. This Benedict Arnold returned to the roof of the aviary some days afterward, looking guilty. He was a bad loser. So I packed him off to the zoo."

Jack cocked up an eyebrow as he concluded: "Still, I used to send him a nice, stale present occasionally. Never let him know where it came from, of course."

10.

What Sky Knows No Storm ?

NOTWITHSTANDING Barrymore's lavish expenditures, the year 1929 found him with an income of $430,000. That he had no unpaid debts seems an amazing circumstance when one considers that, among other things, he was putting a quarter of a million dollars into his estate, and *The Mariner* had succumbed to dry rot, representing a dead loss of more than $110,000.

There had been numerous lesser levies, such as the $25,000 paid out during the first ten months of his bird hobby, and the $8,000 for a plinth weighing some tons. This shaft had a sundial atop it that told time for several parts of the earth (if you knew how to read it). Jack built a thick slab of cement at the bottom of the swimming pool to support the great weight.

The transfer of the plinth from Gould's Antique Shop in Los Angeles to the pool of Jack's Tower Road estate was a problem in transportation and engineering. It had to be taken on a double-truck to the top of the mountain, then lowered by means of block and tackle on a runway built for the purpose. The pool no longer could be used for swimming, but the plinth, Jack said, was beautiful.

He built another swimming pool, upon which varicolored lights played at night. Near it stood a pagoda rest-house of gay colors, and to the north of the pool an electrically controlled fountain, twin cascades falling over fantastically arranged rocks. The pumping system was a complex apparatus, costly to operate. Some $40,000 had been spent in all, because Jack happened to have found a sundial to his liking.

He made two other large pools, in one of which he put salt water and fish accustomed to that medium. In the other pool he placed fresh-water fish. Then he endeavored to re-educate the salt-water fish by gradually lessening the salinity of their pool. They did not co-operate wholeheartedly in the experiment.

One day Barrymore suddenly went into a rage, crying out against actress Marlene Dietrich. "Damn this Dietrich person! Damn her!"

It seems that Miss Dietrich's swimming pool had been accumulating an abundance of vegetable growth. The water-works officials obligingly charged the water system overnight with more chlorine than usual, as a measure to discourage plant life. The added chlorine killed Jack's fish. When he learned what had caused this massacre, he began to denounce all actresses, living or dead.

He should have been happy in his present marriage, it would seem; and in general he was, except for periods of brooding. He reported a quarrel with Dolores as early as May 2 of that year, when his wife suggested that he do less drinking. Jack believed that Dolores' sister, Helene, had inspired the temperance suggestion. Helene now was married to actor Lowell Sherman, to whom Jack had taken a dislike, suspecting his brother-in-law of making slurs against his behavior.

Sherman probably never did anything to harm Barrymore's interests other than try to steal scenes from him in a motion picture.

Sherman seemed cordial toward Barrymore when, on Jack's and Dolores' first wedding anniversary, he telegraphed his brother-in-law:

CONGRATULATIONS ON FIRST YEAR OF THE RUN. IF ANYTHING HAPPENS, REMEMBER THERE IS ALWAYS VAUDEVILLE.

Jack's first severe Hollywood illness occurred in May 1929. Barrymore underwent treatment for a duodenal ulcer. On his way from the Pasadena hospital to the studio on the afternoon of the twenty-third, Jack visited the Hollywood aviaries to purchase some birds. He worked all that night on the motion-picture set of *General Crack*, notwithstanding his illness.

In June his throat began to bother him. A doctor recommended that he have his tonsils removed. Fortunately another medical man, Dr. M. Russell Wilcox, examined Jack's throat to make one of the finest diagnoses since the day when Hippocrates described the face of a child suffering from peritonitis. Said Dr. Wilcox: "Your throat merely is raw from bad booze. I advise you to switch to better liquor. No operation necessary."

Ethel arrived in Hollywood in July. She seemed concerned about Jack's drinking. She asked Hotchener, "Why is he doing it so heavily?" to which Barrymore's manager responded, "I don't know. Is there always a reason?" Perhaps Ethel saw early signs, which others did not then see, of storms lowering over her younger brother's household. She did not reply to Hotchener's question.

For a time Jack became happily occupied in planning a new yacht. He would call it the *Infanta*, a name suggested by Dolores, who now was expecting her first child. Jack commissioned L. E. Geary, naval architect and engineer of Seattle, to design a power-driven, steel-hull yacht.

This steel diesel cruiser was to be 120 feet in length over-all, with a 21½ foot beam, 9 feet draft. The twin-screw vessel was to be powered by two diesels. She would have a cruising speed of twelve knots. She would cost $225,000. Barrymore planned a mint-bed aft the main deckhouse for juleps.

In August Jack made a Technicolor sequence of *Richard III* for the Warner Brothers *Show of Shows*—the first time that Shakespeare came to the sound-screen. This part of the production was beautifully done, and demonstrated that the actor had lost none of his powers when reciting such classics as the *Richard* soliloquy.

In September Winston Churchill called at the Warner Studio to see Jack make scenes for *The Man from Blankley's.* They had dinner that night by themselves. Jack said they discussed the *Hamlet* days in London. The British statesman recalled during this reunion with his actor-friend that the Prince of Wales, Jack, Churchill, and several members of Parliament had visited together at the Whistler house.

"Mr. Churchill and the M. P.'s," Jack afterward explained, "were late that day in reaching the House of Commons for a debate. They had to leave the Prince of Wales behind because royalty was traditionally not permitted to set foot in the House of Commons. Neither was I, traditionally or conditionally; but the Prince was the first to be respectfully dropped on the way. As usual, I stayed on until reaching the historic barriers."

A photograph was taken of Mr. Churchill and Jack on the Warners' sound-stage. Barrymore sent a copy of it to his old friend Max Beerbohm in London. In a letter accompanying the picture, the actor revealed that he had had a recurrence of his ulcer. He informed Beerbohm, however, that he in nowise blamed Mr. Churchill's visit for this condition.

He went on the Sippy diet, and remained home for two weeks, occupying himself by painting adventurous scenes on navigational charts. He often did this sort of work upon charts of his voyages. He thumbtacked the sea maps to a drawing board, then painted upon them scenes illustrating his real or fancied adventures, in the style of fifteenth-century cartographers. He lettered them as of that period, then antiqued the charts. He had begun this hobby as early as 1913, after a fishing expedition to the Bahamas with sculptor John Roude-bush. That map had been titled by him: *The Voyage to the Perilous Island of Andros, the Rum Country, and the Lake of the Flamingos.*

He returned to the studio after a fortnight. He still was not well. His blood pressure was low, one hundred over eighty. His blood pressure seldom rose at any time more than one hundred and twenty mm.

Although ill and overworked, Jack visited the shipyards in Long Beach, where his yacht was building. He had entered upon the plans with some degree of zest. Now, however, as he watched the riveters at work on the hull plates, saw the welders making the tanks oil- and water-tight, and observed the shipwrights, blacksmiths, and carpenters build upon the steel body, he seemed to lose interest in the project.

He could not associate a shell of metal with the sea. It had been different with his sailing yacht. He had a personal, romantic attachment for *The Mariner*. She had been more to him than something of wood and canvas. He personified her, as one might a beautiful woman. Now, with all the elaborate and costly fittings that made the *Infanta* one of the finest yachts of the West, she still did not mean the sea to Barrymore. *The Mariner* had been born of blue water, so it had seemed to him; she had descended from a long line of Gloucester boats that partook of history as well as of romance. A steel hull seems to one who has been under sail as a barnyard hen compared to a bird of paradise.

He did show an alert interest, however, in one item of the *Infanta's* cruising equipment, the galley stove. The yacht's specifications called for a five-burner, single-oven Lange brick-lined range, fueled by diesel oil. Barrymore's cook said that he "could do better work with an eight-burner, two-oven range."

"Give our chef his eight burners," Jack said. "Give him eighty burners if he insists. The most important man on a ship, next to the skipper, is the cook.

"These geniuses of the cuisine are a little nutty to begin with," he added. "Only in France are they properly appreciated for their virtuosity. In that land of gastronomic intelligence, their slightly insane actions are entirely ignored. It is taken for granted that their constant stooping and crouching over hot kettles, pots, and the various flames and soup-retorts addles their wits. They become crazier than ever, these master cooks; but there is a sublimity in their madness. From it they create such wonders as make the belly sing hymns, and the liver dance as if before the Ark of the Covenant. The man who thinks that food is merely something to eat is the kind of moron who would make pen-wipers of the Sistine tapestries, or hang a First Folio in an outhouse. For God's sake, give our ship's cook an eight-burner range for his sanctum!"

A few days after his first wedding anniversary Jack said to his manager, "Let's ascend to the eyrie to talk about affairs of state." They climbed up the narrow, steep iron ladder to crawl into the hideout in the tower. Jack had a bottle in one trousers pocket and a glass tumbler in the other.

"I don't know what to do about Dolores' sister," he began slowly, "but I can always tell when Winkie has been down to see her. As you know, Helene is strongly mental and forthright; she has aggressive convictions about what husbands ought to be and do."

He then went on, as if talking to himself: "Dolores, with her charming naïveté, is easily impressed by strong advices. Of late she is harping on my drinking too much, and says that I ought to get on the wagon."

"That," said Hotchener, "doesn't seem unreasonable."

"No," Barrymore replied, "but I told her that of late I've noticed it isn't so easy to stop drinking as it used to be. She got quite excited at this. Then she said, 'That isn't true; you're just putting on an act when you say that.'"

Hotchener says that Jack slowly repeated, "*Putting on an act!*"

"But is it true?" the manager asked. "I mean true that you find it harder to go on the wagon?"

Barrymore poured himself a drink, looked at the glass for a long moment, then replied, "Yes." He drank, then asked, "What do you think I can do about it?"

"Well," his manager replied, "you're getting older, and the habit stronger. But you do have terrific will power, when you care to exercise it. The question is, do you really want to stop drinking?"

Barrymore looked Hotchener directly in the eye. "I'm not sure that I do." He was silent for a time, then added, "It helps me not to worry too much about the future."

One dabbles one's hand in the small, cool stream. The water that touches one's fingers for the little moment flows on to the reservoir lake. Then it falls at its own time, spills without identity over the concrete shoulder of the great dam. It finds the turbine blade. It is only a little water, now merged with a torrent. Yet of itself it breeds a moment of power, perhaps enough to mean a part turn of a dentist's drill, or one small ray in the microscope of a scientist, or one brief gleam in the stage-border while the great actor stands reciting.

What are words that flow past the lips? Where, how, and why do they sometimes move the mind in strange ways?

"You're just putting on an act when you say that. . . ."

The falling of a ten-cent pottery piece from a cupboard shelf makes enough clatter and loud noise to startle a household. Servants rise from their beds to investigate. The man and his wife go to see what is wrong. Is it a thief entering the house at night, or merely the cat prowling? It is important, this noise; it rouses everyone, the falling of a ten-cent pottery piece.

Yet a man and a woman may sit, their hearts breaking, and no one pays attention.

II.

Paradise Mislaid

IN THE time of his greatest wealth gathering and wealth spending, in the time of his finest screen portrayals, in the time of his possession of a wife's love and her bearing him two children, the son of Maurice Barrymore found no lasting contentment.

He now was forty-eight, still vital, still prodigal and wayward. The next five years, however, would be for him a period of transition from a last dream to a last reality. The wild winds frequently had blown across his heavens, but soon he would know the whole gale, and then the hurricane. He hurled himself against these years with fist-shakings and scornful cries. His prodigious follies, quixotic deeds, intense bursts of labor, together with his disregard of repose, would have felled a god.

Now, in retrospect, and from the record, these five years seem to have been a dress rehearsal for personal disaster. Barrymore strove, in his own Peer Gynt fashion, to keep alive the love that he so gloriously had dreamt. He fleetingly inspired new hopes in Dolores' mind that things again might be as they had been at the beginning of their romance. But soon his good intentions strayed like soap bubbles, floating, shimmering, bursting to nothingness in the air.

In March of 1930 Jack began work on *Moby Dick*, the talking-picture version of *The Sea Beast*. By the end of the month Barrymore's yacht, the *Infanta*, had been launched and fitted, and on April 1 taken for a shake-down cruise to Ensenada. Neither Jack nor Dolores went on the trial run of their yacht; the actor was busy on his picture, and Dolores expecting their first child.

This girl, Dolores Ethel Mae, was born the morning of April 8, 1930. Jack's wife looked up at him to say, "I'm sorry for your sake that it's a girl."

"I wanted a girl," Jack replied. "Doesn't my whole life prove that I get along better with girls?"

Jack became especially restless that autumn. He took a short trip alone to Ensenada; then, in September, he decided to go on a much longer cruise, taking Dolores and their five-month-old child on the sea journey. He would revisit places described with passionate earnestness in his diary nearly five years before when aboard *The Gypsy*. Perhaps with these scenes of an emotional yesterday once more springing up before his eyes, he might re-enshrine his great romantic dream.

Jack employed a woman doctor as well as a nurse to look after the baby's health aboard the *Infanta*. The family sailed from Long Beach September 27, 1930, bound for Cape San Lucas, Mazatlán, and other ports eulogized in Jack's diary. He could not, however, as the voyage progressed, rouse the nodding gods of romance. They had promised, or so it had seemed to him, a life-long blessing at the time of his days of yearning aboard *The Gypsy*. Now they snored, unmindful of incense or of prayer.

Barrymore admittedly possessed everything that a "normal man" could desire: a beautiful wife, a lovely child, a yacht of his own, and what the magazine editors called "success." But he had no "freedom," as he interpreted the word. Everywhere he moved about on the boat, some shadow of restriction fell: a nurse, a doctor, no sails to hoist in fair winds or to shorten when storms outside one's own breast might be ridden out adventurously.

About two months after this southward sailing, Jack suffered a severe gastric hemorrhage. He collapsed from loss of blood. Dolores summoned a medical practitioner in Guatemala. The bleeding was controlled, the doctor given a thousand-dollar fee, then the *Infanta* made for home, her owner stretched out on his bed.

Although extremely ill in his cabin during this homeward voyage, Jack personally attended to professional queries via the *Infanta's* wireless. The Warner Brothers, for example, suggested that *Trilby* be adapted to the screen, and that Barrymore play the role of Svengali. He wirelessed his manager in reply:

> Impress the writer with the fact that the male character must be funny and get lots of laughs, particularly in first part of story.

Although a sinister figure, he is a wise, dirty, glutinous Polish Jew, with no conscience and a supreme contempt for all those nice, clean, straight-thinking English Christians. He has an enormous sense of humor. The funnier he is, in the proper way, the better the picture will be, and the greater contrast to all the sinister part, hypnotism, et cetera, in the last part of the picture. . . .

The female lead must have exactly the correct quality. Otherwise the entire play goes for nothing. The man's is the better acting part, but if the girl is not perfectly right everything he does is bound to be unbelievable and a little ridiculous.

When the *Infanta* reached port on December 2, Barrymore clothed himself fully and disembarked to meet the reporters and press photographers on the Long Beach wharf. Public word of his illness was being withheld.

One of the camera men saw on the pier a sea-turtle that Jack had captured. This shell-encased reptile weighed more than a hundred pounds. The photographer wanted a picture of the actor holding the turtle. Dolores, fearing what might happen to her husband's stomach were he to lift such a weight, started to protest. Barrymore signaled for her not to interfere. He stooped, seized the armature of the turtle, then held it in a pose.

After the reporters had gone Jack entered his limousine pale and weak. He stayed home in bed for the next month. He now suffered headaches on the right side of his head, above the ear, forerunners of neuralgic attacks that recurred periodically until 1940, at which time they abruptly subsided.

One day during this illness he said to his manager, "I am told that if I don't quit drinking I am sunk."

He then spoke to Helios Hotchener concerning the "mystic aftermath of losing one's blood." He wondered if the blood did not irradiate certain spiritual qualities. He had ordered that all sheets and mattresses used by him during his illness in Central America be burned, after the taboo system of certain tribesmen who guard against their hair, nails, or blood falling into possession of anyone who might practice sorceries upon such bodily traces.

Barrymore devised a suitably horrible make-up for Svengali, a beard that sprouted in a hellish curl, and glass eyeball covers to bring hypnotic menace to his stare. The actor's advice as to the selection by the casting director of a seasoned leading woman for *Svengali* was entirely disregarded. An inexperienced girl, Marian Marsh, was assigned to play opposite him in January 1931. Instead of complaining about this, Jack patiently coached Miss Marsh, acquainting her with his own personality, so that she would not shrink from him when he put on his horrendous make-up.

One of the studio officials automatically construed Barrymore's pedagogical generosity as a romantic sortie. This was decidedly the wrong interpretation. Not only was Barrymore capable of platonic interests, but, as was well known among Jack's friends, he never strayed from the woman he currently loved. He still earnestly cared for Dolores, although doubts occasionally rose to plague him, and his outbursts increasingly confused his wife.

In March he began *The Mad Genius*, the last commitment of his five-picture contract with the Warners. Then, in May and August of 1931, Jack, Dolores, the baby, and a nurse cruised off Alaska and among the islands of that territory to hunt kodiak bear.

An American settler on Lemesurier Island, where Jack acquired a totem pole, told Barrymore that to remove such a tribal emblem from its appointed place meant bad luck. During the voyage homeward Jack became concerned about what the settler had told him. Barrymore said that he halfway believed that the tribal gods, in whose behalf the pole had been erected, "might take a notion into their whimsical noggins to wreak vengeance on the thief."

Dolores was expecting a second child in June 1932. Her husband decided to build an addition to the Marriage House, a nursery known as the "Children's Wing." Other alterations and additions were undertaken.

Jack had acquired, at a Glendale antique shop, a Dresden chandelier that once had been in the palace of Archduke Francis Ferdinand. He had purchased this at the bargain price of seventy-five dollars. As in the episode of the plinth, the acquisition of the chandelier set off a train of expensive labors. Jack built a room in which to hang this museum piece, a large octagonal chamber that cost him $3,000.

The Dresden array of cupids and candle sconces was trussed to the roof beams. "I did this as a precaution," Jack afterward said, "against earthquakes and wives." Only he and builder Camomile knew how to reach the anchorage of this masterpiece by means of a cleverly concealed trap door in the ceiling of another room. The branching mass of china could be unbolted in fifteen minutes, once a person reached the roof truss that supported it. Otherwise, the ceiling would have to be removed, and the chandelier in all probability damaged.

Even the purchase of cheeses set off a train of expenditure. Jack's fondness for "free lunch," especially the pungent articles of delicatessen, led him to search for and find two authentic Stilton cheeses. "These cheeses," he said, "are the most important things that English lords possess. The drooling peers hand them down to their eldest sons under the law of primogeniture."

He maintained that he dedicated his rathskeller to the cheeses. At any rate, he did fashion for them a refrigerator. While he was at it, he built a wine cupboard, the door to which had a combination lock, because he lost keys so often through holes in the pockets of his ancient lounging-robe. He mislaid the slip of paper bearing the combination to the wine cupboard. After a legal safe-cracker had twice reopened the cupboard, Jack wrote down the numbers on the wall, where anyone might read them—and did.

The rathskeller had in it an old bar of Wild West history and draught beer on tap. This bar once had been in a Virginia City saloon patronized by Mark Twain. It was an aged shrine and had a bullet hole in its façade. Barrymore decorated it with cigarette premium cards and cigar bands of other days. The one which Jack prized was a John Drew Cigar band, his dapper uncle's picture on it.

This retreat, Jack said, looked like the tomb scene from *Aïda*. Often he would hold his daughter on his lap while sitting there, and improvise stories for her entertainment, fabulous recitals of the deeds of a mysterious people called the "Magoozalums." When Dolores Ethel was old enough to take notice, he installed a motion-picture projection machine in the trophy room, not for the showing of his own photoplays, but to run off animated cartoons.

From a financial standpoint 1931 was the best in Barrymore's career. His income for this year was $460,000. He spent money almost as rapidly as he made it, yet he had no unpaid debts.

The next year also was to be one of professional activity. He undertook the romantic role of the Baron in *Grand Hotel*, on January 9, 1932. Greta Garbo, Lionel, Wallace Beery, and Joan Crawford participated in this picture.

When, on January 16, Director Eddie Goulding introduced Barrymore to Miss Garbo, Jack kissed her hand in the John Drew tradition, then said with Victorian politeness: "My wife and I think you the loveliest woman in the world."

Jack behaved toward this shy, sensitive artist as with a timid bird in his aviary. They became good friends. On January 25 Barrymore and Miss Garbo had a particularly difficult scene to play. At the close of this sequence Miss Garbo electrified the director and the camera crew, *and* Barrymore, by impulsively kissing the actor.

"You have no idea," she said in the presence of the others on the set, "what it means to me to play opposite so perfect an artist."

Miss Garbo, for the first time in her career as a star, now permitted photographers to take her picture off the set and with Barrymore. Jack had a quieting influence upon her. She formerly had hastened from the set to go to her dressing-room, speaking to no one, seeing no one other than her confidante, Salka Viertel. Now she would sit beside Barrymore on the sidelines, waiting for their next scene together.

"I admired him greatly," Miss Garbo said. "Barrymore was one of the very few who had that divine madness without which a great artist cannot work or live."

On April 10 Jack stayed home from the R.K.O. studio where he was making *State's Attorney.* His manager found him "in the dumps." After a quiet ten or fifteen minutes, Jack said, as if in dismissal of some question he had asked of himself: "Well, let's forget it." Then he addressed his manager: "Didn't you say there was an article in today's newspaper asserting that I carry a million dollars in life insurance?"

"Yes," said Hotchener. "That's what the article claimed."

"Well, I'm glad that Joe Schenck was able to arrange it for me."

"I'd be glad, too," remarked his manager, "but he wasn't able to."

"No?" asked Jack. "Then how much insurance do I have?"

"None," Hotchener replied. "I have been politely told that the insurance companies do not consider you a 'good risk.'"

Jack thought this over, then said, "I want to make sure that little Dolores Ethel is taken care of, and the next baby provided for. Winkie has plenty of money of her own; her house on Schuyler Road is clear, but the children . . . I don't know . . ."

"Why not give your wife something to put in trust for the children?"

"Doesn't that need a legal document?" asked Barrymore.

"Yes."

"If I just told Dolores what I wanted," Jack said, "I'm sure she'd do it without any document." Then he added, "She's perfectly fanatical about that child. She's forgetting me entirely in her new love for the baby." He paused, then asked, "Do all women get that way when their first baby comes?" Then, without waiting for an answer, he continued, "Anyway, I'd like to arrange the other matter instantly."

"You have some certificates of deposit."

"That's good," said Jack. "What are *they?*"

"They are formal documents from your bank," Hotchener explained, "stating that you have so much cash deposited with that bank. They are like gold. They are in the safe in your room. Endorse them over to Dolores, and they become hers."

Jack put his name to six certificates of deposit which amounted, with accrued interest, to $70,672.

"It was worth doing," he afterward said, "just to see the smile on her face. I'm glad we did it without any legal document. When I explained the purpose, she simply said, 'You know I'll do what you ask, Jack.' And I know she will."

Barrymore received crank letters in which threats were made to kidnap his daughter. He fenced-in the Tower Road estate and hired a night watchman. One evening, late, the actor heard shots. He ran out doors, clad in his bathrobe and a pair of old red Morocco bedroom slippers, to find his watchman staring confusedly into the night.

"Well," Jack roared, "go investigate the shots!"

"Not me," the watchman replied with conviction. "I'm paid to prowl around this steep yard and punch a time clock; but I don't go off of the property to see who's shooting at who!"

Barrymore himself inquired into the shots next morning to discover that his neighbor, John Gilbert, had fired them. That actor, in brooding over the loss of his once-glamorous career, had grown depressively neurotic. He imagined all kinds of plots against himself, as when, only the week before, he had called the police to say that someone was breaking into his house. The officers merely found a woodpecker at work near the Gilbert bedroom.

Now, as Barrymore learned, Gilbert had discharged a pistol at an automobile parked near his grounds. A bullet shattered a window of the motor car, interrupting the dreams of its occupants, a boy and a girl. It cost Mr. Gilbert a thousand dollars to repair the damage done to the automobile and to the emotions of the romancers.

On the afternoon of June 4 a son was born to Dolores and Jack. The expectant father had been pacing the hall for some time near the delivery room in the presence of a considerable audience of nurses and hospital attendants. He swore that if a son be given him, he would quit drinking.

When the doctor called out, "It's a boy!" Jack gave a glad cry. As he touched his child, Barrymore cried: "Thank God! A son!" He observed in the boy's rather long black hair, sturdy arms, and full chest a resemblance to his own father, Maurice Barrymore.

There now arrived in Dolores' room a large floral piece in the shape of a "wheel of life." A tiny, old-fashioned, child's bouquet was pinned among the lilies of this gift, a nosegay placed there by Jack himself.

Barrymore, looking out from his hospital room next to that of Dolores, saw a group of newspaper men in the corridor. He assumed them to be kidnapers; no one could convince him to the contrary. He sent his manager to Tower Road to find a revolver and bring it to the hospital "instantly."

"I'll stay up all night," Barrymore threatened, "and shoot any bastard that comes within a hundred yards of my son."

When the armed Hotchener returned to the hospital, Barrymore said, "You stand guard a little while. Don't let a soul come near the place unless properly dressed in hospital white. I'm going out for a few minutes."

For a few minutes. . . .

Dolores now asked for Jack. No one knew where he had gone. He stayed away for several hours, celebrating the arrival of a son. The actor returned to his room to sink into a deep sleep with his clothes on.

Dolores again sent word that she wanted to see her husband; but it was impossible to rouse him from his sleep. The wife became heartsick at this backsliding in the light of protestations and enthusiastic words of reform made earlier that same day.

"I swore that if God would give me a son, I would never drink again," Jack said some days afterward. "What happens to a man who makes a sacred oath, then breaks it?"

On July 9 Barrymore began one of the finest portrayals in his screen career, the deranged husband and father in *Bill of Divorcement*. He was supported in this picture by the dynamic young actress, Katharine Hepburn.

Barrymore at once recognized the talent of this intelligent, eager girl. The widely accepted report that he was sarcastic to her is untrue. She allegedly had said to him, "I'll never play another scene with you," and he purportedly replied, "But, my dear, you never have."

This year of 1932 became Barrymore's busiest on the screen. Immediately after the completion of *Bill of Divorcement*, he appeared in *Rasputin and the Empress*, a photoplay in which his sister and brother were co-starred.

A new sound-camera was introduced to the Metro stage for the photographing of *Rasputin and the Empress*. The crew nicknamed this mechanism "Grandma." Ethel Barrymore one day was passing the camera crew on her way to the place where her brothers stood for the taking of the scene. An assistant director, desiring to find out if the new camera were properly loaded with film and the photographer ready to record the sequence, asked, "Is Grandma ready?"

Miss Barrymore, unused to the argot of motion-picture workmen, believed the remark intended for her. She stiffened, slowly wheeled. Then she gave the assistant director and his crew the sort of glare that causes apples to fall from trees. Jack, as a witness to this episode, became so convulsed he was unable at once to play the scene with his gifted sister.

Playwright Charles MacArthur wrote the *Rasputin* scenario, working on it from hour to hour, to tailor it to the measurements of three mighty individualists. MacArthur's job of assuring the Barrymore brothers that he was not favoring one against the other in the dialogue became one of the scenarist's problems.

"One late afternoon," MacArthur says, "a furtive Lionel slipped away from the set to call my office. I met him in a studio alley.

"'That so-and-so brother of mine,' Lionel said, 'is getting too smart. He's doing all sorts of treacherous things behind my back to steal a scene. You've got to see to it that he quits this nefarious practice. Appeal to his better side—if you can locate it.'"

Lionel and MacArthur had numerous beers at a Culver City dive, then started out at night in a taxicab for Lionel's home. The portrayer of the weird monk kept speaking bitterly of Jack's cunning ways, particularly during the scene in which Rasputin counted his money on the floor.

The beer-filled friends advised the taxicab driver to draw alongside some shrubberies of a Beverly Hills estate. Lionel got out of the cab, still grumbling about his brother's rude thieveries. The disgruntled actor decided to lie face down on the lawn to re-enact the money-counting scene for MacArthur.

"And all the while I am down there acting on my belly, playing my scene," Lionel cried out, "what do you think that smug so-and-so brother of mine is doing behind my back? I caught him today red-handed wriggling his ears, pursing his lips, shaking his head, flicking dust from his larcenous backside, and stealing the whole scene from me. . . ."

The owner of the estate, alarmed by Lionel's cries, came out of the house to inquire, "What in hell is going on out here?" Then he said ominously, "I don't care *what* your names are! You'd better get the hell off my property before I call the police!"

One day when Jack, Dolores, and their babies were driving home from a holiday in Palm Springs, the small daughter spied a Manx cat, a tailless, grim female, sitting outside the door of a small store. She began to cry out: "Nookie! Nookie!"

"Stop the car instantly!" Jack said to their chauffeur. "I'm going to buy that rudderless cat for my daughter."

The woman who owned the Manx cat and the store as well informed Jack that the pet was not for sale. It was a cynical, cross-eyed animal, independent of manner, a feminine version of pugilist Tom Sharkey, except that it had no ship tattooed on its chest.

"But I'll give you ten dollars for 'Nookie,'" Jack said to the owner. "Fifteen, if you insist."

"It ain't for sale," the woman said, "and its name ain't Nookie."

"If my daughter, a young lady of discernment, says its name is Nookie, you may rest assured that its name is, or should be, Nookie. However, will twenty-five dollars recompense you?"

When Jack's chauffeur pointed out with some degree of awe that the cat had no tail, Barrymore informed him: "Manx cats have no tails. They got that way when one of Sir Hall Caine's novels fell on the tail of a tomcat in the Isle of Man—Darwin's theories notwithstanding."

"That's a lie," said the owner of the Manx cat.

"Twenty-five dollars for this tabby," and Barrymore displayed a fistful of crumpled currency. "Do I hear 'thirty'?" Finally Jack made a sudden bid of seventy-five dollars. The woman thereupon hysterically parted with the Manx cynic.

The year 1932 brought Jack $375,000 for five pictures made at a fast tempo. His health was not of the best, yet he still held onto his unconquerable spirit, and never lost for a moment his great sense of humor.

A producer, offended by Jack's didos, announced one day that he would "give this great Barrymore a piece of my mind." He marched onto the set to shake a finger in Jack's face.

The actor looked at him, then at the finger. "Don't point at me, if you please. I remember that finger when it had a thimble on it."

Barrymore began the making of *Topaze* in December, a screen adaptation by Ben Hecht of the play of that name. The actor maintained that he still was happy in his marriage. But Hecht said privately, "Jack is hiding something, perhaps his head—or possibly his heart."

The restlessness increased, the drinking increased, the domestic uncertainties, the jealousies, the quarrels increased.

After a summer of hard work and marital unhappiness, the actor began *Counsellor-at-Law* for Universal Studios. Barrymore's role required the fastest and most sustained delivery of lines of any part he had undertaken since coming to Hollywood eight years before.

He successfully finished this picture at Universal, then completed another, *Long Lost Father*, for R.K.O. Studios. He then was recalled by Director William Wyler to Universal for the remaking of a single scene opposite actor John Qualen for *Counsellor-at-Law*.

Jack went with his manager to Universal Studios on the evening of October 30, 1933. He was understandably tired. He had had but two glasses of beer during the day, and about as much the day before. He definitely was not drunk.

Jack seemed wearily confident as he picked up a property silver pencil from the property desk and then began what ordinarily would have been for him the simple redoing of a sequence.

Actor Qualen was letter-perfect, having played his own part on the stage with Paul Muni. After Barrymore had finished one of the longer speeches, and Qualen had made the proper rejoinder, Barrymore suddenly stumbled over his next brief speech. The actor made a comic face. Everyone laughed.

The scene was undertaken again from the beginning. Then Barrymore "blew up" in his lines at almost the same place in the scene as before. A third "take" was ordered, and Jack failed at it. He did not make jokes now. He became quite angry, and threw the silver pencil to the floor.

Barrymore continued to falter during several successive trials of the scene. The effect of his own inadequacy communicated itself to actor Qualen; that performer also "blew." A recess was ordered, the lights "rested," and Barrymore given an opportunity to consult the scenario.

The actors at length resumed their places before the camera. Then Jack again failed to remember the lines he had newly reviewed. Director Wyler and Cameraman Brodine exchanged perplexed glances. Barrymore's manager stood in sad amazement on the sidelines. The actor stubbornly persisted and repeatedly flunked out time and again, hour after hour. At the fiftieth empty attempt, Producer Henry Henigson arrived on the set to inquire into the astounding event. He squinted at the fifty-first take, at the fifty-second, then said to Hotchener, "Is he *that* drunk?"

"He's a little tired," was the reply. "Not drunk."

"Nobody ever got *that* tired," replied Henigson.

"He'll have it in a few minutes," said the actor's worried manager.

Barrymore still was fighting gamely to conquer his scene. He was perspiring. His face was drawn, his jaw set. Finally, after the fifty-sixth successive relapse, Jack's manager intervened to ask: "Why not put it over until tomorrow morning?"

Barrymore smiled mirthlessly. He turned from the camera to walk off the stage. He looked straight ahead.

Hotchener arranged for Jack to appear the next morning for the retaking of the scene, then followed the actor outside to his automobile. Barrymore did not speak all the way home, nor did his manager put any questions to the obviously harassed man. Hotchener left Jack's house at about one o'clock in the morning, with a "get some sleep now; everything will come out all right."

Jack merely nodded. Then he went into his library. What he thought to himself during the next hour, what fears he had of an approaching shadow, we cannot know. But we do know that a knock sounded on his door at two o'clock, an hour after Hotchener had left him. The actor's behavior during the remainder of that morning demonstrated the quality of his manliness, his courage, his greatness of soul.

The knock at Barrymore's door at two o'clock on the morning of October 31 was made by Noll Gurney, the manager of several of Hollywood's foremost actors, and a trusted friend of Barrymore's neighbor, John Gilbert.

Barrymore himself, in bathrobe and slippers, came to the door. "Hello, Nollie, old man. Come in."

"No, thanks," Gurney said restrainedly. "I haven't time." Barrymore cocked an eyebrow as Gurney added, "Jack Gilbert is in a bit of trouble."

Gurney, of course, was unaware at this time of Barrymore's own travail. "Trouble?" asked Jack. "Never heard of the word." Then he said forthrightly, "What can I do for Gilbert?"

"Would you mind coming to his house right away?" Then Gurney added, "I left his Filipino servant to keep an eye on him while I am here."

"I see," Barrymore said. "Threatens to do away with himself. Is that it?"

Gurney nodded. "You'd better put on a topcoat. It's chilly."

"I'll dress myself completely," Jack announced. "We have plenty of time, Noll. An actor will do nothing so operatic as self-immolation without an audience."

During the minutes Barrymore took to clothe himself, and later as they walked to the Gilbert estate, Jack questioned Gurney closely as to his neighbor's confusion of mind. Was he drinking heavily? Yes. Was he having woman trouble? Yes, his third wife, Virginia Bruce, was threatening to leave him. He had become so violent earlier in the evening that Miss Bruce had absented herself from the premises.

"One of the first of Gilbert's setbacks," Gurney said, "came after he signed a contract to do five pictures at $250,000 each, shortly before sound pictures came to the screen. He was permitted to make only one picture. It was hissed by the Stanford students at its Palo Alto première."

"What the hell!" Jack snorted. "Even Caruso once was hissed in Naples. There's something else bothering him."

"Yes," said Gurney, "there is. So many slurs have been made on Gilbert's voice that he's got it into his head that the public think him a softie."

"Well," said Barrymore, "my rugged friend, Jack Dempsey, has a voice like a constipated sparrow; but I'd hesitate fifty light-years before suggesting that he was anything less than a lethal bull."

They now were entering the grounds of the Gilbert estate. Jack suddenly halted to ask, "Haven't the Gilberts a new baby?"

"About three months old. A little girl."

"Did he mention his baby at all when talking about killing himself?"

"No."

"That's because the child can't leave him," Barrymore said. "The wife can walk out on him, but the baby is incapable of such things as decisions, leave-takings, and yowls of recrimination. Therefore, the child is not in a position to hurt your friend's pride." He paused, then added, "This gives me an idea."

Gilbert was astonished when Barrymore entered the house. The unhappy man put on a hollow sort of cordiality, half rose from his chair, held out his hand, then said, "Great to see you. We'll make a night of it."

Barrymore shook hands perfunctorily. "Yes. We'll make a night of it."

"Get drinks for everybody," Gilbert called out to his house boy. "Triple ones!"

Barrymore sat opposite Gilbert, then said quietly to the house boy, "There will be no more drinks tonight for anybody. Understand?"

Gilbert made as if to speak to the bewildered Filipino, as if to assure him that Mr. Barrymore merely was jesting. Barrymore, however, closed off Gilbert's chance to say anything. "Shut up!" he said, "and stay shut up till I tell you to speak." Then he said impressively, "I hear that you've been making a God-damned fool of yourself. Over what? Don't answer! I'll answer for you."

Gilbert's eyes wavered, then his caller continued: "All because someone says this, or says that. Why in hell do actors read the papers anyway? Christ! Do you think the world turns on the importance or the unimportance of a ham? Well, it doesn't!"

Gilbert stared at the floor in a stunned sort of way.

"Why should you give a damn about your voice, good or bad?" Barrymore went on. "You can dig ditches, can't you? Or get a job with Western Union? How old are you? Shut up! Gurney here tells me you are thirty-three or thirty-four."

Barrymore now turned to Gurney. "Noll, I had a grandmother who went broke for the tenth time when she was seventy-two. Did she bump herself off? No. She had guts, God bless her! She went out and got a job." He again addressed his remarks to Gilbert. "It makes me sick when these lollipop Hollywood bastards go around with their heads in the clouds after a taste of notoriety; but at the smallest setback to their egos they put their taffy-coated skulls in their precious hands and begin to wail *Eli Eli*."

He paused. Gilbert now was sitting, his mouth open, as if uncertain what to do. He flushed. He clenched his hands.

"You've got a baby," Jack said. "Never entered your head, did it, that you owe the *child* something? No. The ham always thinks only of himself. Get up! We're going to look at the baby. Where is it?"

"In the nursery," said Gilbert meekly.

"Lead the way," Jack commanded. "It'll do us all good to look at something decent in this God-damned sink hole of culture."

In the nursery, Barrymore directed Gilbert to take the child in his arms. "Don't drop her. Just hold her close to you."

Gilbert held the child. Then Barrymore put his hand on Gilbert's shoulder. He now spoke slowly and with tenderness. "Doesn't that make you feel something? Isn't she more important than a bit of newspaper gossip?"

Gilbert was crying as he held his sleeping child. After perhaps a minute Barrymore took the baby girl from him, and held her for a while himself. He kissed her head, then gently placed the baby back in the crib.

It now was three o'clock in the morning. "You go on home, Noll," Barrymore said to Gurney. "I'll stay here for a while."

Barrymore remained in Gilbert's house until seven o'clock. He left his neighbor asleep, then returned to his own house to dress for the remaking of the scene at Universal.

Notwithstanding the experiences of the night, his own galling failure of memory, the sleep denied him during the Gilbert episode, Barrymore did not falter as he went before the camera. He worked expertly, and with the vitality that he so often strangely summoned from his own depths at times when everyone thought him doomed or lost.

He made the scene without a break, at the first trial. Here was a champion, a man to be remembered.

12.

The Flight

BARRYMORE wrote to George Bernard Shaw on October 30, 1933, a matter of hours before his memory bogged down on the *Counsellor-at-Law* studio stage. Barrymore's letter ostensibly dealt with his desire to make a motion picture of Shaw's play, *The Devil's Disciple*.

In the light of the actor's collapse of memory that same evening, the letter also may have been activated by a premonitory impulse to leave the scene of growing harassments.

Dear Mr. Shaw:

I think of bringing my wife and children to England in the near future, and I have heard from one of the major studios here that there is a chance of doing *The Devil's Disciple*, which I would love to do. I don't know as yet whether or not these arrangements have been crystallized; but I wondered, inasmuch as I am going to be in England anyway, whether it would interest you to have me do one of your plays in the cinema there? You know the ground and conditions better than I do, and I would rather approach you directly, if the idea happens in any way to intrigue you, than to do it in any roundabout fashion. Would you be good enough to cable me, care Beverly Hills (charging the cost to me)? I should like, if I may, to impress upon you the fact that any communication between us will be abysmally confidential, and although I can assure you that our personal relations will be absolutely direct, Hollywood is such an odd place that, if you will not mind my suggesting it, would you couch your cable reply to this letter in terms of rather cryptic analogy? . . .

Shaw replied to Barrymore by cable, but it has been lost from the actor's files. A letter from Shaw, however, bearing a November 14 dateline, arrived at Tower Road.

Dear John Barrymore:

I am out of the film world here, being Victorian and very old, and yet too advanced for the poor things. Until lately the film work done here was not as good as at Hollywood. It is better now, and will be better still later on, as it is the English way to do nothing until others have made all the experiments and found out the way, and then go ahead with it strongly. And it may be that the development of the movie into the international talkie may operate in favor of the studios which are within easy reach of Paris, Rome, Berlin, etc. as against remote Hollywood.

On the whole, I think it is not so much the question of which is the best professional centre as to where you would like to live and have your children educated. And that takes a good deal of consideration. I dare not advise you. The world is in such a mess at present; and our profession is such a desperately precarious one at all times that one can only laugh when one is advised to act prudently.

R.K.O., through [Kenneth] Macgowan, has been sounding me on the subject of films for a year past. I suggested *The Devil's Disciple* as the best selection, provided you could be induced to play Dick Dudgeon. This has just come to a head; and my terms are accepted; but there is one stipulation which I have sprung on them too lately to receive a reply. This is, that Dick must not be represented as being in love with Judith. If you have read the play you will understand that Judith is a snivelling little goody-goody, as pathetically pretty as she pleases, and spoilt and conceited enough to imagine that Dick has faced the gallows for her sake instead of "by the law of his own nature." But the least suggestion that he was prowling after her instead of standing up to her husband would belittle him unbearably, and reduce the whole affair to third-rate Hollywood sobstuff. Unless I can knock this into R.K.O., the bargain may fall through; but by the time you receive this you will either have been offered the engagement, which will show that my stipulation has been accepted, or else the deal is off.

Faithfully,
G. Bernard Shaw.

Concerning Shaw's stipulation that Dick must not be in love with Judith, Barrymore afterward said: "Mr. Shaw has a strange quirk in all his plays of building up a male character, then, like an Indian-giver, taking the drama away from the man and throwing the scenes to the woman. I think that the sublime Irishman's own life-conflicts somehow are the basic cause of this habit, as witness his writing of impassioned letters to Ellen Terry, yet never permitting himself actually to meet that beautiful artist in person until late in her career. I believe that many of the emotional confusions of the vegetarian genius might have been resolved had he deliberately tackled three mutton chops, drunk a glass of porter, and then called instantly upon the lady."

On December 4, 1933, Barrymore again wrote to Shaw in part:

> I am afraid I did not make it clear in my letter to you, a copy of which I have just looked at, that I do not intend to live anywhere but in California, and was just coming to England for a couple of months with my family, and if we could utilize that time in possibly doing something together, it would not only be great fun but lucrative fun at that. . . .

The production of *The Devil's Disciple*, however, was delayed, then finally abandoned. Shaw wrote on January 22, 1934, expressing his opinion of Hollywood.

> I am sorry for the delay of the *D's D;* but it is inevitable. As you know, the differences between first-rate work and shop routine are often microscopic and seem to the routineer to be quite unimportant; but they are just what the first-rate man earns his eminence by. I have only glanced through the opening pages of the scenario; but it has been enough to convince me that I must put in about a month's work (or leisure) on it before any attempt is made to rehearse or shoot it. I can only hope that, when I return to London in May, I shall have something to send you on which you can set to work.
>
> I see I shall have to educate Hollywood. It means well; but it doesn't know how to make an effect and leave it alone. It wallows in it fifteen seconds too long, and then starts to explain it. It can't find the spiritual *track* of a story and keep to it. And it can't tell a story. I've never yet seen an American film that was intelligible to me all through. And it doesn't know the difference between a call boy and a playwright.

On December 11, 1933, a week after Barrymore's second letter to George Bernard Shaw, the actor began tests for a screen portrayal of *Hamlet* in Technicolor. This undertaking promised an enhancement of John Barrymore's artistic fame as well as a significant broadening of motion-picture dimensions. Barrymore's brilliant friend and teacher of the Shakespearean word, Margaret Carrington, and her husband, Robert Edmond Jones, arrived in Hollywood. Jones was to direct the enterprise. The young multi-millionaire, John Hay ("Jock") Whitney, had arranged to finance the project if Barrymore's tests warranted the production.

The afternoon of the *Hamlet* test found Jack ably reciting the "rogue and peasant slave" soliloquy. That evening, after dinner, he invited Helios Hotchener and other friends to see him do the ghost scene. He began the speech from Act I, Scene V:

> *O, all you host of heaven! O earth! What else?*
> *And shall I couple hell? O Fie! Hold, heart;*
> *And you, my sinews, grow not instant old.*
> *But bear me stiffly up. Remember thee?*
> *Yea, from the table of my memory . . .*

Then Barrymore suddenly broke off, as in the October episode at Universal. He put his hand to his head. He could not proceed beyond the "table of my memory" phrase. He was completely unable to remember the next lines, beginning with "I'll wipe away all trivial fond records."

The references to "remembrance" and "memory" seemed to confound Barrymore, to throw him into a psychological deadlock. Mrs. Carrington prompted the faltering actor. It was of no use. Barrymore tried again and again; but each time he reached the "table of my memory" reading, a thick mist would rise to obscure the islands of his recollection. He could not complete the scene.

Jones and his wife, unaware of Barrymore's *Counsellor-at-Law* collapse, wondered if he had been drinking. They watched him with sad appraisal as he walked from the stage to sit beside Helios Hotchener.

"Are you ill?" asked Helios.

"No," he replied, "not ill of *body*."

After a pause he added: "I can remember those lines clearly up to a certain place. God knows I've said them on the stage hundreds of times with no trouble." Then he asked: "Can it be possible that there is some hidden reason for my falling down completely when the word 'memory' is spoken? What centers of the brain are disturbed when a particular word or phrase is being repeated? Am I to be struck down as was my father?"

"Could it not be from fatigue," asked Helios, "or perhaps drinking too much?"

"No," he replied with a dungeon tone. "I've had practically no liquor all day." He thought for perhaps half a minute, then said, "No. I've been frightened for some time by my lapses of memory. My father once told me he had been struck behind the right ear during a fight in a London ring. He developed headaches and stop-

pages of memory when lines on the stage evoked intense emotions."
Again he was silent for a time, then resumed: "I, also, have had
falls and blows and headaches. Headaches where my father had
them, over the right ear. . . . I don't want to see a doctor. I want
to beat back whatever it is myself. And, by God! I will!"

Robert Jones and his wife sadly canceled their great plans for
the *Hamlet* production, then left Hollywood for home.

In February of 1934 Barrymore's talent flared brilliantly. He made
Twentieth Century, the screen version of a zany masterpiece given
to Broadway by playwrights Ben Hecht and Charles MacArthur.
These bouncing aces themselves wrote the scenario from their own
play, tailoring it to suit the comedian abilities of Barrymore.

Then, on March 27, Jack quarreled with Dolores.

Their home life now was straining at the seams. Jack was spending his nights in a big chair in the rathskeller, seldom going to his
bedroom. He was beset by domestic annoyances, whether real or
imaginary. He felt that his daughter's companionship was being denied him, and that he was unwelcome in the nursery where his
young son slept and played.

Sometimes his daughter would slip down to the rathskeller, climb
onto her father's lap, there to sit entranced by his improvised tales
of "the Magoozalums."

Each day brought evidence to Jack that his great dream was
fading. He spoke to his manager concerning a trip with his family
to Europe, possibly aboard the *Infanta*, as a means of salvaging
some marital happiness before it became too late.

On May 6 the actor prepared for rehearsals of *A Hat, a Coat,
a Glove*, for Producer Kenneth Macgowan at R.K.O. studios. Nine
days afterward he began the final reading with the others of the
cast for the first scenes of *Hat*. He seemed listless and low in vitality.

He went slowly from his dressing-room to the set on May 15
to begin the making of the photoplay. He had not been drinking
for the last several days. When Director Worthington Minor called
for the beginning of the sequence, Jack seemed dazed. He swayed
into the scene, knew not a word of the speech he was to give, and,
to the consternation of the director, kept on walking in the wrong
direction, to make an exit not indicated in the script.

Jack offered no comment when work was halted for the remainder
of the day. He seemed unaware of what had happened. He went

home for a night of sleep in his chair in the rathskeller. He sat there, fully dressed, alone.

In the morning his manager awakened him. He apparently had not been drinking during the night. The sounds of his children's voices now came to Barrymore's ears. Breakfast was set before him. He did not eat, but listened to the voices of the children, and perhaps to voices within his own soul.

He went with Hotchener to the studio. He failed again this day. He failed again on the next.

Kenneth Macgowan, a man of friendly discernment, called Hotchener aside to say: "I know that he isn't drunk. His trouble is more serious than that. Please make him take a long rest. We must regretfully cancel the contract."

Dolores now advised her husband to enter the Good Samaritan Hospital. Jack received this suggestion almost indifferently, then yielded. He remained at the hospital from May 17 until June 4 under treatment by Dr. Samuel Hirshfeld, Dolores' own physician at that time.

Laboratory and other tests were made, and it was determined beyond question that Barrymore was not a paretic. We mention this to refute the careless, if not malicious, reports of such persons as have easier access to gossip than to documented facts.

Then, to rule out another potentiality, that of the existence of a brain tumor as a possible cause of Barrymore's memory defect and his occasional uncertainty of gait, the physician in charge called into consultation Dr. Samuel D. Ingham, neurologist, afterward president of the Section of Neurology of the American Medical Association. Dr. Ingham found no organic disease present in Barrymore's central nervous system.

Shortly before this time, in Los Angeles, a man diagnosed as an incurable alcoholic had died. The autopsy disclosed that he had a brain tumor. The doctor attending Barrymore had had nothing whatever to do with this other case, but it was fresh in his mind.

Dr. Hirshfeld said, as others had before him, that drink was the basic cause of Barrymore's trouble, and added that the patient had a Korsakow Syndrome.

The Korsakow Syndrome is a loss of memory of recent events. This condition was first described in 1889 by Dr. S. S. Korsakow, an eminent Russian neurologist. There is not a vast literature on this matter. The most recent available opinion on the Syndrome is that it is caused by a toxemia, the result of a circulating poison that has a specific affinity for brain tissue. It is not, in a strictly scientific sense, regarded as insanity.

It is the opinion of several experts that as late as 1934 Jack could have been cured of his loss of memory and certain other physical ailments, such as enlargement of the liver. It is believed that his memory would have returned unimpaired, with the possible exception of such recollections as he might wish to blot out for neurotic or hysterical reasons.

Drug addiction, it is said, can cause loss of memory. Jack was at no time a user of narcotics. Nor do the authorities whom I have interviewed believe that injuries to Barrymore's head had anything to do with his memory defect.

Subject all his lifetime to extreme and contradictory actions, Barrymore's mentality, aside from the striking loss of memory of recent events, remained uncommonly alert and facile. As the years passed he suffered a diminution of his powers for sustained attention, his memory disorders increased, together with a lack of impressibility. He could hold one of his own questions tenaciously in mind when undergoing an acute phase of his trouble. But any reply to an inquiry put by him rebounded, as if striking against a hard, smooth wall. Then no answer could satisfy his repetitious interrogations. During these Lethean intervals he might ask some fixed question again and again, in each instance uttering it as if for the first time.

He eventually suffered a peculiar type of amnesia, as if he were being intermittently lifted out of the contemporary flux of personal history. Then toward the end of his life he frequently experienced a disorientation of time and place. This defect caused Jack to resort to fabrications and grotesqueries to hide from others his lapses of memory. His affliction became varyingly acute, depending upon the degree of toxicity (and perhaps the lack of Vitamin B, which is thought to be tied up with this condition).

In later years Jack sometimes, but not always, would forget, when halfway through a recital, what immediate subject he was discussing. Then he would enlist his great inherent dramatic art to divert the attention of his listeners. His "ad libs," on or off stage, would arrest the interest of an audience until Barrymore regained the traffic lane of his narrative. It was as if he had skidded off the road to a soft shoulder beside it, then struggled back again to the solid pavement. Sometimes he could not get back. Then it would seem that the roadbed of memory itself had been sabotaged.

When acting in pictures following the *Hat* debacle of 1934, it became necessary for him to read his speeches from blackboards held by an athletic fellow, who would dash about the set, out of range of the camera, but always within eye-shot of the unretentive Barrymore. Even so, he did not always know the story of the play; but by virtue of his immediate art he could give the blackboard line such rich interpretation and inflection as to make up for its dramatic dependency upon what preceded or what followed it. This put a playwright's work to the test; for if the lines had genuine dramatic content one could be sure that Barrymore's quick intelligence in reading them, rather than his over-all knowledge of the scene or of the play as a whole, would spontaneously enliven the characterization or project the story. If, as sometimes obtains among Hollywood products, the dialogue was tawdry, bogus, or superfluous in relation to the play as a whole, Barrymore smothered such speeches with snorts and contortions of feature. These antics themselves sometimes lent a lusty distinction to an otherwise banal composition.

On June 4 it was agreed that Jack might benefit somewhat by a non-alcoholic cruise on his yacht. Barrymore, his wife, children, their maid, and Jack's special nurse left Glendale by train for Vancouver, there to board the *Infanta*.

At the railway station Barrymore asked Hotchener to be sure to keep in touch with him by telegraph or wireless. Dolores, on the other hand, instructed Hotchener "not to try to keep in touch," adding that from this time on she was taking complete responsibility for her husband's health.

Aboard the *Infanta*, and with the usual source of alcohol now denied him, Barrymore drank Dolores' perfume, downed all the mouth-wash available, and even partook of a bottle of spirits of camphor.

A letter from George Grossmith of London meantime had come to Tower Road during Jack's absence. Grossmith, an old friend of Barrymore's, was associated with Alexander (afterward Sir Alexander) Korda in the London Film Company. It was thought by Jack's manager that this letter might lead to a picture engagement abroad.

Then, as if in telepathic answer to Hotchener's ponderings, the actor sent him a wireless message:

WHAT IS EXACT SITUATION REGARDING NEXT PICTURE, AND WHEN DO YOU ADVISE RETURNING? LOVE TO BOTH YOU AND HELIOS.

Henry sent a cryptic reply, advising Jack to telegraph him as soon as possible. Barrymore responded that he would telephone from Prince Rupert on the evening of July 20. On that day, however, he telegraphed Hotchener from Prince Rupert:

MUCH BETTER NOT TELEPHONE. LET US MEET AT GEORGIA HOTEL, VANCOUVER, WEDNESDAY, TWENTY-FIFTH. IMPORTANT.

On the appointed day Hotchener stood on the wharf at Vancouver as the *Infanta* anchored and the Barrymores came ashore in the launch. Jack appeared to be relieved at seeing his manager; but Dolores seemed astonished, if not annoyed.

Hotchener recalls that Dolores asked, "Why did you come?" and that Jack said to her, "Why should he not come? He's my business manager."

When it was explained that the Grossmith letter might mean a London contract, Dolores said, "But Jack is in no condition to discuss business matters."

Barrymore insisted upon hearing the details of the Grossmith letter and his manager's suggestions. Dolores interrupted to say that her husband could not possibly make a picture or do any other work at the present time.

Later that day at the hotel, Jack complained of "feeling tired and thirsty." He asked for a glass of beer. When he said "beer" Dolores told him, "Not a drop of it!" He remarked that a little beer couldn't possibly harm him. Then Dolores announced that if she ever caught him drinking again she would leave him and take the children with her. Jack winced at this, wiped the perspiration from his forehead, then ordered ginger ale.

After Dolores had left the hotel to do some shopping for the children, Jack told his manager that he felt he was "being kept a prisoner on the boat."

"Until today," he added, "I have not been permitted to go ashore. I am being given sedatives, especially when in port. Why?"

Dolores, returning to the hotel, finally was persuaded that a trip abroad might be desirable for the family. Jack at once brightened.

He asked Henry to go "instantly" to the steamship office in the hotel lobby to make reservations on the *Empress of Britain*, which was to leave Canada September 15. Hotchener arranged for the voyage, then left by airplane for Hollywood to continue negotiations by cablegram and letter with Grossmith in London. Jack and Dolores boarded the *Infanta* to resume the therapeutic cruise.

Several weeks after the Vancouver consultation, the manager received a telegram from Jack stating that something serious had happened on the boat. The actor wired that he would arrive alone on his yacht at Long Beach on August 24. The telegram read:

FAMILY LEFT VANCOUVER SATURDAY BY MOTOR TO SEATTLE, THENCE BY TRAIN LOS ANGELES. PROBABLY ARRIVE TONIGHT OR TOMORROW. IF THEY INTERVIEW YOU LISTEN, BUT BE AS NONCOMMITTAL AS POSSIBLE. WILL YOU MEET ME LONG BEACH ABOUT EIGHT FRIDAY MORNING? USE YOUR OWN JUDGMENT ABOUT SEEING THEM AT HOUSE, AS IF CASUALLY, NOT MENTIONING THIS WIRE. REASON FOR THEIR LEAVING, IN CASE OF ANY INQUIRY, WISHING AVOID BAD WEATHER ON ACCOUNT OF CHILDREN. LOVE TO BOTH.

There are divergent opinions as to what actually happened on the day of the "trouble" aboard the *Infanta*. This much is clear: Jack's nurse received a broken nose, threatened suit for damages, and some time afterward was given $3,000 out of court.

Jack's version of the fracas was that he had decided to leave his cabin to go ashore when the *Infanta* again dropped anchor at Vancouver. He declared that the nurse had barred his way, and that Dolores had come to the woman's assistance. In an effort to push the door open, he said, he accidentally put his elbow in the nurse's face; she had reeled against Dolores, who fell to the deck. Then Jack "escaped" and went ashore. Dolores left with the children that evening by train for California.

Jack arrived at Long Beach on the *Infanta* on August 24 to be met by Hotchener. The actor and his manager discussed the nose-breaking episode and its connotations during the motor ride from Long Beach to Tower Road.

"That incident gives my wife sufficient grounds for leaving me for good," Jack said. "The corroborative evidence of Dolores and the nurse will be adequate to gain her a divorce and custody of the children."

When Jack and Henry arrived at Tower Road, Barrymore went

at once to Hotchener's office. He asked his manager to "face the music" for him. Dolores gave Hotchener her version of Jack's "escape." The nurse was present at this interview, her face bandaged. Dolores said a "serious attack" had been made upon the nurse and herself. She considered Jack as being far from normal, and feared that matters were growing worse.

After the manager rejoined Jack at the office above the garage, they had a general discussion of the actor's domestic problems.

While this conference was in progress, Jack looked out of the doorway of the office to see Dr. Hirshfeld entering the gate to the grounds. The actor seemed suspiciously worried, since he himself had not sent for the physician. He remarked that Dolores must have summoned him.

Jack greeted the caller, inviting him into the Hotchener office. There Barrymore asked if the physician thought him able to undertake some radio work to "get back to one's normal vocation." The doctor thought it a splendid idea.

On the following Sunday, August 26, Barrymore called at the Hotchener house and found his manager away from home. Helios also was absent, as she had gone East to attend a philosophical convention. Jack left a note under the door, asking that Henry get in touch with him as soon as possible, that it was urgent.

While Hotchener was reading this note, the telephone rang. It was Jack. He seemed greatly disturbed, and asked that his manager come with all speed to the Barrymore estate. Jack warned him to approach Tower Road as quietly as possible, and slip unseen into the office over the garage.

The manager arrived there to enter upon a five-hour secret conference with Barrymore.

"I am not drinking," the actor said at the beginning. "There are times when a man does not *dare* drink. This is one of them."

Jack alleged that he had overheard on his telephone extension a conversation between Dolores and her physician. He pictured his wife as having been angry and determined. She had said, Jack told his manager, that something must be done to safeguard the children and herself.

Jack added that he had overheard Dolores and her physician arrange for a group of specialists to examine Barrymore. This meant, in Jack's opinion, that he might be judged mentally incompetent.

"This kind of thing," Jack said, "once happened to a close friend of mine in the East. My friend was privately examined by physicians. A few days later a petition was signed by his wife. It was presented to court, then signed by a judge. My friend was put into an institution. Finis! He never came out of it."

"But," said Hotchener, "are there any reasons for your belief?"

"Yes," Jack replied. "Dolores is no longer in love with me." Then he said with slow emphasis, "I deeply loved her, as you know. I love my children and this home. Another domestic smash-up is proving too much for me. I think the fateful seven-year period that dogs my marriages is ending once again. This is the third bus accident, and it doesn't look as though I can bounce out of it."

Then he said, "I would be a damned fool not to get out of California and the jurisdiction of its courts as quickly as possible. Let's blow!"

His tone was cold and deadly as he went on: "I appeal to you, Hank, to help me in this great crisis. Arrange your home and property interests for a long absence with me, if you can. Take Helios along as my guest, too, if she will come. God alone knows where this quest for liberty will take me."

He thought for a time, lay back on the couch and stared at the ceiling. Then he said: "We must get away without letting Dolores have any idea that we are leaving. She would come down on me like a flash if she suspected it. She'll be furious anyway, when she learns it, for no woman likes a man to walk out on her."

He lighted a cigarette. "You have a tough job, Hank, to protect my money, my property, my bonds, my boat. But it's an emergency. We've got to act fast." He then blurted out: "Will she never understand that in a man of my age and temperament, a fixed habit can't be cured by making a prisoner of him and giving him bromides?"

He rose from the couch, calmed down somewhat, then stood looking out of a window, his left hand in his pocket and his feet wide apart. "Dolores will try to pin the blame on you for my leaving her," he said, still without showing excitement in his voice or manner. "But the note I left at your house this morning will show that it is *my* responsibility alone."

Jack decided not to pack anything for the flight. He would not take even a handbag. He would trust Camomile, now the overseer of the Tower Road estate, to send his things on to New York.

Jack asked Hotchener to "see if we can find a day that is auspicious." He added with a mirthless smile, "If ever we needed the assistance of the stars, we need it now."

It was decided that they leave the Glendale Airport by the nine o'clock plane the evening of August 28. His manager reserved seats under fictitious names.

Barrymore's sudden intention to travel by airplane instead of by train is an indication of the man's desperation of mind. He had flown only twice before in his life. On both occasions his life had been jeopardized by near-crashes of the planes. After a second experience, when a plane in which he was riding from a Catalina fishing holiday in 1925 got into difficulties, he had announced that he never would fly for a third time "unless it becomes a matter of life or death." Now he was to go into the sky a third time.

The actor took precautions before his departure to indicate legally that he was not "deserting" his wife, or failing to provide for the family during his absence. He telegraphed Dr. Hirshfeld shortly before leaving for the airport:

FOLLOWING YOUR SUGGESTION, MY MANAGER MADE CONTACT WITH CERTAIN RADIO INTERESTS IN THE EAST, AND THEIR RESPONSE, INDICATING IMMEDIATE OPPORTUNITY, MAKES IT IMPERATIVE I LEAVE WITH HIM TONIGHT. TERRIBLY SORRY TO CANCEL APPOINTMENT WITH YOU AND YOUR ASSOCIATES, BUT FEEL SURE YOU WILL UNDERSTAND, AND WILL NOTIFY YOU THE MOMENT I RETURN.

J. B.

Barrymore and his manager were driven to the Glendale airfield in Camomile's car. On the way there, Jack telephoned Dolores from a drugstore booth. While talking to his astonished wife, he held in his hand a memorandum prepared the day before, a summary of which follows:

He was leaving suddenly because an opportunity for radio work had arisen in N. Y. The doctor had advised radio work, and J. *had* to get to work to support her and the children. He was sending his check for $3,500 to her bank for her use, and instructing the bank to notify him when her balance dropped to $1,000, so he could replenish it. He wanted her to retain Camomile in charge of house and grounds during his absence. He would keep Dolores in touch with his plans and whereabouts.

It was Barrymore's fear that Dolores might reach out somehow to prevent his departure. When he telephoned, he let her believe that he was leaving Los Angeles by train.

Both Dolores and her physician maintain that at no time was it planned to place Jack in an institution for the mentally unfit. Nor was any medical conference discussed "behind Jack's back." The doctor had arranged to have Dr. Carl Rand, brain surgeon, and Dr. Verne Mason, diagnostician, examine Barrymore to rule out all suspicion of a brain tumor. Both Dolores and the physician say that Jack was directly consulted and advised of this appointment for eight o'clock of the same evening he left by plane for New York.

The important thing to consider, it now seems, is that Jack's fears were terrifyingly real to him, no matter who made telephone calls to whom, or who listened to what over an extension. It is understandable that Dolores felt deeply concerned, if not embittered, over recent events; and it is understandable that a sinister river of doubt overflowed the dikes of Jack's brilliant mind in this summer of 1934.

Now, as the plane rolled down the runway, Barrymore seemed enormously relieved. Then, as the flight progressed, new fears assailed him in the night sky. Would he really be safe in New York? Could anyone in California persuade the New York authorities to seize him as a mentally incompetent and dangerous fugitive, and obtain an order compelling his return to the West?

"What if a reporter identifies me somewhere along the route?" he asked. "Flashes the news to the Associated Press, and it appears in the Los Angeles papers? Then maybe a court order will await me at the Newark airport. I ought to have a lawyer there to protect me."

It was decided that his manager's attorney-brother, Maurice, be asked to attend to this confidential matter. The lawyer previously had represented many of Jack's interests in the East. Maurice had been Special Corporation Counsel of the City of New York.

The attorney met the actor and the manager at the Newark airport on August 26. He said he would have a writ of habeas corpus drawn up at once as a precaution if Barrymore were seized. Jack and Henry went to the New Yorker Hotel, where Helios Hotchener greeted them.

On August 30 Hotchener received a wire from Dolores:

I HOLD YOU PERSONALLY RESPONSIBLE FOR ANYTHING UNTOWARD THAT MAY TRANSPIRE.

When the manager showed this telegram to Jack, the actor said,

"Isn't this a clear indication that she thinks me incapable of manag‹ ing my own affairs?"

He then sent the following telegram to his wife:

HENRY HAS JUST SHOWN ME YOUR WIRE TO HIM AND I WISH TO VERY DEFINITELY INFORM YOU THAT THE RESPONSIBILITY FOR THIS TRIP WAS ENTIRELY MINE. AS I TOLD YOU I CAME HERE ON BUSINESS AND I HAD NEED OF MY BUSINESS MANAGER. IT· IS VERY UNFAIR OF YOU TO ASSAIL HENRY. I CAN ASSURE YOU THAT THERE IS NOTHING UNTOWARD IN WHAT HAS TRANSPIRED OR WILL TRANSPIRE AND THAT HIS LONG ASSOCIATION WITH US IS THE BEST GUARANTEE OF HIS GOOD FAITH.

Barrymore's trunks did not reach him for several days. A letter from Camomile, with the trunk keys, arrived ahead of the luggage. Camomile wrote that Dolores had neither hindered nor helped him when he packed the trunks.

The "honeymoon" trunk, as well as the one Barrymore had "borrowed" from Uncle Jack Drew so long ago, finally arrived at Barrymore's hotel suite. He looked wordlessly at the "honeymoon" trunk.

O so white! O so soft! O so sweet is she! . . . You're just putting on an act when you say that. . . .

Now he turned to the old and battered box which had served him for many years. He ran his hand across the tattered labels and the faded initials, "J. D."

"This is the better trunk," he said. "It is part of me."

He was pleased to find that Camomile had packed the *Hamlet* costume, the dagger, and the prompt-book for the play.

Barrymore's attorney advised that he be examined by a recognized authority on nervous and mental disorders as a precaution against possible extradition procedure. The examination was made by Dr. Lewis Stevenson, neurologist and neuropathologist, member of the faculty of the Cornell University Medical School, and associate or consulting neurologist at Bellevue and five other hospitals. Dr. Stevenson's written report follows in part:

The mental status is in every way normal except that there is some slight impairment of memory for recent events, which in my opinion, is due to fatigue. . . . After a careful examination of Mr. Barrymore, lasting well over four hours, it is my opinion that there is no organic disease of any kind in his nervous system, nor is there any evidence, whatever, of any psychosis or any other kind of functional disturbance of the nervous system.

Barrymore announced that he would go abroad at once. He felt that he still was not safe from possible commitment to an institution.

"I want to put a lot of ocean between myself and my worries," he said. "I need a moat for my castle. The Atlantic is just the right size."

He went with his manager aboard the *Berengaria* on September 8, 1934. He promptly locked the doors of his suite. It had become an obsession, a morbid fear which never would quite depart from his mind, that he would one day find himself confined in a sanitarium.

"I'll not rest easy," he said, "until this damned ship passes the Statue of Liberty."

The London scene for a time diverted the man who had made his greatest triumph at the Haymarket Theatre in *Hamlet* almost ten years before.

He spent many of his hours with old acquaintances of the theatre. Among them was actor Richard Bennett, himself a firebrand, an artist of impulse and whim. Jack went one evening from Grosvenor House to call upon Bennett at the Savoy.

The actors had a congenial evening together over some excellent brandy in Bennett's room. Bennett began to recite poetry. Jack asked him who the great poet was who had written the splendid verses.

"It is I," said Bennett. "I have been hiding my light under a bushel."

"Then give us a few more pecks."

Bennett recited until a late hour, then excused himself to go to the washroom. He returned to the bedroom to declaim a fresh ode, but Barrymore had gone. Bennett went to the hallway to look for Jack. He consulted the operator of the lift. No. The operator had taken no one down in the early hours of morning. Bennett concluded that Jack had departed by way of the stairs.

Late next day Bennett awakened partly, and wondered if Jack had managed to get home without accident. He reached out for the telephone on his night-table, and placed a call for Grosvenor House.

The factotum at the other end of the wire seemed vague about Jack's whereabouts. He consented, after some argument, to ring Jack's rooms.

Bennett became impatient. He began to call into the telephone: "Hello! Hello!"

Jack's voice came in reply with a sleepy "Hello!"

"Are you there, Jack?" asked Bennett.

"I think so," Jack replied.

"Well," said Bennett, "are you all right?"

"I'm fine," Jack said. "How are you?"

"Fine. But I've had a hard time getting your room. Are you in it or in the lobby?"

"I don't know," Jack said.

"What in hell do you mean, you 'don't know'? Where the devil *are* you then?"

"Here, I suppose," Jack said, poking his head out from beneath Bennett's own bed.

George Grossmith, chairman of the board of London Film, and Managing Director Korda were frequent callers at Barrymore's suite in Grosvenor House. They signed a contract on September 20 for Jack to do a picture for London Film. He would be paid $60,000 for a six-week term before the English cameras.

Jack suggested to Korda that Ben Hecht and Charles MacArthur write the scenario. Barrymore talked to these friends by trans-Atlantic telephone to Nyack, New York; but the connection was faulty, and besides, the playwrights were up to their mighty chins in ten or a dozen enterprises of their own concoction.

Director Korda visited Barrymore on the evening of September 30. He expressed regret that Hecht and MacArthur were not available for the scenario. Then he asked, "Why not do *Hamlet?*"

Barrymore agreed readily to this. He was pleased.

Then, after Korda's departure, Jack turned to his manager. "I wonder if I am up to doing *Hamlet?* Thousands here remember me in it at the Haymarket. They would be sure to see the film. And if I'm not as good as I was at the Haymarket, it will be just too bad. The flattening out that Bernard Shaw gave me ten years ago would be as nothing to what he'd do this time. He'd have me beheaded in the Tower of London."

Jack now walked over to a mirror, saying, "Let's look at the 'pan.' " He examined his features in the glass, then said, "Well, it would be a vintage *Hamlet*." He turned from the mirror. "But a good camera man might be able to counteract the furrows and the dewlaps of fifty-two years." He was silent for some time, then asked, "We have the *Hamlet* costume with us?"

"Yes," his manager replied. "Camomile packed it in the old trunk."

Now Barrymore looked at his ankles. They were swollen. Then he said, "That is too bad. Too bad for the wearing of tights, I mean. The swelling goes down when I lay off the drinks. But the way I feel now, I . . . Well, drinking helps me not to think about the kids, Tower Road, the yacht . . . and if I'll ever see them again. I think about these things all the time . . . and I wonder . . ."

"Do you suppose you could recall the *Hamlet* lines now?" asked Hotchener.

"That would be easy," Jack said, "because I've done them so many times before. Did Camomile also pack the prompt-book?"

"Yes."

"Then stand by."

He did both soliloquies without trouble. Then his manager turned the pages to the ghost scene, to read back to the actor the lines spoken by the specter of Hamlet's dead father.

And now Barrymore faltered at precisely the same place in the scene as during the test made a year before with Robert Edmond Jones and Margaret Carrington at the R.K.O. Studios.

The actor quietly sat down near a window, stared into the night over Hyde Park, then said, "It looks as if *Hamlet* is out. Do we simply tell Korda it's all off?"

"If we tell him the real reason," said Hotchener, "he'll doubt your ability to do *any* picture for him. Let's think it over first. Sometimes there's a way out."

Jack looked down at his puffed ankles, then said, "It's the first time I ever saw an actor swollen at *this* end."

13.

The Gaunt Yogi

A WEEK after Jack's self-admission that his instability of memory disqualified him for the London screening of *Hamlet*, he announced that he had "found a way out, maybe." He confided to the Hotcheners—Helios having arrived in London from Paris—that he would like to go to India, "instantly."

"All week," he said, "I have been grasping at straws. And now, I think, I've bobbed up with a lotus blossom.

"I've just come from a luncheon with a remarkable Hindu woman and her husband," he went on buoyantly. "The lady is a famous danseuse, so famous that, my memory being the world's most active sieve, I can't recall her name. But she told me of an ancient cure for an ailing memory. Besides, she knows several maharajahs. Claims they would lend me their palaces, retinues, elephants, and other properties if I decide to make pictures in India." Then he asked Helios, "Is there such a cure?"

"There is," replied Helios. "The Ayurvedic treatment."

"Do you think they'd take me on? Whom do we ask?"

"Dr. Srinivasa Murti," Helios replied, "president of the Ayurvedic Conference. He is also a regular physician, one of the founders of the Madras Medical Association, but unless you are in earnest . . ."

After passports had been viséd for France, Italy, and India, Barrymore's manager called upon Alexander Korda to explain that the actor wished to take a holiday in India. The contract with London Film was changed, and *Hamlet* postponed until the next spring.

On October 13 Barrymore sat at a desk in his quarters at Grosvenor House to write a will, the first of three such testaments made by him during the next seven years. The document was drawn up on four sheets of hotel stationery, in writing somewhat larger than his usual hand, the chirography clear and level on the unruled paper:

I, John Barrymore, being of sound mind, and realizing the hazards of travel, declare this to be my last will and testament.

I wish my body cremated and the ashes immediately scattered on the sea.

I wish all of my property both real and personal sold as soon as reasonably possible and the proceeds invested and reinvested in United States Government Bonds.

I wish the Bank of America National Trust and Savings Association in California to hold these bonds in trust.

I wish the income of these bonds divided into equal parts for the benefit of my three children: Diana, Dolores Ethel, and John, and used for their support until each reaches the age of twenty-one.

At that age each shall receive an equal share of the principal, which means that when Diana becomes twenty-one she receives *en bloc* one-third of my estate; when Dolores Ethel becomes twenty-one she receives one-half of the remainder, and when John becomes twenty-one he receives the whole of the remainder. If any of my children dies before the age of twenty-one, his or her share of income and principal shall be divided equally among the survivors. If they all die before the age of twenty-one I wish the entire principal to go at once to the Actors' Home in New York State.

I do not bequeath any part of my estate to my present wife, Dolores Costello Barrymore, for three reasons:

One, because she has a fairly large invested fortune of her own which I have augmented in the past by upwards of fifty thousand dollars ($50,000) which I have caused to be invested in United States Liberty Bonds registered in her own name;

Two, because she has a large house of her own, free of debt, on Schuyler Road in Beverly Hills; and,

Three, because, for a considerable time, we have not lived together as husband and wife, and a legal separation between us is inevitable.

Dated in London, England, this 13th of October 1934.

John Barrymore

Barrymore and his two companions left Victoria Station on October 18 and arrived at Genoa the next morning. They motored in Italy, for Jack wished to revisit places of happy memory. It now was twenty years since Edward Sheldon had welcomed him to Venice and then gone with him on a tour that presaged the man's artistic future.

Edward Sheldon was much on Jack's mind during the whole of this present Italian journey. It was as if Barrymore were recapitulating that prologue to his coronation, when, with Sheldon as his Warwick, the actor decided to take up the scepter and put on the dynastic purple of great kings of the stage. How brief the reign, yet how brilliant it had been! How torrential the surge of years, now gone.

In Florence, and again in Rome, he spoke to his companions of "Ned." He well remembered the time when the young playwright and himself had heard the little girl sing "Tripoli" in the candle-light of the cave-like inn. But Jack could not find that place of medieval enchantment again. Perhaps it was well that he did not find it. The girl now would surely be old with drudgeries, her people dead, the wine of the caves no longer magical, the candlelight not the same. One sometimes must go on to new grapes, new songs, and be content to let the old days stay in the heart only as dreams.

The party stopped over at Rapallo to permit Jack to visit his friend, Max Beerbohm. Beerbohm made a caricature of himself for Jack, a lead-pencil drawing of a Romanesque figure in a toga, with laurel leaves in green crayon crowning an imperial head.

Barrymore suffered from headaches and a heavy drowsiness during much of this journey. He slept a great deal, but when awake seemed feverishly restless, and ate hardly at all.

He obviously had a temperature upon arriving at Naples, from which port he was to sail for Bombay, but refused to consult a physician, or permit his companions to ascertain his degree of fever by means of a thermometer.

He had not heard from Dolores as yet. That fact accentuated his feeling of uncertainty. A letter from his caretaker, Camomile, indicated much unrest at Tower Road. This put Jack into a rage. He wrote Camomile a letter of authority, advising him to see a lawyer if necessary. He added this postscript: "Above all, 'carry on.' Am with you hook, line, and sinker."

Jack and his companions went aboard the Italian Line motor cruiser *Victoria* on October 26. There he met a maharajah, who at once became interested in Barrymore's idea of making a motion picture in India. The potentate volunteered to defray all expenses of such an undertaking.

Jack stayed up nights, and slept during the days. He remained most of the time in his stateroom, but occasionally appeared among the passengers for tea or for dinner, wearing a cerise cummerbund and a smart dinner jacket. He spent his "loose" moments at the bar in the company of a Eurasian salesman from Calcutta, a person of great alcoholic capacity.

One late afternoon Jack saw a little girl of about four years of age on the second-class deck. She was violently seasick and crying. Her mother, also seasick, lay stretched out on the deck, unable to look after the child. Barrymore went at once to the dining-saloon for some orange juice, then passed through to the second-class deck to hold the sick child in his arms. He had no handkerchief. He never carried one, except a decorative kerchief in the breast-pocket of an evening jacket. So now he cleansed the child's face with the sleeve of his white linen coat. Then he gave her the orange juice. Soon she fell asleep, still in his arms.

Each afternoon, thereafter, this little girl would wait for Barrymore to visit her. He brought toys from the gift shop. He held her on his lap and told her stories.

Concerning the rough seas, Jack said, "It's a fine experience to have one's staggering done *for*, and not *by* one." A sudden lurch of the vessel in the sea-trough threw him against a door. He began to swear piratically. One of the women passengers remonstrated. He smiled at her, then said, "Pardon me, madam. It was just a slip 'twixt the ship and the lip."

As the vessel neared Bombay, Jack frequently mentioned his father, and spoke to his companions of the times when Maurice Barrymore had described India's mysteries and beauties, the strangely clairvoyant yogis, the splendid temples and mosques, the fakirs and their hooded cobras swaying to the music of reeds.

And now he expressed a fear that he never was to return alive to the western world. That is why he had written his will back in London. He said he had practically abandoned hope of ever rejoining his wife and children on Tower Road. He added that he felt it was his "last chance," this visit to India, and that in the time-old land of secrets he might find the miracle that would rid him of his weaknesses.

"I know that if I fail this time," he said, "I shall never come upon a cure anywhere again."

His spirits rose on November 5 when, from the deck of the *Victoria*, Barrymore first saw the harbor of Bombay and, inshore, the Moslem architectures rising above the aprons of world commerce. His artist's eye was stimulated, his theatric side stirred by this great back-drop of towers and minarets.

As he left the ship, the child whom he had befriended called out to him. He turned, then impulsively went to her at the gangplank head, took her in his arms, kissed her again and again, and carried her ashore.

A cablegram from Edward Sheldon awaited Barrymore at the Taj Mahal Hotel. Sheldon asked that Jack write him about Agra. The message from his thoughtful friend pleased the actor, who said, "Agra! How I'd like to go there. But I feel that I must first get right with myself, get well if I can. Let us get on with the treatments without delay. Then other things will follow."

Before entraining for Madras on November 7, Barrymore wrote forebodingly to Sheldon: "Whether I ever can come back or not is at present merely moot."

Jack had reserved rooms at the Connemara Hotel to await the interview with Dr. G. Srinivasa Murti.

There was an undated letter from his wife at the hotel desk, the first of her communications to reach him since the flight began. Dolores wrote that she had wanted to reply sooner to his letter and cable, but that both children, ill with colds, had demanded her attention. She went on to say that Jack's plans seemed "so indefinite" that it would be best for her to await news from him upon his return to England before deciding what was "the best thing to do." She closed by saying that "the children send you their love." Jack made no reply to this letter.

He now turned his mind to the "cure."

He was somewhat astonished by the manner and personal appearance of Dr. Srinivasa Murti. He had expected to see in him a patriarchal apostle with white beard and robes. Instead, the scientist who called upon the actor was a middle-aged, smooth-chinned gentleman of brisk military manner. He wore a turban, but otherwise was dressed in occidental fashion. He showed a fine sense of humor, telling Jack that the British soldiers, with whom he had served as surgeon in Mesopotamia, were unable to pronounce his name and had referred to him as "Dr. Murphy."

"This doctor is delightful," Barrymore said later in the day. "I thought he would be prejudiced against modern systems of medicine, and critical of what had been attempted for me in California. He was not. This completely disarmed me."

When Jack offered the doctor a drink, it was declined; but the physician didn't seem to mind when Barrymore mixed two drinks for himself.

"I've been quite a user of liquor," Jack said to Dr. Srinivasa Murti, "and now think it about time to control my thirst."

The doctor asked him to speak frankly about his problem, which Barrymore did.

"Funny thing," Jack afterward said, "it didn't occur to me to mention my bad memory until I happened to ask the doctor for a second time if he would have a drink. He replied that he never indulged. Then I remembered that he had used that same phrase only a few moments before, and I had forgotten it. I asked if this indigenous school of medicine could mend my failing memory. His answer upset some more of my preconceived ideas."

The doctor had replied that if Barrymore were a Hindu, he could almost guarantee that the Ayurvedic treatments would restore his memory. The Hindus had faith in the remedy. Their mental attitude was co-operative at the beginning.

"But, as for a naturally skeptical American . . ." The doctor paused, making a small but meaningful gesture.

"The cures at Lourdes," Jack remarked to his caller, "are based on faith. I can understand that perfectly. I'll at least undertake your treatment with an open mind. I promise it."

The Hindu physician, observing that Barrymore smoked continuously, recommended that the number of cigarettes be considerably reduced. Then he began to explain the treatment.

It consisted of certain spiritual factors together with internal and external medication. The remedies all were herbal, essences and leaves from the Himalayan region, or from transplantings brought to Malabar. The diet was a simple one of vegetables. There would be six weeks of treatment. During the first three weeks the patient would feel debilitated. The latter three weeks of the course promised an upbuilding of the body. No hospitalization was required; the doctor regarded it as a psychological hazard to place his new patient in an environment reminding him of clinical restraint. Dr. Srinivasa Murti advised Barrymore to move to a quieter and less tourist-trodden hotel.

"Because there is no bar there?" asked Jack.

"Not at all," replied the doctor. "There happens to be a bar in the quieter hotel, bars almost everywhere in India. But you must decide for yourself whether or not you can stay away from it or any other bar."

"But if I can't?"

"Then your condition will grow worse in all respects, especially the amnesia; and soon, very soon, you will reach the stage where you cannot be cured at all. And, of course, your life will be much shortened."

"I've made up my mind to try," Jack said.

It was decided that Helios Hotchener take this opportunity during Jack's time of treatment to visit friends living some miles outside Madras. She would return when Barrymore became well enough to continue his travels. Meantime her husband would remain at Barrymore's hotel.

Dr. Srinivasa Murti made tests during the next several days, in accord with modern medical practice. Then he assigned an Ayurvedic specialist and four assistants, all of whom held regular medical degrees, to take charge.

The treatments were begun on November 15 in a room next to Barrymore's sleeping quarters. The specialist and his four assistants brought with them not only their clinical equipment but a quantity of flower petals to strew before a small brass altar. There were several niches in the central pillar of the altar, where brass receptacles filled with sacred oils were set. Tiny wicks in the oil lamps were lighted, and incense burned in a brazier.

The chief Ayurvedic ministrator invited Barrymore to seat himself before the altar, then asked him to keep in mind a desire that health be restored him. The five physicians now seated themselves near the patient and began to intone ancient and rhythmic Sanskrit chants. The Hindu physicians said that Jack might interpret this ceremony in terms of his own religion, that its purpose was purely emotional and psychological, intended to dissipate thoughts of ill health or depression, and turn the mind into invigorating channels.

The ritual done, the doctors undressed Barrymore, then placed him upon a broad slab of highly polished wood. The chief sat at the head to preside over the treatment; the four assistants sat, two on either side of the patient. Now they began manipulations, each physician being assigned respectively to a certain area of the body, then applied warmed oils from Himalayan sources. The massage continued for about an hour.

Now Jack was bathed in a brew of leaves which had been simmering in a tub for several hours, then cooled to body temperature.

It was a fragrant bath of soapy consistency. The doctors next put Barrymore between linen sheets in his own bed, where he lapsed at once into a deep sleep.

These massages and baths and periods of relaxation, together with herbal medication, continued for three weeks. Barrymore's memory began to improve. His ankles no longer were swollen. By the fourth week he had lost his feeling of weakness, his headaches, his indifference to food.

Barrymore took enjoyable drives about the city and its suburbs. He spiritedly resumed his plans to do a picture in India. He would make a reality of his oft-dreamt pilgrimage to the Fort of Agra, the birthplace of his father.

His interest in literature and music revived. He asked that reading matter be brought him from Higginbotham's bookshop in Madras. He played his favorite operas on a small Victrola bought in Rome. He spoke infrequently of the past and its connotations of grief. He surely would do *Hamlet* for Korda when spring came.

Dr. Srinivasa Murti admonished his patient not to misconstrue a new feeling of physical and mental well-being as a notion that he might harmlessly return to former indulgences.

"On the contrary," the doctor warned, "your only safety lies in continuing for a considerable time the abstemious regimen imposed by the cure, until it becomes automatic. The benefits will then be so obvious and exhilarating that you will of yourself desire to maintain them permanently."

Barrymore frequently drove on the boulevard that lay along the beach of the Bay of Bengal. In places the sands spread for as much as a quarter of a mile from the road to the water's edge. There the Madrasis gathered to play games and listen to music.

Jack soon was recognized whenever his car stopped, or he got out in his bathing suit and robe to lie upon the sands. The young people surrounded him. There were groups of students from Madras University or workers employed in educational or parliamentary buildings.

Barrymore greeted them cordially, sometimes joining in their games, or discussing with them all manner of subjects. He was particularly impressed by their questions as to the deep psychological currents of Shakespeare's tragedies. He was told that the Hindus readily and literally accepted the ghost of Hamlet's father, because their own religion taught the continuation of life after death.

The actor frequently questioned the young students about their own lives, their beliefs.

Jack was enchanted by one story told him concerning the Lord Buddha. The Buddha was walking along a road and saw a cobra, its body crushed. "What is the matter, my brother?" the Buddha asked of the cobra.

"Some cruel boys stoned me."

"Why did you not defend yourself?"

"Because," the cobra replied, "you have taught us that under the law of harmlessness one does not hurt another in self-defense."

"But, my brother," said the Lord Buddha, "you might have hissed a little!"

Barrymore was sitting with his manager in their car one December afternoon. Music was playing, and the actor seemed absorbed in it. He sat with one hand resting on the window-well of the car door. He felt a gentle touch, then his hand was turned, palm up. Jack glanced about to discover on the running board an old and gaunt yogi, a turbaned ancient in a loincloth, his bronzed and wrinkled skin draped over a narrow array of bones.

The yogi looked up from Barrymore's palm to say in polite but toothless English: "Permit me to tell your fortune, sahib. Yes?"

"Go right ahead, Gus," said Jack, charmed by the yogi's gentle manner. The actor added banteringly, "I take it you are one of the early settlers of Madras?"

The yogi studied Jack's palm, then said, "Your father and your grandfather would have done well to have remained in India. For that is where you also should have continued to live."

"Continued to live?" Jack asked. "Have I been here before?"

"Oh, sahib, yes!" said the yogi. "You lived here before. And this land harmonizes with you." The old man again studied Barrymore's palm. "You should have been a painter. Instead you have painted your stories, not with colors, but with the sahib's thoughts and emotions. Sahib, you are an actor. Yes?"

"It is my sad impression," said Jack, "that you are a patron of the movies."

The old man was unperturbed by this skepticism. "Your wife and children are now in America," he intoned. "You never were destined to be happy in married life, sahib, nor will you ever be."

Barrymore turned to his manager. "Our friend here seems to have access to our files."

"Perhaps," said the yogi, "that is enough to tell the sahib. Yes?"

"No," and Jack seemed greatly interested in the fortune telling, "you may as well give it all to me, while you're at it."

"You do not seem destined," the old man said slowly, "to live to an old age, and toddy will greatly shorten your life."

"I've just been cured of toddy," said Jack. "That's a horse on you."

"I know, sahib," said the yogi. "But I read writing that is unwritten, and yet it is written here in the sahib's hand. You have planned to travel much in India," he went on. "You would avoid much trouble if you would stay here. But no; the sahib will return to America soon."

The gaunt yogi declined to take the rupee Jack offered him. He got down from the running board with surprising agility for such a bag of bones. Barrymore looked after him as he walked away, frowned a little, then asked the chauffeur to drive back to the hotel.

By the middle of December Jack seemed almost restored to good health. He had had nothing strong to drink. He was not morose. He no longer spoke bitterly of Dolores—in fact, he did not refer to her at all.

He planned to go as soon as possible on a tour of India in a private railway car. There actually would be two such cars at his disposal, one for the narrow-gauge and the other for the standard-gauge right of way. He looked forward to staying for some time at the Fort of Agra.

Then one day, December 15, Hotchener left Jack asleep in his room and went to his own quarters to read for an hour. During that hour Barrymore disappeared from the hotel.

The Eurasian, the Calcutta salesman who had been Jack's bar companion on shipboard, had called at the hotel and gone to Barrymore's quarters. Soon afterward they left the hotel to go to a Madras club, where they had several drinks. Then they visited a bagnio, at which place Barrymore promised the madam a twelve-hundred-dollar fee to close her doors to her usual clientele.

From that day until Barrymore returned to his hotel a week afterward, we have no record of events other than Jack's own robust reminiscences.

"It was an extraordinary place," he would say, "with a madam who looked like Moll Flanders. There were numerous girls, all Eurasians. They had astoundingly happy dispositions. They liked to go on picnics and sing little songs. The most interesting character in the place, however, was the madam's Greek lover, Dmitri. His name sounded Russian, but he was a Greek. Dmitri seemed a rather tragic figure, in that his whole soul longed for expression in cooking; whereas he was condemned, in a manner of speaking, to the patchoulied prison of the madam's affections."

Dmitri, Barrymore maintained, was a frustrated person, rather emaciated, dark-complexioned, and subject to dizzy spells.

"My coming seemed to hearten Dmitri," Barrymore said. "I, too, was interested in cooking, although I am an eccentric eater. We would sit up late in the kitchen, trying out recipes. His knowledge of the French school of cookery was vast. He detested curries, said they reminded him of the madam and her insistence that he remain faithful to her. In fact, she would call out to him, right when we were engaged in some special bit of cooking, and demand that he come at once to their room. I managed eventually to talk her out of this disciplinary action, and Dmitri seemed grateful. What a sad fate for a virtuoso of the cuisine to find himself irrevocably transplanted to another field of art! Sometimes tears would come to his dark eyes as he looked at the pots and pans. He confessed that the jealous madam even had burned a cookbook sent by one of his wives, whom he referred to as 'the Saloniki one.' "

According to Jack, a group of gentlemen jockeys appeared at the door one evening. When they were informed by a servant that the place was closed for the week, the jockeys refused to depart without being given a convincing reason "by the proprietor" in person for this cessation of business.

"With my privacy at stake," Barrymore continued, "I myself went to the door, politely invited the jockeys inside, and used some diplomacy. They thought they had seen me somewhere before, but were not sure. I persuaded them that I owned the place, then *begged them not to believe the story* that was going the rounds that my house had been quarantined by the health authorities. I offered to show them our girls. I appealed to them to trust *their own eyes* as evidence that my establishment was being politically persecuted. The jockeys had become a little pale by this time, and when I called out to the girls to come to the parlor, a spokesman for the disillusioned horsemen neighed wearily, 'Never mind, old man. We'll be moving on, thank you.' "

When Barrymore returned to his hotel, the doctor arrived to discuss with him the consequences of his week-long activities. The actor apologized, promised not to have another lapse, and the treatments were resumed. Then, two days afterward, Jack again disappeared from the hotel for several days. It now became apparent to the doctor as well as to Jack himself that it would be quite futile to continue with the treatment.

All plans to visit Agra or to go to the maharajah's palace vanished from Barrymore's mind. He decided to sail for England to fulfill his motion-picture contract for *Hamlet*.

The actor and his manager left Madras for Bombay on January 7, 1935, where Helios Hotchener rejoined them. She found the actor greatly depressed. Helios did not ask, nor did Jack tell her what had happened, beyond saying that he had lost his last chance for a restoration to health.

During the first part of the return voyage on the *Victoria* from Bombay to Naples, Jack would go daily to the Hotchener cabin to lie on the couch. He said little, and sometimes dozed there. Then he would go out in the early hours of morning to wander about on the deck alone.

He picked up some bar companions, a few days out of Bombay, and his morose mood changed into a seeming gaiety. He neglected to eat. His headaches returned. His ankles again became swollen.

At Suez, where the *Victoria* docked overnight, Barrymore went ashore with a ship's acquaintance. He returned on board the next morning in an agitated condition.

"Give me twenty-one pounds," he said to his manager. "I'm told that I owe it as a gambling debt. I apparently borrowed it from the man with whom I went ashore last night."

"But you never gamble," Hotchener pointed out. "How can it be that you made an exception last night?"

"I simply don't know. I don't remember a bit of last night. I wasn't especially tight, yet I can't seem to recall where we went. But I must pay the twenty-one pounds, for I'm told a complaint is being lodged against me at the British Consulate."

At Naples Jack became quite ill. He said he didn't want to go to England to do *Hamlet*.

"What do you suggest we should do about your contract?" asked his manager.

"Tell Korda that Hamlet is dead, very dead." Then, with a smile, he added: "But there is always King Lear . . . but later, *much* later. Cable Korda that urgent business calls me to America. It does. It calls me anywhere but London."

The actor and his two companions sailed from Genoa aboard the *Rex* on January 20.

"I wonder," he said, as the ship got under way for America, "if that damned old yogi in Madras didn't have more to tell me than he did? Much more."

CANTO FOUR

The Stag at Eve

I.

The Dervish Dancer

THESE were the seven last years of a lifetime. The personal
phases of that lifetime were a Gothic holiday of flowers,
of verses, and of wine, with rains and thunders too, when,
toward the close of day, the landlord spoke above the storm
to remind the unthinking guest that no one feasts for nothing or
is sheltered free at the inn.

Now at an ailing fifty-three, Barrymore began to pay at the usurious
rates demanded of a man of public name and of middle years when
he does not conform to the gospels of exemplary behavior. Condemnation by others went unnoticed by him; he seldom read the newspapers, and listened to warnings not at all. He forfeited his material
belongings. He lost in health. But his spirit remained essentially young
and unconquered.

He paid as much attention to adverse criticism as might a turf
champion were a delegation of stewards to appear at the thoroughbred's box-stall to say: "Look here, old fellow, we didn't like the way
you whinnied after winning the Preakness this afternoon."

Barrymore ignored even the good criticisms. Ashton Stevens recalls
that Jack, when informed of Percy Hammond's laudatory notice of
Peter Ibbetson, remarked: "I'm glad Percy liked the performance, but
I wish he wouldn't write about me as though we were just married."

It is a Ben Hecht theory that rulers, once dethroned, have a tendency during their last years to become caricatures of their former
selves. Hecht surmises that Barrymore in 1935 began deliberately to
lampoon his once great loves and his career of artistic eminence. He
burlesqued the gods of romance and good fortune as mere money
lenders and pimps.

He had come to Hollywood ten years before in possession of no assets other than his magnificent talent, his fame as the new Hamlet, and a contract with the Warner Brothers.

During the following ten years he earned $2,634,500. Of this Hollywood fortune he expended $538,646.97 in income taxes. He purchased a home costing in all $250,000. He bought two yachts, one of which became a dead loss of $110,000. The other stood him $225,000. In all ways his style of living was lavish.

Let us make a random choice from the complete file of checks, ledgers, and other documents at hand, and take for the purpose of example the figures for 1933. That year happened to have been his third most lucrative twelve-month. During that period he received $335,500 from motion pictures and $9,550 from bonds, a total of $345,050. His income taxes for the year 1933 amounted to $116,722.74; his agent's commissions $33,290; his alimony to Blanche Barrymore (Michael Strange), together with insurance policies for his daughter Diana, $13,557.30; his household expenses $46,250; his manager's salary $10,400; his telephones, telegrams, and photographs $1,750. The *Infanta's* maintenance for this year required $34,947.25. Purchase of a lot near Tower Road, the building of walls, pools, and other structures came to $67,549.08. Additional expenses, such as club dues, chauffeur's wages, storage charges for the *Hamlet* scenery, legal fees, vacation trips, and incidentals brought Barrymore's total expenditures for 1933 to $335,086.45, as against earnings of $345,050. This left him the comparatively slender credit balance of $9,963.55 for the year.

Even to such of us as are not public accountants, it becomes quite clear that this degree of spending does not coincide with the precepts of thrift. It seems remarkable that, notwithstanding the ten years of extravagance and heavy taxation, no debts whatsoever had been incurred as yet on Jack's Tower Road property or on his yacht.

In 1934, the year of the flight, Barrymore's gross income had shrunk to $74,264.42: the combined proceeds from one picture, *Twentieth Century*, two radio broadcasts, and the yield from bonds. As against this decrease in income, he spent $288,497.76! From 1935, the time of his homecoming from India, he kept on spending at a maharajah's pace.

His financial position on his return from India on January 31, 1935, was as follows: He had physical assets (his Tower Road home, his yacht, and a lot in Beverly Hills) to the amount of half a million dollars. He possessed negotiable securities in excess of $140,500. He had no debts outstanding. He had ready cash to pay February bills amounting to $15,108.14.

Barrymore had moored his yacht first off Guaymas, Mexico, and afterward on the Atlantic seaboard, beyond the threat of seizure by California authorities.

The stocks and bonds had been moved from California by the self-appointed fugitive as a precautionary measure at the beginning of the flight. He had placed them for safe-keeping in the vaults of the Sterling National Bank & Trust Company in New York. Dolores' bonds, representing her own earnings, amounted, together with gifts from Jack, to approximately $163,500. These of course had remained in her possession.

Upon his return to America Barrymore opened an account with the National City Bank in New York City. To allow ample scope for his financial whims, he instructed the Bank to notify the Sterling depository to sell bonds whenever his cash balance dropped below $2,500.

We are now about to see how a fortune melts under the high temperature of a man's caprices.

While in New York during the last ten days of January 1935, Barrymore's already depleted physical condition began further to deteriorate. News reaching him of domestic bitterness at Tower Road merely stimulated his reckless nature to headlong indiscretions. An occasional nurse attended him during such times as when he returned to his suite at the New Yorker Hotel after nights of philandering.

Jack's lawyers advised him not to answer telephone calls from Tower Road, fearing that he might make undiplomatic statements. He insisted, however, upon writing Dolores a "letter of farewell" on February 7, and composed the following document:

> Dear Dolores,
>   This is rather a difficult letter to write to you, but believe me, I do it after having considered everything very deeply. We might as well face the fact like two civilized people that it is quite evident for your own happiness as well as mine that our life together has come to an end.
>   In fact, as you know, our proper relationship as husband and wife really terminated about a year ago.
>   Therefore let us get together to make the necessary legal arrangements in as friendly a fashion as possible for our own sakes

as well as for the children. I think the sooner this is started the better, and, as certain picture negotiations require me to remain in New York for the present, I have asked Senator McAdoo's partner in Los Angeles, Colonel W. H. Neblett, to act as my legal representative to hand you this letter and to meet you to discuss some plan by which we can get our affairs in order.

I hope that in a few weeks I can settle the business matters that keep me here now, and come to California to see you and the children before going again to England. But meanwhile I hope that rapid progress can be made in settlement of our problems, as the English picture may start sooner than is now planned.

Jack.

Barrymore's lawyers prevailed upon him not to send this letter. He then seemed to forget his "farewell" until next day when, in response to an anxious telegram from Lionel, he wrote in part as follows, addressing his brother by nickname.

Dear Mike—

You know I can't put in a God-damned *letter*—which are *foul* things anyway—one-tenth of what I want to say to you, but I don't think that's so damned necessary as you can supply most of it yourself. The whole thing is cold and worse than that—and from something I vaguely remember . . . you won't be *unduly* surprised!! Nobody knows better than you how difficult in a way this kind of letter is to write—but I know I don't have to write *you* anything as your bean and your soul don't need it.

Everything is all right and I feel fine. Ever so much love to you, Mike . . . and don't *worry*. Everything will be *Jake*.

Much love,
Jack.

On the same day that Jack wrote to Lionel, Barrymore's manager left for Hollywood, where he learned that Dolores had moved most of the furniture from Tower Road. Jack's personal possessions were left on the premises. Objects in the trophy room, such as the dinosaur's eggshell given him by explorer Roy Chapman Andrews, two Ecuadorian human heads, shrunken and mummified, and a pickled spider were not claimed by the departing wife. The earthquake-proof chandelier remained in place. Dolores and the children took up residence in the Wilshire district of Beverly Hills.

When Henry Hotchener returned to New York on February 17, he found Barrymore in extremely bad health. A cable was sent to Korda to cancel the London contract.

At noon on February 26 Barrymore's nurse knocked at Hotchener's door. "He's in a most dreadful condition," said the nurse. "I can't find his pulse. I'm afraid that his heart is about to stop beating."

Hotchener telephoned to Edward Sheldon, who immediately sent his own physician, Dr. Kenneth Taylor, to Jack's hotel. That evening Dr. Taylor placed the stricken actor in New York Hospital. Jack's manager took a room across the hall from Barrymore's suite.

The actor remained at the hospital until March 21. He had no liquor (except for one incident, when a bottle was smuggled to him by a lady he had met aboard the *Rex*). He underwent dietary and light and heat ray treatments.

It was during this time of hospitalization, early in March, that a young student at Hunter College, Miss Elaine Jacobs, first became acquainted with the sick actor. This stage-struck young woman entered Jack's suite, and also entered what was left of his life.

When the doctor and nurses protested their patient's reception of a stranger, Jack announced that Miss Jacobs was his protégée. He said that he was going to help her to become an actress. She soon announced her new name, Elaine Barrie.

Now we come to a much publicized time of Barrymore's winter of discontent.

The publicity inspired by the Barrymore-Barrie association did not restore any laurel leaves to the actor's molting crown. He, of course, paid no attention to the subsequent furor of print, and Miss Barrie did not seem to take pains to avoid public mention. She was but nineteen years old, at an age when a sudden emergence from prosaic privacy sometimes brings with it the illusion that notoriety is fame.

With Barrymore's ledgers, or photostatic copies of all the pages before me, and with every canceled check for his ten years of prodigious spending at hand, and with full access to the medical records, as well as to the pertinent legal documents and to the Hotchener daily diary, it is an inescapable deduction that Jack, who seldom spent wisely, now began to spend wildly.

The canceled checks indicate that from April 17, 1935, to May 15 of that year he took a sudden interest in buying women's apparel. His personal checks made out to the Saks New York stores during a period of a lunar month amounted to $4,811.15. In addition to that amount, and on one day, he purchased gowns and coats at Milgrim's costing $1,051.31. For whom? Not for himself, surely, for he was not a female impersonator.

These are but specimens of the man's spending spree. Whatever the provocation, and whoever may have benefited by it, it is not for us to say. The record, however, shows that by September 11, 1935, less than five months after his leaving the hospital, Jack had to sell bonds to the amount of $124,068.77 to meet his regular obligations and to satisfy his King Ludwig vagaries. Then, his resources low, he moved his remaining bonds and his bank balance of $3,151.08 from New York. He took these remnants of his fortune to Weehawken, New Jersey, there to deposit them secretly in a provincial bank.

During these five months of headlong spending, Jack earned but $5,000 for two radio broadcasts, an average income of $33 a day. During that same five months he spent at the rate of $827 a day!

He permitted his yacht and its crew of ten to remain idle much of this spring and summer at an East River mooring at an average expense of $3,000 a month. He himself chose, during a season of oppressive heat, to reside in a small New York apartment instead of enjoying the comforts of the owner's suite aboard the *Infanta*.

Let us concede that the man brought upon himself a King Lear transition. Let us own that his waywardness and capricious nature, together with the inroads of illness, caused his collapse of fortune and of home. And above all, let us not point a moral, nor assess the motives or the actions of his companions. But do not ask us, prithee, to accept this cavorting of the stag at eve as a minuet painted on glass.

While still in the hospital in March, Barrymore was visited by old friends, among them Herbert Bayard Swope, Jack Prescott, and Al Woods. Michael Strange and her then husband, Harrison Tweed, called, as did Jack's daughter Diana, with several of her girl schoolmates.

Barrymore entertained Diana and her young friends with gay accounts of his travels. He then invited his daughter to come with him for a voyage on the *Infanta*. The girl was delighted at this prospect. Her stepfather, Mr. Tweed, agreed to accompany Diana on this voyage.

Commentators have created some mystery over the fact that Mr. Tweed now became the temporary lessee of the *Infanta*. The reason for Tweed's drawing up of a protective contract was that he legally could take the yacht's management out of Jack's hands if the actor's

condition should become such as to make that course advisable when
at sea.

Barrymore left the hospital on March 21, went across the river to
Newark, there to board a train for Miami, Florida, where the *Infanta*
was moored.

Before taking the train at the Newark railway station, where Diana
and Mr. Tweed were awaiting him, Jack spent some minutes at the
telegraph desk. His lawyer asked him point blank what new record
he might be making to complicate his already muddled affairs. The
attorney was shown a telegram which Jack had composed to Miss
Barrie. The actor was prevailed upon to reword the message, merely
saying in it that he would get in touch with his protégée upon his
return from the cruise.

It might be well to state that until now there had been no publicity
bearing on Barrymore's interest in Miss Barrie's theatrical or other
aspirations. It was pointed out to Jack that he should stay away from
pens, pencils, ink, paper, and other implements of communication until his troubles with Dolores might be resolved.

The party sailed from Miami for a fishing trip to the Bimini and
Andros Islands in the Bahamas.

Meantime, Jack's manager and the California attorneys were conferring with Dolores' lawyers in regard to a property settlement and
other terms of separation. It became a slow, tedious, stubborn business. When Barrymore returned to New York from the cruise, he
was informed that divorces are not to be had "instantly" in California.

Jack conferred with his manager about this problem on April 12
at the New Yorker Hotel. Hotchener's diary for that day indicates
that the voyage had not improved the actor's health.

On April 26 Ethel called at the hotel to see what, if anything, she
could do to help her sick and troubled brother. Miss Barrymore had
just completed a tour, working hard as always. It was not encouraging to one who loved Jack so deeply to see what her brother was
doing to himself.

Jack slipped away from the hotel, leaving his sister waiting there
for hours. He was not heard from until the following evening, when
Miss Barrie and her mother, Mrs. Edna Jacobs, appeared with the
actor at the N.B.C. radio studio, to do a scene from *The Jest.* His
manager says that Jack looked worn and tired, and had a temperature
of 101 degrees.

The next morning Hotchener received a telephone call as well as a note from Barrymore, asking him to pack the actor's bag and bring it "to the following address, Barrie, 280 Riverside Drive."

In early May Jack again sent his shuttling manager to California to try to reach an amicable settlement with Dolores.

It at once became clear that the first flood of publicity regarding Jack's appearance with his young protégée in public was not conducive to Dolores' peace of mind. Moreover, she was in no mood to enter a lenient property settlement or make other concessions to her hopscotching spouse.

While Hotchener was in the midst of trying to persuade Dolores' attorneys that two plus two equal seven and a half, he received a telegram from Jack. The wire recommended that Hotchener hasten once again to New York. The manager now was asked to negotiate a radio contract for Barrymore to do a scene from *Twentieth Century*. Elaine Barrie was assigned a role in this broadcast.

The day after the widely publicized radio debut of the young woman, Jack, Mrs. Jacobs, and her daughter boarded the *Infanta* to sail for Miami and Havana. Shortly before the departure of the yacht, Barrymore received this telegram from his Los Angeles attorney, Colonel William H. Neblett:

MRS. B. FILED DIVORCE COMPLAINT THIS MORNING CHARGING HABIT-
UAL INTEMPERANCE AND EXTREME CRUELTY.

Barrymore looked at this message, made no comment other than to ask the ubiquitous Hotchener to fly to California to help the lawyers prepare a reply to Dolores and protect Jack's interests as best he might.

Jack and his guests returned to New York from the Havana cruise on June 15. Hotchener again had come East. Barrymore visited his manager at Essex House on June 16. The actor was grave. He said there had been some unpleasant incidents during the voyage. He added that he might need legal advice. Among his troubles was the aftermath of the Havana purchase of an $1,800 canary diamond. He added that no one had taken the precaution to declare this ring to the Customs authorities. Jack requested that Hotchener consult his brother Maurice, which the manager proceeded to do. Barrymore soon afterward paid the Government $3,200 for the duty, the fine, and the penalty for failure to declare the yellow gem.

Hotchener now, as was his practice, placed before Barrymore a statement of moneys recently expended by the actor. Jack noticed one item: "Cash to Elaine, $1,000." Concerning this, he said, "I have no memory of giving Elaine a thousand dollars. I'll ask her about it."

He telephoned the Jacobs' apartment, and was heard to say that he had not intended to give Miss Barrie a cash present of a thousand dollars, and asked that it be returned.

On June 20 Hotchener, in his capacity as business manager for Barrymore, received an envelope delivered at the desk of his hotel. The envelope contained a handwritten message signed "Elaine Barrie," and a check for $1,000.

> Enclosed find the check made out by the East River Savings Bank. Will you please send some books of blank checks immediately, as Jack has no more left from the National City Bank. Thanks so much.

The "one-thousand-dollar incident," Hotchener says, was followed by a coolness toward him on the part of Mrs. Jacobs and her daughter. He adds that he now found it increasingly difficult to reach Jack by telephone, a voice answering each of Hotchener's calls with "Mr. Barrymore is out."

Miss Barrie telephoned Hotchener, saying that Jack wished to see him on an important matter. Henry arrived at the Jacobs' apartment to find Barrymore in a nervous mood. The two women, Mrs. Jacobs and her daughter, also seemed tense, apparently waiting for Jack to speak. Then Barrymore said that he had promised to help Miss Barrie's dramatic career. He wanted Hotchener to act as her business agent as well as his own, and obtain radio and motion-picture contracts for the protégée.

Hotchener regretted his inability to undertake this assignment. He advised Barrymore to pay more immediate attention to his own jeopardized career than to the discovery of talent in others. For example, the manager cited, he had been trying for some days to get in touch with Jack to obtain a statement to offset the doubts of Dolores as to her husband's sudden new role of dramatic coach.

As an outcome of this visit, the following affidavit was sworn to by Elaine Jacobs late in the evening of that same day, June 18, 1935, before Mortimer M. Seluff, notary public:

State of New York
County of New York

Elaine Barrie (Jacobs) being duly sworn says:
"I am the daughter of Edna Barrie (Jacobs) and have been

acquainted with John Barrymore since sometime in March 1935.

"With regard to the personal relations between Mr. Barrymore and myself I state most emphatically that they have been and are of a strictly platonic nature and only on the basis of the professional artistic relationship, indicated by the fact that we have already made a radio appearance together and are planning to do theatrical work jointly in the future.

"Mr. Barrymore and I have not been together privately under conditions that could justly arouse suspicion, but have always been in the company of either my mother or my father or some trusted friend or employee."

Hotchener, the transcontinental envoy, now left for California, to remain there until an urgent call from Jack brought him again to New York in August. Barrymore informed his manager that he was "willing to settle with Dolores on her *own* terms," as he felt he no longer could tolerate this legal obstacle to a marriage with Miss Barrie.

Then, on September 12, Jack telephoned his manager at Essex House to say that he had had "a serious quarrel with Elaine." He added that they were going to dissolve their friendship. Would Henry come instantly to the Jacobs' apartment to help him move out?

Hotchener and his brother went to the apartment together. They found Barrymore's trunk already packed. The actor and his two advisers then went to Essex House, where Jack engaged a suite.

The next day brought the actor a letter and a telephone call from Aaron Sapiro, a lawyer representing Miss Barrie and Mrs. Jacobs. This letter contained certain demands for reparations. It referred to properties Jack allegedly had brought to, then taken from the Jacobs' apartment, in particular the canary diamond and a robe brought by Jack from India. The Sapiro letter admonished Barrymore as well as Hotchener not to leave New York until these reparations had been adjusted.

Now Jack again was possessed by "the flight motif," but he had no place to go. His lawyer called into consultation attorney Frank Aranow, a former partner of Sapiro. It was at this time that the actor moved what was left of his ready assets to the Weehawken bank, and moored his yacht beyond the reach of possible attachment.

On the day he moved out of the Jacobs' apartment, Jack and his manager discussed the severe drain upon the actor's resources during the past five months. He was advised to "retrench."

Jack now sat at his desk to write the following letter to Diana, his daughter by Michael Strange:

Dearest Diana—

It's a long time since I have seen or heard from you, although I suppose you know that some weeks ago I tried my best to see you—or didn't you know?

This letter may seem a little odd to you, but believe me it is of great importance to us both, and you know we love each other so much we can talk perfectly frankly with one another.

You probably know I have been having some "domestic trouble" and that, mixed up with it, I have not earned anything for about the last year and a half. Therefore, as you can well imagine, my funds aren't what they were. However, even all through this lean period, I have done my best to see that you should be well provided for.

My best recollection is that for the last ten years or so I have paid for your use something approximating one hundred and eighty thousand dollars. Don't you think that in view of *that* and of the fact that it is *I* who now need some consideration, that you could do without any further payment from me, at least until I can get to work again and begin to earn once more?

As you can imagine I have felt very reluctant to write you in this fashion, but I am sure that if these amounts I have paid you have been properly taken care of, you need not want for anything.

I hope you will understand the spirit of this letter, my dear baby, my own dear funny thing, and that you will—as they say in the classics—"drop me a little line," saying that you *do.*

This will mean a *great deal* to me, and I know damn well this is all I need to say to you.

All my love—fuzzy dear one.

Daddy.

Barrymore sketched a small head near the written words "funny thing," in this letter to Diana. No reply to this appeal ever reached her father.

On September 16 Jack received from California, for his signature, the property agreement in Dolores' suit against him. Its principal terms were:

Barrymore was to keep the stocks and bonds in his possession, "not in excess of $100,000."

Dolores likewise retained hers, "approximately $163,500."
The wife was to have the Lincoln and Chrysler automobiles.
Jack would hold title to the Tower Road house, *subject* to a
trust deed for $50,000, held by Dolores. Jack also would own
a vacant lot in Beverly Hills, subject to the same trust deed.
The actor retained the *Infanta.*
Barrymore was to pay Dolores monthly for the support of
the two children $850. Also the premium on life insurance
policies for the children's benefit amounting to $235,000.
Mrs. Barrymore to have custody of the children.

It seems incredible that on the same day of the receipt of this agreement, and in the midst of his New York confusions, Jack, chancing
to be reminded that the morrow was his wife's birthday, sat at a desk
in his Essex House suite to compose this telegram to Dolores:

DEAR WINKIE, HAPPY BIRTHDAY AND LOVE TO THE CHILDREN. I
WOULD LOVE TO THINK THAT YOU ARE AS LONESOME AS I AM, BUT
THAT IS AS IT MAY BE. ANYWAY, MY LOVE TO YOU AND THE BABIES.
YOU MUST ALWAYS REMEMBER THAT ONCE WE HAD LOTS OF FUN
AND DON'T LET ANYTHING EVER MAKE YOU FORGET IT. PLEASE
BELIEVE I MEAN THIS, BABY, AND WE WILL BOTH FEEL BETTER.
MUCH LOVE.

JACK.

2.

Over Niagara Falls in a Barrel

BARRYMORE announced that he would not undertake any
screen work during the next several months. He planned to rest.
Two legal developments permitted him to leave New York,
and, if he so desired, to return to California without danger of collid-
ing with bailiffs or psychiatrists. The property agreement with Dolores had been signed by each party to it. The reparations demanded
by Miss Barrie and her mother were to be resolved out of court. Both
coasts now seemed clear.

The reparations involving the yellow diamond and the robe from
India would cost Barrymore $3,500. Two thousand dollars of this

peace offering would go to Aaron Sapiro, attorney for Miss Barrie and Mrs. Jacobs. The remaining $1,500 was to be paid to Sapiro's clients.

This diamond became a somewhat expensive trinket. It originally had cost $1,800 in a Havana shop. The customs levies and fines, after the yellow gem had been imported without the formality of declaration, had been $3,200. Now, with $3,500 in reparations, the stone represented an outlay by the actor of $8,500. Perhaps the jewel was a distant and mulatto cousin to the Hope Diamond.

The gem and robe were placed in escrow with the Trade Bank of New York, to remain among the vaults as an earnest that Miss Barrie and her mother refrain for a year from giving interviews to the press. The two women signed an agreement to this effect.

Jack advised Helios and Henry Hotchener to resume their holiday in India. Camomile would look after him until the return of the manager from the Far East.

Barrymore left New York on a train for the Pacific Coast on September 19, 1935. Miss Barrie followed him by airplane to Chicago, but failed there to head off her tired idol. He took a slow train out of Chicago instead of boarding the limited on which Miss Barrie had been led to believe he had made reservations. The lorn young woman proceeded to Emporia, Kansas, there to plead, by means of the radio, that Barrymore consider her lonely heart and speak to it from Kansas City. The only speaking he did in Kansas City was to a waiter, in regard to some cracked ice and ginger ale.

Barrymore arrived in Beverly Hills on September 25 to go to the house of his brother in Roxbury Drive. Lionel gave him sanctuary, then listened somewhat dubiously to Jack's vows that the association with young Miss Barrie was "cold." The elder brother said nothing by way of censure or approval. What *was* there for him to say? What is there to be said by anyone, ever, when a fifty-three-year-old colleague has fed upon the loco weed of romance?

That same night, after Barrymore again had assured his brother, as well as his manager and a delegation from the press, that a giddy interlude was done, he made a long-distance call to the East. The next morning he admitted that he had telephoned Miss Barrie in New York.

"I have decided," he said matter-of-factly to his manager, "that I am going back to her. When can we start?"

"But it's only six days," the astonished Hotchener said, "since we left New York. You then were of a mind to take a rest in California, and suggested that Helios and myself resume our vacation in India."

"I had forgotten that completely," the actor said. "Can't you postpone your trip?"

Hotchener replied that he had arranged his own property interests, reserved a cabin on the steamer, and planned to depart the next night for the port of San Francisco.

"The long and short of it," Jack remarked, "is that you are leaving me when I need you most."

"There are no contracts for you in New York," Hotchener pointed out to him, "especially since you have had such odd publicity. Camomile will take care of your Tower Road interests. When you are again ready to work, cable me. I'll return at once to make your contract."

Barrymore seemed troubled at this pronouncement, then angry. When the Hotcheners reached San Francisco, however, Jack sent them a telegram that all was well.

Dolores Barrymore obtained an uncontested divorce on October 9, 1935. Miss Barrie and her mother soon thereafter arrived in California. Their lawyer, Aaron Sapiro, now became Jack's attorney-manager. New brooms began to function. Captain Otto Matthies was ousted from the pilot house of the *Infanta*, after having served for ten years as Barrymore's skipper. Camomile, too, was dismissed from Tower Road. In August of the next year a mortgage of $40,000 was placed on the *Infanta*.

There are several divergent opinions as to the degree of helpfulness that Barrymore's new associates brought to the last years of his life. He had been surrounded frequently by persons bent upon the reforming of his morals and the supervising of his career, but never before had he been so harassed by conflicting forces.

Each faction of the several Barrymore regimes has a point of view. When an observer comes upon a controversial tableau such as this, he might bear in mind that a lamb, traditionally regarded as the mildest, most harmless of creatures, could seem, from the point of view of a clover blossom, nothing less than a predatory fiend. Which is the lamb here, and which the clover blossom?

While stoutly defending their respective points of view, none of the aspirants to Barrymore's favor seemed able to satisfy his question, one which he asked again and again: "Where is all the money I have made? Who has it?"

Wherever the money went, and for whatever purpose used, the canceled checks indicate that the spending continued at the rate of a Mississippi flood. Let us take, for example, the Barrymore bank statement for April 1936, made by the Hollywood-Highland branch of the Bank of America.

It is captioned "*John Barrymore (Aaron Sapiro, Power of Attorney)*." It shows that the actor, on April 1, had $22,629.17 in cash on hand. The statement indicates that Jack and/or his new attorney-manager disbursed $17,312.84 of this sum during the one month of April, leaving a balance on April 30 of only $5,316.33. He or his agencies were spending his money at the average rate of $577 a day during this April.

Some of the checks for this month may be of passing interest. His telephone bill was $1,691.07. There were two checks, both made out to "Cash" on April 21, bearing the endorsement, "Elaine Barrie," and amounting to $950. There were five checks dated variously during the two weeks from April 1 to 14, drawn to and endorsed by Aaron Sapiro, amounting to $4,222.27.

Barrymore, in May of 1936, obtained the part of Mercutio in the M.G.M. production of *Romeo and Juliet*. He was not the star. He supported Miss Norma Shearer as Juliet, and the late English actor, Leslie Howard, as Romeo. Jack was returning to the screen after a year and eight months of absence from it.

Barrymore now permitted himself to be placed in residence in the private West Los Angeles sanitarium of Mrs. Louise Simar Kelley. Mrs. Kelley's husband, Jim, was Barrymore's "guard" during the months at the sanitarium. Jim also accompanied his charge to the motion-picture sets, and watched over him during occasional social expeditions.

The Kelley establishment was a retreat for gentlemen of jangled nerves. Young Mr. Kelley was a slim, dark, rather silent chap, who looked like an assistant curator at an art museum. When, however, any of his patients became unruly, he could and did reveal an astonishing familiarity with oriental wrestling holds. Mr. Kelley's calisthenics bewildered but never maimed the guests.

Barrymore's introduction to Kelley involved a whirligig ritual. The actor had erroneously presumed that the quiet Kelléy was neither a strong nor an energetic person. Jack made an interesting suggestion as to what Kelley might do with a hat, then lunged at his new acquaintance. The next moment Barrymore found himself in a knapsack position on Kelley's back, and dazedly on his way to a bedroom.

Ben Hecht and Charles MacArthur now were keeping friendly eyes upon Barrymore during such times as he took recess from the sanitarium or his preoccupations with Miss Barrie. I myself had gone to Damascus to buy a sword in May of 1935, and returned to Los Angeles early next year to learn from Hecht and MacArthur that our friend was subsisting on one can of beer a day. I was told by the playwrights that Jack seldom received anyone in private other than his new mentors. They added that Barrymore, when informed by them that his present romance could be seen almost daily in big journalistic headlines, seemed amazed, then splendidly detached about the whole business.

It was early in 1936 that Camomile wrote to the Hotcheners, in India, that Aaron Sapiro was beginning suits against Warner Brothers, Camomile, and Henry Hotchener for an accounting of Barrymore's funds. This was the first intimation to reach Hotchener that Jack had dropped his pilot. The ex-manager returned to California in April, but was unable to get in touch with the actor, who was ill. Hotchener immediately transferred all the financial records of his ten years of Barrymore's business to his own attorney, who voluntarily placed them in the custody of the court.

When the case came to trial, Hotchener's testimony caused the judge to order the suit dismissed. Barrymore then wrote a letter to his former business manager, saying in part:

> These records indicate that all of my cash and securities have been fully and properly accounted for by you, and have furnished a complete answer to the charges against you.

After having had the entire Hotchener file analyzed by persons more fitted than myself to study such figures, and notwithstanding my complete affection for Jack and my sympathetic familiarity with his prejudices, I think it proper to report that none of my advisers has found the least irregularity in the voluminous records. It is upon the basis of this survey of the Hotchener dossier, and from my own reportorial study of its documents, that I have accepted it as reliable source material. The authorization to use these documents, as well as Jack's sea log aboard *The Gypsy* and *The Mariner*, was given by Barrymore in legal form to Hotchener, together with the right to make it available, upon Barrymore's death, to any writer of Hotchener's choice. That right never was revoked.

We should have had a brief colloquy at the beginning of this work as to how and why this book came to be written. But, being a nonconformist in letters as well as in life, I shall now say these things:

I did not, during any part of Jack's lifetime, tag after him with pencil and notebook, a minor-league Boswell. I had not intended to write this or any other book, other than a last memoir, to which Jack himself offered to supply a foreword, and got this far with the composition of it:

> If you find this book hard to read, please consider, it also was hard to write it.

I had become weary of roller-skating in the purgatory of letters. I sometimes wished I had stayed where I belonged, an unambitious peasant behind a plow on the Colorado prairies. Now I wanted to sit in my garden with my tuberous begonias and my dog, and think upon what, if anything, I was going to tell God.

My friend was dead. He had named me, together with his brother Lionel, and his last attorney, Gordon W. Levoy, as an executor of his derelict estate. He had liked me, not for any special reason I presume, but we were good companions. Perhaps it was because we never had to explain things to each other. Perhaps it was because we both had been reared by grandmothers. Sigmund Freud had not, so far as either of us knew, extended the Oedipean inferences as far back as one's grandmother. We felt a great lack of psychoanalytical *verboten* here, as if the savants had slighted us.

I recall having said to Jack one night: "I liked to sleep with Granny." To which he replied: "Christ! So did I with mine!" But we both became a bit sad to think that anything either of us had done, and enjoyed so much, had escaped censure.

Perhaps Jack liked me because he properly could address me as "Pride of the Rockies." My grandmother used to make my underwear from flour sacks. These sacks came from a mill that manufactured flour known to the trade as *Pride of the Rockies*. Somehow this label always found a place across the seat of my homemade underpants, and it didn't fade for a long time. It enchanted Jack to learn that his friend had been so nobly lettered athwart the rear. And I have tried hard—well, reasonably hard—to live up to my billing.

After my great companion died, I began to receive advices from many friends of Barrymore concerning the writing of his life. Could I, I asked myself, write of him objectively? And should I write of him at all, or so soon after his own robust gaiety had gone out of the world? Then Ashton Stevens, Richard Watts, Jr., and many other men and women mentioned during the course of our narrative offered to give me of their advice, their time, their material. They opened their files to me, as did numerous doctors and attorneys, within the limits of ethical usage.

I now became rather frightened; for with such material at my disposal, it meant that I, who never cared much about succeeding at anything, now *must* care. I was called upon in my own coming twilight to commit such drudgeries as please no one but the sheriff, who appears so many times at the doors of authors. Still, I was again to see, in rich recollection, the face of my friend; to hear his gay, brave voice once more. I sought to fashion a green wreath, with few false leaves, and now I place it beside the crypt upon which his brother carved the words:

Good Night, Sweet Prince

And now, as Jack used to say, "let us return to the libretto."

Whenever Barrymore asked, "What has become of all the money I've made?" his tone was not that of a man rooked at the gaming table. He never cried out to excite a pity that he would have despised, or to inspire a mercy that he neither expected nor desired. But bills sailed like confetti through the air, and, oddly enough, here was a man who wanted to owe no one a cent.

Perhaps, even at his own rate of spending, he thought it strange that yammerings so often rose all about him concerning his lack of funds. He had made $2,600,000 during his first ten years in Hollywood. The days of his fabulous contracts now were done; still, he would earn another half-million dollars, $3,100,000 in all. He sometimes went to work when half dead, with only his stout spirit to sustain him on the motion-picture set, the stage, or at the radio microphone.

It is a curious thing to observe that while he had invested in a few great luxuries, such as his yachts, his house, his hobbies, he spent comparatively little on himself in the sense of personal maintenance.

He cared not at all for clothes. He didn't own a watch. He wore no rings. He entertained infrequently. He much preferred to eat a herring in the kitchen or, if possible, in some friend's kitchen, to sitting in costly fashion at a restaurant table.

To be sure, he had drunk much in his time—640 barrels of "hard stuff" during his last forty years, according to an estimate made by Dr. Hugo Kersten—but even so he was not a connoisseur of wines. Indeed, he had a beachcomber's taste for the cheaper grades of liquor, and now his physical tolerance for alcohol had become so slight that he drank far less than was believed of him.

He once had had a large capacity for drink, but by 1936 a few ounces would affect him noticeably. Many, many times he was accounted drunk when the fact was that he was ill, genuinely ill, yet kept doggedly to his feet when a less spirited man would have been whimpering for the doctor and the priest in the same hot breath.

As for money itself, I am sure that Barrymore never accorded wealth the importance given it by some. Aside from his almost fierce desire to see that his bills be paid, he did not appear to bother much about money. And, perhaps, even his desire to meet his obligations should not be interpreted as a nobility, but rather as a wish not to be beholden to anyone, a symbol of freedom of soul.

He seldom had much pocket money even when affluent. Now, in 1936, he carried less. It was said in explanation that he was not given money lest he wander off from the Kelley sanitarium to spend it on something more fiery than the single can of beer permitted him each day.

He did "wander off" frequently, to the worriment of Jim Kelley. Mr. Kelley even became afraid to bathe, for each time that Barrymore's guard stripped himself for the tub, the resourceful actor would flee the premises. The nude Kelley could not very well pursue him into the street. Then Hecht, MacArthur, or myself would receive the news from Kelley over the telephone: "The Monster has broke loose again!"

We had come to call Jack "The Monster." If anyone is so stupidly dull as to think this was not said with affection, and is not being recorded here with affection, then . . . but why should one explain such things?

He, on his part, had nicknames for each of us, the mildest of which consisted of "bastard," draped with fulsome adjectives. He sometimes saluted us with a fine old word associated with the chinaware of mid-

Victorian sleeping quarters, employing that term instead of relying upon the more conventional "Monsieur" or "Señor."

MacArthur, Hecht, journalist Sidney Skolsky, and myself were sitting one June day in 1936 in a corner of the Beverly Hills Brown Derby. It was the lunch hour. Mr. Skolsky, who never drinks, Mr. Hecht, who simply cannot become intoxicated no matter how hard he tries to convince you to the contrary, Mr. MacArthur, who had had two or three Rum Collins, and myself, as stiff as a teakwood board, were looking at whatever it was we were looking at, when an alarum sounded from without.

Mr. Barrymore was entering, up-stage center, with the slightly informative but rather loud announcement: "I am on my way to a fencing lesson!"

The food munchers, some of them noble tourists, reacted variously to Mr. Barrymore's next remarks, which had to do with thieves and charlatans. He gave it as his expert opinion that Hollywood was well populated by both groups. As a person of quick eye, he saw one diner shaking his head rather sadly. He paused at that gentleman's table to say, "You are making a monumental mistake, my friend. No one gets anywhere in this cultural center by shaking one's head. This is the Land of Nod."

He now gave attention to a lady of haughty curiosity, who sat in one of the horseshoe-shaped booths near a window, studying the actor through rimless eyeglasses. He bowed over her menu with a courtly manner and asked, "Madam, would you be good enough to direct me to the gentlemen's room?"

He now saw us waving to him from the corner booth, then whooped happily, and said to the lady, "Never mind. I see where it is," and came at once to our table. The greetings, embraces, the calls for refreshment, caused several patrons to leave the near-by tables. Then the Monster finally settled down to some happy reminiscences.

Mr. Skolsky had a sober presentiment of disaster, but, with the courage of a war correspondent, stayed on the field.

I had not seen my friend for more than a year. Yet he spoke of things he had heard about me, showing that he had islands of recollection thrusting up from the sea of his impaired memory of recent events. He questioned me at some length concerning my children, especially about my thirteen-year-old son Will, who recently had started a riot while being baptized in the River Jordan.

During the christening Will had made a religious sign over a Mohammedan Arab's head. A battle with camel-sticks followed this mischief. My older son, Gene Jr., entered the fight rather happily. Then my fifteen-year-old daughter, Jane, came into the fray with such amazonian ferocity as to confuse everyone. She began to practice high kicks. The thing that amazed the some thirty combatants on the banks of the sacred stream was that the young lady was impartial: she attacked *both* factions, Christians as well as Mohammedans.

Fortunately, a call to prayer now was chanted from a minaret. The true believers left off fighting for the love of Allah. After a judicious distribution of *bakshish,* Papa pried his warlike children from the field.

Barrymore spoke of the "phenomenon of impulse," and of how men's lives were deeply affected by either the smothering of impulses or the yielding to them.

Then someone at the table mentioned *Hamlet,* and Barrymore said:

"One time, when we were on tour with this Elizabethan oddity, I went to my dressing-room after having dragged in the body of Polonius for the curtain's fall on Act III. By some obscene oversight, I had not been drinking for several days. I had become tired of the grind. I had a sudden impulse. I obeyed it. I enlisted the musical aid of one of the members of the cast, who liked to play a saxophone during his off-scene moments, and together we went before the curtain. He began to play a little ditty on the saxophone, and I, in my tights, began a tap dance. Soon the audience heard of this unheard-of thing and hastened back to the theatre from the smoking room and the foyer. Then I did a cake-walk, and next a jig. Then I went into a waltz with some unseen being, perhaps the ghost of Hamlet's father. It was a better performance than I had given so far that day, for I had become stale and surly. Then, when the curtain rose for Act IV, I really did myself proud. Everyone appreciated *Hamlet* the more. I had got an impulse out of my system—as usual, I fear."

The restaurant by this time was almost empty. Barrymore began to tell some raucous stories. And now a young man at a table near the door rose from beside his companion, a young lady, to come to our table to announce sternly: "Mr. Barrymore, my wife and I are on our honeymoon, and . . ."

The actor interrupted him with: "What a droll place to bring a bride! Haven't you something more exhilarating on your agenda than mere gourmandizing?"

"You've been talking loud," the young man said. "Talking loud, and . . ."

"So are you," again interrupted Jack, "but not saying anything. At least nothing of a deathless quality."

The young man became quite angry at this. "My wife is a lady!"

Barrymore rose. "Before I can rule intelligently upon that claim," he said, "I demand to see her credentials, all birthmarks, tattoo signs, et cetera."

The young man grimly left the table, paid his bill, and took his bride outside.

"I am confident," said Barrymore, "that they are impostors."

Journalist Skolsky worriedly informed Jack, "I hear that the young woman is related to one of the heads of the police force."

"Excellent!" cried Jack. "Barricade the doors. We shall resist the police."

I afterward was informed that a deputation of police *did* call, but by this time Barrymore had come with me to my house in North Bedford Drive.

My daughter had no pleasant welcome for either Mr. Barrymore or myself. She had met Jack when she was ten years old, and it had been one of her fondest memories, his rising, bowing, his taking her hand and greeting her, not as a child, but as a grown lady. Now, at fifteen, Jane was undergoing a sudden aloofness, a ladyhood, and it spoiled an illusion to see the great cavalier in robust mood. Besides, she was at this time a strict prohibitionist.

"Will you serve us one small drink?" I asked my daughter. "We have just had a trying experience."

She looked at us with a Carrie Nation glare, then said, "I'll get you something. I'll get you *both* something special."

While Jane was on her way to the kitchen, Jack said of her, "Spirit! Great spirit! It is written in her eye." The sound of bottles and other glassware from the direction of the kitchen caused him to say reverently, "The Angelus!"

We did not know, of course, that the young woman was mixing for us a potion of Worcestershire Sauce, tabasco, spirits of ammonia, onion essence, and a dash of peppermint.

"She has such a gentle manner," said Jack, "that one finds it hard to believe that she kicks Arabs in the chin."

"Yes," I admitted, "she is an especially sweet child."

Jane returned with two whisky glasses filled to the brims. She set them before us. I complimented her for her hospitality, her breadth of mind. While I was lifting my own glass, Barrymore tossed off his drink with delicacy, but with speed. Then his eyes opened wide. He began to make desperate, swimming motions, first the breast-stroke, then the trudgeon, and finally a frantic Australian crawl. When his windpipe lost some of its paralysis, he rose to his feet and gasped: "My God! I'm in the house of the Borgias!"

His good friends MacArthur and Hecht went East on business late in June 1936. They were to return to California in August. I remained on in Los Angeles, sent my three children to Fire Island, where I ordinarily spent my summers, and moved to the Talmadge Apartments.

For recreation I rode a police automobile at night, the K2 homicide car of Lieutenants Joseph Filkas and William H. Baker. These tours were of interest to an old reporter, and when necessary the detectives could deliver me speedily to Barrymore, wherever he might be.

Jack had gone back temporarily to Tower Road to live with two servants, a man and a woman. During this interlude, following his completion of *Romeo and Juliet*, few persons showed interest in his flattened purse.

July 19 was my wedding anniversary. I was to have had a late dinner with Harry and Sibyl Brand, my neighbors at the Talmadge. We were on our way out of the apartment house lobby when the desk clerk said there was a telephone message for me from Barrymore.

"I wondered if you were coming up to see me tonight," Jack said over the telephone, then added, "I'm not exactly in the pink."

This statement disturbed me. It was the first of two times during our acquaintanceship when I was to hear him say that he felt ill. No matter how sick he ever seemed, he always would insist that he was feeling "fine." So, when he now said over the telephone that he was "not exactly in the pink," I became concerned. I excused myself to my companions, then put in a call to the police switchboard.

Lieutenants Filkas and Baker, and one other detective of the homicide detail, arrived in the police car within a few minutes. We then raced westward along Wilshire Boulevard, the siren sounding, then cut north to Sunset, and then turned to our right on Benedict Canyon, and to our right again on Tower Road. We now climbed most of the way in second gear. The city at night danced below us, a spangled ballet dancer whose broad skirt swirled with sequins of yellow, red, and green, flashing as if in a great stage glow.

Filkas took his hand off the siren button, merely leaving the red headlight on as a warning. We did not wish to disturb Barrymore's neighbors on the hill, and besides there now was no traffic on the winding road.

We left the car at the lower gate, then entered the grounds after a servant inside the house released the buzzer-lock. We climbed the steep terrace to Liberty Hall.

We found Jack seated at a refectory table inside the narrow reception hall. He seemed dull and forsaken, but rose to his feet with an old-world politeness as charming as it was automatic whenever he greeted anyone, friends or strangers, to his own home. Ill though he obviously was, and deserted and stripped the house wherein he briefly was staying, his John Drew mannerisms dominated the social moment. He suddenly became the host. His Victorian formality was real and picturesque, a part of his nature, a reflection of all the Drews and of the old household in Philadelphia.

Tonight, among the somewhat bleak remains of his hillside palace, Barrymore seemed gaunt. His face was not as puffy as it recently had been. Instead, the cheeks were gray and fallen in, as if hollowed out by round stones. It seemed remarkable, always, that he could change so noticeably in appearance, so swiftly from day to day, even hour to hour, now seeming gay, almost robust, then suddenly hunched over, haunted. He lived many parts, a great Protean, as if life itself for him were a stock company of long season.

One highball glass, surrounded by numerous cigarette butts, stood on the table near a fireplace long unused. Ashes had formed gray islands on the man's unpressed blue trousers, and there were holes burned in the tweed coat, which was out at the elbow. Plaid socks, a rather gay note in the ensemble, and an extraordinarily smart pair of square-toed, custom-made boots from Hellstern's of Paris, somewhat disguised the swelling of his ankles. But his fine manners and his personal charm made everything else in the scene subordinate to the man.

Having shaken hands with his callers, Jack asked them to sit in an assortment of chairs at the refectory table. These creaking chairs, together with the veteran table and a scanty array of other down-at-the-heel objects, had been left on the premises by generous usurpers of Tower Road's more sumptuous properties.

A brown bearskin rug lay on the floor-boards of the reception hall. One eye of lackluster glass remained in that trophy head, an eye turned with myopic fixity toward a welter of books with broken bindings and some sea charts from the *Infanta*, all heaped together in one corner of the room.

The door to the kitchen off the foyer was ajar. A wall telephone could be seen just inside this opening. Many telephone numbers, names, and an array of doodling sketches penciled by Jack made a plaster notebook of the wall near the telephone. In the kitchen background, two tired servants were standing as if placed there a year before by a taxidermist and then forgotten by him.

One of the detectives seemed interested in a second doorway, beyond which, in a brighter light than that of the foyer, there could be seen an old iron bedstead with blistered enamel, and a rickety chest of drawers, upon which two silver-framed pictures rested. On the wall above the ill-kempt bed hung a large crucifix. The cross was of antique, polished brown wood. The figure of Our Lord nailed upon this rood had been magnificently achieved in ivory. The face was compassionate in its pale agony.

While Barrymore was telling his policemen guests of his hunting expeditions in Alaska, Lieutenant Filkas said to me, in an aside: "Shouldn't I ring for an ambulance? He's in awful bad shape."

"No," I replied in an undertone. "Forget the ambulance. But while I slip out to the kitchen to see that his drinks are cut, bring up the subject of murders you have solved."

"Murders?" Filkas asked. "Are you kidding?"

"No. It will keep his mind away from his troubles."

With three such experts as the detectives present, it was not hard to get the homicidal reminiscences under way. As I had anticipated, the gory experiences of the sleuths proved a tonic to the sick man, whose greatest illness, I always have believed, was loneliness.

We sat until long past the time for the detectives to go off duty. At about three o'clock in the morning Jack motioned for me to go to the bedroom. I obeyed the sign. He came into the bedroom, closed the door, then took up one of the silver-framed photographs on the chest of drawers. It was a picture of himself holding the infant Diana in his arms. He put down this picture, then picked up the other one, that of his two children by Dolores, his son John and Dolores Ethel.

Now, still holding this picture, he said: "I have two questions, and I've got to know the answers. You'd tell me, if you knew, wouldn't you?"

"I don't think so," I said. "You probably have the answers already."

There was nothing to be gained by coddling him when he entered these moods. Nor were lectures of the least use, ever, and I was not by nature a lecturer, nor by force of circumstance and moral stature in a position to call any other man's kettle black.

"You think," he said petulantly, "that I'm wanting to go back to Dolores and the children. Is that what you're thinking?"

"I think," I said, "that you're brooding about it tonight, this minute, but tomorrow you'll be heading the other way."

"I'd give anything to see the babies," he said. "That's what is on my heart and mind."

"We're all alike, Jack," I said. "All of us want to eat our cake and have it. That's you, it's I, and it's that other battered polygamist, John Doe."

He restored the picture of his boy and girl to the chest. "If she'd only let me see them," he said, "I think I could work things out."

"It will have to be the other way around," I said. "If you can work things out, as you say, for just four or five weeks, and *then* make your appeal, I think you can see the children. Women, when wronged, usually demand blueprints, proofs, and all manner of evidence that the humble prodigal has been purged of his sins."

He thought for a time, then said, "But the second question worries me even more than getting to see the children. You don't know what the second question is?"

"It most likely has to do with your so-called romance of the moment."

He shook his head. "Nothing of the sort. It has to do with locks and bars, and gentlemen with eyeglasses, who look in from time to time to say 'yes' to all your questions, but then say 'no' to the few friends who ask if you are being let out next Christmas."

This was the first time I had heard Jack discuss his obsession. I had known of his fears, of course, for as a matter of fact I had been living with Dolores' physician, Dr. Hirshfeld, at his Monte Mar Vista home, back in 1933, and again in 1934, at the time when the doctor diagnosed Barrymore's condition of memory before the flight to India. I had asked the doctor concerning Barrymore's mental status. I had received from him the reply: "No one as yet has satisfactorily defined insanity. But I assure you that your friend absolutely is not a paretic."

I now said to Jack, "I know that you are serious about this locks-and-bars delusion . . ."

"It's no delusion!" he cried out. "It's God's honest fact! They wanted to put me away two years ago, and now they'll be after me again."

"I'll tell you what," I said. "I'll give you my word that no one ever will put you away as long as I live. And, if anyone tries, I'll get you out of it somehow. So forget it."

He looked at me for a long moment. Then he said something that seems rather meaningless when set down on paper; and I don't know how to interpret it by means of words; but something in his tone, his manner, conveyed to me his great relief, his trust in my promise, as he said, "I *see* you."

I then advised him to go to sleep. Although he was eight years my senior, he somehow seemed a child at times, and then I would feel toward him as I did toward my own sons.

I now assured him that no sleeping pills were being given him, and added that he might have not one but *two* drinks at his bedside. He didn't take the second drink. I sat there until he fell asleep, and heard him say in his sleep, "Mum Mum." I finally turned out the light and left the room. Then Joe Filkas drove me home in the early morning.

In November, with Jack preparing to do *Maytime* in support of vocalists Jeanette MacDonald and Nelson Eddy, he suddenly decided to elope with Miss Barrie. MacArthur and Hecht sought to dissuade him from this enterprise. They gave a long list of reasons why he should not, at fifty-four, again draw on the bee-keeper's veil of matrimony.

This two-hour conference occurred at the home of Countess Dorothy di Frasso in Beverly Hills. The actor stood leaning against a mantelpiece. He remained calm and amiable as the two playwrights harangued him. Whenever he appeared in that frame of behavior, politely silent, it was a sign that nothing could be done to sway his intentions.

After the earnest and perspiring lecturers paused, a pair of Clarence Darrows at the close of a summation, Jack said slowly and with finality: "Gentlemen, you are talking to a man who is about to go over Niagara Falls in a barrel!"

The next day he flew with Miss Barrie and Attorney Sapiro to Yuma, Arizona, to be married to her there by a Justice of the Peace.

3.

Passion in the Desert

THIS fourth honeymoon of our friend seems to have assumed a Donnybrook flavor. A separation occurred after one month and twenty-three days of dissonance.

A public skirmish occurred between the husband and wife at midnight of December 31 at the Trocadero, rendezvous of Hollywood's élite. Barrymore's name-callings, directed at his young mate, rose above the happier sounds made by celebrants of the New Year of 1937, the popping of wine corks, the tootling of toy horns, the voices of cinematic stars singing "Auld Lang Syne."

Five hours after this set-to, Barrymore telephoned to Attorney Henry Huntington. This good barrister was but slightly acquainted with his early morning telephonist. Nor was he at this time one of the actor's admirers.

Huntington, attorney for Mrs. Simar Kelley, in whose sanitarium Barrymore now again was a guest, had met Jack in 1936. Huntington then had been on a duck-shooting holiday near Mecca (California's Mecca, not Mohammed's) and stopped over at an Indio café to pluck, draw, and cook his bag of wild fowl. He chanced to go from the kitchen to the bar of the café. There he saw Jim Kelley, husband of his client, standing with Barrymore. Kelley explained that Jack and he were on one of their occasional "trailer tours."

Kelley had an automobile trailer attached to his car. Whenever Jim took his sanitarium guest on a junket, the actor would snooze in the trailer between ports of call.

Barrymore and Kelley finished their beer at the Indio café, then said good-by to the lawyer-sportsman. Huntington took hold of Jack's arm, thinking to assist him to the trailer. The actor shook off this aid, straightened, then said icily: "Why don't you go back to your ducks?"

That first meeting did not endear Barrymore to Huntington. Now, on this New Year's morning, and having been to a party himself, the lawyer was in no humor to be disturbed by the actor. Huntington, however, listened to Barrymore's announcement that his wife had left him, and that she was contemplating the filing of a divorce complaint. She had gone alone to their rented home at Number 1020 Benedict Canyon, where the Barrymores, Mrs. Jacobs, and three servants had been residing. Jack asked Huntington to come "instantly" to the sanitarium for a conference on this and other business matters.

The reluctant attorney went at dawn to the Kelley establishment, there to learn that Jack knew nothing of his recent business affairs, and that Aaron Sapiro still had Barrymore's power of attorney.

On January 2, 1937, Huntington appeared early at the courthouse to file a revocation of Sapiro's power of attorney. Then "things" commenced to happen. Creditors began to pound for immediate payment of bills. Huntington's records show $161,503.82 debts outstanding, including the mortgage of $40,000 on the *Infanta*. The actor had signed a paper for this lien on his yacht on August 6, 1936, the debt payable one year from date at seven per cent interest. He now told Huntington, however, that he had no memory of having done this. The list of recent unpaid bills for the seven weeks of his fourth marriage amounted to $10,108.90, of which $511.83 appeared to have been spent on himself.

The actor could have undertaken ordinary bankruptcy proceedings to escape his debts, other than liability for taxes or the support of his children. He preferred to do otherwise.

"I want to owe no one," he told Huntington. "We'll pay up."

On February 16 Huntington filed in Jack's behalf a petition, under Section 74 of the Bankruptcy Act. He represented to the court that his client had physical assets on land and on sea worth $261,597.05. It was indicated that all Barrymore sought of his creditors was time for a proper liquidation, so that he might pay his debts dollar for dollar.

It was almost two years before these claims eventually reached settlement, and the bankruptcy court honorably discharged the debtor. Barrymore paid in all $111,503.82; then, in accord with his hole-in-the-pocket philosophy, he went deeply in debt again, and again endeavored to dig out of his caved-in pit of obligations.

Between February 1937, a time when Barrymore undertook payment of his debts in full, and the date of his first clearance of financial obligations, November 13, 1939, there were days of tumult and trouble. At times it seemed that no one, not even he, could survive the travail of ill health and harassment.

Miss Barrie's representatives served a divorce summons and complaint on Barrymore the middle of February. Her attorney, Leo L. Schaumer, also attached to these papers a temporary restraining order to tie up her husband's property and possible funds. Mrs. Elaine Barrymore asked for $2,500 a month alimony, listing her necessary expenses at the Benedict Canyon home at $2,225 a month.

Following his completion in December 1936 of *Maytime*, Barrymore's professional star went behind the clouds, there to stay hidden a year or more. His faulty memory, his unpredictable health, his untoward publicity, caused producers to hesitate during 1937 to risk employing him. How was he to meet the self-assumed terms of Section 74 of the Bankruptcy Act?

It was now that MacArthur, Hecht, and one other friend actively assisted Attorney Huntington in trying to untangle the affairs of the never-whimpering actor. He still seemed to them a great man, and he always would seem no less. Huntington, now a fierce admirer of Barrymore's, says of him: "He was the most completely honest person, in all ways, I ever have met."

On the day before it appeared certain that Jack would lose title to his yacht by foreclosure, one of his friends placed enough money in Huntington's hands to pay the interest on it. This friend was accounted quixotic for supplying this sum merely to postpone an inevitable loss of property. Barrymore, it was pointed out, never again was likely to set foot on the deck of the *Infanta*. But what others did not understand was that his yacht remained a symbol to him, as the Alchemist's Corner had been, and as Tower Road also stayed a symbol. It is important, when all else is lost, that a man of great imagination be permitted to keep the relics associated with his dream-world.

Tower Road, like its master, had come to a run-down condition. Jack had not been there for some time when early in 1937 I called upon him at Kelley's to suggest that he visit his estate. He brightened at once.

As he walked slowly up the hill Barrymore spoke happily of the "old days." Each landmark reminded him of some adventure or experience. The totem pole, the sundial, the aviary, the now stilled fountains, the drained pools, all these seemed matters of pleasant excitement to him. He said little of the changes, the lack of life about the place, the House of Usher stillness, the stripped rooms, the cobwebs in the rathskeller.

One thing, however, did disturb him. Someone had removed the John Drew Cigar band from its place of honor among other cigar bands pasted against the façade of the old Wild West bar.

"That," he said, "was worth more to me than all the rest of the things put together." He paused, then added sardonically, "I wonder why they didn't take the crucifix? Afraid to?"

Barrymore presently found an old set of North Pacific charts among the mound of books on the floor of the reception hall. We sat at the refectory table for an hour or so, to plan in detail a cruise on the *Infanta*, a voyage that I knew, and he must have felt, never would be undertaken. Still, we spoke of it as a bright reality, and argued as to ports we would touch and those we would avoid, and for how long we would stay in each haven. Then he said: "We shall sail into Arctic waters, permit ourselves to be frozen fast, and never come back at all."

Reports frequently reached the newspapers that Barrymore was extremely ill, that he was not expected to live. Such rumors had persisted since 1936 when, in July of that year, I received a query from Ward Greene of Hearst's King Feature Syndicate: "Chicago reports John Barrymore dying. If he does, would you write his life story for us?"

To this I had replied: "The Barrymores never die. It would be against the family tradition to do anything so commonplace."

Ben Hecht made a fine effort in 1937 to write into a scenario a part for Jack. It was to be a role in David O. Selznick's *Nothing Sacred*. Selznick had an intelligent admiration for Jack both as an artist and as a personality. It was Selznick's opinion then, and it still remains, that Barrymore's enactment of the crazed husband and father in *Bill of Divorcement* was the greatest all-time performance on any motion-picture screen.

The producer agreed that if Jack would memorize but one speech of twenty lines and recite it for him, he would place the actor in the part written by Hecht. Selznick's main concern was that Barrymore might not be able, in his present state of memory, to master the long, swift-spoken dialogue demanded by the scenario. With only his single can of beer a day, and after a week of painstaking rehearsals at the sanitarium, Jack went to the studio. He failed this test.

"As a matter of fact," Hecht informed me, "Jack didn't know a word of the speech; but he got off one of his own, ten times as good as mine; then he read like Coleridge from the script. Still David couldn't take the risk."

Trips to the desert near La Quinta were prescribed for the actor. Kelley took him there in the trailer. A remote house was found, and these holidays among the dunes seemed to benefit him.

Soon thereafter I received a call from Edmund Goulding, who had directed Jack in *Grand Hotel*. "I am about to do a picture for the Warner Brothers," he said. "But I hear that Barrymore has to use blackboards for all his speeches. Is that so?"

"We are tapering him off," I replied. "We've got him down to *slates*."

Goulding agreed to give Jack a part in his forthcoming picture. I afterward learned that he had been urged to do so by Gordon Hollingshead, now an executive at Warners'. His friends were at pains to see that Barrymore gain this role, for there now remained no funds to maintain him properly. Here was a chance for him to make at least $30,000 for two weeks' work.

Notwithstanding Hollingshead's and Goulding's intentions in Jack's favor, other studio officials became dubious as to the actor's condition. They demanded that he take a screen test before being assigned the role. I sent the following wire to Barrymore, in care of a lumber company at La Quinta, four miles from the actor's isolated camp in the desert:

EDDIE GOULDING EXPLAINS TO ME THAT HE IS HAVING CERTAIN DIF-
FICULTIES WITH THE DOUBTING THOMASES OF BURBANK. HE HESI-
TATES, FOR FEAR OF OFFENDING YOU OR UPSETTING YOU, TO SUG-
GEST THAT YOU COME IN AND MAKE A TEST SO THAT THE BOYS MAY
SURVEY YOU WITH THE NAKED EYE. STRONGLY SUGGEST WAY OUT
OF DIFFICULTY IS FOR YOU TO SEND WIRE TO EDDIE, VOLUNTEER-
ING THAT YOU BE TESTED. BY THIS I MEAN CELLULOID, AND NOT
BLOOD. LET ME HEAR FROM YOU IN ENGLISH. REGARDS,
                                                GENE FOWLER.

This matter remained in abeyance until late in April. It looked as if Jack simply would not be given studio consideration. It was explained to his friends that, among other things, no insurance company would underwrite a picture in which the ill Barrymore might have a part.

Then, on April 23, Mrs. Elaine Barrymore received an interlocutory decree of divorce. Jack again went to the desert. He was undergoing frenzied urges to rejoin his fourth wife, together with intermittent cries against her.

I sent the following telegram to Director Goulding on this disconcerting April 23:

DEAR COMMODORE. CAN YOU ISSUE FROM YOUR IVORY TOWER LONG ENOUGH TO CONSIDER THE GUTTER SORES OF OUR FRIEND, NAVARRE? HE IS HAVING A DIVORCE DECREE FLUNG INTO HIS CLASSIC FACE TODAY. THIS WILL BE QUITE A SURPRISE TO THE GENTLEMAN, AND, IT IS HOPED, WILL SHOCK HIM OUT OF HIS AMOUR. WE ARE SHIPPING THE REMAINS TO THE HINTERLAND MONDAY. WE NEED AT LEAST FIFTEEN HUNDRED DOLLARS FOR THE WAR CHEST. CAN YOU DROP YOUR GILDED MEGAPHONE, PUT PERFUME UNDER YOUR ARMS, AND CONTACT THAT CERTAIN CROESUS [Douglas Fairbanks, Sr.] WHO ONCE OFFERED US A GRAND, AND, TO OUR PRESENT HORROR, WE SPURNED? HIT HIM WITH A GOLDEN BLACKJACK, AND MEANWHILE I SHALL RAISE THE REST FROM MY OWN PRIVATE SUCKER LIST. LET ME HEAR FROM YOU BY INDIAN RUNNER. REGARDS,

GENE FOWLER.

A day for the test was assigned and Jack returned to the sanitarium. Goulding himself "inspected" Barrymore at the Kelleys' in the presence of Huntington, MacArthur, and myself.

On the appointed day for the test I received word from Kelley that "the Monster has broke loose." It seems that when the guardian got into the bathtub Jack darted off the reservation to join a lady, waiting for him by prearrangement in a taxicab.

I next received news that Barrymore and his companion were having wassail in the dining room of the Beverly Wilshire Hotel. I hastened there, rather angry to be sure, to find him and his blond friend having cocktails. I berated the young woman, in fact I God-damned her, for this mischief. I then did likewise with the Monster, who rose in a Chesterfieldian manner to say: "I simply cannot permit you to use such language in the presence of a whore."

When Jack appeared at the studio, Goulding was reluctant, for Barrymore's own sake, to begin the test. The director turned perplexedly to Gordon Hollingshead, who had recommended this part for his old friend.

"Don't humiliate Jack by refusing to let him go through with the test," Holly advised the worried director. "And *don't* have any film in the camera to record a flop."

Goulding never let Jack know the real reason the test failed. The director merely announced to MacArthur and other of Barrymore's friends: "He was fine. Really fine. But he made the star a bit nervous, and the studio, you know, has to consider her wishes in regard to whom she plays opposite. Don't worry. We'll keep an eye out for another picture for Jack."

It was during this time of despond that two of Barrymore's friends again financed him, so that the actor might have a change of scene. MacArthur promoted a loan of six thousand dollars from producers L. B. Mayer and Eddie Mannix. The note was signed for by the playwright together with one other close friend of Barrymore's. Afterward it was forgiven.

The Kelley trailer was provisioned, books provided, and the actor taken again to the desert. Letters arriving from Jack indicated that he was bouncing back to a semblance of health and spirit. He wrote to Huntington in July:

> Thanks very much for your encouraging and charming letter. It was like a wind from the sea (not a broken wind, my dear fellow) but a breeze with a tang in it. Incidentally I am fuller of "tang" than I've been for ten years, and am raring to go! For the first time in my life I want to "show 'em," and don't think I won't!

He wrote again to his attorney this same month, reviving the idea of doing *Hamlet* in the Hollywood Bowl.

> Dear Henry:
> The Bowl dimension has possibilities that would be unforgettable. They have never been properly utilized in drama there. I'll just sit tight, and try not to go screwy.
> Meanwhile am writing to Clarence Locan, the publicity man at M.G.M., to use his judgment when to splurge it. Personally, I think that will stop gossip of various kinds. The only possible thing in its disfavor is that it might give some other ham the idea to beat me to it. It is imperative it be registered immediately, but then, that is only for a movie. If anyone gets the idea of doing it, as I can't do it till September—not in the Bowl, and I don't think that can be done, on account of the concerts—but there is the Auditorium, and God knows how many theatres might leap at it. Possibly the best thing is not to say a damned word about it till a short time before we do it, and then make the "advance notices," as we say in this amiable profession, "intensive."

Personally I am forced to think, from long experience in the theatrical business (a judicious combination of banditry and harlotry), that the lower we lie till we strike, the better.

Much love to you—
Jack.

I received at this time a letter from Jack, wherein he seemed to be turning various professional projects over in his mind.

Limbo—on the Dunes.

Dear Gene:

Someone—I think it was Sam T. Jack, the eminent buttock impresario—said "God works in mysterious ways His wonders to perform." As I remember (a thing, thank Christ, I'm not very good at!) it was a farewell banquet in honor of four sisters—large girls all, who, having been, to coin a phrase, the mainstay of the troupe for many years, were laden with honors and hernia. We retired to the patchoulied twilight of the Everleigh Club. It was a really great moment, and reminded one of Napoleon's farewell to the Old Guard at Fontainebleau. (*No*— I wasn't *there*. You bastard—I merely heard about it from somebody who was—a director.)

I don't know why I ramble on this way, but Elba is kind of quiet today, and the bees are droning lazily around the one-holer. Two dogs of frail parentage are lolling in the stink-weed patch, and all Nature seems waiting with finger on lip for some portentous event or cataclysm to occur. It wouldn't surprise me at all if it were *The Master of Ballantrae.*

Oddly enough, I have always wanted to play that ophidian and fearless son of a bitch, and went so far as to have a long interview with Lloyd Osborne on the subject. He said he had frequently "coquetted" with the idea (that was his expression), but something had always intervened. Then Walker Whiteside did it, and it was a bit of a flop, and *why not?*

Whether or not Lionel can be seduced into playing it, I don't know. Of course that would be great. I have, more times than I can tell you, broached the subject to him, and he has always dexterously evaded it. *You* might have better luck, even intimating it might be a bridge to terra firma for his little brother, who is at present in a state of slightly swirling levitation.

If, however, that combination, which would be imperial, with you and Charlie [MacArthur] writing the script, prove hopeless, and Lionel prove inexorable, the idea is too gorgeous to give up. We could get some swell person to play the other brother. There *must* be more in this than meets the eye, as I have thought about the damned thing so intensively for so many years.

It is a quaint conceit, but I have always regarded you and Charlie as two bawdy and libidinous guardian angels, a proper complement as it were to my somewhat static and sacerdotal self! a sort of *Balance Wheel*, as it were, to phantasmagoria.

I am eating my gruel at regular intervals, and dreaming as infrequently as is compatible with celibacy; and, while we are on the subject, put aside a *little* every day, in spite of your riotous living, toward a stained glass window for Mrs. Kelley and Jim. Since your letter, oh, Ishmael! Or P—Pot, as you prefer, I live again!

Love,

Jack.

A second letter from Jack touched on more social aspects of his proposed return from the desert:

I am coming to town (which sounds a little Georgian!) if one can call that dermoid cyst, *Hollywoodus in Latrina*, a town, Thursday, to see Eddie Mannix. And, oddly enough, my evening is free, if the constabulary has not been forewarned of my approach. I thought, if I prepared you in time, we might do it together. The latter part of that phrase perhaps indicates more promise than meets the eye. . . . I'll call up Thursday before twelve a.m.

Till then, a pox on the Whigs—

Jack.

P. S. I enclose a little picture, to be used at children's lantern-slide parties, entitled, "Do not Sojourn too Long on the Desert," by Lafcadio Hearn.

The "little picture" was one of the most comical things I ever hope to see. It showed the Monster in a yachting cap, embracing a donkey. He had written a caption on the margin of the photograph: "A desert version of the Foreign Legion's production, *A Midsummer-Night's Dream*. Meet my leading lady, Mrs. Siddons."

It was decided that Jack remain a while longer in the desert, but he was reported to be growing restless. He sent Macedonian calls for "even the Platonic company of some fair conversationalist with a vocabulary of not more than six words."

MacArthur and myself debated the question of enlisting some young lady, who might be trusted not to take liquor with her, for the Platonic mission. We consulted experts, one of whom said, "I know just the right person. For a slight fee, she would consider it a privilege to lighten Jack's moments."

"Send her over for evangelical instructions."

A pleasant young woman, of the build of a young sequoia tree, arrived at our hotel quarters. She became somewhat obdurate about an emolument of one hundred dollars, but eventually settled for all the cash we had on hand—fifty-six dollars, as I recall it—and promised not to let Jack even read a whisky advertisement.

When we sought to impress upon her the danger that Barrymore might seek to charm her into helping him escape to some desert community bar, she looked at us rather pityingly, and said, "Boys, I *think* I know my business."

The next morning Mr. MacArthur and myself were sitting at the hotel, feeling noble. We had done a Samaritan deed. A friend had called (by the proxy of Jim Kelley and the U.S. mails) from the Tibetan wastes.

"He would have done the same for us," I sighed, a little enviously. "I'm sure he would have."

"If he were to think of it, yes," said MacArthur. He beamed at his glass. "Right now, I can picture the Monster making sheep's eyes at this Amazon, and even proposing a trip to a bull-fight in Madrid."

"I now wish," I said, "that we had given her the hundred dollars without quibbling. We could have borrowed it from the hotel management."

"Now," said MacArthur, "don't go having a guilt-complex, like the time you lost the corpse in Chicago."

"It's not that," I said, "but I hate to see an artist short-changed. Painters, composers, writers, and women are constantly being rooked. People don't appreciate . . ."

The telephone rang. "I hope it isn't Howard Hawks," and MacArthur rose to answer the telephone. "I haven't written a line of that scene I promised him yesterday." He said into the telephone, "Hello." Then he paused, listening attentively. His mouth froze in a Caledonian smirk. He twirled his forelock, as is his custom when shocked or pondering a sudden problem. Then he asked, "When?" and said, "I see. Uh, huh! Uh, huh! I see. Well!"

He hung up the receiver, then sat down, a little stunned.

"Was it Hawks?" I asked.

He shook his head. "It was Jim Kelley."

"Trouble?"

"I think we should keep our heads," he remarked, "like Marie Antoinette used to say in all futility."

"He's escaped!" I cried out. "How? When? Damn it!"

MacArthur sat like a ventriloquist's doll, murmuring, "He knows where we are. Carries this address and room number on his person at all times." Then he added, "He's spent it, of course, but he'll have to come to us eventually."

"Spent what?" I asked. Then I wheedled my companion, "Now, listen, I have a general feeling of catastrophe, but you can confide the details in me. I'm a grown-up boy—in some respects."

"It was passion in the desert," MacArthur said, having risen to go again to the telephone. "An Honoré de Balzac situation. Passion in the desert."

"Now don't fly off the handle and notify the police," I advised him. "Come back here and sit down like you did in France during the War."

"I'm only calling downstairs for drinks," he said. "You'll want one, too. Passion in the desert. Hmmm. . . ."

I permitted him to order the drinks without interruption. Then he came back to his chair and addressed the ceiling. "The bare facts are as follows: While the naïve Kelley was looking for some desert flowers, out of season, too—and by lantern light, of all things —the cunning Monster charmed the lady into lending him the contents of her purse! Our money. Can you imagine? Then he made a bolt for her car, commandeered it, and hasn't been seen since."

"But he hasn't been at the wheel of a car since he turned over in one five years ago," I pointed out to MacArthur. "I know that for a fact. He has a great superstition about driving one. Claims it would be curtains for him."

"Then," said MacArthur, "prepare yourself for a neat little shock. The young woman claims that the car is *stolen*, and that *we* are responsible. Accessories before the fact."

We waited all day. In the afternoon the telephone rang. "It's Jack," I prophesied confidently. "Probably has a flat tire, or is on a flagpole or something."

MacArthur again went to the telephone, saying en route, "If it's Howard Hawks, I have a mind to tell him to go to hell."

It wasn't Jack, and it wasn't Hawks. It was the young woman!

"I'm going to sue both of you!" the wronged hoyden yelled

into MacArthur's ear. "I've been gypped and humiliated. And I'll never trust no actor again, or trust whatever it is you and that other wise guy claimed you was. See?"

"But," MacArthur remonstrated, "you yourself said that you knew your business, boys. Cut us off while we were advising you to . . ."

She had hung up. MacArthur ordered more drinks, then came back to his chair to pick up a placard from the floor.

"It says here," he announced, "that you can get your laundry back in twenty-four hours, if you mark it 'Special.'"

We waited until nine o'clock that night. We had sandwiches sent up to us. MacArthur was reading aloud from the Gideon Bible when a gentle knock came on the door.

"Come in," MacArthur called out, "unless you are particular."

The door opened, and there stood the Monster. He was garbed in a soiled trench coat. His yachting cap was perched on one side of his head. He looked coy, but somewhat ill-kempt.

"I saw a candle burning in your window," he said, "and knew that it was meant for me."

"Jack," I asked, "where did you park the car?"

"Car?" he asked with some affront. "What would I have been doing in a car?"

"It's not what you have been doing *in* a car," I said. "It's what you have done *with* the car you took from a young lady."

His eye lighted. "She was enchanting," he said. "Find Huntington instantly. I intend to remember her in my will." He turned to Mac-Arthur. "It is good to be back again with you, my bonnie lad. What are you drinking?"

"We are not speaking," MacArthur said.

"Don't worry about a thing, gentlemen," Jack said. "The car of which you speak is now being rebuilt by the finest mechanics."

"Good God!" cried MacArthur. "You *wrecked* it?"

"Dented it a little fore and aft," said Jack. "But when I gave your name as my reference, the kindly garage man promised to have it right side up and running like a mink within the fortnight."

The car matter eventually was settled without litigation. We never again subsidized a lady to brighten the hours of our friend.

When Attorney Huntington took Barrymore as a client, he did so with the proviso that whenever Miss Barrie re-entered the actor's life in a positive fashion, the relations between lawyer and client would automatically cease.

Early in August of 1937 Jack received a telegram from Miss Barrie. She was arriving at the Glendale railway station from the East. Would he meet her?

He did meet her, with flowers. Then on August 9, 1937, the interlocutory decree of divorce was dismissed. Exit, Attorney Huntington.

4.

Up from Twenty Fathoms

THE diver comes up from the sea floor where the hull lies twenty fathoms deep off wintry Provincetown. He suffers a temporary paralysis, a palsied, blue suffering. He has the "bends." His colleagues carry him, his weird helmet now off like a discarded world, his leaded feet dragging the deck as he is half hauled into the decompression chamber of the salvage ship. There he must remain in a stepped-up atmosphere until the blood vessels of his nervous system recover their caliber and tone.

Barrymore, it seemed during 1938, had come up from twenty fathoms under with the "bends." The only decompression chamber available to the now fifty-six-year-old man was the romance of his own choice and the out-and-out commercialization of a great family name.

Apparently no one with access at this time to the actor and his affairs reverenced the century and a half of shining tradition which had been passed on to Barrymore, and by him briefly but brilliantly enhanced. The actor himself properly wished to meet his debts. To this purpose he permitted himself to be exploited in an array of claptrap motion pictures and a series of raffish broadcasts, which, save for an occasional Shakespearean gleam, made him seem a buffoon in the minds of a new generation.

Late in 1938 it was decided that he return to the stage with his fourth wife as his leading lady. The vehicle chosen was a work described by Ben Hecht as "a grasshopper's dream." It was called *My*

Dear Children, a comedy. Barrymore submitted this play to his old-time producer, Arthur Hopkins, who declined the issue.

This comedy had its première at the McCarter Theatre, Princeton, New Jersey, on March 24, 1939. The theatrical firm of Aldrich & Meyers produced the comic valentine; Otto L. Preminger directed it. The company manager was Captain Pierce Power-Waters, whose wife, Alma Power-Waters, afterward wrote a book, *John Barrymore,* published in 1941 by my friend Julian Messner.

I was in the Orient, then voyaged among the South Seas during the autumn and winter of 1938. In the spring of 1939 I returned to America to reside for an isolated time at Ben Hecht's home in Upper Nyack, New York. I was completing a book, and watching the tulips come to bloom while Ben and his wife, Rose Caylor Hecht, stayed in California. My near neighbors were Charlie MacArthur and his wife, Helen Hayes. Charlie informed me that Jack was again on the stage, but not exactly as Hamlet. It was not practicable for me to see Barrymore's play, nor did I greatly desire to witness the abdication.

The shorn Samson had a few good friends who managed on occasion to ply a needle and thread on the patchwork of his remnant destiny. The intimate recollections of this period, as given by these friends, form a report of Barrymore's last theatrical feat, the pulling down of the pillars of the house of his art.

Barrymore's old-time confidant, Jack Prescott, attended Jack during this springtime of 1939, when the *My Dear Children* company went to Washington, D. C. A road tour was planned as a sequel to this experimental stand on the Potomac.

Prescott arranged that the actor go to the Hay Adams Hotel while in Washington. He says that Miss Barrie countermanded this order, and that Jack then countermanded his wife's order. When Barrymore neglected to appear at the Sunday-night rehearsal in Washington, Prescott went to Jack's hotel, to find him ill with laryngitis. The play opened the next night, but the stricken and fevered actor barely could speak. Prescott states that by Wednesday's performance, his friend was in whispers.

"I had Barrymore's chauffeur drive Elaine to New York," Prescott recalls. "I bought railroad tickets for Jack, then sneaked him onto a New York train. I then notified Captain Power-Waters there would be no evening performance. I came down the next day with the finest attack of shingles any white man ever had. I got back to New York, and was laid up at The Lambs for two months. The show closed for three weeks, and then Jack shoved off for Rochester. He got as far as Memphis, Tennessee, where he called me by long-distance telephone at The Lambs. He said he was going to kill Elaine."

Charles MacArthur, at about this time, decided to examine the Monster first hand. He afterward reported:

> As you know, *My Dear Children* opened in the sticks, and stayed there whilst the authors and producers warily sniffed the New York breezes for tell-tale odors of hot tar. All of them expected public lynching.
>
> Jack had no illusions about the piece. A year before, he had sent me the script, asking not how good, but how bad I thought it was. The production was Elaine's idea, and even she didn't think too highly of it. She explained rather blandly that it would serve to introduce her to New York, and prepare the way for a production of *Macbeth* later in the season, when she would appear as Lady Macbeth. Of course Jack would be the Gloomy Thane. She was thwarted in this ambition by the management, which prudently kept the turkey out of town most of that year.
>
> The first performance of *My Dear Children* (after Jack recuperated somewhat from Washington) was perpetrated somewhere down South. A few days later I had a call from the Monster, who wanted me to come at once, as the script seemed to need a little fixing.
>
> This cry came at four-thirty a.m. after a hard night for me at the Stork Club. Even so, my recollection of the script was quite clear. I told Jack that I would see him in hell before I touched the dramatic whimsy with a ten-foot pole, but that if he wanted to visit with me I would be delighted to make the trip. I promised to call him in the morning on this point, and asked him what town he was in. He repeated the question apparently to someone in his room, and then replied, very distinctly, "Atlanta."
>
> I instructed the hotel operator to wake me at ten, and remind me to call Mr. B. at Atlanta. I was duly aroused by a pair of bellboys at that hour. The call was put in, but nobody in Atlanta seemed to know of Jack's whereabouts. We checked on the earlier call, and found that it had come from another city in another state—Chattanooga, Tennessee. And that is where we located him.
>
> He asked me to fly at once to Nashville, if only to look at the show. I was nervous at this suggestion, as my objections to the script had created in the past a slight barrier between me and

his co-star, Elaine, and I felt sure that nothing I might see on the stage would improve my relations with her. I mentioned this possibility to him.

"Are you, perchance, referring to my fourth wife?" he replied with such emphasis as to give me my earliest intimation that the dew was off the rose. I agreed to take the first plane.

Jack was at the airport, his coat collar up, and he needing a shave. He was waist-deep in small Southern nose-pickers slugging him for his autograph. When he saw me totter out of the plane he loudly hailed me as the humblest of crockery bedroom utensils, then waded through the small fry to embrace me. The horde followed, pushing their autograph books into my face under the misapprehension that anyone Jack would go to the trouble to meet must be Important. When I refused to tell them my name they appealed to Barrymore. He seemed amazed.

"Children," he said, "is it possible that you do not attend school?"

They assured him that they did. He inquired into the nature of their studies, then deplored that History was not one of the required courses. This they denied, whereupon Jack pointed to me and roared:

"And you do not recognize the Bastard Son of St. Louis, Henri the Fourth of France? *Kneel!*" A smallish section of the crowd (those under eight) knelt while I signed their autograph books "Navarre." I signed a dozen before a friendly cop broke up the demonstration. A cab driver asked for directions, and Jack said, "the Country Club."

MacArthur narrates that he naturally assumed Barrymore to be a guest of the club, but Jack informed him that Tennessee had never repealed prohibition, and that ruses of this sort were sometimes necessary when on quest of a julep. The Monster assured Charlie that southern hospitality in this regard made no distinction between members and perfect strangers. MacArthur added:

The Nashville Country Club is by way of being an architectural jewel, a bit Grecian in line, like most of the town's principal monuments. We approached this noble pile, then ascended its marble steps. Jack remarked the beauty of the surrounding dogwoods and the distant hills.

Two elderly colonels were sitting on the veranda, sipping at frosty juleps. Whether Jack's beard put him in the General Grant class, I can't say; but both of the old gentlemen betrayed some alarm at our approach. They rose and took strategic positions before the classic portal. One of them gently asked if we were expected. Jack bowed from the waist as he said, most certainly we were expected. The colonels looked at each other, then asked if we were guests of a member.

"Of course," said Jack, gilding his perfect diction with a faint southern *patine*. When they asked the name of the member whose guests we were, he held forth for twenty minutes while he tried to think of a name that would get us admitted.

It was one of those "a man who" speeches that you hear at bum banquets and national conventions, but such a flight of pure southern oratory that the colonels listened as to the song of a lark. A group of colored servitors now had gathered in the doorway. The colonels were deeply impressed, but firm about getting the name of our supposed host.

MacArthur describes how Jack got his second wind, glared at the juleps, then started out again.

In accents more southern than before, the Monster declaimed that our sponsor was the Noblest Son the South had yet produced, a man whose charm had enslaved the North, erased all bitterness between the States (and here I noticed that his seeing the Negro servitors in the doorway had given him an idea) a man whose Life & Works proved that breeding heroes and racehorses were secrets known only to the South. And what name do you think he pulled out of the hat? None other than that of the dark-skinned friend of our youth, that genius of his race, Bert Williams!

The Negroes standing in the doorway became silently convulsed, MacArthur continued. The colonels said no Colonel Williams was a member of the club, nor had they ever heard of any Colonel Bert Williams. Jack seemed shocked at this. He asked coldly, "Have you heard of General Robert E. Lee?"

MacArthur drew one of the colonels aside to explain that this was John Barrymore, who had spent the previous day in Chattanooga, where he doubtless had been asked by some Colonel Williams to visit the country club in *that* city.

The colonels changed their tune immediately, ushering us inside like royalty, and proceeded to prove their words by surrounding Jack with juleps. But when they tried to sign the tab he wouldn't hear of it. He insisted that their fellow southerner, Colonel Bert Williams, wouldn't like it—"wouldn't like it at all, suh!"—and signed Bert's name to every tab. The colonels attributed his stubbornness to inter-city confusion, and told the waiters, with a wink, that Mr. Barrymore was to have his way. The waiters kept their faces straight, but the minute they hit the kitchen you could hear them rolling on the floor.

Shortly before curtain time, according to the reminiscent Mac-Arthur, Jack left the club greatly refreshed. "On the way out," Charlie says, "he pinned a note to the bulletin board, proclaiming Bert Williams the First Gentleman of Dixie, and the Noblest Nubian of Them All!"

A quarrel between Barrymore and his fourth wife occurred when the company reached St. Louis. Miss Barrie left the company.

Jack telephoned from St. Louis to Henry Hotchener in Hollywood at midnight April 30. The long-time manager quotes the actor as saying: "Can't we get together again on the same basis as before?"

Henry Hotchener and his wife left California by plane to join Barrymore at Omaha, the theatrical company's next place of performance. It had been more than three years since they had seen him.

"This time it is final," Jack said of his troubles with his wife. "You may count on that definitely. I shall never see her again."

Barrymore then advised Henry to scrutinize his business affairs. He added that when his wife departed the troupe he had not money enough left to pay his hotel and telephone bills.

Barrymore, Hotchener says, was hazy as to how much cash he was receiving each week. He had left such details to his chauffeur, Kurt Wehnert, now serving him in the triple capacity of chauffeur, dresser, and manager pro tem.

"Kurt and his wife," Barrymore explained, "are traveling with me, keeping track of things material, looking after my food and clothes, and taking good care of me. I don't know if Kurt keeps any accounts. You might ask him."

Jack became somewhat concerned about a home he had bought in Bellagio Road, Bel-Air, after his fourth marriage. He wondered if it "could be taken away" from him. He decided to telephone his Los Angeles lawyer to ascertain "instantly" if the house were still in his name, or if anything had "happened to it."

The attorney informed Jack that the Bellagio property was neither in his name nor his wife's, but in the name of a third person. After some incendiary language on Barrymore's part, there was another telephone call between lawyer and client. The attorney now told the actor that the house was in Mrs. Elaine Barrymore's name. The confused Jack said to Hotchener: "Can't you and Maurice do something about all these things? It seems that I am not a realtor."

Barrymore made a radio broadcast in Omaha on this May 1, and in it offended many cornhuskers. That night at the theatre, in a curtain speech, he deplored marriage as mankind's greatest calamity, and spoke of women as lacking in mental ability. He said there were fewer women artists than men, because "it is difficult to ride Pegasus side-saddle."

From Nyack MacArthur got Jack on the telephone the next night at Sioux Falls. Jack said: "Everything is squared away. I made a fine curtain speech, and all is well."

MacArthur learned from the New York office of the company, however, that Barrymore's curtain speech had been another tirade. He had spoken of marriage as "merely a bad tooth that could, and should, be extracted whenever the pain prompts a visit to the dentist."

When the company reached Sioux Falls Henry Hotchener asked the co-producer of the play, Mr. Myers, for a statement of the weekly expenses of the production. Upon examining this paper, Hotchener ventured an opinion that the outlay seemed rather large. Mr. Myers pointed out that $500 of the weekly overhead was being paid to Mrs. Elaine Barrymore. He added that her contract provided for this stipend, whether or not she stayed on with the troupe as an actress, and that Jack himself had approved the arrangement.

Barrymore loudly denied that he had signed either this document or the Declaration of Independence. When the agreement was shown him the actor found to his amazement that he *had* signed it.

"It looks," he said, "as if I had two strikes called on me even before I came to bat."

Hotchener reports that as the company reached Des Moines on May 4, there was an air of defeat among the troupe. Audiences had not been large. Jack seemed bewildered when informed by Hotchener of this box-office condition. Until now he had been of the belief that the play was a success. The actor predicted that business would pick up when the company reached Chicago, adding, "That is a Barrymore stronghold."

At Cedar Rapids, on May 5, Mr. Myers submitted to Hotchener a detailed financial statement received from the New York office. This showed a loss of $7,000 to date for the play. Mr. Myers said that his firm "could not carry this show much longer," then added that Chicago was the only hope for its continuance.

"Have you told Jack," Hotchener inquired, "that the show is on the verge of failure?"

"No," Mr. Myers replied. "We were afraid it might depress him, and make him unable to give a good performance at the very time we needed his best."

"Then," said Hotchener, "you do not know him as I do. He always wants the truth, and often works his best when the odds seem against him. Don't you think he is entitled to know that you are running low in funds for this play, and that in a few days he may need to find another job?"

Hotchener broached this situation to Barrymore at the actor's hotel. Jack sat quietly for a few moments. A bellboy knocked on the door to deliver a telegram from Pandro Berman, at that time a producer at R.K.O. Studios in Hollywood. Berman offered Barrymore a motion-picture contract, and asked for an immediate reply.

Barrymore and Hotchener discussed this message favorably. Jack said that he would reimburse the Aldrich & Myers firm for its losses once he had returned to the films. The actor agreed with Hotchener that his return to Chicago and New York as a "low comedian" in the present play would be an "unfortunate contrast to the Hamlet of fifteen years ago."

Jack now said he felt that he should discuss the situation with Mr. Myers as a matter of courtesy. He did so. Then he asked Hotchener to rejoin him in his hotel room, where he announced:

"I have changed my mind. I think it important to prove that I can make a success of this play, particularly since Elaine has left the cast. Let us, therefore, inform the R.K.O. people that I shall give them a definite answer within the week. By that time I'll be in Chicago, and we shall all know if the play will make good there."

Ethel Barrymore, now touring with her company in the mid-West, telephoned to her brother on the evening of May 5. She informed him that she had read adverse criticisms of his activities. She said she wished to give him her love and encouragement.

After he had hung up the receiver, he said, "I want to send her a wire." He then dictated this telegram, addressing his sister, as was his and Lionel's custom, as "EEthel":

DEAREST EETHEL: I HAVE ALWAYS LOVED YOU MORE THAN ANYONE SINCE MUM MUM WENT. MY ADMIRATION STARTED WHEN WE

WERE KIDS, AND YOU SUDDENLY WONDERED WHAT YOU WOULD
LOOK LIKE IN A PARTY DRESS. YOU TOOK SOME WHITE LACE CUR-
TAINS DOWN FROM A WINDOW AND DRAPED THEM ABOUT YOUR-
SELF IN SO AMAZINGLY DEXTEROUS A FASHION THAT I THEN AND
THERE FELL IN LOVE WITH YOUR BEAUTY. YOU LOOKED AS DIVINE
AS SOMETHING OUT OF HEAVEN, AS INDEED YOU WERE AND ARE,
AND I NEVER FORGOT IT. DEAREST LOVE TO YOU AS ALWAYS.

JAKE.

Three days after the play opened in Chicago on May 8, 1939,
Henry Hotchener left for California with the intention to look after
Jack's affairs in the West. It was Hotchener's understanding that the
actor desired a restoration of their long-time business and personal
relationship. This, however, was not to be. Whether or not the actor
was influenced against Hotchener after the former manager's departure for the West is a matter of conjecture. We do know, however,
that Jack was a person of sudden change; and once he "turned," he
could be most obdurate. He soon became embittered against his
former manager, and the briefly renewed relationship came to a cool
termination.

My Dear Children remained in Chicago for thirty-four weeks.
During that successful run of the play Ashton Stevens, foremost of
the "Barrymore Pioneers," watched over the man who first had
come to him, late on an April night in 1906, in the editorial rooms of
the San Francisco *Examiner* with a letter of introduction from Ethel.

That had been thirty-three years ago, a long time; yet it seemed but
yesterday to the veteran critic. The years are short. Only the days
are long, as our lifetimes move on hidden wheels.

5.

A Tale of Two Cities

BARRYMORE had sent an importunate wire from Peoria to Ashton Stevens in Chicago. Perhaps this sagacious dean of the drama critics was in a better position than any other observer to behold what the years had done with Jack, and what Jack had done with the years.

Stevens and his wife, Kay Ashton-Stevens, met their friend at the railway station. Barrymore looked like a beleaguered Etruscan. He had had nothing strong to drink during his days in wineless Iowa, still his eyeballs were congested.

"Jack could barely see," Ashton says. "So we took him at once to a hospital. There the oculist was willing to blame the redness of Jack's eyes on a strain, a cold, anything but drink."

Stevens stayed within call of his long-time friend until the opening night of *My Dear Children* at the Selwyn Theatre. There a nurse attended Jack backstage, awaiting his every exit with eye-drops.

"But the redness remained," Stevens recalls, "and the first-nighters, with innocent faith, believed that Jack's every pause for a line in the script, and every blurt of a line ad libbed by him, had been blown in the bottle. His role in the crude comedy practically amounted to an autobiography of the Barrymore of first-page fiction and gossip columny and radio self-caricature. He hammed and hawed the role to their hoarse delight."

With a more benign insight than others, Stevens knew from long experience that he was not seeing on-stage the real Barrymore, but looking upon one who wore his Sunday shoes in the mud.

"He falsely enriched his voice," the dean reported. "He flagrantly fiddled and faddled his hands. He strutted and dragged not only the foot but many of his lines. And always and ever for the laugh."

Ashton recounts that Jack visited him the next day to ask if the critic thought the "show would run." Stevens assured him that it would, and that everyone else in Chicago thought as much.

"Cynics," Ashton adds, "came to sneer, but presently wore friendly smiles; for, what was left of the most fascinating actor of his day still held some of the old magnetism. Quicksilver would gleam again in strange moments of this strange impersonation of a lightweight father in a lightweight comedy, wherein Hamlet became not only Prince Hal but Falstaff too. Jack would pause in the play, then intimately bespeak by name some pal in the audience. Or he would lose his line, and say, ever so casually, 'Wait a minute; I'll get it,' and then get it. And 'repeaters' presently learned that this was as much a part of the show as were his asides in criticism of his own acting and that of his associates."

Barrymore knew what the customers wanted and gave it to them, Stevens said, but gave it only in part.

"I say 'in part,' because he did not die on the stage of this Chicago playhouse, where, it is to be feared, more than one 'repeater' came again and again with that dire prospect strongly in mind. He was ill, visibly and audibly ill. There was a period when the show had to be temporarily closed, notwithstanding the loyal stage-doorkeeper's brave avouchment: 'Barrymore? He's here by eight every night—dead or alive!'"

Concerning the barley-corn topic, Stevens pointed out:

"A little liquor went a long way with Jack Barrymore at this stage. That is one of the tragedies of the hard drinker; his resistance softens, until what would be moderate drinking for another becomes active alcoholism for himself. The lad who served Jack as first-aid with the restoratives poured but little whisky for the long highballs. But when that factotum went on some errand and Jack poured his own, that was another performance, and another story."

Barrymore had "poured his own" following one of the matinees, then went to dinner at Henrici's with Mr. and Mrs. Stevens, actress Laurette Taylor, and Jack's daughter Diana. Miss Taylor and Diana were playing in a revival of *Outward Bound*.

A double cocktail, Ashton says of this dinner gathering, didn't jumble Jack's speech, but it played tricks on his memory. The word "frightened" came into the conversation. Turning to Kay Ashton-Stevens, he informed her that the most frightened face he'd ever seen was her husband's, the time Barrymore crawled fifty feet along the tenth-story cornice which ornamented the exterior of . . .

" 'It was the Sherman Hotel, right over there,' Jack pointed. 'I had a yen for a high yaller girl I'd seen on that floor. The only way I could get into her room was through the window.' "

Stevens went on to say that Jack's reminiscence became somewhat off-color as well as anachronistic, but the critic did not reprove the gay raconteur.

"The hotel where he had played the human fly," Ashton says for the record, "was not Chicago's Sherman, but San Francisco's St. Francis. The lady he risked his neck to visit was anything but an octoroon. She was a glacial blonde, who made him feel, as he said at the time, like an explorer who had just conquered the Northwest Passage. But the frightened face of the story always was mine in Jack's varied narrations of this episode."

Stevens declared that Barrymore liked to watch his daughter's expression when he talked of "lofty cornices, high yallers, and a wastrel youth." Ashton then went on to say:

"Jack told me this might be an antidote for Diana's infantile worldliness. Now that he'd seen her act, he thought her more realistic on the stage than off. But he never moralized to Diana, nor to anybody. He altogether lacked the supreme urge of the moralist, the sense of guilt. I never knew another man who sinned as innocently as Jack Barrymore."

Toward the middle of May of this year, Barrymore learned that his fourth wife was again suing him for divorce.

"Soon I shall be unable to count these things on my fingers," he said. "I must rent an adding-machine from the local Burroughs' agency."

Jack Prescott came on from New York to stay with Barrymore in suburban Glencoe after a severe illness struck down the actor. The great mime lay beneath an oxygen tent. Prescott says that Barrymore spoke to him through the folds of this canopy concerning his fear of a mental collapse.

Ashton Stevens says that upon Jack's recovery it became a long, sad season. "But it was my sadness," Ashton was quick to add, "not his. He never contrasted past with present; never looked at the great days with envy, or even admiration; or gazed with regret at his own clownish crucifixion. He was the least vain of all the famous actors of his time. Acting was in his blood and breed, but he never, in a hundred talks with me, seemed to regard playacting as one of the major arts. The only notices he ever had seemed aware of were the 'bad ones,' at which he laughed. He did, however, once comment on a gushy page in a Sunday supplement, referring to the writer of it as 'the enruptured reporter.' "

Stevens says there were many nights during this Chicago reunion when Jack was himself, "even his young self of old."

"Then," recites his reminiscent friend, "he would swing back the clock and relive the fine, foolish nights in San Francisco, where he was first housed in lodgings above the twenty-four-hour Mason Street saloon of Billy Pratt and Matt Tierney. Here, in a spacious back room, the Texas Tommy and the Bunny Hug were supposed to have begun their infant toddle. Here gathered the all-night women and the wits of that sinful city's undisguised and hospitable Tenderloin."

Jack at that time was barely out of his boyhood, Stevens recalls:

"But he gleamed among his elders, and without striving to do so. That was his charm for men from the papers, the Bohemian Club, the polo field of Burlingame, as well as for the ladies of the lily field. He was an eloquent listener. His eyes spoke so much oftener than did his lips. I remember the youthful eyes of Jack Barrymore as not only the handsomest but the most alertly expressive eyes I ever saw in a human head. Even those hardlings, drinking up the dawn at Pratt & Tierney's, fell for the flattery implied in Jack's sensitively listening eyes. Maybe he became a great actor because he was also a great audience."

Stevens believes that girls of Jack's youth "were just girls to him—the plural suited better than the singular."

"His magnetic listening was a loadstone for their confidences," Ashton continued. "Even Margie O'Brien, the headlined Queen of the Tenderloin, was moved to tell Jack how she had traded to Nat Goodwin the key to a flat that did not exist, in exchange for an expensive European edition of the recently invented horseless carriage.

"And, one wonderful sunrise, I heard Margie tell Jack of the night she had met and felled the aristocratic and difficult Billy MacDonough, the youthful sportsman-scion of a house of gold. Billy had bought, and brought to his native California, England's world-famed stallion, Ormonde, only to discover that the noble animal's reproductive powers were nil.

"Billy, as fine a youth as ever lost an eye in the playful duels at Heidelberg, had sworn by his glass substitute that Margie O'Brien would never rook *him* as she had Nat Goodwin.

"But, there he lay one night in a room above the bar of Pratt & Tierney—the room now occupied by Jack. He lay at full length while, in this very room, and in the hallway outside, and downstairs, and in every reach of bar and café, and piled like cordwood, there were empty champagne bottles that had been emptied at Margie's order but at Billy's expense. There were hundreds of bottles, perhaps a thousand, for the whole neighborhood drank nothing but MacDonough's champagne that night. And there he lay, the one-eyed sportsman, dead to the planet in every member but his artificial orb, on which the lid had refused to fall.

"Margie described this epic night to the delight of Jack, then said, 'Ashton hadn't believed I could entertain Billy MacDonough, so I telephoned the *Examiner* office. Ashton had to climb over the empties to view the living remains of the sportsman!'

"Jack interrupted Margie's story to exclaim, 'Even more horrible than wonderful!' "

Ashton Stevens urged Margie: "Yes, but tell Jack what you then said to me!"

"Oh, all that I said to Ashton," Margie remarked modestly, "was 'Allee samee Ormonde.' "

"You never died if Jack liked you," said Ashton Stevens, as he tuned up his banjo. "He loved Lou Houseman, Chicago sports writer, fight promoter, theatre manager for Al Woods, and closest friend of William A. (Billy) Pinkerton. Lou Houseman's was the first local name sounded and saluted by Jack at the Chicago première of *My Dear Children*."

The dean played a few chords, then went on to say of the première:

"Jack seemed now to be seeing Lou's little, thick-set, cab-like figure humped over right there in the third row. I, who had been one of Lou's pallbearers a dozen years back, turned to look where Jack was looking, and almost expected our old crony to swap smiles with me.

"Often, during the long run of the preposterous play, Jack seemed to see Houseman among the audience, as he interpolated his name jocosely but affectionately. One night at dinner he told Kay a Houseman story on which he doted, and on which she will dote for the considerable balance of her years."

The dean gently played mood music on his banjo as he repeated Jack's tale of Houseman:

"It was the story of what befell Lou's working capital following the Jeffries-Johnson fight at Reno. Houseman had collected some $15,000 and a partial champagne amnesia. Upon regaining consciousness during the train ride home, he found himself with barely enough money left to pay the ministering porter and the waiter who brought the antidote to his compartment in a coffee pot.

"Mr. Houseman arrived home feeling worse than the conquered Mr. Jeffries. And home he stayed for several days, lest the gibes of the Loop open his wounds. All Lou had brought back, save his sorry self, was a suitcase full of soiled linen. His wife was making ready this lot for the laundry, when he told her not to send the turn-down collars. Because they, he said, like their owner, were frayed.

" 'There's only one thing to do with a frayed collar,' Lou told his wife. Then he showed her. He ripped a collar its full length. And out fell a one-thousand-dollar bill! Each one of twelve more frayed collars returned to their ripper a thousand-dollar bill. He had hidden, then forgotten, his treasure inside these collars. Thirteen grand in all."

The critic-minstrel now began to play a glad little mazurka on his banjo.

"Jack," he continued, "said to my wife during the Chicago reunion: 'Kay, weren't you with Ashton when he helped bury Lou Houseman from his home in North Hollywood?'

" 'Yes,' said Kay, 'and so was Jim Jeffries, and eleven others. Lou had thirteen pallbearers.'

" 'It was Fate,' Jack sighed, 'that had me too many miles away from the funeral. I would have spoiled Lou's day by being the fourteenth pallbearer. From the day he tore the frayed collars to the day he breathed out, his favorite number was indubitably thirteen.' "

I now said in a wander-thought moment to the musing banjoist: "Ashton, Jack once told me you used to part your hair in the middle." He struck a chord, then replied, "I did until thirty-some years ago. You see, Ethel told me she didn't like it that way. So I changed it."

"Your speaking of funerals," I said, "reminds me of Tommy Meighan, who took Jack to one of those somber events. Jack found himself in a black car after the entombment of someone whose name slips my mind. He seated himself beside an elderly, crotchety man whom he did not know. The old boy made loud objections when Jack took a little nip from a flask. As the car started off toward the cemetery exit, the man rasped: 'You *might* have some respect, if not for the sacred surroundings, at least for my age.' To which Jack asked, 'And will you confide in me what that age might be?' The old boy replied crossly, 'I am ninety-seven.' Jack gestured toward the environment of marble and sod, then said, 'There doesn't seem to be much point to your leaving the place.' "

Stevens said that the last Loop performance of *My Dear Children* was the saddest of the Chicago engagement. Jack was to go to Pittsburgh, Cleveland, Detroit, then return to Broadway after an absence of more than fifteen years.

In speaking of the Chicago farewell, Ashton recalled that Jack said, "You can't drown yourself in drink. I've tried: you float."

"He had been worrying about New York first-nighters," Ashton continued, "especially the Broadway critics. Most of them, other than Burns Mantle, had been in knee-pants when their predecessors acclaimed his *Hamlet*. To these brilliant young gentlemen, John Barrymore would be a stranger—or worse, a picture-actor, and a decayed one at that.

"Anyhow, Jack fortified himself beyond his limited capacity for the parting. The simple, honest, friendly, grateful speech he had intended had fled his memory by the time he was to speak. He forgot this was a 'farewell'; forgot the loyal 'repeaters' out front; forgot everything but the presence in a near row of a pair of youthful night-club performers, whom he had applauded and consorted with the previous after-night. To these widely unknown small-timers, the grand old-timer addressed his spattering speech.

"I, who was to have spent the balance of the night with him, was not the only one who left the house before the stage manager persuaded him to let the curtain fall. I couldn't stay. I had grown more or less hardened to the caricatures he visited on himself—but this wasn't Jack Barrymore at all: it was the complete obliteration of Dr. Jekyll by Mr. Hyde. I went into the street, with great, gawky, sentimental tears salting my face."

Barrymore returned to Broadway late in January of 1940. The play was to open at the Belasco Theatre the last night of that month.

It was understood that Ethel Barrymore would stay with Jack at Bayside, Long Island, in a place remote from the "gang," then Prescott would arrive to "carry on" when the play opened on Broadway.

Ethel watched over Jack until the time for his New York debut at the Belasco Theatre. Prescott sat in Jack's dressing-room during the first night, to protect him between acts, and then, after the play, to surrender him to Diana. She was to take her father to the apartment of her half-brother, Robin Thomas, where a few friends would greet him at a supper. Prescott was to call there at about two o'clock in the morning, together with Jack's male nurse, Karl Stuevers, a huge though amiable young man, again to take Barrymore in tow.

The play itself was a disappointment to the New York audience. One of the first-nighters, Spencer Merriam Berger of New Haven, a long-time admirer of Barrymore, said of it:

A profusion of the great and the near-great turned out for the première, a few a bit wistful about spilt milk and such, but most of them ready for anything that came. I'm certain that the majority expected the curtain to rise on Jack removing his trousers while tossing off Oscar Wilde epigrams.

What followed was an unbelievably baleful performance. Somewhere Barrymore had got the notion that his return to New York called for decorum with a capital D. The dazed audience snickered perfunctorily for a time, soon gave up, and I think that some began to wonder if it were too late for a refund.

The final curtain brought the first spontaneous reaction of the evening. Relieved that the show was over, yet anxious to demonstrate their affection for Jack—however strained that affection might be at the moment—the audience gave him a thunderous ovation, to which he responded with bows and tears.

Now, I thought, when this quiets down he'll cut loose with a speech that will make amends. But the moment he opened his mouth, onto the stage there popped one Bert Freeman, "an unemployed actor," clad in what might have been a Kresge conception of a Hamlet costume. This fellow in green tights proclaimed himself to be Hamlet's ghost.

"I've always wanted to play *Hamlet* with you, Mr. Barrymore," said the interloper.

Jack, startled, but ever the master, put his arm around the man, and agreed that it was an enchanting idea, but suggested it be postponed until the following evening. Many in the audience had meanwhile assumed that this was a planned epilogue, which would prove as unfortunate as the play, and went out.

The curtain cracked down, Freeman got the hook, and a minute later Jack told a half-empty house that this was "the happiest evening of my life." Brother, that was acting!

Jack Prescott says that Mrs. Elaine Barrymore entered the theatre shortly after the beginning of the first act. After the performance she started backstage to Jack's dressing-room.

The room now was filled with Barrymore's old friends, among them the artist, James Montgomery Flagg, who was accompanied by a handsome young lady. Jack looked at Flagg's companion appraisingly, then said, "Well, Monty, you're still quite a picker." To this, Flagg replied, "Yes, Jack, and you used to be, too." It was at this remark, as on cue, that Mrs. Elaine Barrymore entered the dressing-room.

"Jack immediately chased everyone out," Prescott says. "That is, everyone but myself and Elaine. I protested against this reunion. Jack told me that I could leave, which I did. I stood in the hallway outside his dressing-room. Finally Jack called out to say that Elaine was leaving, and that he was going with Diana, as previously arranged, to a supper party. I took Jack's nurse, Karl, down to the Players Club. Diana was to telephone us when Jack was ready to leave her party."

Prescott says that at half-past two in the morning he received a call from Diana. He reports her as saying: "For God's sake, come and get my father!"

Prescott found Jack, Diana, and Miss Barrie at the club Monte Carlo. The two young women were at odds over possession of Barrymore's good graces.

"At six o'clock in the morning," Prescott continued, "Jack and I retired to Elaine Barrie's apartment in Fifty-Ninth Street. After seeing them safely in these quarters, I look reprovingly at Jack, who said, 'Well, after all, I am not committing a statutory offense. She is still my wife!' "

After the third New York performance of *My Dear Children*, Barrymore's nervous depletion sent him to Mount Sinai Hospital.

"Elaine drove us there in a car," Prescott says, "Jack and I in the back seat, at about one o'clock in the morning.

" 'Who am I to be at the hospital?' Jack asked me.

"I replied, 'You are Mr. Wellandstrong.'

"He hesitated for a moment, then you could hear him screaming for a mile away. He laughed long, then said, 'Well, you would be the one, you sweet-scented so-and-so, to dig up a character of Charles Hoyt's, and pin me with it.' "

Prescott stayed with Jack that night at the hospital. The next day he was excluded from Barrymore's room. "I sat on the mourners' bench," Prescott continued. "I knew where the orders had come from. I went to an outside phone, and called: 'This is Ned Sheldon trying to get Mr. Barrymore.' Jack came on the phone. I told him that I had been stopped from entering his room, and that I knew who had given the orders. Very quietly, he said, 'Come back in five minutes, you sweet-scented bastard! And just say you want to see me. You will not be stopped.' And I never was again."

After some days at the hospital, Jack resumed his New York appearance in the play at the Belasco. Miss Barrie resumed her role in it, supplanting Miss Doris Dudley. The play ran for four months, with its chief actor vacillating between poor health and worse.

Barrymore had periods of morbidity, was reluctant to go out of doors, and had a habit of standing at a window, looking out, saying nothing.

"Sometimes," Prescott added, "he would snap out of it, and for a while be the gay fellow that you and I knew, only again to slump back into this deep, dark cavern. His great difficulty was to remember if anyone to his liking had called on him or was about to do so. Such a person might have been known to him for years, and, while that person was with us, Jack would be as intimate and delightful as possible; but after the caller had left, Jack would look at me with a stricken expression, then ask, 'Who was that?' or, 'Do I know him?' Such an incident happened in Chicago with Jim Kirkwood, whom I had brought out especially to see Jack at Glencoe. Jim spent the afternoon with us, but after he had left, Jack had no recollection at all of Jim's having been with us."

Sometimes Barrymore and Prescott would prowl about New York late at night. It occasionally suited Jack's whim to put on tails, a white tie, and an old opera hat. On one of these nights the two formally attired friends found themselves in Tenth Avenue. When Prescott asked if Barrymore knew where he was going, the actor insisted that he did. He said that years ago there used to be a place between Eleventh and Twelfth Avenues that was "tougher than hell," and that it would be fun to go there again.

"We finally found a basement dive," Prescott recalls. "I am positive that Barrymore never had seen the place before, and I know that I hadn't. It was the lowest sort of dump. We breezed in, stepped up to the bar, and Jack asked for a little brandy. The bartender a little scornfully scrutinized our silk hats, but said nothing. He reached behind the bar, then put a bottle on the woodwork. Jack, in one of his delightful moods, now asked the bartender if he was not taking chances in trusting two men with a bottle of brandy. The taciturn bartender merely shook his head.

"We probably were there ten or fifteen minutes when Jack said, 'Don't look now, but I think we are in hot water!' I glanced over my shoulder to see, approaching us slowly, three of the toughest-looking fellows I ever glimpsed. Jack and I remained standing at the bar, trying to appear detached, when the biggest one of the three reached over between Jack and myself, to plank down a dirty envelope and a pencil. He said, 'Mr. Barrymore, wouldja give us yer autyграpht?'

"At this, Jack let out a great yell: 'Give you my autograph? Christ! I'll marry you!' "

My Dear Children closed toward summer. The now fifty-eight-year-old actor had received a film offer from Twentieth Century–Fox Studios in Hollywood. He spent his last night in New York with Prescott. He expressed a wish to go to the Hotel Knickerbocker, where he so often had met friends at the bar, above which the Maxfield Parrish painting of *Old King Cole* was hung. He frequently had been the guest of Enrico Caruso, a resident of that hotel. They had sat up late, discussing the merits of caricature, of which branch of art the great tenor had been a talented amateur.

Prescott explained to the incredulous Barrymore that Caruso had been dead these nineteen years; the old Knickerbocker long ago had been torn down; *Old King Cole* was now the property of Vincent Astor, and was hanging in the St. Regis bar.

"Then," Jack said, "let us proceed to the St. Regis to see the portrait of the flatulent monarch."

When the friends dropped in at the St. Regis, only a few patrons were on hand. Barrymore and Prescott sat at a table near the bar, ordered spicy food, had drinks, and looked long at the picture of *Old King Cole*.

Barrymore pretended that he saw standing at the bar the famous characters of yesterday. He said to Prescott, who understood his mood exactly: "There is Jim Hackett. But who is that little sprite with him? Oh, it's Oliver Herford. And here comes Uncle Jack Drew with Nat Goodwin. They'll drink the place dry. And do you see

Herbert Kelcy, Ezra Kendall, and Kid McCoy? Our friend Caruso looks a bit stuffy today. Probably his physician has cut him down to five plates of spaghetti."

He saw, in his mind's eye, Jim Corbett, Thomas Meighan, Kid Broad, the Considines, Frank Worthing, Ferdinand Gottschalk, and all the gone great figures of a time that was on Broadway.

He now spoke of the still living men, friends whom he had not seen too frequently of late years, but they were in his heart: George M. Cohan, Sam Harris, David Belasco, James Montgomery Flagg, Joseph Cawthorn, Willie Collier, Frank Craven, David Warfield.

"Flagg first saw me when I was a sixteen-year-old atrocity," he said. "I was stark naked, peeling potatoes down in Greenwich Village. The artistic side of the talented Monty was immediately aroused."

The night became long, and many present-day patrons began to arrive at the St. Regis bar; but Jack had eyes only for the pageant of yesterday, and for the *Old King Cole* painting, which had seen Broadway in its green and salad days.

Then, at last, Barrymore and Prescott parted company, never again to see each other, or together recreate a dream of other days.

The play in which Barrymore had achieved the greatest anticlimax of his career earned, according to the figures published by Mrs. Alma Power-Waters, wife of the company manager, $666,519.06. Barrymore, preparing to return to Hollywood, and after long months of work, had left as his share of these proceeds $5,000. It was a check, not payable to him, but to his Japanese gardener Nishi. Jack had thought it advisable for Nishi secretly to hold this "nest egg," so that no one might get it away from him.

"I remind myself of Grantland Rice's destitute ballplayer friend," Jack said. "That wastrel veteran of the diamond told Rice that he had enough money to last him the rest of his life—provided he drop dead on the spot!"

6.

The Grampian Hills

I SHOULD have paid closer attention whenever he said that he was "looking for the Grampian Hills." It seems, in retrospect, to have been a most poignant reference to his innermost yearnings.

The chance reading of a letter addressed to my younger son quite suddenly calls back to mind Jack's Grampian Hills. It is like an old tune, long forgotten, springing to the lips of the whistler. Note for note, the melody rises, seemingly unbidden, from the staves of the past, as songs oftentimes do. Each strain brings with it a full restoration of the setting for the long-stilled tune. You recall in clear detail that night of long ago, the girl you took to the theatre, against her mother's wishes, to see John Mason in *As a Man Thinks*, her flower-scent, the touch of her young hand. How right it seems to be nineteen again, if only for the duration of a remembered song. That was your own first glimpse of the Grampian Hills.

I now recall, belatedly enough, that whenever Jack spoke of these hills, a far-away spell would possess him, as if he were beholding some enchanted highland blue with distance, and hearing fabulous pipes being played beyond the horizon. His voice would take on mysterious inferences. Then the mood would pass.

The letter that stirs this laggard reminder of the Grampian Hills was written by Barrymore in July 1937. At that flustered time he was contemplating the purchase of the Bellagio Road property for his fourth wife, who did not choose to reside at the now-deserted Tower Road estate.

That letter, addressed to my son Will, said:

> We have found a house which, if we can only get it—as the owner is in Mexico, probably being shot—will have a murderers' room with a concrete base, where you and I, and those cognoscente of whom we approve (I need scarcely say an excessively attenuated roster!) can cavort and have our being undisturbed. It will also have a swimming pool that will wind tortuously among overhanging trees. *And* a pool table, at which we will fleece the neighboring bumpkins! Give my best love to your father and mother and the rest of the family. Soon I

trust we will all be tending our flocks together on the Grampian Hills—where the cows really *do* come home. . . .

I remember a lung-pink map in the schoolbook of liverish binding, a prosaic barrier behind which I spent sly hours with adventurous Nick Carter. That map informed us perfunctorily that the Grampians divide Scotland's Lowlands from the Highlands, with Ben Nevis the tallest of that mountain chain. This geographical connotation, however, was not in Jack's mind at all, nor did he have reference to the literary locale of Scott's *Lady of the Lake,* nor that of Bobby Burns's poems, nor Barrie's *A Window in Thrums.*

"He had in mind quite another thing," Lionel said as we talked of Jack, "and quite another kind of place. The Grampian Hills meant to him a final retreat, where all would be wonderful and right. It was during our childhood that we first heard from Papa himself concerning the Grampian Hills. Papa used to stride up and down the room in his zebra undershirt, his eyes bright, his long forefinger leveled at some fabulous world unseen by mere mortals, and recite:

> "My name is Norval; on the Grampian Hills
> My father feeds his flocks, a frugal swain. . . ."

"It is from John Home's early nineteenth-century play, *Douglas,*" I informed Lionel. "A lady at the Public Library settled the matter for me, after I had supplied her with the cue. Took her all day to do it."

"It's news to me what it is," said Lionel, "or where it comes from. It didn't matter to us then, nor would it now; we were not a family for research. Jack never knew what the Grampian Hills actually were; but he knew what they *meant.* What they meant to him. Our father's grand inflections made them appear to us what Utopia must have seemed to Sir Thomas More; what the Promised Land, Arcadia, the Elysian Fields, the Garden of the Hesperides, Zion, and all the rest rolled together, meant to the groping, dreaming men of the ages. It was a place where caravans rested; where time itself stood still."

Now in 1940, and once again in Hollywood, the home-coming actor did not find himself among the Grampian Hills. Instead, and realistically enough, he entered for a second serfdom into a bankruptcy arrangement. Somehow, between the time of the comparatively recent payment of old bills—his honorable discharge by the bankruptcy court on November 30, 1939—and that summer of his home-coming to Hollywood in 1940, he had incurred another $110,-000 in debts. This amount did not include the neglected payment of alimonies and child support, arrears estimated variously in court recitals at between $50,000 and $100,000.

Of the creditors' claims, almost fifty per cent represented fees for attorneys and business management. The debtor once more shook his head like a tired bison, then voluntarily undertook the payment of these newer liabilities. And although he subsequently was to earn $241,085.18 by means of picture work and radio broadcasts, he still would be adjudged a bankrupt *after* his death but not before it.

We shall now have done with a further detailed presentation of Barrymore's finances as pertain to the two last years of his life. There were many just debts, of course, and just creditors, also; but the picture in the main is not a tidy one. And we find ourselves unable to fire away at certain of these claims without striking other than biographical targets. Were we to enter into an analysis of Barrymore's harassment by fair-weather leeches and foul-weather bleeders who drank at the veins of an impaired memory, it would be to write an essay on parasites, a monograph more vitriolic than scientific.

During his more alert days Jack had not stirred himself to any great degree to ward off the beaks of such cormorants as hover about a man of fame, ready to pluck out his eyes, once the pockets are rifled. Even had he desired it otherwise, he now was powerless to withstand the last carcass-swarming onset by the fetid crew. They crawled over him with duns and writs. They quarreled among themselves. They still sulk when reading his epitaph.

Let us turn our eyes away, as he did his, from this obscene tableau. His eyes were upon the Grampian Hills, where no one ever sees the greedy littleness of man.

The two last years of Barrymore's life, notwithstanding the many illnesses and the squabblings of the law, became for him a reunion with several companions who represented the gay days. They brought him moments of boisterous gladness, a grand reprise.

The private meeting ground for these Barrymore cronies was, more often than not, the studio home of John Decker, the artist, in Bundy Drive. Decker, in his own youth, had been an art student at the Slade. School in London, where Barrymore himself had been enrolled. Decker had painted scenes for Sir Herbert Tree's His Majesty's Theatre, working in the lofts of the red-nosed, white-bearded

W. T. Hemsley, who used to fall with astounding regularity into the whitewash tub. Hemsley's chief ambition was to own a white horse instead of the senile black palfrey that was his means of transportation. Decker one day whitewashed his employer's steed, then left the metropolis at Hemsley's insistence. The young artist returned to America.

Decker, now in New York, designed and painted the scenery for the *Greenwich Village Follies*. He also served as theatrical caricaturist on the art staff of the *Evening World*. As such, he made Barrymore's acquaintance at the time of *The Jest*. Afterward they met again in Hollywood, where Decker was becoming recognized as a modern artist of versatile talent. He was regarded by Barrymore and by others of the actor's group as one who would become instantly famous on his deathbed.

"The first time I ever saw Decker was in 1932," I told Jack. "I had a hangover that was being appraised skeptically by my cinematic collaborator, Rowland Brown, himself a teetotaler, who nibbled at cookies stored in an umbrella stand in the hallway of his house. We were en route to the studio that day to compose a scene for one of your less than significant motion pictures. We chanced to see in Gower Gulch a harried gentleman in a condition similar to my own. He was hatless. A flock of blackbirds could be seen flying down again and again to gather hair from the gentleman's head for the upholstering of their nests. He was batting at the industrious birds, and cursing them."

"That would be Decker," Jack said. "Aside from his art, which I admire no end, I find him enchanting, because he dislikes sunsets and his mother. And I believe that we both owe him a great personal debt for exhuming that museum piece, Sadakichi Hartmann."

The Mr. Hartmann to whom Jack had reference was an habitué —together with actors Thomas Mitchell, Roland Young, John Carradine, Fannie Brice, Tony Quinn, author Ben Hecht, and other western sojourners—of the studio in Bundy Drive. Sadakichi, author of *The Last Thirty Days of Christ*, had been an art critic of parts, a poet, a dancer, a fuming savant. He was half German and half Japanese, a circumstance that did not enhance his popularity during martial times.

He now was squatting among the rusty tins of his memories, in a shack of his own manufacture on an Indian reservation near Banning, California. When a windstorm tore off the roof and up-ended it in the middle of his shack, Sadakichi calmly placed a doorway in this relic of the gale, and now had two rooms instead of one.

"The elements," he said with bronchitic laughter, "are a matter of indifference to me. I defy them."

The aged Sadakichi's burst of coarse hair made of his head a gray chrysanthemum. He had a long, bony face, with mummy wrinkles in the umbery skin, a little copse of a mustache, and the longest fingers ever seen, and active hands incapable of an ungraceful movement.

This husk-and-shanks that was Sadakichi's physique belonged to a tattered but fierce egotist. Benjamin De Casseres once described him as "half Hooligan and half God." For almost sixty of his seventy-two years he had pranced like an accelerated zombie among the easels and the inkpots of the elite, entering the ateliers without knocking, stepping on the toes of apostles, heckling his personal benefactors, drinking on the cuff, dancing with gargoyle attitudes, and mumbling his own weird rondels over the briskets of dowagers slumming in Greenwich Village, where, early in this century, Sadakichi Hartmann had set himself up as King of the Bohemians. He had been Walt Whitman's amanuensis for the writing of letters to foreign lands. He had known Paul Verlaine, Stéphane Mallarmé, Claude Debussy, and Paul Heyse. He had followed Whistler on the London streets, then written a book on his art. He had peered over Ibsen's shoulder in a coffee house, and crouched behind the screened box at the Munich theatre several times when the mad King Ludwig attended rehearsals. He seemed a bamboo bridge from the past.

Sadakichi had fathered thirteen children and given them the names of flowers. Still, he decried parenthood and frowned upon all sentiment. He deplored German music as an expression of Teutonic philosophy, and proclaimed it the raven-call for continuous world unrest.

Now in 1940 Sadakichi sat like a praying mantis in Decker's studio. Barrymore enjoyed many hours with the old and snarling pessimist. Sadakichi said that he had known the actor's father quite well. Then he added, to Jack's delight: "Your father was a sublime actor. I cannot say the same for his stupid younger son. Hah!"

Jack replied admiringly: "What a wonderful part you would be for Lionel!"

During June and July of 1940 Barrymore was making a motion picture at Twentieth Century–Fox, a celluloid delicacy instigated by Jack's latter-day legend. He pretended, when on public view, to be robustly undisturbed by this cartoon, or by the radio caricatures he weekly draped about his person. This was a papier-mâché suit of armor for his illness and for his personal turmoil.

Such onlookers as saw him in the studios or abroad among the cafés assumed that Barrymore was a person of little sensitivity or fine feeling. But when away from all this, he sometimes seemed wilted and deeply hurt by the horse-play demands of his work. There were a few persons who knew that even a tricky memory did not altogether shut out from Jack's own ears the echoes of yesterday's empty laughter.

Decker, Sadakichi, and myself were visiting Jack at the Twentieth Century–Fox Studio one morning. We found him quite sober. He seemed concerned about something. He asked me to go with him to his dressing-room during the noon recess. He was wearing a Hamlet costume, God forgive everyone concerned! He telephoned from his dressing-room to his fourth wife at Bellagio Road.

After a fairly long conversation with her, he hung up the receiver, then turned to me worriedly. "Can't you get me out of this?"

"What good would it do?" I inquired. "You would immediately throw yourself again on the spears."

"No," he said, "I've got to shake myself loose from this Promethean predicament. Rather, I've got to be shaken loose. I find it intolerable."

"All you have to do," I replied, "is to walk out, but this time *stay* out."

"It's not as simple as all that," he said. "I've got to be *made* to stay away." He looked at the telephone as if turning over some purpose in his mind. Then he said, "I'd call Lionel, but he's through with the whole business, and I can't blame him. Can't you think up something weirdly effective?"

Lionel remarked recently: "I suppose both Jack and myself would have been happier if we had been made differently. Whenever Jack got in the way of love, he would put halos over the heads of his women. He'd hold these halos up by means of broomsticks. I never had the effrontery to point out to him what he was doing. I even went so far at times as to help polish these halos, or shine an electric light on them. He eventually got tired of holding the broomstick, and then he'd prop it on a chair, and fall asleep. But the last halo was too much even for me."

Early in July 1940 Barrymore visited Decker's studio to find Sadakichi there. Sadakichi had had a hemorrhage at the Indian reservation. He had lain there in a seizure, he said, for more than sixty hours, without water or other attention. He finally had revived, then taken a bus into town to escape the hot dust of the desert.

The old stoic this day was reclining on a beach-chair in Decker's back yard, watching the artist, who had on a hay-seed hat and a paint-smeared shirt that hung outside his trousers and partly concealed a huge rent in the seat. Decker was solemnly waiting for ripe plums to drop, one by one, from a tree, while Sadakichi made cynical comments.

A portable radio commenced playing "The Dance of the Hours." Sadakichi began to wave a fly-swatter in time with the music. "It is a very difficult piece to dance to," he said to Jack, "because of the change in tempo. Perhaps I am the only one who can do it right." Then, as a coughing fit seized him, he added, "But not at this time."

Sadakichi then began to denounce me to Barrymore for not having purchased him a coffin. He had intended to use this piece of furniture as a bench at the reservation, he said, and then employ it for another, eventual purpose.

"Have you no proper defense," Jack asked of me, "for refusing this amiable as well as practical request for a sarcophagus?"

"I did shop for one," I replied. "I interviewed numerous experts, then finally earmarked a coffin, a rather snappy number it was, too. The wholesale price was seventy-five dollars, not including the hardware, which, as I understand it, nowadays usually is merely lent for an occasion. But there was a hitch in the negotiations."

"Please!" and Barrymore raised a hand. "Don't hedge about it. No excuses can be accepted. There shouldn't be any hitch to such a simple transaction. Our friend here is apt to depart this life at any moment. The least we can do is to provide him with a suitable cocoon against the day of his immortality."

Sadakichi pointed at me, and cried out wheezily: "Not only is he hedging, but his wife absolutely refuses to sew a slip-cover for my coffin."

Barrymore pretended to be deeply shocked at this. "I can't believe any woman to be so ignoble. She might be condescending enough to contrive some little makeshift, if only a flounce of dotted Swiss. I'll draw up a petition. We'll all sign it."

"The hitch to the whole business," I explained to Jack, "is that I have run up against some mortuary ruling that a coffin bought by a layman at wholesale positively cannot be used for a subsequent burial."

"Nonsense!" Jack objected fiercely. "Sadakichi is *not* a layman. I invite you to glance at him dying there, and then look me in the eye and dare to tell me that *his* dying is not the work of a great professional."

Later that day Sadakichi was missing from the main room of the studio. A search of the premises resulted in his being found in the garage. He was seated behind a huge gilt picture frame, like a portrait of himself.

One evening early in September 1940 Decker, Will, and myself received word at the Bundy Drive studio that Barrymore was becoming increasingly unhappy at Bellagio Road.

"Then why are we sitting here?" I asked.

Will drove us to Bellagio Road. A maid answered the ring at the door. We entered the living room. Jack, in an old bathrobe and slippers, came downstairs. His nurse, Karl Stuevers, followed him.

"Welcome to the Halls of Montezuma!" Jack whispered. "Or perhaps the shores of Tripoli. No matter."

"You want to join us?" Decker asked.

Barrymore pointed overhead, then whispered, "Even the ceilings have ears." Then he raised his voice. "Wouldn't think of it, old man. It's late, you know." Then he whispered, "Get me the hell out of here, quick!"

"Collect your things, Jack," I said. "We're on our way."

"I don't think I'd better go upstairs myself," he said in an undertone. Then he looked at his nurse. "Would you be so kind?"

Karl assembled an outfit, then Jack dressed himself hurriedly. He put on, among other things, a tall-crowned Tyrolean hat, with a jaunty brush in the crown band. Now he insisted, before being driven off in Decker's car, upon inspecting an olive tree in the yard. This was the ancient olive tree he had brought to Tower Road some years back, and recently had his gardener, Nishi, transplant it in the grounds of the Bellagio place.

"Let us take this noble plant with us," Jack said of the tree. "Did you gentlemen bring derricks and spades?"

He was dissuaded from this nocturnal uprooting of the old tree, but took from it a sprig for his hat-hand, saying that it was "an emblem of peace."

He now spied, as we were driving along, a light in the window of a neighbor's home, that of W. C. Fields. "Uncle Willie is all that makes this neighborhood bearable," he said. "I don't like to leave him. He has such an excellent pool table."

We soon arrived at Decker's. There in the artist's studio Jack seated himself in a red-velvet chair, snorted, then said that he wanted a divorce "instantly." He also wished to recover the ancient olive tree, which seemed an important symbol to him. He afterward talked much of the tree, but never got it back.

We stayed up until late, then went to my home in North Barrington Drive near by. I began to fold up toward three o'clock in the morning. Decker went home, and I left Jack with Will. Before I struggled upstairs, I instructed my sprightly son: "From this night on, you are to take up with our durable friend whenever your brittle and aging father leaves the field. Don't ever return him to the place where we found him tonight. Tower Road is where he belongs."

Jack and Will left our house for Tower Road at about four o'clock in the morning. They inspected the grounds of Jack's estate by flashlight. When they entered the deserted aviary, Jack said, "I've always wanted something. Did you ever want anything with all your heart?" Will said, yes, a pipe organ. To which Jack replied, "Precisely. And I want a pool table. I want to install one in this aviary. I've wanted a pool table all my life."

He never went back to Bellagio Road, and never returned to the partner of his fourth bus accident.

Jack retained the services of attorney Roland Rich Woolley to bring a divorce action. Mr. Woolley filed a complaint on September 23, 1940. An answer and cross-complaint was filed by the fourth Mrs. Barrymore's lawyers on October 25. An agreement was reached on November 26, and a divorce granted to Mrs. Elaine Barrymore by default in court the next day.

Karl Stuevers stayed on for some months with Jack at Tower Road, and Decker also kept close to his friend. The artist and his wife,

Phyllis, frequently made Barrymore welcome at the studio, and I believe that Jack spent the happiest moments of his fading days among friends in Bundy Drive. There his drinks would be cut to a small alcoholic content. His cronies would gather about the red-velvet chair to brighten his nights. Here he seemed to relive his own time as a painter. He watched Decker at work, sniffed the turpentine happily, and spoke of James Montgomery Flagg and of other artists of the New York days.

"I still have a feeling," he said to me one night at Tower Road, "that certain people want to put me out of circulation."

"What? Again? Don't be ridiculous."

"It's constantly on my mind," he said, "and besides, the creditors are planning to take Tower Road away from me for keeps."

"I think both these hurdles can be cleared," I said.

"For God's sake, how?"

"Have you known of a single instance," I asked, "of anyone ever being committed when regularly earning big money?"

"They're always sending people to the brig," he replied, "claiming they are incompetent to handle their own fortunes."

"That's an entirely different situation," I said. "If Aunt Bessie retires with a full sock, and no longer earns money, she is a cinch to be put away. But never if she is regularly making money each week. I am informed that you now are making, at the moment, six thousand dollars a week . . ."

"Then where in hell is it?" he interrupted.

"Keep on the beam," I said. "It goes, most of it, to your creditors. But I think they are letting you have a few florins of it now and then for pin money. Now, if you keep on working, no judge is going to rule that a person smart enough to earn a thousand dollars a day is nuts. The judge himself would seem nuts to make such a ruling. He could be impeached on the ground of judicial paranoia . . ."

"By God!" he said. "You are right for once! I'll just keep on working."

"Now, as for Tower Road, if you threaten the creditors to quit work entirely . . ."

"You're reversing yourself," he said. "I must keep on working to stay away from the chicken-wire."

"Just a moment. You won't actually quit. You'll merely threaten to do so. The creditors will be so flabbergasted at the prospect of losing a huge sum each week that they will let the golden goose stay on its nest."

"I shall burn a candle to you," Jack said, "in some great cathedral. I shall, of course, burn it at both ends."

Such creditors as had objected to maintaining Jack in the Tower Road house were persuaded by Attorney Woolley that the actor should be permitted to reside there unmolested. Mr. Woolley pointed out to them that otherwise he himself would retire the actor to the Woolley ranch until Jack regained his health.

Toward Christmas of 1940, Jack fell ill on the day he was to make a broadcast for the Rudy Vallee program. Woolley called in Dr. Hugo Kersten to attend the unconscious actor at Tower Road. The physician arrived early in the afternoon to examine the patient. Dr. Kersten said that the actor should remain away from all work for some time. It appeared that Barrymore could not, unless miraculously restored, rise to his feet for several days.

The actor's agents explained to the reluctant physician that "a whole radio world" rested upon Barrymore's resuscitation in time for a seven-o'clock broadcast that night. They assured Dr. Kersten that his new patient was more stout of heart than other men, and that "he always gets up for any emergency."

The dubious physician administered restoratives, then telephoned to an athletic club for a wrestler known as Tony. Tony arrived at Tower Road to commit the inert Jack to a course of massage and baths. Then, shortly after five o'clock in the evening, the actor roused somewhat to ask, "Where is Earl Rogers?"

He was referring to that brilliant criminal lawyer, now long dead, who had known Jack in the days when the actor was playing stock at the Belasco Theatre in Los Angeles. Perhaps the present scene reminded Barrymore of the time when the famous lawyer defended him for having felled a barber (a not unusual thing for him to do in his days of theatricals). Jack and the attorney had stayed up all that night, and the actor had wondered next morning how either of them was to get as far as the courthouse steps. But Rogers, Jack said of the incident, stepped out, after a tussle with the bathroom faucets, as fresh as a rose, dressed himself, then went to court, spoke brilliantly, and won Jack's case.

And now at Tower Road, with Tony the wrestler working over him, Jack floated back to a more modern world. At six-fifteen he dressed himself, somewhat laboriously, then walked to the automobile that was to take him to the broadcasting station. He gave what was regarded by the officials as a "spirited show"; then, in his dressing-room, he collapsed.

Back at Tower Road that night he was carried by Nishi in a chair up the steep terrace. Jack's heart action seemed weak. He became unconscious three times before morning. Then, to the astonishment of everyone, he grew suddenly vital by breakfast time, but had no memory whatsoever of the illness of the previous night.

One of the actor's agents said to a confrere, "We'd better give out a story that he has only a little influenza." Jack looked up to say, "Well, *isn't* that what I have?"

There were numerous repetitions of this type of sickness and collapse during the following months. Then Barrymore had a recurrence of a gastric ulcer. He was placed on an appropriate diet, given injections to control hemorrhage, and assigned to the care of nurses. Lionel meanwhile substituted for Jack on the radio program.

On the day the nurses left him, Barrymore prepared to report at the radio station for rehearsal. He spied a bottle of aromatic spirits of ammonia in his bathroom, and downed enough of this medicine to incur a severe hemorrhage and a condition of shock.

An ambulance hastened to Tower Road. It was a new vehicle, but it broke down on the way to Hollywood Hospital, with Jack unconscious inside it. The doctor, speeding after the ambulance in his own car, drew alongside, then got out to administer emergency aid to Barrymore while the ambulance was being changed under the stricken actor.

It seemed that Jack might die this time. Still, when I called upon him at the hospital next day, he sat up to say, "I trust that the good public will forgive me for recuperating."

He began to scratch his chest with a military hairbrush, for he had eczema among his several other ailments. "Don't you suppose," I asked, "that the hospital gladly would provide something more suitable than a hairbrush for your eczema?"

"Do not ring for unguents," he said. "I prefer this technique."

The telephone bell now sounded, and Lionel asked about his brother's condition.

"The Monster seems a bit more chipper today," I told Lionel. "He is at this moment scruffing his torso with a hairbrush."

"Tell him to comb it straight back," Lionel said.

"I was wondering," I remarked to Lionel, "if this hairbrush antic is some hereditary trait handed down to the menfolk of the Barrymore clan. Do *you* do it?"

"Hell, no!" Lionel shouted over the telephone. "I keep a cat."

That night, late, I received a telephone call from Decker. "The Monster is out of the hospital."

"You're crazy!" I said. "Why, he's hardly able to sit up. I saw him myself at the hospital today."

"He's reported at the Club Ugene," Decker said. "We'd better go there on the double-quick to investigate."

We not only found Jack at the Club Ugene, but were alarmed to see him partaking of a sardine sandwich with cold kraut. He was conversing brightly with Producer Earl Carroll and a group of that gentleman's delightful show girls.

"I do not remember even one nuance of any hospital experience," Jack said to Decker. "Of course, if it amuses you to conjure up such a preposterous legend in your own Neanderthalian skull, I'll be the last to gainsay it."

Inquiry at the hospital disclosed that Jack had been wandering down the hall. He was garbed only in an open-back nightshirt, and calling for his nurse in picturesque terms. An interne accosted him with an order to "pipe down." Jack replied with such vigorous, Elizabethan fluency, that no one sought to prevent his dressing or leaving the scene "instantly."

In November of 1941 Jack was again in the hospital. There he received a bouquet and a note from Miss Elaine Barrie. Their interlocutory divorce decree was to become final within a few days.

It is Miss Barrie's recollection that Jack telephoned her to urge that they be reunited, and once more prevent the divorce from becoming final. She refused to go back to him.

The actor, however, left the hospital with plans for a reunion. He announced that he would give a private dinner of reconciliation at Tower Road. Covers would be laid for two. He restored his fourth wife's photograph to the silver frame from which he had torn it in a rage almost a year ago. He ordered flowers and wine. He barred the gates of Tower Road to his friends. Only Nishi remained on the premises to witness what went on in preparation for the potential love-feast.

Nishi telephoned half-hourly bulletins to Decker and myself, as we awaited news of the peace conference at Jane Jones' café on Sunset Strip. Nishi reported Jack as being dressed in formal attire, chilling the wine, staying sober, arranging the flowers . . .

Then, at about midnight, Nishi flashed us word that Mr. B. had gone into a rage. His patience had evaporated. Miss Barrie had not appeared at the feast. Finally, at about two o'clock in the morning, Nishi reported that the wine had been drunk, the flowers were in the fireplace, the picture again had been torn from the frame. King Lear was declaiming on the Heath. The curtain at last had fallen on this romance.

Barrymore now seemed utterly to forget his fourth wife. He never again sounded the strange cries that had presaged his several returns to Miss Barrie.

Jack went to Palm Springs for a "rest." While there he fell in with some companions who ignored the advice that his drinks be diluted. He swallowed twenty old-fashioned cocktails, then collapsed.

He now entered his final year of markedly failing health, but got to his feet again and again, with a gameness seldom observed in any other man of our time. Nor did he complain of being ill. He *acted* the part of a well man, not the least effective of his many roles.

Dr. Kersten realized that it was impossible to keep his patient entirely in line. The physician did the sensible thing of substituting for Barrymore's stronger drinks a light, domestic vermouth, watered considerably. Jack would carry this refreshment in a black overnight case, a ladies' model. It accommodated four drugstore bottles of vermouth, a flask of aromatic spirits of ammonia, and the hairbrush. Whenever he went out for an evening, to Decker's, to Ben Hecht's, Earl Carroll's, or to the broadcasting studio, he would have with him the black bag.

"The only objectionable feature to this," he said, "is that the citizens constantly are mistaking me for a politician with a bribe case. Even so, it is the finest luggage a man ever had."

It now became quite apparent to his doctor that Jack had cirrhosis of the liver and a kidney involvement. He caught cold frequently. He had chronic chills. But he held his chin high. Ben Hecht, at whose Hollywood house Jack spent a night of unclouded brilliance, said of him:

"People are mistaken when they pity Jack for his many ailments. He doesn't remember these aches and pains at all the next day.

Think how fine it would be for all the invalids of the world, mooning over yesterday's attacks and dreading a revisitation of sickness again today, if only they could be stripped of this overshadowing fear that intensifies each disease. Jack will never die of fear. Perhaps he will never die at all."

Sometimes I suspected Jack of remembering much more than he seemed to salvage from the immediate past. In fact, he said as much to me during his last trip to the camp of Ruth Curry Burns and her husband Eddie, near Mount Baldy. Jack had an unexpected surge of memory of recent events during that rainy night.

"I'll have you know," he said, "that it suits my fancy to let most things slip past without my batting an eye. You hear more that way, see more, than if you let the Philistines know that you are on guard."

The world-of-now seldom entered Jack's mind during this last year. He sometimes sat at Decker's, a newspaper shielding his face, but he was not reading; he was hiding behind the newspaper whenever some stranger entered the studio.

He knew little of the World War, other than for the passing moment, as when he said to me on December 7, 1941, after the radio had brought to us the news of Pearl Harbor: "It looks as if our great literary project, *The Life and Times of Sadakichi*, might be slightly out of place, like finding an antelope in the top dresser-drawer."

Decker one day handed Jack a letter from a Pennsylvania innkeeper. The boniface wrote to ask if Barrymore would sell his bed, together with appropriate testimonial evidence, as one of a collection of couches of historic lovers now being assembled at the inn. Barrymore promptly sat down to write:

> I was charmed by your letter, and also about the idea of the testimonial, which has exquisite possibilities. I am devastated to have to inform you that the bed is still in use—and will continue to be, I most sincerely trust—for some years to come. When I have no further use for it, I should be most happy to consider your offer, although it is practically committed to the Smithsonian Institution.
>
> I feel sure, however, that a man of your astuteness could achieve some *blanket* arrangement with them to transport the bed to your hostelry during whatever is your busy, or mating season.

Diana, Jack's daughter, came West in January 1942. He placed her photograph in the frame from which he had torn the picture of his fourth wife. He spoke of how happy he would be at last to play the role of father, "and mean it." The actor and his daughter appeared together on the radio, in *Romeo and Juliet*. He sent a telegram to Diana's mother, Michael Strange:

DEAR MICHAEL: THIS IS MERELY TO TELL YOU THAT DIANA HAS TAKEN THIS FLATULENT CAVE OF THE WINDS KNOWN AS HOLLYWOOD BY STORM. EVERYBODY SEEMS TO ADORE HER. I MUST SAY SHE IN EVERY WAY JUSTIFIES OUR SLIGHTLY CYCLONIC COLLABORATION. ALL THE BEST TO YOU.

FIG.

Then, quite suddenly, the temperaments of father and daughter collided. He removed Diana's picture from the frame.

At the beginning of 1942 Jack's memory of recent events became still more loosely seated than before. He had experienced another onset of illness, with an internal hemorrhage so severe as to warrant blood transfusions. But he got up to walk again. He stayed on at his radio work, and even appeared in a motion picture.

It was said by attorney Gordon W. Levoy that had Jack undertaken two more motion-picture assignments, together with his regular radio work, he soon would have been able to meet all his debts. Mr. Levoy, with bankruptcy expert Judge Earl C. Moss, now served Barrymore as counsel, having succeeded Attorney Woolley as such in the autumn of 1941.

Jack's impairment of memory did not remain at a constant low level even during his latter months. Volcanic islands of remembrance would rise one day, to disappear the next, in the sea of his forgetfulness. He did have moments, sometimes minutes, yes, even hours of clear recapitulation of events that might have occurred as recently as the day before, or even a week.

For example, when he learned one day that the opera, *Manon Lescaut*, would be given in Pasadena the next week, he invited Will to accompany him there. The young man agreed to do this, but presumed that Jack soon would forget all about the appointment.

Will was pleasantly astonished a week afterward when Jack called him by telephone to say: "Get your evening coat on, Your Highness, or redeem your father's moth-eaten jacket at the pawn shop, and call for me instantly. We're going to that opera in Pasadena."

They drove to Pasadena, got lost, then saw a group of young persons in evening attire at the doorway of a structure which Jack positively identified as the opera house. The music-loving companions went into the place to find themselves at a dance being given by the Junior Chamber of Commerce!

Jack and Willie never got to the opera. They returned to Tower Road at five o'clock the next morning. They sat in the rathskeller, where a widow spider now was the main tenant. They talked through the dawn.

"Remember the time," Jack asked, "when you were in high school, blowing a tuba? Or was it a flute? And your mother gave your father merry hell for letting you stay up with us at all hours? Claimed you were getting galloping consumption, or something?"

"Did you ever know what finally happened?" asked Will.

"No. A divorce?"

"Not quite. I came home from Tower Road at about two o'clock one morning to find my father propped up in his bed, reading a horror story. You know his tastes in regard to literature?"

"He can barely read," said Jack. "But go on. Was he sober?"

"Strange to say, yes. As I approached his room to bid him good night, or good morning, I overheard my mother say: 'Now, look. Barrymore may be a genius, although there is another school of thought on that. But I'm not going to stand for your keeping *my* son up *all* the time. He's a growing boy.' I heard my father reply: 'Well, if the lad can't take it, I want to know it now. I've practically never had a wink of sleep in all my life, and he's no better than I am.'"

Will added that when his mother saw him standing at the door she gasped: "Look at him! That's what I mean!" Then Will said that his father, looking up from his horror story, exclaimed: "Good God! You're right! The younger generation *can't* take it!"

Jack, sitting with his young friend in the rathskeller, howled: "I know the answer to that!"

"Sure you do," Will told him. "It was the same night you rehearsed me for the First Gravedigger for our high school *Hamlet.* You got together some chalk and burned matches, and made me up as a death's-head."

Will says that he found, penciled on the wall of the rathskeller, the combination numbers to the wine closet. He turned the dial. The door opened. Jack and he lighted a candle to go inside the vault. There they found an old bottle of wine on its dusty side in a corner of the closet. The two friends uncorked it. The wine was flat, and a little sour. Yet they happily drank it together, toasting their fathers.

"What impressed you most about Jack?" I asked my son. "What seemed to you his outstanding characteristic?"

"He was so young," Will replied. "He never seemed old, never at any time, and that was a wonderful thing."

7.

Bell of Requiem

THIS man whom Arthur Hopkins called "The Dazzling Sojourner" prepared to leave Tower Road late in the afternoon of May 19, 1942, to go to the rehearsal of his weekly radio program. He spent some time on the telephone with a friendly linguist. This interpreter obligingly spelled out for Jack the German equivalent of seven English words submitted by the actor.

Barrymore wrote this translation in pencil on a scrap of white paper. Jack's borrowed German maintained that "All this world is full of" that thing which Victor Hugo represented a general as thinking of out loud when called upon to surrender. Barrymore signed this motto "Schiller," as though it were a quotation from the works of that eighteenth-century Teuton.

Next, he penciled on a pink memorandum slip in English, "I have a rendezvous with death." He then drew a line from left to right on the paper, and beneath it added a notation, "Recite this on radio."

He placed these two notes—the last ones he ever was to write— in his night-table drawer. He then announced that he wanted no breakfast (a not unusual decision for him to make), dressed himself slowly, then called out for Nishi. There was no response to his summons.

Nishi no longer was at Tower Road. He had been sent weeks before to a camp for enemy aliens at Manzanar. But Jack had forgotten all about that. He likewise had forgotten the day of leave-taking when the belongings of the gardener and his large family were piled high at the doorway. He had forgotten how he himself had protested, when it was explained to him that, with America at war with Japan, Nishi must leave California. Jack had asked, "But is there a war on with Nishi and his family?"

He still thought of Nishi as being in his employ. Barrymore went out of doors to look for his gardener on the bowling green which the painstaking Oriental had laid out at the actor's command, but which never had been used. He sought for his long-time servant in the Victory Garden. The Nipponese ground-keeper himself had urged its planting in compliance with the patriotic campaign for home-grown legumes. When the gardener had inquired what vege-tables Barrymore wished him to plant, the actor replied, "Horse-radish!" The obedient and literal-minded gardener planted whole beds of horseradish, and nothing else, and this pungent herb now grew luxuriantly and uselessly on the estate.

Jack, on this afternoon of May 19, telephoned my house to say worriedly that Nishi could not be found. I did not see fit to burden his mind with oft-repeated details of war regulations. I merely said, "He'll show up eventually."

I detected a hoarseness in his voice today, a shortness of breath. I ventured to break the rule of never asking an actor or an athlete concerning matters of health.

"How do you feel?"

I became concerned over his reply: "I feel like hell. That's pre-cisely how I feel."

This was but the second time that I had heard him admit feeling other than "in the pink." I reported his conversation to Lionel, who also became worried, and said, "He never admits he is ill. I'll keep an eye on him."

Barrymore's secretary-attendant, Ehrling Moss, now reminded the actor that it was time for him to go down the hill to the broadcasting station. With Ehrling at the wheel of the automobile, Barrymore was driven toward the upper gate, looked at the totem pole and then at the abandoned concrete water tower that gave high, winding Tower Road its name.

He settled himself in the seat of the motor car. He shivered inside his camel's-hair overcoat, although the late afternoon air was not chill. He did not stop over today at St. Donat's Restaurant in Sunset Drive for a Pimm's cup, as he regularly had done of late when on the way to a rehearsal or a broadcast. Oftentimes he spent a quiet hour or more in this English-style eating house, talking to the proprietor, Ella Campbell, or watching the patrons playing at darts.

Barrymore had had a bad head-cold since March. He was coughing when he arrived at the broadcasting studio for the rehearsal, but said that he was "fit." He had not been drinking for the last two or three days.

After the rehearsal of his lines, Jack left the broadcasting chamber to go to his dressing-room. He became lost. He almost collided with a group of sightseers in a corridor of the building. They paused in their tourists' march to watch him as he tiredly leaned against the wall for a few moments. Several of the sightseers shook their heads as though in disapproval of the moral character of the man. Some of them handed down an immediate opinion that he was "drunk again."

These citizens then went on their way to examine some other free marvel; and the greatest actor of our time went on *his* way, which soon was to lead him beyond anyone's censure or praise.

He wasn't able to locate his own dressing-room. He entered the first door that yielded to his hand. It so happened that the place in which he now found himself had been assigned to John Carradine. That actor at the moment was broadcasting elsewhere in the building as a guest of the Edgar Bergen–Charlie McCarthy program.

It was a curious happening, this chance entrance by Jack into the room of a young actor who for years had regarded Barrymore as his beau ideal. Only two weeks before, Carradine had sought Barrymore's advice on how to play the character Louis XI in a revival of *If I Were King*.

Carradine, having concluded the broadcast with Edgar Bergen, now returned to his dressing-room to read the newspaper notices of *If I Were King*. He had opened in that stage revival at the Philharmonic Theatre in Los Angeles only the evening before. The young actor had brought the newspapers with him to the broadcasting station, but had not yet had the opportunity to read them.

Carradine was amazed upon entering his room to find someone lying on the couch, the newspapers spread over him or scattered about on the floor. Carradine was still further astonished to see Jack himself rising from among the journalistic litter.

"How are you, old man?" Jack asked, as he sat up slowly.

"Why, hello, Jack," said Carradine. "Are you all right?"

"Never better," Jack said, but Carradine saw that he was gray with illness. Barrymore coughed. He had difficulty in breathing. Carradine was too confused for the moment to do other than mutter something about having "opened in the play last night," to which Jack said, "Of course; and I take it that you received splendid notices."

"I haven't read them yet," said the younger actor.

"Good," Jack said. "Actors should never read them. If you don't believe the bad ones, why should you pay attention to the good ones?"

There was a long silence, then Carradine mentioned that he had played the role of Louis XI in accord with Barrymore's advice of two weeks before. The older actor now began to discuss the younger man's career, as if he himself were not ill, and the playing of Louis the only thing in all the world that mattered.

"Tell me," Jack said in reference to King Louis, "are you having fun with the old fellow?"

"Yes," said Carradine, "but I want to tackle the other play, the one Irving did about Louis. Think I could get away with it?"

"You could get away with anything, you lean, cadaverous bastard! You could play . . ."

He broke off, dreadfully weak, and gasping. Dr. Kersten now arrived at the studio in response to Ehrling's call. Jack was half carried to his car. He was driven to Hollywood Hospital. There it was learned that he had bronchial pneumonia in the right lower lung. He lost consciousness.

News of the severity of the actor's ailments was withheld from public knowledge for a time. Lionel took his brother's place on the next radio program.

Ethel, touring New England with *The Corn Is Green*, was advised of Jack's illness but not yet told of its gravity. She kept in touch with the hospital, however, by means of long-distance telephone.

The primary cause of Jack's collapse was cirrhosis of the liver. There were secondary conditions, such as the failure of kidney function, chronic gastritis, ulceration of the esophagus which hemor-

rhaged, hardening of the arteries, and chronic eczema. The pneumonia was the terminal event of the man's long-standing illness.

Because of a breakdown of the kidneys and a failing circulation,
his body became water-logged. Fluid collected in his chest and ab-
domen and embarrassed the heart. Somehow that great heart beat
on against all these odds.

How he outlived this night of May 19 still remains a matter of
wonderment to Dr. Kersten, who said in a statement ten days after
Jack's collapse:

> The fact that Mr. Barrymore survived this attack for more
> than a few days, instead of hours, is more of a tribute to the
> patient's amazing vitality than to any medical science practiced
> in his behalf. Perhaps this unexplained vitality had something
> in common with the several other matchless qualities of this tal-
> ented and courageous artist. As his physician, called to minister
> to him upon several other occasions when his condition was, to
> say the least, critical and alarming, I was compelled to wonder
> at a spirit and a will that belied his sixty years.
>
> In exploring his physical history, and taking into account his
> chronic carelessness in getting proper rest, or his observing even
> a semblance of diet, I also became acquainted intimately with the
> man himself, his fine mind, his opinions, his philosophies. I found
> that his great personal strength and courage, even his foolhardi-
> ness, cloaked in fact the gentlest sort of soul, tolerant, generous,
> without conceit, and almost childlike in honesty of thought. It
> is not for a medical practitioner to say that these qualities have
> any bearing whatsoever on a man's physical fortitude at the
> threshold of death. Yet, who knows?

Barrymore never had undergone any surgery. Now, when urged
to submit to a tapping procedure, he said, "All right. Stick a stiletto
in my belly!" He then became unconscious again. His blood pressure was low. He had a temperature of 102 degrees.

He was given a local anesthetic early in the morning of May 20.
A trocar was introduced through the abdominal wall, and fluid with-
drawn. I saw him soon after the procedure. He had asked, during one
of his intermittent moments of consciousness, that I come to his room.

I had not intended to do other than remain with the loyal Decker
across the hall, or with Lionel who sat in another near-by room. The
elder brother was sleepless, agonized of spirit, but stoically wordless
except for an occasional self-addressed remark, such as "Why in God's
name can't *I* do something for him?"

I entered Jack's room to find him breathing like the sound of a cloth being slowly torn. His mouth was half open; his eyelids were half open, the eyeballs turned upward, with only the congested whites to be seen. I came in as quietly as possible. I thought him unconscious. Still, he said hoarsely, "Yes, Gene." Then he resumed the breathing.

I had seen him on several other occasions when it had been thought that he could not live the day. Always I had denied that he would die, for I felt that somehow he would get up again. And he always had. But now, as I stood beside him, something seemed to say to me, "Your friend is going to die. Your great friend is dying."

Almost angrily, for my resentment of death is as wildly strong as it is futile, I left the room to rejoin Decker across the hall. The artist stood looking out of the window at the various doctors and nurses coming and going in the courtyard below. Then he went in to see Jack again. And Jack roused, as if miraculously, to say to this loved friend: "Somehow, I never feel bankrupt as long as you are within call. Nobody could foreclose on our friendship, try as they would."

I did not want to be alone, and I could not sit still. I looked in on Lionel in the near-by room. I sat beside him there. His head was bowed.

We didn't speak for some time, then he looked up to ask, "What do you think?"

"I think the same as you do," I replied. "There's no need for us to lie to each other."

"No," he said. Then he asked, "Would you be so kind as to see the newspaper reporters for me?"

The news of Barrymore's actual condition had begun to circulate. The reporters set up a death-watch at the hospital. The young men and women of the press, with here and there a veteran reporter well known to me from my own newspaper time, were kept informed of all happenings during Jack's ten days at the hospital. And, in return for this simple courtesy, they gave a great man the dignity of an exit.

Jack again underwent a tapping procedure on Thursday. He occasionally thereafter roused temporarily from his coma-like condition, and then the great spirit of mischief that was his weapon against all tragedy would lance through the darkness for a little time. Whether or not he knew that he was dying, I cannot say. It is untrue that he announced that he would "play a death scene for Diana" when she called at his bedside.

On Thursday, he again had asked that I come into his room. I found a nurse combing his hair. He roused to ask her, "What are you doing to me?"

"I am combing your hair," she replied.

"Oh!" he said. "How droll! I thought you were leaning over to kiss me."

Then he said that he was going to recite a poem dedicated to all women. He got as far as "Oh, woman! Beautiful beyond . . ." then once more became unconscious.

On Friday his doctors thought his pneumonia to be subsiding. They issued an encouraging bulletin. This seeming improvement was transient, for soon Jack's condition became worse.

One of his old friends, a priest, the Reverend Father John O'Donnell, looked in on Barrymore. Then Father O'Donnell went down the corridor to sit with Lionel for a time. The priest recalled that he first had met Jack at a circus.

The cleric learned that Jack was expected to die soon. He returned to the actor's room, this time not merely as a friend but as a priest. And now Barrymore received the last rites of the Catholic Church.

But Jack still lived on valiantly. I again went into his room that night to find a nurse endeavoring to brush his teeth. She looked up from the small basin held beneath the patient's stubble-bearded chin to say, "He simply won't open his lips to let me brush his teeth."

"Well," I inquired, "should you do it? Is it necessary?"

"It would make him feel much more comfortable. And the doctor has asked that it be done."

I whispered to her, "Is he conscious?"

"I'm inclined to think so," she replied, "for he is stubbornly clenching his jaws."

"Then stand in a corner," I said, "close your ears, and we'll see what can be done."

The nurse complied, a bit dubiously. I leaned over Jack, and said, "Listen, you obstinate bastard! A beautiful woman is trying to brush your teeth, which, by some miracle, still remain in your possession. Open your eyes and see for yourself what you are missing, you . . ."

The Monster opened his eyes, then his mouth, and the nurse had no further trouble in brushing his teeth. Thus encouraged, the young woman held a glass of mouthwash to his lips. "Now please rinse your mouth with this, Mr. Barrymore."

He promptly swallowed the mouthwash, to the consternation of the nurse. She worriedly reported this happening to the doctor, who hoped for the best. Decker came in to advise the nurse: "Never give him anything in a small glass, unless you know it can be safely taken internally."

Jack suffered a severe gastric hemorrhage the next day. But even the nurse did not blame this calamity on the mouthwash.

On this seventh day, I again sat in the corner of Jack's room. Barrymore once more was seemingly unconscious. The nurse said that he had been in this condition for several hours. After I had sat there for some minutes, Jack said distinctly, and without opening his eyes: "I thought you were closer."

Believing him to be talking in a haze, I did not reply. I sat looking at his pale face and the still hands that rested, palms down, on the white covering of the hospital bed. . . . What superb bone structure his head and face owned, I thought, no matter his years or the devastating illness. . . . He now called me by name, his eyes still closed. I went over to him.

"Will you hold my hand while I sleep?" he asked. I held his hand. Then he spoke of my children, somewhat incoherently, and then of Ned Sheldon. I did not know Sheldon at the time, but Jack always had taken it for granted that I had seen the playwright during my several journeys to New York.

He lapsed again into his coma, but breathed more easily than before. I stood there, his hand in mine for several minutes. The hand was cold, yet the grasp of it tenaciously strong, as his hold on life had always been.

Now he began to mutter. I could understand few of his words other than "Mum Mum." Obviously he was speaking of his grandmother, for that is what the Barrymores always had called Mrs. Drew.

Now he made another of his amazing returns from the depths. He opened his eyes. They seemed for the moment to sparkle as of other days. He even raised an eyebrow.

"Lean over me," he said quite clearly. "I want to ask you something."

I was unprepared for other than some last request by a dying man. I should have forseen that this mighty fellow would not surrender with a sentimental, prosaic statement. The cocked-up eyebrow should have warned me that mischief never sickened in his soul.

"Tell me," he asked, "is it true that you are the illegitimate son of Buffalo Bill?"

I was so abruptly jolted out of my sorrow that I laughed. He had made me seem ridiculous to myself, and not by any means for the first time. And that had been his purpose, I am quite sure, for he must have felt that I was grieving. And he never wanted his friends to grieve.

"Yes," I replied, with a solemnity that seemed to please him, "I am told that Colonel Cody was my natural father. But we mustn't let anyone else know of it."

He smiled, then said, "I have always thought so," and promptly became unconscious again. These were the last words he ever said to me.

I looked in on him the ninth day. Now he was in what seemed to me to be a delirium. The nurses had placed white mittens on his hands, to keep him from scratching his inflamed skin. It was as though he had put on the boxing gloves to meet the dark foe. Nurses now found it necessary to restrain him. He showed surprising, quick strength. He was trying, it seemed, to rise with the instinct of a knocked-down champion, his senses beaten, but his spirit never. He fought as only the young fight against this last antagonist, for the old seldom come to blows with the final aggressor. They slip away, as if on some quiet journey into the night.

I now found myself unable to look at him again. I sat with Decker across the hall, in the event that Jack might call for us. We could hear him breathing, and calling out unintelligibly. The breathing now had changed in timbre. It came like the sound made by a knife-blade being ground on a stone wheel.

He roused only once again, to say something to his brother. Lionel asked him, "What did you say, Jake?"

"You heard me, Mike," he replied; and, so far as I know, those were his last words to anyone.

At nine o'clock on the night of May 29, Decker went in to see Jack. He made a sketch of his friend. Then, at ten-twenty, Barrymore's breathing no longer could be heard across the hall.

After sixty restless years, he had found the Grampian Hills.

Ethel Barrymore wrote:

> I am feeling—as I am sure you know—laid low. So many memories of my little brother—so long ago—when we were all so young, and knew and expected so little—and it didn't matter.

Good Night, Sweet Prince.

CURTAIN

Index

Index

471